THE PUB AND THE PEOPLE

ONE WEEK LOAN

D1354678

THE PUB AND THE PEOPLE

A Worktown Study

by

MASS OBSERVATION

faber and faber

TO
MARY ADAMS

who made Government and Parliament
recognize the value of social science
methods

AND
EVERETT JONES

who saw the full implications that social
research can and should have for the
future.

This edition first published in 2009
by Faber and Faber Ltd
Bloomsbury House, 74–77 Great Russell Street
London WC1B 3DA

Printed by CPI Antony Rowe, Eastbourne

A CIP record for this book is available from the British Library

ISBN 978-0-571-25095-0

INTRODUCTORY NOTE

WHEN TOM HARRISSON lent me the proofs of this book, and let fall that owing to blitzes they were the only copy in existence, I felt seriously alarmed to have them in my desk. For the work embodied in them is not merely interesting stuff about one of the nerve-centres of human behaviour—it is much of it unique, and now forever incapable of duplication. Far from being "out-of-date" (because the field work took place mainly in 1938) it represents, for that very reason, the diary of some travellers on perhaps the last excursion-trip made intelligently to a Lost World. Events have turned it, in the Accountant's phrase, into "a Document of Record".

There are two ways in which it can be read. I have once myself, by very different methods, tried to analyse the place of the public house in the working-class life of a great city.[1] It was therefore necessary for me to read this "Worktown" evidence as a serious contribution to an almost completely undocumented subject. Much of it astonished me. Sometimes I thought the mode of presentation so clear and so robust that Truth could hardly escape without a flea or two in its ear. But I had no doubt at the end that, even among those research-workers whom it heartily annoys, this book will stand as a permanent and irreplaceable source-work about the place of pubs in British life.

The other way to read it is as one would read *Vanity Fair*. Everyone is interested in people, especially if they are behaving discreditably. And here is a book that is a magic casement on a foaming fairyland of ale and cakes. It brings home, with the clarity of a dream, a world where there were lights and thoughtlessness and, above all, an absolute stress on private life.

You walk back into a warm bright room and marvel that in 1938 we never knew that those spittoons were in Arcadia.

I am grateful for this book to Mr. Harrisson and his friends of Mass-Observation, and I think that, apart from its serious value, a good time will be had by most.

BASIL D. NICHOLSON.

[1] *The New Survey of London Life and Labour*, Vol. IX.

PREFACE

I happened to spend the years 1932–35 exploring some of the most primitive and uncivilized parts of the world, including Central Borneo and the great chain of islands stretching down the Western Pacific. I spent also a year living among people who were still eating each other, on the island of Malekula in the New Hebrides Group. I found no difficulty in being financed by the Royal Geographical Society, the Royal Society, the British Museum and other bodies to go anywhere in the world in search of rare or previously unknown birds from mountain tops, or to make notes on strange manifestations of human behaviour among peoples with coloured skins. It was gradually borne in upon me that the things I was doing, at great expense, in these difficult jungles, had not been done in the wilds of Lancashire and East Anglia. While studiously tabulating the primitive, we had practically no objective anthropology of ourselves, despite many "social surveys" on a statistical basis. I determined, therefore, to devote as much as possible of the rest of my life to studying the so-called civilized peoples of the world. With this object in view, on my return from the Pacific I went to the industrial North of England (until then strange to me) and spent many months working in different jobs, trying to pick up the threads of mass life in Britain in much the same way as one does when visiting a little known country. Early in 1937, when I had been doing this for six months, I met Charles Madge, then a newspaper reporter, who had many of the same aims in view, but thought the best way to make such studies was through a nation-wide system of voluntary informants, reporting upon themselves, rather than by specialized study on the spot.

This is an old story, just worth recalling in this rather personal way, because this was the origin of Mass-Observation, which has (I think) become in a very small way a significant feature on the intelligent landscape of British democracy. During the past five years we have worked with increasing support, and have at several points been able to exercise some constructive pressure by supplying relevant facts, not available elsewhere, about ordinary people to Government departments, voluntary bodies, M.P.s, periodicals, factories and informal groups. The structure of Mass-Observation remains very much as it was at the beginning —a team of whole-time paid investigators, observing others objectively; and a nation-wide system of voluntary observers providing information about themselves and their everyday lives. Madge, alas, has since the war been engaged on other work, so that the responsibility for both sides has rested mainly with me. The trained investigators operate from London (82, Ladbroke Road, W.11), though of course they are at any one moment distributed about the country on different studies. But for three years this team concentrated its whole attention on one town in the North, "Worktown".

We have called it Worktown, not because we take it as a typical town or as a special town, but because it is just a town that exists and persists on the basis of industrial work, an anonymous one in the long list of such British towns where most of our people now earn and spend. For three years in Worktown we lived as part of the place. For the first two years we were practically unnoticed, and investigators penetrated every part of local life, joined political, religious and cultural organizations of all sorts, worked in a wide range of jobs and made a great circle of friends and acquaintances at every level of the town structure from the leading family through the Town Council to the permanently unemployed and the floating population of Irish dosshouse dwellers.

The original team of investigators came in simply because they were enthusiastic for the idea of making an anthropological survey of ourselves. We presently received generous and entirely disinterested support from two Northern industrialists, Sir Thomas Barlow and Sir Ernest Simon, for whose early confidence in our initial efforts we cannot be sufficiently grateful. Further help then came from Dr. Louis Clarke (now Curator of the Fitzwilliam Museum, Cambridge), from the late General G. H. Harrisson, from Mr. Michael Higgins and from an anonymous senior civil servant (who constantly came to our assistance in days of need). Then Mr. Victor Gollancz gave us sufficient support to enable us to work on a proper basis preparing a series of four volumes on Worktown life, of which this is the first—the others being more ambitious and extensive volumes on politics and the non-voter, on the religious life of Worktown with its numerous sects, and on that tremendous climax of the industrial year, the week's holiday in Blackpool. The present volume was in proof when the war began; the others were in draft. The war necessarily drew Mass-Observation on to other problems. We are therefore forced to leave completion of the other volumes until after the war, when it is our intention not merely to produce them, but to produce them with additional material, bringing them up-to-date and showing the changes which the war has brought about in the institutions studied—politics, religion, leisure.

In the meanwhile, we offer this volume with some diffidence. As a matter of fact, I had adopted the view that it would be better to leave it over, too. It was not until, by chance, I showed it to Mr. Basil Nicholson (who has written the most intelligent study of the pub in his section of the *New Survey of London Life and Labour*) that he strongly urged it should be published now; he has contributed his own views on this subject in an introductory note. It did seem, thinking about it again, that as well as the possible interest of the field material, a useful purpose might be served after three years of war by recalling in this particular way one small section of the thing we are fighting for, or away from. Moreover, plans are being made about the future of Britain, and these are often being made as if the prejudices and habits of ordinary people can be ignored; publication might serve some constructive purpose in reminding the planners, in their valuable work, of one of the habits they most often ignore. I say this with some feeling myself, as since the war my family have lived at Letchworth Garden City, one of the key towns of the planning movement, and one of the few places in England where no pub is allowed: this book could not have been written at all if Worktown had been Letchworth.

The book speaks for itself. And through it some of the people of Britain speak for themselves too. For the extent to which we fail to appreciate the real quality of that large section of the community who do not write to the newspapers—often do not even vote in a General Election—is so great that the full integration of our democratic culture is endangered. There remains in Britain a gulf between the top people, the leaders, and the rest, the led.

One of the basic institutions in British work life is the public

house. Many books have been written about it; they are referred
to and listed in this volume. But there has been little attempt to
make an objective, unbiased appraisal of the pub, and especially
of how the pub works out in *human* terms of everyday and every-
night life, among the hundreds of thousands of people who find
in it one of their principal life interests. Mass-Observation has
no interest either in proving pubs are good or pubs are bad.

We do not suppose, of course, that Worktown pubs are
"typical", any more than Professor Malinowski considers the
Trobriand Islands typical. The object of our studies in Worktown
was to take the whole structure of the place and analyse it out.
This cannot be done in more than one town at once, and the inter-
relationships *within* the town, irrespective of relationship to other
towns, were the broad basis of our study problem. The obsession
for the typical, the representative, the "statistical sample", has
exercised a serious limitation on the British approach to human
problems and is largely responsible for the generally admitted
backwardness of social science in this country. The real issues of
sociology can only be faced if the sociologist is prepared to plunge
deeply under the surface of British life and become directly
acquainted with the mass of people who left school before they
were 15, and who are the larger subject-matter of British social
science. The issues cannot be fully viewed by statistical inter-
viewing, the formal questionnaire, and the compilation of data
on the library level. That, at least, is Mass-Observation's view,
the incentive of our particular line of approach. There is room
for every sort of sociology in this country, because there is so
little of any one sort. There is no need to criticize other sorts;
but it is necessary to stress that at present the social sciences
are still rather one-sided and rather more academic than the
subject itself requires and deserves.

The reader will notice that in this volume there is not, for
instance, any attempt to make a statistical sample of interviews.
There is not one single direct *interview* in the whole book, though
there are many reported conversations with informants of all
sorts. There are plenty of statistics; they are nearly all statistics of
observation. Mass-Observation, as its name implies, considers that
one of the clues to development in the social sciences is the actual
observation of human behaviour in everyday surroundings. We
cannot afford to devote ourselves exclusively to people's verbal
reactions to questions asked them by a stranger (the interviewer)

in the street, without running a grave risk of reaching misleading conclusions. What people say is only one part—sometimes a not very important part—of the whole pattern of human thought and behaviour.

Main stages in the Worktown survey were thus:

a. Public house reconnaissance and description; preliminary penetration. 3 months.

b. Penetration by observers into all parts of Worktown pub life. 2 months.

c. Observation without being observed. 10 months.

d. Work conducted more openly; active co-operation with all sorts of people in all spheres of local life. The study of individuals, letters, diaries, documents. 3 months.

e. Data from important people. 2 months.

f. Studies of statistics, organizations and published sources. 3 months.

In preparing this book for publication, a source of difficulty has been the dispersal of the unit which originally undertook the main part of the Worktown investigation. John Sommerfield, who led the fieldwork, has been two years serving in the Royal Air Force, is now stationed overseas. Bruce Watkin was first in the R.A.F., and is now engaged on special scientific research. Walter Hood won the first Trades Union travelling scholarship and left the Worktown unit, to be caught by the war in Australia, where he remained and is playing his part. Woodrow Wyatt is a Staff Captain in the army, Brian Barefoot a doctor, Herbert Howarth in Egypt, Gertrude Wagner works in the Ministry of Information's Wartime Social Survey, and so on. This has produced complications in proof reading and in the checking of certain points. Every care has been made to ensure accuracy in this respect, but minor errors may perhaps be forgiven on that account? It is a matter of the greatest regret that the superb pub photographs taken by Humphrey Spender cannot, under present conditions, be reproduced.

The picture ends with the war. The book stands, with trivial modification, as completed in 1939. No attempt has been made to cover the wartime period which is bringing many significant new developments. The consumption of beer has increased very considerably in Worktown since the war, and the social structure

of the pub is subject to great new pressures. The last war transformed pub-life. There were drastic restrictions upon the hours
during which pubs could be open, drastic increases in the price
of drink (between 1914 and 1921 duty on each barrel of beer
rose from 7s. 9d. to 100s.), a considerable weakening of beer's
alcoholic content, a considerable decrease in the amount of
beer drunk, and a 600 per cent fall in the number of convictions
for drunkenness. These changes, brought about by the war,
remained. They became accepted as pub normality. Numerous
local and other restrictions (such as the "no treating" rule which
was an attempt to alter the basic pattern of pub life) were tem-
porary, and produced no post-war effects. A competent and well
documented account of these restrictions is to be found in Arthur
Shadwell's *Drink in 1914–1922*. Further changes are now afoot.

Even for those of us who took part in the investigation, there
is something strange and remote about reading the results again
now. Will the highly technical cult of pigeon-racing ever reappear?
Shall we see again the esoteric rites of the Buffaloes? And the
strange way they play dominoes in Worktown? And the elaborate
class structure of the pub, which changes every week-end?
Swiggling, standing rounds, the spittoon, the complex system of
bookmakers' runners, the annual booze-up on Trinity Sunday,
the "Diddlum Clubs", the trend towards bottled beer—what
of all these things now? Already it is probable that much that is
described here is part of history, the past. If so, we shall indeed
have done one of the principal jobs which we set out to do five
years ago, when we determined to attempt to describe and record
history as it was made. The first Mass-Observation book, published by Faber & Faber in 1937, was a detailed study of the
Coronation. Since then we have learnt a lot in the technique of
collecting and presenting material in logical patterns. But since
then also we have tried to follow the main social changes of our
time. During this war, while engaged in doing immediate, war-
helpful jobs of social research, we have been able at the same
time to put down week by week files of detailed material on how
the events of this war—greatest crisis in the story of civilized
mankind—have impacted upon ordinary people. To ensure the
carrying on of this long term side of our activities we have a small
office in the country, Mass-Observation's *War Library*. The War
Library collects not only the verbal and behaviour reactions
of people from day to day, but also the documentary story of the

war, in posters and postcards, wrappers and pamphlets, menus and bills, programmes, Christmas cards, war books, popular tunes, film scripts, sermons and public speeches.

While in these years of energetic work we have never been successful in obtaining one shilling of support from academic quarters, we should like to take this opportunity of thanking individuals in Universities and elsewhere who have given us invaluable help and advice at many stages. We should like especially to thank Mrs. Mary Adams, Kingsley Martin, Prof. P. Sargant Florence, Prof. T. H. Pear, Dr. E. O. James, Prof. John Hilton, Julian Huxley, Bertrand Russell, H. G. Wells, Tangye Lean, Dick and Zita Crossman, Tom Driberg, Everett Jones, Lord Horder and Max Nicholson. Without their moral support and critical guidance at many points, we should have deviated from the job in hand even more often than we have done; it is not their fault we have not done better.

For guidance as regards technique of investigation, we have turned principally, when puzzled ourselves, to field work that has been done in America, where sociology is so much in advance of anything yet seen in Europe. Here we should like to acknowledge our indebtedness particularly to Prof. E. W. Burgess and the Faculty of Sociology in the University of Chicago, which has published several fundamental studies in this field; also to the work of Dr. Dollard, Dr. Elton Mayo and their associates. We were fortunate, in the later stages of our Worktown study, to be visited by several American sociologists who were most helpful and we should particularly like to thank Prof. H. C. Brearley of South Carolina.

Finally, we owe more than we can ever show—more, indeed, than we can ever know—to the people of Worktown. I think I speak for most of the 80 people who came especially to Worktown to help in these studies, when I say that we found an almost unfailing pleasure, honour, hospitality, among the hundred thousand people of this great, smoky, anonymous industrial town. Whatever we thought of the pubs individually, all of us found there friendliness and the company of British working life. There are many other sides to Worktown's story not dealt with in this study of the pub though fully analysed in the other studies in the series. Whatever these people's limitations, and whatever our own, there emerges unmistakable through this research a basic goodness of heart in the individual, confused with an indecision of purpose and function in the community, which provide the ground both for hope and for concern about a future which can and surely must be based on the satisfying of the normal, social, psychological and physical needs and hopes and dreams of the ordinary people who drink and laugh, occasionally fight, cry and die in the pages that follow.

The main work on this study was done by *John Sommerfield* and this is really his book. *Bruce Watkin* also did a great deal of the hard work. Only the circumstances of war have prevented them seeing it through into publication more easily and effectively than I have been able to do the job. My own effort to edit and correct have been completed in a barrack room shared with 29 other privates and without any minutes of privacy. It has been particularly difficult to revise the first three chapters. It is possible to start reading at Chapter IV. (page 67) without seriously damaging the continuity, because the preceding chapters are by way of background and basis to what follows.

August, 1942.   TOM HARRISSON.

CONTENTS

DIAGRAMS

The diagrams are by Pamela Bocquet, Beatrice Lawrence and Molly Moss.

I

THE PUB

IN WORKTOWN MORE people spend more time in public houses than they do in any other buildings except private houses and work-places.

Why?

Of the social institutions that mould men's lives between home and work in an industrial town, such as Worktown, the pub has more buildings, holds more people, takes more of their time and money, than church, cinema, dance-hall, and political organizations put together.

The pub, reduced to its lowest terms, is a house where during certain hours everyone is free to buy and drink a glass of beer. It is the only kind of public building used by large numbers of ordinary people where their thoughts and actions are *not* being in some way arranged for them; in the other kinds of public buildings they are the audiences, watchers of political, religious, dramatic, cinematic, instructional or athletic spectacles. But within the four walls of the pub, once a man has bought or been bought his glass of beer, he has entered an environment in which he is participator rather than spectator.

In six religious sects (five of them new), the ordinary man or woman has also a higher degree of participation, even extending to speaking in tongues. They are the only other institutions in Worktown which supply a similar participation, except the "clubs"—and the word "club" has become synonymous locally with drink; and especially with obtaining drink after hours.

The relation of the pub to the place as a whole may be indicated by a general account from a person who has been working with the study unit; his impressions are thus:

> There are 300 pubs in Worktown: 200 police: nearly 200 churches and chapels: 30 cinemas: about 24 prostitutes: 180,000 other people.
> The major industry of this industrial town is cotton, but iron, leather, machinery, coal, and tripe are also important

industries. Chimneys are the outstanding landscape feature. Most of them smoke, and all day long soot dirties all the faces. It is the most prosperous of all the cotton towns, for it does fine spinning, and so has been least affected by foreign competition. In 1938, 15,000 workers were unemployed, which is approximately one in every nine of the working population. Work is predominantly done in the mills, whose employees include a high percentage of women (with high maternal and infant mortality rates). There are extremely few "upper class" people: there is a constant tendency for people who are economically or intellectually successful to leave the town and the district. The M.P.s are Conservative. There is very little local art, and if you go into the municipal Art Gallery, the attendant comes and has a good look to see that you are all right. The local evening paper is the intellectual dominant, reaching some 96 per cent of homes: it is "impartial", with a strong liberal-conservative slant, old established, first-rate journalism and production. The Unilever combine sales departments regard this as one of their black spots. Local patriotism is strong; though the town (incorporated as a borough in 1838, now getting a strong city urge) is one of an endless chain across the north, it in no sense identifies itself with other adjacent towns. It has a culture essentially its own, and available for uniform study— the solid background and smoky foreground of the industrial revolution and the vast, intricate technical civilization that has grown up around the basic industries. Worktown has a saying which has been heard from two consecutive mayors in public: "What Worktown says to-day, the North says to-morrow, and London the day after." Neither the tram service labyrinth that greets the new arrival outside the huge, hollow station, nor the architecture along the main streets (wider than in other towns), nor the women's hats, lend much colour to this thesis.

Very few workers have holidays with pay. Sunday is strict, and no trams or buses run in the morning. There are some 55,000 houses, and the same number of Co-op. members. The houses stand mainly in long, continuous rows, with narrow backs, across which washing flaps, soot-gathering, on Mondays.

The streets are mostly cobbled—and so is the bed of the town's river, the only paved river in England. Innumerable clogs clatter before daylight on their way to cotton's 48 hour week, cotton spinners with wages from 18 to 80 or so shillings, weavers averaging 32. A third of the workers are in Unions. There is no local branch of the Catering Section of the Transport and General Workers, the Union that takes in barmen. The Isolation Hospital and the Technical School are years out of

date, must soon be replaced to save local disgrace. Water
supply good. Rates just up 1s. 2d. partly because of the new
huge extension to the Town Hall, white, ornate, Bradshaw,
Gass and Hope (architects) crescent, with lions and arcades.
This is in town centre, bordering a huge waste space, fringed
on another side by the new and very striking cinema, and a
decomposing interstitial industrial belt, with slums immediately
adjacent—they also run off from the main shopping streets.
The Casual Ward is in the town centre too. The Public
Assistance Committee's Mental block is well outside, though,
and inadequate; people have to be recertified every few weeks
in accordance with law because there's nowhere to shift them to.
Most people are sane, pleasant and straightforward, without
southern sophistication, local-minded but curious, reasonably
credulous, reasonably optimistic, fairly mean and suspicious—
these generalizations don't really mean much about any town,
and equally cover all.

The dialect is at first unintelligible to the stranger. Full
of fine shades of meaning, reversed grammar, and regular good
humour. On the whole people care about their own homes,
and their few personal dreams (security, a holiday week at
orientalised Blackpool, a fortune in the Pools) and nothing else
matters very much except the progress made by the town's
famous football club, whose stadium draws each Saturday
more people than go into pubs or churches, in a once-a-week
mass manifestation of enthusiasm, fury, and joy.

Things are made in this dirty town. That justifies it. Why
they are made no ordinary citizen knows. In this mess of goodwill, misunderstanding, effort, insecurity, thought for the day,
Victoria the Great as biggest film draw of the year, the pub stands
on any corner. The frequent tide of adult folk sends long tem-
porary pseudopodia into the doors of each, to drink and talk,
then retract in darkness to smaller but not dissimilar houses
where they sleep. Why do they go there? Because people have
done before? Because other people are there? Because there are
things there that are nowhere else? Because people go everywhere
there is to go? Because the pub is as much a part of this civilization as the font or forge or diesel engine? Because they like
to change the rate of living, to alter the tempo of muscle and
eye, trained now in such exact and even exacting routines—
but people with no such exactness, cannibals and so on, also
take rate changers, stimulants, drugs? They go there to drink.

But there is more to it than that.
It is no more true to say that people go to public houses to

drink than it is to say they go to private houses to eat and sleep. These are the things that people do in pubs:

SIT and/or STAND

DRINK

TALK	about	betting
		sport
THINK		work
		people
SMOKE		drinking
		weather
SPIT		politics
		dirt

Many PLAY GAMES

cards
dominoes
darts
quoits

Many BET

receive and
pay out losings and winnings.

PEOPLE SING AND LISTEN TO SINGING: PLAY THE PIANO AND LISTEN TO IT BEING PLAYED.

THESE THINGS ARE OFTEN CONNECTED WITH PUBS . . .

. . . weddings and funerals.
quarrels and fights.
bowls, fishing and picnics.
trade unions.
secret societies. Oddfellows. Buffs.
religious processions.
sex.
getting jobs.
crime and prostitution.
dog shows.
pigeon flying.

PEOPLE SELL AND BUY

bootlaces, hot pies, black puddings, embrocation.

Also

LOTTERIES AND SWEEPSTAKES happen.
PREJUDICES gather.

All these things don't happen on the same evenings, or in the same pubs. But an ordinary evening in an ordinary pub will contain a lot of them.

Here is a characteristic record of such an evening:

This pub is at the corner of a block of brickfronted houses, whose front doors open directly on to the pavement. The road is cobbled; the bare, flat façades of the houses are all tinted to the same tone by the continual rain of soot from the chimneys of the mill opposite and the chimneys of all the other mills that stand in all the other streets like this.

The pub isn't much different from the other houses in the block, except for the sign with its name and that of the brewing firm that owns it, but its lower windows are larger than those of the others, and enclosed with stucco fake columns that go down to the ground; and the door, on the corner, is set at an angle; it is old-looking, worn, brown; in the top half is a frosted-glass window with VAULT engraved on it in handwriting flourishes; at the edges of the main pane are smaller ones of red and blue glass.

The door opens with a brass latch, disclosing a worn and scrubbed wooden floor, straight bar counter brown-painted with thick yellow imitation graining on the front panelling; at its base is a scattered fringe of sawdust, spit-littered, and strewn with match-ends and crumbled cigarette packets. Facing the bar a brown-painted wooden bench runs the length of the room.

Four yellowish white china handles, shiny brass on top, stand up from the bar counter. This is important, it is the beer engine, nerve-centre of the pub. Behind the bar, on shelves, reflecting themselves against mirrors at the back of their shelves, are rows of glasses and bottles, also stacked matches and Woodbine packets. Beer advertising cards and a notice against betting are fixed to the smoke-darkened yellowish wallpaper; and on the wall, beside the door, is a square of black glass, framed in walnut, that has painted on it, in gilt, a clock face with roman numerals, and the letters NO TICK. (The clock can't tick, it has no works; but if you are a regular the landlord will give you credit.)

Five men, in caps, stand or sit, three at the bar, two on the bench. They all have pint mugs of mild.

From the back parlour can be heard the sound of a man singing a sentimental song. In here they are discussing crime, man-slaughter, and murder. A small, thin man (whose name subsequently turns out to be X) appears to be a little drunk, and is talking very loudly, almost shouting. Another chap, called Y, also has a lot to say.

X (to Y): "If a man says you're a jailbird he's no right to say it—if he *is* a man."

Another man: "He can have you oop for defamation."

Y: "I've seen cases in the paper where a man's been found guilty and it's a bloody shame."

X (very slowly): "I'll tell you a bloody case, I'm telling you . . ."

Y: "Awright."

X: "There were two navvies——"

Another man, who has been quiet up to now, suddenly says, in indignant sounding tones "No, they weren't navvies", to which X simply replies "Ah'm sober enough" and goes on, apparently irrelevant—"There isn't a law made but what there's a loop'ole in it. Marshall Hall said that afore 'e was made a Sir—some big trial it were, for murder, an' it lasted a week, he'd strangled 'er wi' a necklace, it were that Yarmouth murder. He 'a won t' case, too, but for that courtin' couple, they were passing and they 'eard 'er screamin' and they thought they were only, you know, 'avin' a bit. Instead o' that 'e were stranglin' 'er. D'you know why there's a loophole in these 'ere laws. Well, them there M.P.s—'ave you ever noticed there's always some lawyer puts up. Now the reason for that——"
He looks up and sees, through the serving hatch at the back of the bar, a man going into the parlour, and shouts out "Eh, Dick, lend us two an' six. We're skint". Dick shouts back something inaudible and goes on into the parlour.

X stands silent for a moment, beerswallowing. One of the men on the bench says to him "Are you workin'?"

X: "I'll never work no more. I've an independent fortune every week."

Questioner turns to the barmaid, who has now come in from the parlour, and says "Molly, you don't know Mr. X, do you?" (Meaning that she knows him pretty well.) She laughs and replies: "No, I don't know him".

X: "None of that, Mr. X. I call 'er Molly, not Mrs. . . ."
He trails off, not knowing her surname.

The chaps begin to talk about swimming. X, irrepressible, knowing everything, chips in "I'll tell you 'oo were a good lad—Bob Robbins".

The singer in the parlour, who has been steadily working through three verses, now finishes with a prolonged and loud note, and there is the sound of some clapping.

The talkers have now divided into two groups, one around X, the other around an old man who is arguing about the age of the swimming baths. He keeps on saying "I remember it being built", to which another chap replies, disagreeing, "My father works there."

X: "That lad could fly through t' water like a bloody fish."

Y: "Bill Howard, that's 'is name."

X: "Goes into water like a bloody fish."

Old man (loud): "I remember it being built."

X: "I'll tell you what 'e could do—you know when you're walking along the towing path, you an' me walking along the towing path, 'e'd keep up wi' you, you an' me, walking decent tha knows, 'e'll keep up wi' you."

X stops, drinks, and the old man can be heard stubbornly reiterating: "I remember it being built."

X: "I'll tell you the hardest feat that was ever known—for a man to fall off the top of the bath and not go to the bottom and not go to the top, as long as 'e can 'old 'is breath—I've seen (name inaudible) do that. 'e could do a 'undred yards in eleven seconds—wi'out any training. What could 'e do wi' training? I'm telling you, he could stay in t' water, not go to the top and not go to the bottom—an' I'll tell you 'ow 'e did it."

Y (interrupting): "'ave another."

X: "Aye."

While he is getting his drink a chap stands up, and says "I swim that road", demonstrating convulsive sidestroke movements with his arms.

The old man looks up from his argument and remarks "I go left 'and first". And returns to the swimming bath discussion.

X, now with another beer, carries on: "He'd drop into the water and neether go to the bottom or go to the top . . ."

In the parlour they are singing the chorus of a jazz song, which the barmaid hums loudly.

It is now half past eight, and more people are coming in. Two old men arrive; both have gaps in their front teeth; wearing clogs, dark scarves knotted round pink wrinkled necks, white hair raggedly protrudes from behind their old caps; their coats, trousers, and waistcoats are all different yet appearing alike to be made of a shapeless greasy grey-blue cloth. They sit together, talking in undertones. Their beermugs are placed on the edge of the bar counter, and they have to reach forward, half standing up, to get at them. They both smoke pipes, from which drift the ropey smell of cheap twist. At regular intervals they shoot tidy gobs of spittle across into the sawdust. They reach for their mugs together, and drink the same amount at each swig. The mugs stand untouched for several minutes, with a last inch of beer in them; then one of the men stands up, drains his mug, and bangs it on the counter:

> The barmaid has gone out, and the landlord takes her place. (He is large, redfaced, clear blue eyes, about 45, wears a clean dark-grey suit, no coat, clean white shirt, sleeve rolled up, no collar or tie.) He draws off two halfpint glasses from one of the middle taps; the old man pays him, and the two empty the glasses into their mugs. During this transaction no one has said anything. Both men, standing, take a long, simultaneous swig, and sit down. One remarks, suddenly loud "Well, of all the bloody good things at Ascot t'other week anyone following Aga Khan t'other week would 'ave 'ad a bloody picnic".
>
> X bawls across at him "What dost tha know about bloody horses. I'll bet thee a bloody shilling and gie thee two thousand pound start an' I'll 'ave bloody Lawson agen 'im. Why, 'e's seven bloody winners at meeting, you bloody crawpit." The old man says nothing.
>
> A group of four men has gathered round the table, and is playing dominoes. Each has a pint mug at his elbow. At the end of the round they turn the dominoes face downwards and stir them noisily. They play with a lot of loud talking and joking.
>
> One says "'oo went down then?"
>
> "Jimmy."
>
> "Oh, Jimmy went down."
>
> "I did."
>
> "My down—one an' one."
>
> "If we're down we're down, that's all. What's the use of worrying."
>
> "Come on, man, don't go to bloody sleep. Th'art like a bloody hen suppin' tea; when th'art winnin' it's awreet, but when th'art losin' it's all bloody wrong."
>
> They talk about the holidays, which begin next week.
>
> "I'm not savin' oop twelve bloody months for t' sake a gooing away fer a week. Wife's always asking what I do wi' me overtime, and I towd 'er—why, I bloody well spend it, what dost think—and she says—Tha owt t' 'ave more bloody sense."

So on, until, at about 10.20, they leave; standing for from one to three minutes outside, and calling "Good night" as they walk, at about two miles an hour, to their private houses, which are seldom more than three minutes' walk away.

We shall presently come to all the different things that are done in the pub, from brawls to Royal and Ancient Order of Buffalo initiations; from the fading folk-lore of Pigeon Racing to the growing rage for darts. It is only necessary to point out here, that betting and gambling are largely centred in the pub, with a whole social group around the bookmakers' runner; but that the other things are found to some extent in other institutions. There are few things which are peculiar to the pub in Worktown, other than draught beer and spittoons. It is essentially a social group around widespread and commonplace social activities. These attain new angles, new point, and a close integration with other aspects of industrial life by being pressed into the service of satisfying, or dissatisfying, these numerous small communities bound together by the bond of beer habits.

There are, on the other hand, certain things which are not found in pubs in Worktown, though they occur in pubs elsewhere. The following might be expected:

> Billiards.
> Whist Drives.
> Dances.
> Skittles.
> Shove ha'penny.
> Literature.

Billiards, dancing and whist drives never occur in Worktown pubs. They are a regular feature of church and political life, and often a major source of church and party revenue. There are also separate dance and billiard halls, well patronized: interest in billiards tends to decline, in dancing to increase. The patrons of both are often regular pub-goers, and frequently leave the halls to have a drink. Skittles and shove ha'penny are apparently unknown in the town, and the pub has apparently given up its one-time function of a reading place; few even have an evening paper for their patrons. Bearing these qualifications in mind, it should incidentally be possible from the particular study of Worktown pub life to appreciate something of the function of the pub in all English industrial communities.

II

DRINK

Beᴇᴇʀ

For almost everyone in Worktown Drink equals Beer.

BEER IS BEST proclaim the boardings along the main roads. Showcards in pubs announce "A healthy appetizing drink that will help to keep you fit. The best refreshment".

Oatmeal stout is "Thoroughly sound and well brewed from the finest quality Malt, Hops, and Oatmeal. Free from acidity and GUARANTEED PURE."

A local firm makes and publicizes "Vitamin Stout". And William Younger's is "Just what the Doctor ordered!"

But—says a pamphlet given away by the Rechabites, local temperance society—"Beer is the most harmful of alcoholic drinks because it is the most seductive."

And—of a leading brand of beer a landlord said to an observer—"Anyone who can drink ——'s mild must be able to feed on rats."

An old female rag sorter, when drunk, remarked to an observer, "I've supped ale till I'm sixteen and I'll sup it till I die."

Others write of it with fondness too. Says a letter, sent in answer to an inquiry conducted through the local press on "Why drink beer"—"I drink beer to keep me fit it do's the stummick good, and there is only one good reason I Drink Beer it is because I cannot eat it."

Differently looked upon, and analysed, beer is $3\frac{1}{2}$ per cent alcohol, $3\frac{1}{2}$ per cent malto-dextrins, with traces of volatile acids, proteins, organic acids, and mineral matter.

But beer is over 90 per cent water.

The main local brewery announces that, since 1853, they "have been brewing good wholesome English beer, using only the choicest malt and finest hops. The natural aperient and tonic values of the hop cannot be excelled by better means THAN A GLASS OF BEER".

Hops (*Humulus lupulus*), condemned by Henry VI, were let in by Henry VIII, introduced from Flanders to Kent, still their centre, though the king banned them in ale because they did "dry up the body and increase melancholy".

THE BREWERY

Observers went to the brewery to see. Their report:

The building is large, red brick, with towers, from which all Worktown is visible. In tower is water tank. The town water goes up to it. Sacks of barley are hoisted to the top floor. Pipes, vats, furnaces, pumps, blowers, cooling pipes, grinding machines, make beer from this water, gradually, from floor to floor, down to the barrelling and bottling rooms.

Only yeast is permanent, taken from cold storage rooms, put into fermenting vats for 52 hours, sucked off, dried, and restored to its dark cold solitude.

The water is bought from the town; once a well was bored; they spent three thousand pounds, went down for eleven hundred feet, then gave up. An extra, and very large water tank was put in the other tower. It is empty, has never been filled.

Barley, in sacks, comes up the hoist, is cleaned and polished; big magnets pick out the old nails, etc. Mechanically stoked furnaces boil a mash of barley with water—some brought in tanks from Burton to the brewery siding.

Above the boiling vats are domes of polished copper. Peering through inspection window the seething shiny liquid darkness of hot stout is visible. Carbon dioxide collects in the dome, is drawn off, stored under pressure, used for aerating bottled beer. (What's left goes to mineral water, puts life into lemonade.) After the boiling vats the half-way-to-beer liquid is drained off through complicated cooling pipes into the open, fermenting vats. In these huge tanks, the liquid stands bubbling, while foam gathers on top in snow crags that turn brown, collapse, and form a scummy crust that stays while underneath yeast works for 52 hours.

Then the now "almost-beer" goes down to the next floor, into more tanks. In both rooms half the vats are empty. Some, the brewer who shows the observers round says, have not been used for years. The big vats hold 180 barrels; perhaps ten are filled every week. The brewer was rather evasive about this. What he liked showing and talking about were the air conditioning and constant temperature arrangements. For the fermenting rooms they are essential, but they are everywhere.

About 150 people work here. Hours are variable. Men have to stay around all night and through the week-end to nurse the fermenting. The biggest concentration of workers is in the bottling plant. Here are machines for bottling, washing, labelling—all American, very expensive. The brewer exhibits pride in them, takes out a washed bottle for inspection, and de-tailed discussion.

Conveyers take the bottles straight through to the crating department. During bottling carbon dioxide is injected. Women work on this, mostly aged 35 to 45. They wear blue aprons, and look healthy.

Next is washing room, where high pressure containers on wheels, looking like enormous vacuum cleaners, are standing about. These are for yeast that has been removed from the fermenting vats; it is pressed, and the squeezed-off liquid is drained back into the vats. This is done to save tax, because revenue men come round to measure amounts in the fermenting vats. At one time the extra liquid was thrown away.

Observers go down in lift to a room full of crates. The brewer says there used to be twice as many of them at one time. Here the head brewer is encountered; he is tall, with long white coat, bowler hat, red face, reminding observers of a horse breeder. With him is unnamed short, squat, very wide man with a wide felt hat. At the back of the crates is a small table with bottles and glasses. Observers are given strong ale.

Next are the cellars, where again the complaint is made that they are only half as full as they used to be. Then to the huge white barrel-shaped vats where the beer stands, waiting, until it is ready to be barrelled. Here it is icy cold.

Adjacent is the yeast room. A heavy insulated door opens to a small bare cell. In it are four small containers about the size and shape of dustbins. Each is half filled with yeast. There is nothing else in the room, except cold air. But this is the most important place in the brewery. The yeast is 25 years old. It goes on for ever. It has been the active principle in making the beer that some have died from drinking too much of a good long time ago. Kept at the right temperature and properly looked after there is nothing to prevent it going on indefinitely. The brewer worries about the possibility of it going bad, though. When asked what would happen if it did he says that they would have to get some more, and it might be worse than this lot. (He never refers to anything being not so good as something that exists in the brewery, but always talks about it as being "worse" than what they have already.)

From this cold sanctuary the party is taken to a small semi-underground room with two large barrels, a table, glasses, and rows of sample bottles, handwriting labelled. The brewer leans against the wall, lights a cigarette, and becomes social. Different kinds of beer are brought out and drunk. Observers think, and remark, that they taste rather or a lot better than the same taps in the local pubs. The brewer drinks "best mild". The small, cheerful, saturnine man in attendance has some too. He is a beer apologist, and attempts to give the observers an intellectual beating-up in conversation about pubs and drinking. His job is to go around the pubs and look into complaints, also to see that their beer is kept decently. He says that the landlords are responsible for bad beer; some men come into the trade and don't know anything about it. He quoted landlord of the —— Arms, who used to be a commercial traveller. Observers gain face by pointing out that the beer there is always too warm. Brewer says that within his memory at least four small firms have all closed down.

Everybody comes out of here in social mood, and find themselves in the engine room, where there is a steam engine that was christened after the boss's only son at the age of three. The son never visited the engine (it has the most peculiar valve gear) and there appears to be feudal feeling about this. Brewer says "We've made a mistake here, not having any sons in the business".

There are yet garages and stables to be seen. The harness room, full of past glories of dead horses, is looked after by a pensioned-off old man, who has enormous ears.

The brewer leads the way down to a railway siding where there are trucks full of Burton water. He props up a ladder against one of the trucks and insists that observers should climb up and look in (to see that it is really there). On top of the truck is a manhole; inside, the tank is empty, except for enormous quarter-inch thick flakes of rust strewn over the bottom. Last is the coopering shop. Barrels are still made by hand. The men have nearly all gone home by now, because, the foreman says, they get paid by piece-work. It is quite different here to any other part of the place—old-style craft-work—a difference that is summed up in a remark made by the brewer, who refers to something as "one of these economy stunts", while in speaking of every other rationalizing device in the brewery he had been enthusiastic.

This firm has a capital of £600,000 in ten pound shares. Dividends for the last five years are—10 per cent, 6 per cent, 8 per cent, 10 per cent, 10 per cent; "Information as to the number of licensed houses owned is not available" says the Stock Exchange Year Book.

When the firm was asked for information about this their reply was laconic and obscure.

Workers in this firm are largely unorganized, though at one time many of them belonged to the union[1] (now 40 members, none paid up). Another local brewery firm has its chairman also chairman of the Conservative Party.

Beside making beer they also bottle Guinness, wines, spirits, make cocktails, and soft drinks. They own a number of pubs in Blackpool which, during the holiday weeks, are crammed with Worktowners.

KINDS OF BEER, COSTS, CUSTOMERS

Says the *Encyclopædia Britannica* (14th ed.) speaking of different kinds of beer:

> The essential difference . . . lies in the flavour and colour, which depend particularly on the type of malt and the quantity of hops used in brewing them.

Beyond a certain stage of fermentation the chemistry of beer is a mystery—highly complex, not yet known. Brewers proceed empirically. Differences between different kinds of beer can be shown on the basis of their alcohol carbohydrate and proteid content.

	Alcohol % by weight.	Carbohydrate and Proteid %.
Strong Ale	5·15	9·6
Bottled Pale Ale (best quality)	4·44	4·24
Light Bitter	3·28	3·06
Mild { From	3·45	4·44
{ To	2·58	2·80

Mild is the most commonly drunk beer in Worktown. It costs fivepence a pint—minimum price. In parlours and lounges, the pub's best rooms, patronized by hat and tie rather than cap and scarf, all beer prices are a penny a pint more.

Most of it is supplied by Magees (a local) and Walkers (a nearby) brewery. Other firms are Threlfalls, Hamers, Cornbrooks . . . But Magees and Walkers dominate the local pub scene.

As well as mild there is "best mild", penny a pint more, stronger, and in observers' opinions, nicer than the common

[1] 1931 census gives 472 brewery workers in the town.

mild. It is light in colour, like bitter, which is seldom drunk here.

Other draught beers are strong ale, I.P.A., stout. So that Worktowners' choice is:

MILD	5d.	a pint
BEST MILD . . .	6d.	a pint
I.P.A.	7d.	a pint
STRONG ALE . . .	11d.	a pint

Draught stout no longer counts. At one time commonly drunk, it now is extremely rare here; we have only seen it sold in one pub. Strong ale is not often drunk; when kept it is displayed on the bar counter in a little barrel.

I.P.A. is interesting. Originally a light bottled ale brewed in this country to be sent to India, specially suitable for hot weather, its introduction to English drinkers was the result of an accident. Hodgson's India Pale Ale was the standard drink of Englishmen imperializing in the east. In the 1820's Bass came in on this market. (They were able to do this as the result of a "misunderstanding" between Hodgson's and the East India Co.) By 1827 shiploads of Bass's I.P.A. were walloping their way down the Irish Channel. One was wrecked. But much of its cargo was salvaged and sold at Liverpool. There, the local drinkers acclaimed it, and Bass's developed a good market in the whole of the area. A bar selling I.P.A. at the 1851 Great Exhibition launched it as a world drink.

But, now, in Worktown, I.P.A. (which is to-day made by all the main brewers)—only sold in bottles in most places—is largely draught. It isn't drunk very much except in a few pubs, is considered to be very intoxicating and to give you a bad hangover. Of it, a barman in a pub that sold it said, "It's a good appetizer —but I wouldn't like to have a lot of it".

Draught beers, on the other hand, are served through pumps, whose handles, sometimes wood, sometimes brass and china, plain, coloured, or patterned, stick up conspicuously upon the bar-counter. The average pub has three or four pumps; these used to be used for mild, best, and stout. Now one or two are often disused, and the others connected up to barrels of mild.

AMOUNTS

The biggest local brewers were asked for relative figures of different types of beer sold. It was useless to ask them for actual sales; these are surrounded with the utmost secrecy; brewing firms send men to hang round the yards of their competitors and watch their lorries; also they try to take on rivals' employees —all to find out the sales figures.

This is what they replied:

Dear Sir,—In answer to your letter of the 30th November, we have to say that the information that you ask for is confidential, and further, our staff is too busy to be getting out fanciful statistics.

A director of Messrs. Guinness who is personally known to one of us, replied (courteously) pointing out that it was impossible for them to know what their Worktown sales were, as they were not made direct, but to the local brewing companies, who did the bottling and distribution themselves. In general, we found these data surrounded either by secrecy or uncertainty.

We tried the barmen. One, in a typical, small corner beerhouse, said that their sales of bottled beer were about a third of those of draught beer, and gave the following figures:

AVERAGE SALES PER WEEK

2½ barrels of mild.
16 doz. of bottled ale.
12 doz. of Guinness.
4 doz. small bottles stout.
1 doz. minerals.

The yearly sales of this pub are as follows:

SALES OF MILD
(In barrels, weekly orders)

Jan.	Feb.	Mar.	Apr.	May	June	July	Aug.	Sep.	Oct.	Nov.	Dec.
5	2½	2½	1½	2½	3½	4	3	2½	2½	2½	2½
3	2½	2½	1	2	2½	4	3½	4	3	2	2
2	1½	1½	3	3½	2	3	4	4	3	2	3½
1½	2½	2½	3	1½	2	1	1	3	2½	2½	2½
				4		1½	1½		2½		4½
11½	9	9	8½	13½	10	13½	13	13½	13½	9	15 Totals

YEAR'S TOTAL, 139 barrels

This barman wrote "There is so little demand for bitter and draught stout that difficulty is experienced in obtaining them in the meaner quarters of the town".

Some landlords' statements about the relative quantities of beer drunk are:

(a) "I should reckon 93 per cent—no, 92 per cent mild."

(b) "We have plenty of women at night—they drink stout, Guinness, or Brown Pete. I should reckon 60 per cent of the women drink Guinness. Some men drink Guinness as well, but not many." . . . "No best mild; we mix the mild and the bitter."

(c) "I should reckon 60 per cent drink mild."

(d) "The people here drink more best mild than mild—only women drink the Guinness—and port—very little I.P.A. and strong ale drunk—whiskey when they can get it."

(e) "Re proportions of various drinks consumed, I think 90 per cent mild, the other 10 you can work out, but I should give Guinness 5 per cent. You see, the heavy drinker is the man in the vault and taproom, and he consumes 200 per cent more than the customer in the best rooms."

The Brown Pete referred to above is the usual term for Walker's Brown Peter, a bottled brown ale. Their light ale is called Falstaff, and popular with Worktown Irishmen; and they also sell a bottled stout. Magee's bottled beers cover a similar range, the light ale being called Crown. Landlords are not supposed to split pint bottles between customers (prices being $7\frac{1}{2}d$. a pint bottle, $4\frac{1}{2}d$. a half bottle) but it is often done.

The general estimate of about 90 per cent mild is borne out by all our observations. The *gill* is the common unit of drink, the only Worktown term for a half-pint.

QUALITIES

Choice of brand and type of beer is limited. Most pubs stock only mild, and bottled ales and stout. And most people live within walking distance of only Magees' or Walkers' pubs. (Later we show that 90 per cent of pub regulars don't walk more than 300 yards to get to their usual pubs.)

That most people drink the cheapest beer points to price rather than taste or quality being the deciding factor of their choice. At week-ends, when drinkers have most money, more bottled beer is drunk. We have plenty of observations on men starting off their Saturday night drinking with a round of bottled Crown or Falstaff, before going onto draught. And nationally the consumption of bottled beer has gone up 300 per cent in the past ten years. This shift has tended to alter brewery work, and is an increasing factor in pub organization. So far in Worktown, bottled beer has made no major inroads on the dominance of draught.

Men are guided by price first. Women, who often have men pay for them, go more for taste and the externals. It is more "respectable" for women to drink bottled beer, mostly bottled stout or Guinness, seldom mild. Brewers have found nationally a preference for beer in amber bottles, rather than green bottles. They don't know the reason. An important factor is the tradition of beer, tradition's drink, as amber-coloured; looking green through the bottle, it isn't absolutely beer. In a random count (May), 43 per cent women were drinking beer or spirits, 57 per cent bottled stout or Guinness.

How is beer drunk? Do people take much notice of it as beer? Later we will go into the complicated and important habit-patterns associated with the act of drinking. For the moment let us see what beer-drinking looks and sounds like.

The following is a report by a local working-class man, a non-pub goer, who was told to go into a small beerhouse and give his impressions of beer-drinking:

> When I got in nobody takes any notice beyond two of the men turning to look very quickly at me. I called out "A gill, mild," this was put on the mahogany topped bar, no polish on this, owing to the constant swilling of the top with the beer given in full measure and spilling as it is lifted to the mouth.
>
> Gill was pushed on to the top from the Pump by the chap of about 40 who was in his shirtsleeves.
>
> None are sitting at the form near the door, but when I sits to try my first drink of beer ever I am joined by a man called "Jack", he says "Good evening, chum, never seed thee before in here". I told him that I used to come round that quarter some ten years before, he replied, "Aye, this bloody street has never been the bloody same since the mill shut up, there's bugger all doing round here now, th'art lucky wi' a good job these days, same wi' t'bloody beer, it's nowt but piss and chemicals, it's not so bad here, they keep it well though, I'll say that for him."
>
> We were joined by another man who began to tell me of what he did and where he used to work. "I only come in here

on Sunday neets, tha'll not see me in this place for another week, I've gettan a good home and a good wife and family, I've nowt to complain of only my own bloody silly self, that's reet, isn't it Jack, if I'd been sensible I'd have been in the —— now, I was theer for 27 years, they cawn't make bloody beer these days, then they could have etten they bloody meight off the floor then, they kept them pumps clean and everything were all reet."

The other chap in the blue-suit cut in with "Well, it were thee own bloody fault thee should a looked after theysel, still it's noan the same since that Jack H—— geet it".

"Aye, then we used to put gradely Hop dust in the vats then, and when that government chap came round he used to say it weer good, nea they are always watching, they know they play about wi' it. I've seen times when thea could stick a bloody spoon up in it and it would stand up, God strike me dead it were like bloody black treacle."

"Thee tak it frae me, keep to what theat suppin nea, common beer, keep away from spirits and bitter, they're no bloody good to anybody."

As we talk the men are all talking at the top of their voices, now it's about the Wandrers and two are talking about the Army, then it gets to "Thee just see, before long they'll have us all on munitions before long, them and all the bloody women, they'll not let so many men this time on it, it'll be to the bloody front, theer's no beer theer." At this they all laughed, one said "We bet em last time and we'll a to do it again."

They are all ordering their beer like this. "Fill it up, pint o' bitter this time." Then the man held the glass and put to the pump and the handle was pulled down, the glass in nearly every instance was filled to the brim, as it was put down it spilled, sometimes he got the cloth and wiped it up.

Another man called out, "Thea thinks I've gettan a good job, well thee be up every neet on my job, one Saturday neet off in a month, I get to bed when the wife gets up, it noan reet, neet time's the time to be in bed and get some fresh air in't day time."

A chap in a blue suit came to sit near. "Havin it filled up again wi me, Christ, I've had 18 pints in one neet and noan ben any the worse for it, theat reet though, enoughs as good as a feast." Another man of 50, muffler on, "I went into . . . and it were sludge at bottom, I towd him about it, he said tak it or leave it, so I walked out wi't wife, we should a spent 5s. that neet, they're like that till they find they're in debt to the brewers."

"THERE'S NO BAD BEER"

Though beer is a common subject of pub talk, the conversation is mostly quantitative rather than qualitative—when, where, how much, and by whom, it was drunk, rather than about its goodness or badness. There are, however, drinkers who do care for the quality of their beer, and who will congregate at pubs whose landlords keep the beer in good condition (more about this later). And some will go out of their way to try a brew that is new to them, as this case shows:

> The landlord here says he gets his beer from a small brewery in Derby Street. He doesn't care for large breweries, says "It's all done with chemicals". He likes, when possible, to let the barrel stand for a day or two before he taps it. Tells observer a story of how he once ordered a barrel of bitter, but no one asked for it until, six months later, a stranger called in and ordered a bitter. Landlord said that he had some, but it wasn't any good, it had been kept too long; but if he liked he would draw off a little and let him try it. The stranger said that it was wonderful—"like wine". This man took to calling in regularly for it, until the barrel was finished. It went soon, because he told his friends, and they came in for it too. In the end he said he was sorry that he had let them in on it. The moral of the story, according to the landlord, is that beer from the big breweries goes off in no time, and if it had been ——'s bitter it would have been absolutely undrinkable.

Serious drinkers will watch the pumps while their beer is being drawn, to see that it is pumped properly and that no stale liquor is being put into it—a habit that they say is common. We have observed on busy nights in some pubs a bucket half full of beer standing just inside the bar, beside the serving hatch; and the waiters empty the slops from their trays into it. Theoretically all the slops, and beer left in glasses should be collected and returned to the brewers. A landlord writes of this:

> Re condition of beer. Well, this varies, some brewers send it badly conditioned, and it takes three or four hours in that case before ready for use. It takes beer weeks to go off unless something is wrong in the brewing, it is returned if not suitable and replaced, mind you, Brewers do not like a landlord to return anything and they expect him to have the intelligence to dispose of it (someway). Re glasses returns. That also

should go back into the barrel and be returned to the brewers, but I question very much if this is done in most pubs.

Some pub-goers give this reason for preferring the "vault" to other rooms, because only in the "vault" can you watch your beer being drawn off. (But you can't know what slops have gone back into the barrel from last night.) About 15 years ago a new type of pump was introduced into one local pub; these pumps were out of sight of the customers and they disliked them; after a few months they were taken away and the old ones replaced.

For the great majority of drinkers, taste and quality of beer are not the major factors; were they so most of the big popular pubs in the town would have to go out of business. The general attitude is nicely summed up by the following correspondent:

> There is, I think, many different brands of beer which so far I have not had the Pleasure of Tasting. Those I have, such as: Magee's, Walker's, Hamer's, Cunningham's, and one or two others, have all a nice Flavour, and I enjoy a glass of beer. The Price question I will not Dispute, because I do not Drink Excessively, so I don't favour any particular Beer, and so I always say: There's no *Bad Beer*, only sometimes Indifferent.

Most pub-goers simply drink the cheapest available beer, while a minority exists for whom quality is most important. This is in agreement with the findings of Basil Nicholson, author of the section on Drink in the London Survey (also republished separately by the Church of England Temperance Society). We cannot trace any other work in this field to which we might refer our conclusions.

HOW MUCH BEER IS DRUNK

It would be little use to answer the question:—How much beer do Worktowners drink? with a figure based on statistical averages. In any case, it is impossible to find from official sources the real total amount of beer consumed in the town for any specified period; the only people who are in a position to know are the brewers and excise officers, who keep records of local sales; but these, as we have already seen, are jealously guarded secrets.

On the basis of national figures (Government Statistical Abstract for 1936) beer consumption per head of population is 17.58 gallons a year. Population of Worktown for that year is 174,000—making on that basis a yearly consumption of almost

three million gallons (2,958,840). As far as other national statistics
go, of drunks in pubs (per ten thousand of population) Worktown
is below average. (Pubs, per 10,000, Worktown 17.58, England
and Wales 18.29. Convictions for drunkenness, Worktown 7.58,
England and Wales 10.9.) So we will probably not be far wrong
in assuming that the year's beer-drinking of the statistical
Worktowner is about seventeen and a half gallons. But what we
really want to know is what section of the 180,000 odd population
can be expected to be sharers in the year's three million gallons.
Obviously not children. Sample counts of 7,172 people in a wide
range of pubs showed an average percentage of 16 women.
Age group counts (see page 136) showed that over nine-tenths of
drinkers were above 25.

In Worktown, in 1936, there were 52,400 males over the age
of 25 (age and sex proportions based on national figures of last
Census). Field work indicates that some 15 per cent of males
are teetotallers (mainly the town's strong Nonconformist element,
circa 18,000 chapel-goers). Let us then, on this basis, assume that
the maximum *potential* number of drinkers is between 50,000 and
60,000. If they drink three million gallons a year their statistical
average per head per day will be about one pint. (Max. 1.1.)

Now let us examine how much people actually drink in pubs.

On one Thursday evening (27/7/37) the amount drunk by every
one, from opening to closing time, in the bar of a beerhouse, was
noted. (See graphic representation of this on page 195.) 28 men
between them put back 88 pints, an average of 3·16 pints per head.
This average was made up as follows:

Pints	0–1	1–2	2–3	3–4	4–5	5–6	6–7	7–8
Men	3	6	6	7	4	1	0	1

A similar set of observations on the following Saturday showed
an average of 3·45 pints per head. This, however, was not made
up in the same way. 29 men were observed, but 15 of them went
on to other pubs—a common Saturday night habit. The 14
who did all their evening's drinking in this pub averaged 4·57
pints per head. Week-end drinking is always heavier than on
week nights, and far more people visit the pubs (see Chapter V).

These observations were made on "regulars", that is, men who
visit the pub regularly, either on every night or most nights of

the week, who always stay about the same time and drink about the same amount. Their drinking is heavier than that of the occasional casual who drops in to "have one", but, in averaging out the casual's low consumption will be cancelled by the occasional booze-up on special occasions, such as the celebration of a long-priced winner. Outside the town-centre pubs, the majority of people seen in pubs are regulars.

Very few landlords would give any estimate of the ordinary regular's average drinking. Landlord A.H. writes:

" Re quantities of drink. During the week night average 4 pints per night, Saturday probably 12, Sunday 12, including noon."

Drinkers' own verbatim statements give rather a different picture. About six out of ten said that they were regulars, and gave the name of the pub they used; 2 in 10 said that they went to any handy pub; the rest were less definite.

The answers of some who specified amounts drunk are:

Pints	0–1	1–2	2–3	3–4
Men	6	6	1	2

5 said the following variable amounts:

Gills: 2–7, 2–5, 3–7, 2–10, and 8–12.

10 said that they drank more on Saturdays, including one who said he usually got drunk.

(This small check compares well with figures later on, where 58 per cent of drinkers are regulars. The question of drink is so inhibited by teetotal antagonisms and tradition that direct personal data are exceptionally difficult to obtain. Some data was collected by a newspaper competition. One woman came to the offices of the local paper through which the competition was organized, indignantly brandishing a questionnaire, and proclaiming that she had never been in a pub in her life, and was an abstainer. When asked why she had entered for the competition she said that she thought it was a chance to be first for once. We may be warned by this of the serious dangers inherent in any form of direct, verbal, crude sociology.

Another set of clues to the amount pub-goers drink is given by examining the quantity of beer sold by a small corner pub. Earlier (p. 32) we give a table of the sales of a pub right through a year. This amounts to almost 4,500 gallons. Accepting the bar-man's statement that their bottled beer sales are a third of this, we get the figure of almost 6,000 gallons, or 923 pints a week.[1]

Who drinks this? We have a list of the regular customers of the pub. There are 62 of them; some are only week-end regulars.[2] We have not exact figures for casual customers; but certainly there are very few of them here. In these local street corner beerhouses (which comprise two-thirds of the town's pubs) strangers are suffic-iently unusual to excite comment. The amount they drink only represents a small fraction of the total sales, and for the purposes of this estimate can be neglected. Therefore, we will base our weekly average on the 62 known customers. From this we get a figure of 14·89 pints per person per week, or 2·13 per night. This is certain to be slightly lower than the real amounts consumed by the regulars, as many of them will during the week and especially at the week-end probably have been into the town centre pubs.

Summing up, we can say that the average of 1·1 pints a day based on the town's share of national beer consumption divided out among a maximum number of 60,000 people, is lower than the consumption of the average pub-goer. Observation of regulars in one pub shows an average of 3·16 pints in a night. Only a tenth of pub-goers from all over the town say that they drink less than a pint, and some say that they take more than four pints. And all the figures other than those of our first estimate can only be considered real when it is taken into account that, since the ordinary drinker does not necessarily go to his pub every night of the week, a man who drinks 28 pints in a week will have more than four pints on any given night, and a man who drinks four pints a night may consume less than 28 pints in the week.

The most likely deductions from our data are that the regular drinks around three pints a night, but not necessarily every night; but there is a section of drinkers who consume a good deal less than this, and another of heavy drinkers whose nightly average is above four pints. Also, the majority of all types drink more at week-ends. More data relevant to this later.

Since the lowest average is above 1·1 pints a day, we can there-fore infer that the figure of 60,000 potential pub-goers is too high

[1] Multiplied by total number of pubs this gives circa 2,000,000 gallons a year; but about 100 pubs are larger than this one, and thus there is a reasonable agreement with the estimate on other data.

[2] Other material, given later, shows that this is a good average figure for the ordinary beerhouse regulars (p. 110).

N O T E : Colin Clarke estimated national expenditure for 1935 had 6 per cent income spent on drink (with 27·1 per cent food, 3·5 per cent tobacco, 10·3 per cent clothes). Even if we took our minimum figure of 1·1 pints a day for 60,000, this would amount to 3s. 2½d. a week, which is 6 per cent of 54 shillings. M'Gonigle and Kirby, in their work on food and other family budget items, ignored alcohol, which is not mentioned in their book; it was not included as an item on their enquiry schedule (p. 195). "Small items . . . such as newspapers, cigarettes and amusements" are referred to (p. 196) and classed with "money available for food". The authors comment: "Individual tastes vary so much and habits of carefulness or extravagance are so purely personal that it was not found possible to assess what sum could or should be allotted for these little extravagances or amenities." But these "little extravagances" do not, in our experience, vary any more markedly than do individual tastes in food and housekeeping economy. Our own budget data, scanty so far, shows average 14 per cent on these amenity items, minimum 2 per cent, maximum 25 per cent (see a later volume). Harrison and Mitchell in *The Home Market* (1939) similarly ignore alcohol or pub-going, so did the Liverpool University's *Survey of Merseyside* (1934).

The majority of Worktowners work in or connected to the cotton trade, whose average 1937 wages were 32s. 5d. a week—20 per cent get less than 30s. But Bowley and Hogg (p. 148) showed that half Worktown's families had more than one wage earner. A spinner with two sons and two daughters can afford to drink a lot more when they become old enough to go out to work, but not old enough to leave home.

Basil Nicholson says: "From observation and available figures it is possible to say with some certainty that an average London family (excluding abstainers) with an income of from £3 to £3 15s. a week, spent (husband and wife included) about 10s. to 12s. a week on drink in 1934."

He also quotes (in the London Survey) the Colwyn report: "These estimates are admittedly only hypothetical, and they refer to the whole country . . . but the table for 1923-4 agrees remarkably closely with such family budget figures, including drink, as it has been possible to obtain in the course of the present enquiry, and with a wide series of estimates made by both members of the trade and its opponents, as well as with published estimates by impartial writers."

The Colwyn Report figures that he uses are actually thus:

Income	Combined consumption of husband and wife			Cost	Approx. % of income
	spirits (bottles)	beer (pints)	wine (bottles)		
£100–150	—	650	—	£16 5s.	under 16%
£150–200	5½	800	6	£24 7s.	under 16%
£200–250	7½	900	12	£29	under 15%

Finally Chisholm gives other calculations. National drink (all drinks) figures for 1937, £232 million, cf. £248 for 1936-7, which is more than furniture, coal and footwear together. Increase on 1932 was 7 per cent, less of an increase than in other retail distribution commodities—papers upped 10 per cent, tobacco 13 per cent, furniture 24 per cent. Drink comes third item on the nation's bill —food is first, £1,305 million in 1936-7.

The Report of the Commissioners on Customs and Excise showed an increase of 5½ per cent beer consumption in 1937-8, £3 million more paid in beer duty. In March and April 1939 the amount of beer brewed fell 90,000 barrels as compared with the same months of 1938.

REASONS WHY PEOPLE DRINK BEER

There are two sorts of explanations as to why people drink beer. One is really the explanation of why men drink, why they go to pubs. It is the answer to what is called the "drink problem". This we won't attempt to give until near the end of the book. But the reasons that people themselves give for drinking beer are a different matter. A competition in the local press (organized by us) brought a number of replies relevant to this.

Reasons of health and/or beneficial physical effect, the factors recently stressed in brewers' advertising, were given by the majority; and the greatest number of actual references in the letters were to these reasons. 52 per cent mentioned them. Their references (some gave two or three reasons) are classified as follows:

Health Reason Given	Percentage Giving This Reason
General health-giving properties	24%
Beneficial effect in connection with work, or refreshing after work	17%
Good effect on appetite	14%
Laxative effect	10%
Sleep inducing	10%
"Nourishing"	6%
"Tonic"	8%
Valuable properties of malt and hops	6%
"Vitamins"	6%
"Diuretic"	2%

35 per cent of people gave social reasons—drinking for companionship. Other kinds of statements were made. One communication, in capital letters on a small piece of paper 4½ inches square, said: "My reason for drinking beer is to appear tough. I heartily detest the stuff but what would my pals think if I refused. They would call me a cissy." This may be meant as a joke, or even an invitation; but it may far more likely be a genuine cry of distress.

Compare this with the statements of football pool addicts and smokers, quoted in *First Year's Work*, by Mass Observation (1938); there (in the Pools section), typical statements: "Everybody has a do, thart nor in t' fashion if theau doesn't," and "Everybody practically bets o' t' Pools"; plus the Editors' remark: "It is not surprising that 95 per cent Poolites state that all or nearly all of their friends go in for Pools too." In this same report's section on Smoking:—"In answering the question 'Why did you start to smoke?' half the observers gave social or imitative reasons such as:—'In order to be sociable.' 'Because other people did.' 'My chief reason for starting to smoke was that most of my friends were smokers and I felt rather an outsider as long as I was not. . . . I did not get any great pleasure from the actual smoking.'" And Rowntree, whose 1900 survey of York throws so much light, concluded (p. 379):

> The large proportion of persons who stayed in the (public) house for more than a quarter of an hour shows how to a large extent the house is used for "social drinking".

One correspondent wrote us that he only went into the pub with his friends for the sake of their company—"otherwise I am sure I should never set foot in a public house . . . actually loathing the taste of every glass of beer that I drink". This is true of others; beer is often spoken of as "an acquired taste".

A letter from a woman who certainly has acquired it, is the following:

> My reason is, Because I always liked to see my Grandmother having a drink of beer at night. She did seem to enjoy it, and she could pick up a dry crust of bread and cheese, and it seemed like a feast. She said if you have a drink of beer you will live to one hundred, she died at ninety-two. I shall never refuse a drink of beer. There is no bad ale, so Grandma said.

A man aged 66 wrote:

> Why I drink Beer, because it is food, drink, and medecine to me, my Bowels work regular as clockwork and I think that is the Key to health, also lightening effects me a lot, I get such a thirst from Lightening, & full of Pins and Needles, if I drink water from the tap it's worse, Beer makes me better the more I drink better I feel, neither does it make me drunk, when a Boy a horn of Beer before Breakfast was the foundation for the day.

Another man:

> Why I drink Beer is there is hops in which is good for you, also Barm in which keeps your Body in good health.

Many people make use of the phrase "Beer is Best". This is a clue to the large number of references to its health-giving properties; phrases like "it is body-building"—"picks a man up"—are direct reflections of brewers' advertising. In the days before mass beer propaganda people drank considerably more than they do now; the history of the last hundred years of drinking in England is a history of decline. These letters definitely show how advertising phrases intended to keep up consumption have become part of pub-goers' mental attitude to their beer.

The clichés of the hoardings provide what the ethnologist calls "stock answers" to a searching question—the question Why do you drink alcohol? There is a considerable sense of guilt attached to alcoholic activity. We shall deal with this in its religious context, later on, and need only note here that it was shown in earliest days of the pub, in Greece and Rome, when some people slunk shamedly into inns, St. Paul shunned them, pagan groups encouraged them. But it is worth indicating now the wider nature of such oppositions, for the pub and anti-pub one, which goes on as much *within individuals* as within the community, keeps on cropping up in inconspicuous forms throughout this work, and its reports and statistics. In Worktown we have found nine major oppositions which cut across the life of the community in all sorts of ways, and often cut across the life of a family or even of a married couple. These are (on the positive side):

> Betting (including pools)
> Smoking
> Dancing
> Fishing
> Drinking alcohol
> Gardening
> Working
> Cosmetics
> Vegetarianism.

Common to all these issues on which persons apparently alike in respect to income, age, appearance, knowledge, etc., may violently differ, may violently resent in each other, are the following:

(1) They involve some positive manifestation.
(2) This is easily expressed.

(3) They involve social intercourse with other people—even betting, lipstick and smoking are essentially social, and so is gardening in Worktown (where gardens are hedged off or exclusive, the antagonism between those interested and those uninterested is generally negligible).

(4) They do not involve any direct or conscious competition between the different people involved; in betting, of all sorts, the competition is focused on the person or thing betted about and the person who accepts the bet; in working, the competition is with time, the machine, the boss. In every activity there is, of course, always a potential of direct competition—even in swilling or sanctity.

Oppositions of a different kind are those between groups within the same general framework of social activity—between rival football teams, church sects, political parties. But we have not been able to find any similar opposition between football players and non-football players, whist players and non-whist players, between coffee and non-coffee drinkers, fish-and-chippers and nons. In later volumes we shall discuss the importance of this fully. It is relevant here because the pub-goer is conscious of non-pub-goers, of propaganda against pubs, which particularly comes from about a third of the leaders in the town's public life. Notices outside churches tell him alcohol is a peril to his liver and/or his immortal soul. In the papers he can learn that chaps get so bad they need Turvey Treatment. Drink is directly and publicly attacked at meetings and services. On the other hand, the brewers, like the bakers and the milkmen, say their product is best, is the way to health, implying even that beer is better than anything else in life. They provide him with a sanction; they point out that millions do it, that it is the done thing. At the moment, they are showing on Worktown hoardings a lawyer in wig and gown, drinking stout. The law does it; the army and navy do it; it is the done thing; indeed, it is the best thing to do. . . .

Beer, more than anything else, has to overcome guilt feelings. That is why its advertising is simple, insistent, fond of super-latives, visual, and often showing other people drinking the stuff, radiant with good cheer or good looks—"Beer is socially service-able". The opposition, by making drink equal sin, have made those interested in promoting drink for personal profit, provide a simple rationalization for the drinker. The brewer is now in an ideal position—he has a one-point political platform which covers everything, and is, to say the least, difficult to argue with

in terms likely to influence millions of people. The whole basis
of the ancient argument has been shifted. The same sort of thing
has happened in politics in many countries.

It is this that makes the reasons people give for pub-going so
especially "unsound". As a sample of the results of direct
questioning on the subject:

We asked a local pub-goer (ex-policeman) to go round and ask a
few chaps in the pubs he visited why they liked beer. This was
done indirectly in the course of conversation. The following is his
verbatim write-up of the results:

8.15 p.m. Man aged about 40 says "I drink beer because
I think it does me more good than doctor's medicine, it keeps
my bowels in good working order". This man was of the
engineering type.

Navvy type of person aged about 35, says "If I get three
pints down me I can . . ." (What he said is the sort of thing
considered "unprintable". It amounted to the fact that when
he went home he was able to have sexual intercourse with
his wife with the maximum of efficiency, and when he woke
up in the morning he was able to repeat the process with
the utmost satisfaction.)

A young man aged about 25, well dressed in the latest cut
suit, says "This stuff gives me a good appetite and puts plenty
of lead in my pencil."

An aged coalbagger says "Eh, lad, two or three pints every
neet (night) and a pound o' chops and I could knock a bloody
mon off a horse."

A young man, a piecer, says "I don't take too much, about
a couple of gills every neet, it seems to put a bit of bant (energy)
in thee for t' following day."

A middle-aged man of about 40 of labouring type says
"What the bloody hell dost tha tak it for?" I said for my
health, he said "Th'art a —— liar." I paid for him a gill.

A man fairly well dressed looked to me like a lady killer
says "If tha comes in 'ere and pays for who tha fancies a
couple o' stouts tha's no need to get wed."

A young man about 23 says "I only drink this stuff because
I come down to t' barracks about three times a week, if I
weren't in t' artillery I'd ne'er bother."

A navvy type of man about 38 says "This is a bloody habit
with me an' I think if they stopped me tap I should bloody
well snuff out tomorrow."

A young man of shop assistant type about 25 says "What can

a chap do in a one-eyed hole like this, he'd go off his chump if there were no ale, pictures, and tarts."

The factor that emerges here, that was not mentioned in the written material, is the effect of beer on drinkers' *sexual* powers. While convention forbids reference to this aspect of beer drinking on other occasions, there is an element of facetiousness in the pub replies that stresses this sort of reason, a very real one.

NOT-BEER

43·5 per cent of the local pubs are full licences. That is to say, they are licensed to sell wines and spirits as well as beer—more expensive drinks with a higher alcohol content than beer.

But not-beer does not play a conspicuous part in the drinking that takes place in these pubs:

> Friday, May 7, a smallish pub in Higher Bridge Street, midday, two working class men of about 30 come into the vault and order small ports. This causes a profound sensation, the landlord literally taking a step backwards, and repeating in an incredulous italicised voice *"Small ports!"*

In July, 1937, outside a Methodist Chapel, a large notice was put up saying "WINE, ESPECIALLY RED WINE, RETARDS DIGESTION".

> Bar of the Grand Theatre, April 19. Eight women and two men, all sitting, 15 men standing. Jewish woman next to observer changes her order to gin and lime, then doesn't know if she will have water with it. "I'm not used to gin," she says. Barman makes her take soda with it.
>
> One of the town's leading upper middle-class families, on June 20, have sherries all round before dinner. During the meal the old man has Sauterne, followed by five goes of port. Mrs. has Sauterne, the young scion beer and two goes of port. Old man has whiskey shortly afterwards; goes up to bed at 10.30 taking the whiskey decanter with him, speaks of having a "posset".[1]

[1] Significant, in relation to this, is the yearly Worktown socialite revue organized by this family. While nearly all local and Blackpool music hall drink jokes and references are about beer, alcohol in this show was mentioned in a song:

> "Whiskey makes you pawn your clothes,
> Whiskey there, whiskey everywhere."

Unreality of this section of the community singing about pawning clothes is paralleled by the actual set up of the song, given by two men dressed in a peculiar kind of boating costume, holding TANKARDS, standing by two small BEER barrels.

S—— Inn, Mar. 31. Two women order ginger wine. Barman says "I've been here a year—that's the first one I've seen".

F—— Vault. Jan. 22. Yorkshireman, wearing Clarion cycling club badge, says to observer "They're sloppy pubs 'ere". He doesn't often drink, he adds, but when he does he "likes something decent". Is contemptuous because "They haven't got any chartroose whiskey—you'd expect it in a pub this size."

NOTICE

MAGEE'S VAULT PRICES

Whiskey, Rum, Gin	6*d*.
Magee's Ballyhooley Irish,	
Old Souwester Rum	9*d*.
No. 10 Liquer Scotch	10*d*.
Port, Sherry, and Empire	
Wine	3*d*.

In 1935 alcoholic liquor national consumption per head worked out at

Beer	17·58 galls.
Wine	·31 galls.
Spirits	·19 galls.

(Census of Production figures)

That is, the volume of beer drunk is 90 times that of all spirits. But comparison by volume is not realistic. A gill of beer contains about five times as much liquid as the ordinary pub single whiskey. So we can say that for every drink of spirits sold about 18 gills of beer are drunk.

Four out of seven Worktown pubs don't sell spirits. Therefore if this national proportion of spirits to beer drunk holds good for pubs, those with spirit licences will have to sell far more than one spirits to 18 beers. Do they?

A very popular medium sized pub, outside the town centre. Observer asks how much whiskey is drunk. Landlord "Under 1 per cent". Later, after drinking three rounds with observer, he reconsiders this and says "I reckon 2 per cent".

A landlord who gave 5 per cent spirits, and all bottled beers except Guinness, said:

The average person drinking spirits today is suffering from some ailment which necessitates spirits as a medicine, and cannot stand long drinks, or probably a Business man who is being hard pressed by work or financial matters, falls to spirits as a quick consolation to forget matters.

Town centre pub, landlord takes observer into cellar, to reckon up sales by inspection of empties. This is the landlord's estimate.

Mild. 7 loads a week. (A load is 36 gallon barrel.)
Bitter. 1 load.
Old. 2 quarter loads.
Blue Label and Oatmeal stout. 150–200 bottles.
Guinness. "Very poor selling."
Whiskey. 7 or 8 to 10 bottles.
Gin. 4 bottles.
Rum. 4 bottles. (Sold in bottle—"Mostly a sailor and an old woman".)
Port. 8 bottles.
Sherry. 9 bottles. "I drink a lot myself."

This is a pub with a rather special type of custom. It is not used by the ordinary working class pub-goer and many women (non-beer drinkers) go there. Relatively more spirits are drunk here than in almost any other local pub. Yet to approximately 330 gallons of beer only 35 bottles of wine and spirits are drunk. That is over 5,000 gills to between five and six hundred drinks of wine and spirits. (18–20 single whiskeys are got from a bottle, and about 12 glasses of wine.) That is, the chances are ten to one that anyone will order not-beer in this pub.

In another pub, which has a very big custom, especially of young people from the nearby dance halls, an observer reports:

The waiter-on says they drink a lot of whiskey here. When asked how much he meant by a lot he said "I reckon he (the landlord) does eight bottles a week".

We can conclude that the drinking of wines and spirits by ordinary pub-goers is very small. Though in the Wine Bar, which has a special type of customer, wine is drunk on a large scale especially a sticky-sweet concoction called Sweet Mountain Wine which sells at $2\frac{1}{2}d$. a large glass. There is also a good sale of spirits from the barrel here.

DP

The national figures quoted earlier certainly do not represent the relative amounts of wine and spirits to beer drunk by Worktowners (and presumably by working class pub-goers in other industrial districts). This must be made up by middle class (especially non-pub) drinking. Whether this is due to the price factor we cannot go into now, but the enormous volume of gin drinking amongst working people in the days when gin was very cheap seems to show that if spirits cost no more than beer today a lot more of them would be drunk.

Orders from the lounge of the town's best hotel, whose customers are non-Worktowner in habit, many being the better paid class of commercial traveller and business man, plus a number of mostly plump, made-up women of between 30 and 40, show a distinctly different selection from that of other pubs. The following is a list of the orders (in the succession given) for the lounge during half an hour, compared with those of the vault of a large pub nearby:

Lounge, Best Hotel	*Vault orders in ordinary pub*	
2 champagne cocktails	3 milds	1 mild
1 Bass	3 milds	1 sherry
Grapefruit	1 Crown	2 milds
Two best (milds)	4 milds	2 milds
2 Brown Ale and 1 Guinness	2 milds	1 best
1 Guinness and 2 best	3 milds	2 milds
2 grapefruit	1 mild	2 best
2 Guinness	2 best	2 milds
1 best	1 mild	1 mild
2 Guinness	3 best	1 mild
1 ginger ale and 7 I.P.A.s	1 mild	1 best
2 best, 1 whiskey and lemon	1 best	1 mild
2 Guinness and 1 lager	2 milds	
2 "Tenpenny cocktails"	1 mild	
2 oatmeal stouts and 2 sherries	1 mild and 1 best	
2 gin and lime	2 best	
2 best	7 milds	
2 Bass	2 milds	
	1 mild	

The lounge drinks average out at 6*d*. a head, those of the vault at a shade over 2½*d*.

The grapefruits are drunk by the ladies while they are sitting about waiting for the gentlemen. Minerals are not in general thought highly of, e.g. Lounge of large town centre pub, woman drinking tonic water, man asks her "What's that you're drinking?" to which she replies "It's the same as water, it's tonic".

On holidays (principally spent in Blackpool) there is a change for some people in their qualitative drinking habits, as well as their quantitative ones—everyone drinks more then—lots more—but there are also changes in pub behaviour and types of drink consumed.

A barman writes:

> As a general rule people on holiday drink more expensive drinks. G.S. Drinks gin and it at Blackpool—in Worktown mild beer. W.M. Guinness only at Blackpool, and mild beer in Worktown.
> F.A.S. No difference. Objects to wife's preference of Guinness.

Here is a Blackpool pub patronized by Worktowners:

> 8.30 p.m. Majority of men are drinking mild; female Guinness consumption going strong. 2 women are drinking advocaat, 2 have small bottles of Moussec, and 1 contemplates a Bass.

Advocaat, mostly ordered under the name of egg flip, is a thick yellow sticky liquid supposed to be made from eggs and brandy, and reputed to have an aphrodisiac effect. Later that evening 15 orders for it were recorded in ten minutes. In another Blackpool pub:

> Plenty of bottled beers are being drunk, female Guinness and small ports, also some cyder (never seen in Worktown). Many male whiskies.

In Blackpool the unprecedented spectacle of two unattended women ordering whiskey *at the bar* (absolutely tabu to women in Worktown) has been observed. However, this increased wine and spirit drinking on holidays is, as a change from the normal, not anything like as noticeable as many other important changes in drinking habits that happen then. (This is discussed later.)

We began by saying that, for the ordinary Worktowner, drink equals beer. We can repeat it, and add—mostly mild beer.

NOTE.—We have not allowed for consumption of beer in *clubs*. This amounts to 6 per cent of the national drink consumption. Worktown has 65 registered clubs, one for every 2,727 of the population, while the general average for county boroughs is nearly 3,000. Estimates of the kind we have made are not sufficiently accurately delimited to allow for this low percentage. This also applies to off-licence sales.

III

DRINK-SERVERS

Essential link, connecting beer, pub, and drinker, is the landlord and his staff. Throughout this book reports quoted will contain accounts of pub staff, particularly in their relationship with pub-goers; this material will supplement that which is presented here.

Writes a landlord:

Re procedure to become a landlord, first of all produce business qualifications, then references, and above all security. This they do for their own specific reasons, you know what I mean by that—a source of income to brewers. . . . I should say a good average wage would be about three pounds a week, house, light, and coal.

An ex-publican writes:

Publican more of a spare time job, a means of adding to income from other sources. Whether from private resources, pension, or work. A grown up family an asset to assist in rush hours, besides bringing grist to the mill in wages. Questions asked of would-be tenants:—How much money have you— how many children—and their ages. There are frequent changes of tenants. Drink addicts made through drinking with customers, and having so much within reach. Constant losses through lending and credit customers which tenant has to bear. Managers have to contend with spending among customers to keep them, especially the sticker type. If you don't, they go where the landlord is more free . . . the good landlord is of a type who would lead a pack. Birds of a feather. Person who has achieved notoriety in sport preferred. Leads the easily led. He along with his wife are in a position of importance, made so by law. This has the inevitable effect on their characters, dress, and bearing, etc., and they are a type. Grotesque in the lady, coming out with flashy dress and speech in the more choice specimens. Must be of some religion as there is a preponderance of in the neighbourhood. And be thoroughly orthodox.

This man said that the landlord paid on the percentage basis gets around £3 a week in the ordinary pubs.

In the bigger and more profitable pubs the brewers usually put in a paid manager. In these big pubs there is a head barman who is mostly in charge behind the bar; he gets £3 a week, or 30s. if living in. The manager or landlord is supposed to be allowed 15s. a week for food for members of the staff who live in the pub.

The national secretary of the Catering Section of the Transport and General Workers' Union, who was asked for information as to the wages and conditions of pub employees, wrote:

The average pay for men and women is 25s. a week, with Board and Lodging, the food supplied is very poor, in fact in many circumstances uneatable, often including the leavings from Customers' Plates; one house has a staff of 13 and the cost of food per head runs out at 6s. Staff wages are actually lower today than they were in the year of 1931. The comfort of the staff is fairly good in the new Houses, but it is deplorable in the old houses, being overcrowded, badly ventilated, verminous, the work is considered unhealthy, the insurance premiums are about 5 per cent dearer for this Industry than for other Industries, caused through long hours, poor food, constant indoor life, statistics show a greater percentage of Ill Health than elsewhere. Barmen and Barmaids scrub floors, and wash shelves before opening time, others are forced to do House work, girls ordinary domestic work, the men cleaning Windows, Gardening and other domestic work. The combined profit for this trade, including Brewers and distillers, Hotels, etc., was £62,000,000 during the year of 1936.

Mr. Parker's letter indicates the bad health conditions prevalent among pub workers. The tuberculosis rate is exceedingly high, and the mortality of pub-workers in general is heavy. On March 16, 1939, Mr. John Parker, Labour M.P., put a question in the House of Commons about this, asked if the Minister of Health would investigate the whole subject of T.B. among pub emploeyees. Mr. Walter Elliot's reply is a good example of a particular sort of official complacency. The barman serves those who enjoy something which, in the long church versus pub fight (described in later sections), has become, if not a sin, at least tinged with a lower moral standard in the eyes of those who don't pub-go. As such, pub's pander, the barman is no fit subject for special investigation in the formal view, which replied to Mr. Parker:

> "I am aware from particulars published in the last Decennial Supplement published by the Registrar-General that the death-rate from respiratory tuberculosis amongst barmen, though showing a decline on earlier periods at every age up to 45, largely exceeds the rate for the general male population. Other causes of mortality, however, are also excessive for the same occupational group, and I do not think that an investigation respecting tuberculosis would serve a useful purpose."

With low wages, work from 6 in the morning to at least 10.30 at night, much of it standing, and requiring concentration, good manners, careful handling, barmen and maids die unusually fast, and often from diseases unconnected with drinking anything. A Worktown landlord wrote:

> Staff Wages; the majority of Staff are spare time employed, barmen living in in most firms. Pay about 45s. a week, spare time meaning just evenings, Sat. noon, and Sun. noon, at about 4s. 6d. a shift, or probably 30s. a week. Waiters standard 3s. a night, Barmaids about 24s. a week and keep. Re time off, one half day per week is the usual thing. Re starting time. 6.30 a.m. The barman starts in the bar and is responsible for all the bar pumps, the glasses, Brass work, and the cellar. He cleans his bar and then gets his beer ready for 11.30, gets himself ready dressed for opening time. Same applies to bar-maids, who generally help the landlord in cellarwork. The other maids, or oftener than not, a lady employed as cleaner, does the mopping out, etc., empties spittoons, etc., daily.
> . . . many customers link up with barmaids, I think it is very detrimental to the publican, I personally would not allow it, it can cause any amount of intrigue, both by using the till to the advantage of their own pocket, create jealousy amongst the other customers, and also make the maid indifferent to her responsibilities, a good barmaid is uniform to all her customers. If the barman and barmaid link up, and are working at the same pub, I should say split them immediately, but if they are at different hotels I don't blame them for looking to the future of a profession they would both like; under these circumstances the two would stand a good chance of becoming publicans.

Compare this with the following:

I come up to London and fall to be some tapster, hostler of
a chamberlain in an inn—Well, I get me a wife; with her a
little money. When we are married, seek a house we must.
No other occupation have I but to be an ale-draper. The
landlord will have £40 fine and 20 marks a year. He knows
by honest courses I can never pay the rent. What should I
say? Somewhat must be done, or we undone.

That was written, 1592, in Chettle's *King Hart's Dream*.

PERSONALITY

In the ordinary small pub most of the work is done by the
landlord and/or landlady; if they have children old enough they
will usually assist. If not, then an extra waiter-on, either male
or female, is engaged for the busy times (week-ends).

It is difficult to assess the importance of the landlord's personality. Customers' remarks such as:

"He's a coarse fellow, in his shirt sleeves always, he looks
as if he's just got out of bed."
"He's alright, he's been a working man round 'ere 'imself,
not like some other landlords, everybody speaks well of
him."

These do not correlate with the amount of pub custom. (The
latter, for instance, only does a small business.)

"We don't consider the landlord. Any bloody bugger'll do.
It's the company that matters," is another view.

While a report of a conversation with the landlord of the
pub where the last remark was made:

He says that 50 per cent of the goodwill of his sort of pub
depended upon the popularity of the landlord, but in hotels of
any size this was not so, as many regular customers did not
see the landlord in such places for nights on end.
Gave as an example of his own success that he dare not have
a fixed night off, as his customers would start making it a
night of non-attendance. He himself had to be good at cards,
dominoes, and an authority on all sporting matters, he had also
purposely to lose at these games sometimes. He had to be many-
sided to agree with all and sundry, and often left the room when
he was going to find himself in direct contradiction with them.
Went on to say he would tell the state of trade of the works

opposite by his takings, and a bad week's work for the men made a difference of £10 to his takings in no time. Said that what with bad trade and the Chief Constable's attitude there were more landlords keeping pubs than there were pubs keeping landlords. He said as a proof of his argument that a good landlord made a good pub, there are two pubs right across the road, both better furnished, with all kinds of upholstery and covered floors, yet people preferred his stone floors and bare forms.

Our observations bear out his remarks.

In one of the most successful of the smaller town centre pubs the landlord is unpopular with his staff and own wife even:

Landlady drinking with female regular, and the barmaid, who looks up, sees into the lobby where the landlord has just arrived, and says "Here he comes—with his black face", and the landlady repeats to her friend "Charlie's just come in, with his black face".

BEAUTIFUL BARMAIDS

But two of the barmaids here, daughters of Charlie, are both attractive, with well-conditioned reflex smile to all customers. The pub is always full of youthful customers. Barmaids with sex-appeal are a great draw. Some are "uniform to all their customers". Others not:

Observer leaves in company with two youthful drunks, who have been playing darts and flirting with the barmaid from 8.30 until just before closing time. She accompanies the group to the lobby, and then on to the doorstep. One of the drunks and the observer both kiss her good night. The kisses were long and interesting.

Another, smaller pub, which has a considerable "tough" youthful week-end custom:

Two young men play quoits with the barmaid, who is, thinks observer, attractive in a coarse way. She is good at quoits anyway, and wins. One player leaves. She plays again with the other, winning again. This chap, young, redfaced, blonde, healthy-looking, unshaved, cap on one side of his head, face washed but hands dirty, is apparently on fumbling relations with the barmaid.

When they have finished their game he talks friendly to observer, shows him a trick with a penny, making it disappear into a fold in his trousers. He also does two card tricks, then goes out to the lavatory. The barmaid takes his pint pot and hides in the front parlour, which is empty and unlit. He doesn't notice its absence until he has been back for about three minutes, then has byplay with her, both eventually departing to the parlour to fetch the beer. They didn't come back for the rest of the evening, and the lights didn't come on either.

Later the landlord comes in, says he has been to the Old Soldier, and that there had only been three people in, though it is usually full. He has been round some other pubs too, and they're all the same, things are very slack. He starts complaining about how music isn't allowed in the pubs. Thinks the Chief Constable is too young for the job. He complains about the police and how there are always plain clothes men hanging about this neighbourhood as if they were all criminals. He is very fed up and says he is going to retire before next licensing sessions, take a cottage in the country and start suing people, makes dark hints about chaps who owe him £3,000, because he's been too soft with them. He returns to the police, and says you've got to allow them (the customers) a little liberty, but his pub is as decent a place as anywhere. "You can come in any night and you won't find anything going on". (Does he really mean this?) "And the Chief Constable needn't talk."

It is quite common for landlords to drink in other's pubs and go round drinking in each other's company. Recently one fell dead in another's pub. The news that he drank there surprised many friends. The Old Soldier, referred to above, is well-known as a publicans' drinking place.

Conversation about landlords in the taproom. B.C. tells a story about a widow landlady, who got herself a "fancy man", a young chap who lived at the pub and was drunk all the time. He came to a sad end, tottered off to sleep one night in a condition of near-coma, fell into bed on one side and out of it the other, with his head jammed into the chamber-pot. He lay there, unconscious, and died "drowned", says B.C.

The company discusses various landlords' habits of drinking at the Old Soldier, at least six are mentioned, and observer also knows one who does. No one knows why they do it, lot of ruminating until one man suggests "It's ancient tradition." and everyone laughs.

A landlord who complained to an observer of having a thick head said he didn't do any serious drinking in his own pub. Landlords complain—about the Chief Constable, about teetotallers, about clubs, about the brewers. Barmaids too. . . .

> Observer has a drink with barmaid, who is landlady's daughter, and goes out to a job during the day. She drinks grapefruit. Is fond of dancing, goes to the main Hall, went to the Licensed Victuallers' Ball, that was held there, says "it was lovely".
>
> Talks pubs with observer. She stresses, which observer doesn't believe, that the piano playing here is unpaid. Says the K. Arms "is a nice pub. The landlord's a friend of ours".

Constables they scandal about, transferring the sense of guilt and subjugation. After all, things have improved since the times when in Rome tavern-keepers were not admitted to military service, their wives exempt from adultery laws; then innkeepers were classed with thieves and gamblers—now only the second applies.

Clubs they hate. . . .

A club can start up for a few shillings, does so—no heavy pub license taxation; this report reflects the pub reaction:

> Landlord drinks Crown ale with observer, also talking across to his wife and a small group of regulars who are sitting in the lobby. Conversation about the price of whiskey, the weather, and clubs. He hates clubs a lot, says that people come out of them at (pub) opening time so beastly drunk that he doesn't like to have them in. So he doesn't serve them and they go on to some other pub. Later he forgets that he's said this, and refers to having them in the pub and what a nuisance they are there.
>
> There is a calendar on the wall, with a motto on it, saying the Last Great Scorer doesn't count if you have lost or won, it's how you play the game. The pub bookie pokes his head round the side of the lobby hatch and sees it, says what a fine sentiment it is, and how it goes for him all right. It then turns out that this calendar was given to the landlord for Christmas by the bookie's wife.

And the brewers often have the landlord's ill-will:

> "The majority of the brewers won't give allowance for waste. You take a pub like mine, I wouldn't do anything wrong to the beer . . . 'e never told me directly what to do. The

idea was that I should put water in it. They never told me direct." He went on to say it's only the publican who isn't really honest with his customers who can be successful from the brewer's point of view. "'e gets in his cellar and gets his doctoring done, some of them use isinglass, some stoop to the method of having special glasses—the genuine landlord would fall to that before he'd fall to watering the beer."

The point of the isinglass is to bring the specific gravity of the watered beer back to normal.

CREDIT

Credit, vital in pub economy, they complain about. . . . One landlord says of this:

> "Credit is the biggest evil to a publican. The one who is the most generous is the one to come unstuck. Credit varies according to the conscience of the landlord. I should imagine five bob a week is a good average. The landlord is the only sufferer, but I think a great many have cut out the practice. These credit customers come and go, they make a practice of getting and not paying."

About this, a barman writes:

> Strapping, or Putting it on the Slate. In spite of the fact that there is no redress from people allowed tick there is still a small amount of business done in this way. There are people whom the landlord feels he can trust, even so, they often leave an account and go to some other place. Knowing the landlord's helplessness a bigger proportion of bad debts accrue than in other traders' accounts because the other trader can bring the law into operation.
>
> They generally start through the following, either they run short in the course of an evening through getting in a treating ring, will call the landlord on one side and make their request, or will ask for a bottle to take home on credit. Fearing to lose the customers he generally accedes to it, and once in they go to increasing amounts until holidays or sickness causes them to stay out because they can't pay, and the landlord says "Done again".

Sometimes the request is made in writing like this—handed over to a barman "Tom, give 2 Pints one gill for Boxer. Give me the Change for 2s."

The ancient custom of writing it on the slate is seldom found now. The "slate" of these days is any old piece of paper, kept behind the bar.

The following is a list of the people on the slate in a small pub who get, or have got credit during December:

A. Woman whose husband is getting a good wage, she regularly sends children round for small amounts, from half-a-crown to sixpence. Sends Co-op checks over. Now owes about 30s.

B. Owes 10s., has not been in for three months.

C. Described by barman as "a demure young lady". She used to say "A pint of beer, please", and when served, add "It's for my father". She would come about three times in the course of one evening. Paid up regularly for about six months, until one week-end when she said she would pay next week, and could she carry on. She came as usual during the next week, but did not turn up on pay-night and has not been seen since.

D. Labourer, orders a pint for which he paid, then asked for another on credit. Had several more and took two bottles home. He lasted three months, and left owing 6s. 9d., has not been seen since.

E. A man who is so trustworthy that the landlord does not trouble to put down what he owes, as the man puts it down himself, in a small book that he carries with him. This has been going on for twelve years.

F. A carter, who runs up exactly ten shillings credit every week. He doesn't like to let the other customers know about this and gets the landlord to give him the money in odd half-crowns. He always settles up, has been doing this for ten years.

Another angle on credit is given in the following report:

The landlord was very anxious to please and said that he had been told by his brewers that he must stop the slate trade of this pub, and whilst he thought that a landlord's popularity had a lot to do with a pub, he thought that good management had more. He lost a lot of customers when he stopped the credit side of the business, but now he had a lot of strangers coming in who told him that they did not like to be classed with the credit customers, and that is why they had kept away during its last tenancy. This landlord was new to the game and took me to see how he was studying to be master of it. He was busy reading three volumes—*Licensed Houses and Their Management*.

RESPECT

But the landlord gets respect. Writes a barman:

In the vault people invariably turn to the landlord or his susbstitute when talking or arguing, as if to seek confirmation for what they are talking about.

And a local drinker says:

"Why do people appeal so much to the landlord to settle any particular problem in argument. This has happened several times this evening, and the landlord has on each occasion prevaricated—presumably to retain the goodwill of all and favour no one."

There are two landlords and a brewer on the town council, and another recently lost his seat. The landlord of one small pub has started a Magician's Club, and himself delights clients by producing pennies from all parts of his and other bodies. Two ex-members of the famous local football team are landlords. Politician, magician, footballer—they attract custom by personal prestige not connected with the pub. But in Worktown such landlords are rare.

WORK

Most of the work of the pub staff consists of walking about. This is a detailed report of their movements during a slack half hour:

Room empty when observer enters. Landlady sitting by herself at table near bar. She is 50–60, with red face, dark red jumper, dark blue dress, black hair. Waiter-on comes (from other room) to serving hatch, calling out the order before he gets there, puts down his tray and some empty glasses. Landlady takes glass, holds it under nozzle of beer engine, gives two pulls at handle, the first short and sharp, the second longer and slower. Puts full glass on tray. Waiter-on goes off, comes back, switches on lights. Three people come in and sit down. Landlady walks over to table, stands at the back of the chair, takes orders, walks round behind bar, takes glasses, two at a time, fills them up, walks to far end of bar and puts glasses on tray, takes Guinness bottle from shelf, uncorks it in uncorking machine, puts it on to tray. Then walks over to get another glass, which she puts on to tray beside the bottle. Comes out from behind the bar, walks right round to the end where she left the tray, picks it up, and takes it over to table. Gets money, walks round behind bar to cash register, gets change, walks back to table, gives change to customers, walks back again to behind the bar and pours herself out a Guinness. Stops walking about for a little and leans on bar looking at the shelves behind. Then walks over to serving hatch, stops, looks down passage, goes out, comes back with waiter-on, and sits down at the table again.

At 8.30 a barman comes on duty, man of about 35, brown suit, red, puffy face, smooth, shining brown hair. He now takes most of the orders, but when there are several at once the landlady gets up from the table and goes round behind the bar and helps. Barman draws all draught beers, but the waiter-on takes the bottled beers, opens the bottles and puts them on the tray himself.

Barman keeps wiping his hands on towel at every opportunity after he has drawn off some beer. When he smokes he takes a puff, puts cigarette down on ashtray and leaves it there for a long time. This, observer thinks, is because he has got a sort of reflex about smoking behind the bar—when he is busy he is only able to get time to smoke in short puffs like this, both his hands being occupied and wet.

Both he and landlady pick up glasses in threes, between thumb and first two fingers. Glasses are washed by being dipped in sink and left on draining board until needed. The water in the sink was not changed during this half-hour's observation.

(Another barman's reflex observed is this:

Barman, standing in doorway as observers leave, is holding his tray. There is no room to pass, but instead of lowering the tray he holds it up above his head, balanced on the tips of his fingers, as if he was carrying glasses on it.)

A barmaid's conversation with a customer—this one semi-technical:

Man about 30, comes in, wearing green hat, dirty but good mac, blue-striped shirt and collar, smoking fag. Greets barmaid, says "This weather's very changeable. I went out wi'out shirt on Sunday and look at it now—I was up at the Albert."

"Did you see Mr. Wood?"

"What? Boss? No, I didn't."

She says she had a job at the G. & D. when this chap (i.e. Mr. W.) was landlord there. "He was there two years."

"How long was he at the Albert?"

"Two years last September."

"I heard a great tale of woe—all the girls sacked last night for some reason."

"Well, what's going to win the Derby? . . . I've a bet on anyway, better price than it was today."

"It were a miserable afternoon, but I enjoyed myself in the evening."

Another man comes in.

Barmaid. "Still raining?"

Man. "Wasn't when I came in."

Barmaid. "It's stopped!" (Turns to other man.) "It's a big place, the Albert. Did you notice the floor. It's new since I was there. It's new, very nice and clean."

The pseudo-flirtation is common:

Two young labourers, begin to talk to barmaid asking her where she is going for her holidays. The unsober one starts in on an obscure, allusive verbal flirtation with her, which culminates in the suggestion that she should sleep up in a tree and he would come along and shake it until she fell down in his arms. She said she would be too heavy, which was true enough, but he could have her if he could carry her on his back up the hill at the end of the street. Observer doubts if he could.

And the landlord or lady talks, sitting and drinking, with friends and regulars, during slack times:

Lounge nearly empty, few lights on, a young man drinking with Rudolph Valentino. (Note: This barmaid is called Rudolph Valentino because she is supposed to have had so many abortions! Local pub folklore includes a sad story about her. She was found walking home, near the centre of the town, at five in the morning, stark naked. A young man had taken her out into the country on his motor cycle, taken all her clothes off, and driven away with them. The reason for this unkind act was that she had given him the pox.) Now a middle-aged woman comes in, sits in her usual place, orders Guinness. Landlady greets her, sits down alongside, and has a Guinness too.

Landlady: "It's awful, isn't it, Tuesday night." (i.e. quite).

They talk about racing. Landlady: "It's just a horse that I saw and I backed it. I wasn't really interested in the race . . . front room's just got busy, it's the fellows just come in. . . ." She talks about her cough. Friend, sympathizing, also suffers, "It's my throat, the chest . . ." (Puts her hand to her throat.) She then says "Very quiet."

Landlady: "Unusually quiet."

Friend: "Time's dragging since tea, and nothing to do."

Landlady: "D'you know what's on at the Palais, I didn't notice the paper. Hasn't it been cold today, what a change."

Friend: "Terrible today. I noticed it as soon as I got up. I mustn't get a cold. I soon get chilled through. . . . I haven't had the kitchen window open today. (Yawns widely.) I'm yawning."

Two men who have been drinking exactly level finish (11 minutes) and go. Landlady and friend are talking clothes and materials. Before they have finished their glasses landlady says to Valentino "Will you bring two glasses, love." She gets them, sits at table with them; they whisper. Rudolph Valentino says " . . . for about the first twenty minutes he couldn't leave me alone."

.   .   .   .   .

Inaccurately intelligent is a leader in the *Daily Express* (17/5/38):

The barmaid needs to be a philosopher. Her job certainly helps her to become one. She sees the customer who is going up in the world, and that one who is slipping. She sees some that *could* go up and others that are finally down. "Regulars" and "strays" alike confide across the counter their troubles, joys, hopes, and jokes. The last are the worst.

It is a generally accepted idea that barmaids and barmen drink a lot, get a lot of drinks stood them. A few enquiries showed that this idea may be exaggerated. Out of five barmaids (in big pubs) one said she got three a week, two said they got seven, one "two or three a night"; and one five or six on busy nights, and on slack ones, one or two. Another said she didn't drink, is asked about twice a week whether she'll have one and takes a packet of Woodbines instead. She doesn't smoke either, but keeps them and gives them to her boy friend. Four barmen said that they got stood about four drinks a week, and one that he got twelve.

Both barmen and barmaids get drinks stood them by men, usually regulars, usually the same regulars every week. One said that sometimes he gets a drink "from strangers such as you" who want to talk to him for company.

SUMMED UP

The staff-customer relationship can be summed up as follows:

1. The basic relationship of serving drink. This need not entail any social contact at all. (See later—"the silent regular".)

2. Development of 1. When drink is served conversation takes place. This can vary from a random remark to a stranger, about the weather, to a long conversation.

3. Social contact not directly arising from the serving of drink:

a. When talk with customers goes on while the landlord, etc., is standing behind the bar and not serving drink to the people he is talking with.

b. When the landlord, etc., comes out from behind the bar and joins the customers. This can vary from conversation carried on by him with a group of which he is not a member, to his participation in a group that is sitting down and playing games.

The third category is the only one that represents a real social relationship between staff and customer. This, however, cannot be directly correlated with the degree of "affability" that exists between customers and staff; size of pub is most important factor. In the average small beerhouse conversation between landlord and customers is the general rule, and it is common to find him sitting down with them to a game of dominoes, and only getting up to go behind the bar when more beer has to be drawn.

But as more customers come in he is increasingly busy and has to stay behind the bar. The relationship then cannot go beyond 3a. And the more drink and people he has to serve, the less he is able to converse with the drinkers, until at the time of maximum drinker conviviality, the staff-drinker level of social intercourse is at its lowest.

But other factors tend to negate this. Most pubs, during peak hours and peak days, have extra help. (Either "waiters-on", or more of the landlord's family coming into operation.) This frees the landlord once more, so it is possible to find him during the most busy hours sitting and drinking with customers in rooms right away from the bar.

In the biggest pubs, where there are plenty of workers, the landlord is free for conversation and games almost whenever he feels like it. And whether he feels like it or not, it is important for him to do it, as already quoted remarks have shown. In fact, one of the reasons why the landlord has to take on extra help is that he should be free of work during the busy times in the pub.

But, in the largest pubs, even if the landlord is completely free from having to do any drink-serving work, if his social intercourse is not confined to small groups, it will have to be spread out over a large number of people in different rooms, so that there cannot be so much of it per customer.

Again, in the majority of pubs, where the landlord himself helps the work behind the bar, his social intercourse is confined to the vault drinkers (and lobby men, if there is a lobby).

The mutual relationship between those working behind the bar, within working hours, is governed by the same factors. (Also cf. remarks about barmen and barmaids.)

Relationship between the staff of different pubs mostly takes the form of landlords drinking together. Barmen-maid marriages resulting in the pair setting up together in a pub of their own are not uncommon.

In some respects the landlord:pub:regular relation can be compared with that of the parson:church:congregation. Further material will later illustrate this. But one important and significant difference between the landlord:regular and parson:congregation relationship is that there are no class distinctions between the landlord and his customers—mostly he is with the poorest section of them, and they meet on terms of outward equality, usually addressing each other by Christian names. But most parsons are "better" class than their congregations, are never addressed by Christian names—and very seldom by their surnames.

THREE LANDLORDS' REMARKS

"I wouldn't like my daughter to know my life, she's 17. My wife's the best woman on earth."

"Aye—there is some rum buggers in this town . . . there is and all."

Landlord summing up a long conversation: "It's nice round 'ere in the summer time—when it's nice."

IV

DRINKING PLACES

Dear Mother, dear Mother, the church is cold
But the Ale-house is healthy and pleasant and warm.

(WILLIAM BLAKE)

GEOGRAPHY

In 1936, when we came to Worktown, there were 304 pubs
in Worktown (Chief Constable's Report to the Watch Committee).
In some parts of the town there are plenty, in others few, in others
none. We mapped the distribution of 277 of them.[1] A first glance
showed that their greatest density was in the centre of the town,
and along the main routes that radiate out from it. The following
table shows their relative densities in circular areas of $\frac{1}{4}$, $\frac{1}{2}$ and $1\frac{1}{2}$
miles radius, with the Town Hall as their common centres.

Area	No. of Pubs	No. per Sq. Mile	% of Total	
			Area	Pubs
A. $\frac{1}{4}$ mile circle	55	280·6	2·7	19·8
B. $\frac{1}{2}$ mile circle	134	173·1	11·1	48·3
C. B. less area included in A.	79	133·9	8·4	28·5
D. $1\frac{1}{2}$ mile circle	277	39·17	100	100
E. D. less area included in B.	143	22·75	88·9	51·7

Note: E. is traversed by seven main roads, on which are found 56 pubs.
This leaves 87 pubs, not on main roads, in an area of approx.
6·3 sq. miles—13·8 to the sq. mile.

The most striking fact that emerges here is that 11·1 per cent
of the total area contains 48·3 per cent of all the pubs. Even
more strongly marked is the relative density per square mile—
that of the central quarter-mile circle being almost seven times
as much as the general average.

But this distribution is not even; and the unevenness is not
simply due to the fact that the whole area included does not
comprise a homogeneous built-up area.

---

[1] Our analysis of pub distribution is based on 277 pubs included in a circle
of a mile and a half radius; these have been mapped from material supplied
to us by the local Town Planning Committee. Outside this circle lie three
suburban areas which are under the jurisdiction of the Town Council. The
actual map shows 268 pubs, the odd nine lying outside the continuous built-up
area but within the mile and a half circle.

In 1931 J. N. Reedman made some analysis of the pub distribution in Sheffield. He came to the following conclusion:

> There is of course a great concentration in the older parts of the city, and particularly the centre, while reluctance of the magistrates to grant a licence at all on the new housing estates . . . has greatly accentuated the unevenness of the distribution.

By taking the number of pubs per head of population in different wards Reedman shows that density of population is not correlated with pub density. Our study shows quite clearly the same can be said of Worktown. We will return to the question of the age of areas in relation to their pub density.

The ecological approach, used by a school of American sociologists in studying the growth of cities is the best approach to the study of pub distribution. R. D. Mackenzie[1] says:

> Human ecology is fundamentally interested in the effect of *position* in both space and time, upon human institutions and human behaviour. . . . A great deal has been written about the biological, economic and social aspects of competition and selection, but little attention has been given to the distributive and spatial aspects of these processes. The plant ecologist is aware of the effects of the struggle for space, light and food upon the nature of a plant formation, but the sociologist has failed to recognize that the same processes of competition and accommodation are at work determining the size and ecological organization of the human community.

Finding no direct correlation between pub and population distribution, we can look to other factors, such as the presence of factories, the effects of main roads, railways, shopping districts.

There is a dense but not altogether even distribution of factories throughout the town. No correlation between their density and that of pubs can be observed. (There are, however, important factory-pub relationships, which are dealt with later.)

The effect of railways cannot be assessed directly; pubs are not either noticeably present or absent along their routes; neither do they form boundaries between areas with different pub densities. But we cannot say that they are a negligible factor, since we do not know just what are the effects of the railway on the whole development of the areas through which it runs.

[1] In *The City* by Park, Burgess and others, one of the University of Chicago's sociological series, essential books for the fieldworker.

Main roads and shopping districts—these are the channels of the town through which flow the greatest numbers of people. And it is here that the maximum pub density is found. Nine main routes emerge from the edge of the mile and a half circle. Lettering them from A to I (going clockwise) the next table shows the number of pubs on each route.

Route	Pubs		Total
	(within ⅓ mile radius)	(outside ⅓ mile radius)	
A.	5	11	16
B.	7	4	11
C.	21	4	25
D.	11	2	13
E.	11	13	24
F.	13	6	19
G.	—	1	1
H.	—	4	4
I.	—	12	12
Total	68	57	125
% all pubs in area	50·7	39·9	45·2

That is, nearly half the total pubs in the town lie on nine main roads. The variation in the numbers on the different routes is, of course, not only due to the different characters of the routes themselves but also to the relative distances traversed by them within the given areas.

The following table shows the distribution from the point of view of mileage.

Area	Roads	Mileage	Pubs per mile
⅓ mile circle	Main roads	3·3	20·6
	Not main roads	19·6	3·4
	All roads	22·9	5·8
Built up area outside ⅓ mile circle	Main roads	11·1	5·1
	Not main roads	85·4	1·0
	All roads	96·6	1·5
Whole built up area	Main roads	14·4	8·7
	Not main roads	105·2	1·4
	All roads	119·6	2·3

Note: Mileage was worked out with map measurer on 6 in. scale map, and a high degree of accuracy cannot be claimed for it.

The main shopping and "brightlight" district (cinemas, dance halls, etc.) lies within the ½ mile circle, the area of the greatest pub density.

An examination of the relation of the pub with the shops surrounding it shows that the pub is nearly always found where there are most shops. A detailed analysis of all the shops within a 50 yards and a 75 yards radius of 25 pubs (in different parts of the town) gives the following results:

Within 50 yards around the pub there is one shop in every 58·8 square yards. Within 50 to 75 yards around the pub there is one shop in every 74·2 square yards.

Or, putting it another way, 65 per cent of all the shops within a 75 yards radius of 25 pubs were in 58 per cent of the area around the pubs—this area of greater density being within 50 yards of the pubs. To every 100 shops in the outer radius there are 126 in the inner.

To do this we had to make a special "user survey" map for ourselves. The following is an example of a strip of main road containing 5 pubs:

Pub	Shops	
	Within 50 yds.	50–75 yds.
A	17	3
B	14	3
C	3	1
D	2	nil
E	1	1

Naturally, there is considerable individual variation in the number of shops, both total and relative. But our figures show that the pub is positively correlated with the local shopping centre.

Do these facts, then, mean that the density of the population *in* the streets (walking about in them, not living there) determines the pub density? We would rather say that the two factors are correlated. And as we get outside the central area of the town not only is the pub density sparser, but far more irregular; one group of main routes containing 11 or more pubs, another group 6 or less. The populousness of these roads will vary, but there is nothing to show that their variation is either as wide as, or bears any direct relation to, the variations in their pub density.

Reedman says of Sheffield:

In certain districts the congestion of licensed premises stands out very sharply in contrast with other areas where extensive boundaries and large populations either have very few or are entirely without licences. Populous districts which have very few licensed premises are either older, better class residential suburbs or else post-war housing estates.

This is true, too, of Worktown.

It is the oldest part of the town that has the most pubs, and the newest the least. On a map of Worktown lined to show the edge of the town's built-up area in 1890, in the whole of the area outside this line (i.e. built since 1890) there are *only* 20 *pubs*, of which 15 are on main routes. What this amounts to is that, as the town developed and spread outwards, pushing tentacles of built-up area along the main road routes, the amount of new pubs built in the newer areas was proportionately very much less than in the older districts. And those 20 pubs do not all represent new licences for the new areas; most of them must have already existed at road junctions and small villages swallowed up by the growth of the town. The diagram on page 75 shows that the number of pubs actually grew less while the population was still increasing.

The short term explanation of this is to be found in the steadily increasing strictness in the application of the licensing laws and a growing unwillingness to grant new licences on any pretext.

This implies that, in comparing areas of equal populousness, the pub density will depend upon the age of that area. (In towns with a more varied social composition than Worktown this would not apply directly.) An analysis of how this has happened will be found in the next part of this section.

FULL AND BEER LICENCES

Another point should be made before we draw conclusions from this material. We have not differentiated between fully licensed premises and ordinary beerhouses. Existing figures and writings have made this a fundamental differentiation. While in regarding the pub from a purely administrative point of view this may be necessary, from the point of view of the "pub and the people" rather than "the pub and the authorities" its importance is not fundamental.

Reedman says "Generally speaking, it is true to say that fully licensed premises are found on main streets". He does not give figures for this. Now the issue of new full licences (i.e. licence to sell wines and spirits) is rare, and their number has been far more constant for the last fifty or sixty years; their presence in any area is some indication of its economic status, in the same way that shops with a wide range of goods are not found where there are few shoppers. That the number of full licences in the centre of the town is high can be said to be due to the fact that there is a far larger "market" for non-beer drinking in that district than in any other. But while this market is maintained by the personal motives of Worktowners, the fact that it can be supplied is due to licensing laws and *conditions of fifty years ago.*

But if most pubs on main roads were "full licences" a far more direct economic explanation than this would be possible. The proportion of full licences to beerhouses is as follows:

Pubs	Full licences	Beer licences
On main roads	48·1%	51·9%
Not on main roads	39·3%	60·7%
All pubs	43·5%	56·5%

That is, there are relatively more full licences on main roads than on non-main roads. This is inconclusive, since a high proportion of that percentage is made up by the small dense concentration in the centre.

We can say, then, that the distribution of pubs in Worktown is dependent on two sets of factors—the age and the populousness (not population) of the district. The second is the direct economic factor of market and profits, and the first is its historical background, which helps to shape the market by imposing restrictions and/or stimulations. This could equally be said of the distribution of any outlet of consumer's goods. *Only no other market has been so divorced by legal restrictions from direct response to demand.* Consequently it can only be fully comprehended by taking into account pub history.

DEVELOPMENT

In this book historical material is only being used to illustrate facts about the contemporary pub, and not for the sake of trying to include a "history of the pub" as such. Now, in order to understand more fully the factors of pub distribution, and to deal with the basis of the different types of pub that are examined later, we require some relevant history.

Some Worktown pubs can be traced back from before the Industrial Revolution. There is a list of 61 names and addresses of pubs existing in 1824. Nineteen of these are still in existence, same names and addresses.

Mackies *Worktown Directory and Almanack* for 1849 gives the following list:

Inns	117
Beerhouses	188
Beerhouses supposed to exist *without* a licence	15
Inns and Beerhouses where *thieves* and *prostitutes* resort	20
Inns and Beerhouses where *gambling* is practised	13
Inns and Beerhouses having musical entertainments	14

That is, ignoring the pubs without licences, Worktown had *one more licence in* 1848 *than in* 1937. Only, then there were 170 inhabitants per pub, now 559.

Said Mr. Taylor, Coroner for the Borough, 1848, in a speech to the licensing magistrates:

> These ale and beerhouses would hold every man, woman, and child in the Borough . . . there is a drinking place for every 25 houses . . . such are the present resources for selling drink—or poison—some called it by one name, some by the other.

By 1854 there were another 25 beerhouses in existence, though the number of full licences had remained the same; and the absolute number of pubs continued to rise, until in 1869 there were 452 of them.

By then there was also a powerful and militant temperance movement in existence. At a packed meeting of 2,000 people in the new Temperance Hall the Rev. C. Garrett declaimed "No working man in Lancashire need be without clothes, but if he will insist in clothing the landlord and landlady in purple and fine linen, he must be content to remain in poverty and rags".

Since 1830 there had been no restrictions whatever on the issue of beer licences; this policy remained the same for 39 years, when the Act of 1869 empowered the magistrates to refuse to grant the renewal or issue of beer licences; and another Act of 1872 still further restricted the conditions of issue and renewal of licences. The general basis of the present day licensing system had been established.[1] From that time it is possible to trace statistically the ratio between pub and population variation.

Though in 1869 there were nearly half as many pubs again as there had been in existence twenty years earlier, the amount of full licences had only increased by 6, from 117 to 123. Next year, when the Act came into force, 69 beerhouses were abolished right away. The diagram opposite shows that the population: pub ratio has never subsequently decreased, steadily rising from 210 people per pub in 1870 to its 1935 figure of 559.

For nearly thirty years after the new act came into force, the absolute number of pubs continued to fall, while the population was still rising. In 1898 the borough boundaries were enlarged, which besides adding to the population increased the number of pubs by 61. (The break in the curves on the diagram, that are joined by dotted lines, indicate this.) For a few years the absolute number of pubs increased again slightly, but after 1903 began a long, steady fall, decreasing on an average by about three pubs every year. And in 1928, after a period of stagnation, the population too began to fall.

Nothing could show more clearly than this how the growth of the town has not been paralleled by the growth of its pubs, and consequently, how the age of a district is an important factor in determining the relative frequency of pubs in different areas. And we have seen that this falling ratio of pubs to population can be accounted for by Act of Parliament. *The pub today plays a smaller part in the life of the town than it ever did:* and there does not seem any likelihood of that part ever becoming greater as long as this culture continues to develop along the contemporary lines. These figures, the figures of drunkenness, of amounts drunk per head, the change in the hours of drinking, the frequent references in records to the amount of prostitution, thieving, fighting and gambling in pubs, compared to the state of affairs today show how great a change has taken place in pub-life during the past hundred years. This change, which both reflects, and is reflected by, the change in peoples' lives over that period, cannot

---

[1] We do not intend here to go into the intricacies of licensing law history; a large range of literature upon it exists already and there is no need to add to it. A very competent précis on the subject will be found in Professor Catlin's *Liquor Control*, and the subject is covered in detail in Sidney Webb's classical work on it. (See bibliography.)

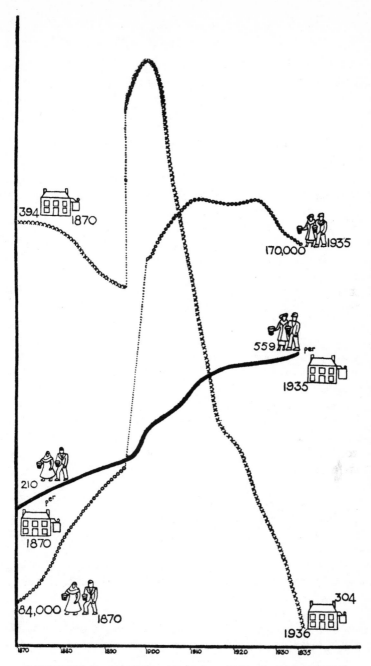

394 1870

170,000 1935

559 per 1935

210 per 1870

84,000 1870

304 1936

VARIATION IN NUMBER OF PUBS, SIZE OF POPULATION,
AND RATIO OF INHABITANTS PER PUB

The solid line = people per pub
The line of Xs = number of pubs
The line of Os = number of people

simply be accounted for by Acts of Parliament. Laws do not come out of a vacuum. They are the result of social forces, and to attempt to account for any social change on the basis of administrative measures alone is superficial.

ALL DECLINE TOGETHER? SOCIAL DECAY?

The restriction of pub activity by law, and even more by direct taxation, is a type of restriction that has been widespread. And the decline of the pub as a factor in town life today is not peculiar to the pub at all. *All the older institutions are declining.* It is a main feature of the contemporary scene. The Church in recent years has suffered, numerically and thus economically, far more than the pub. The political machine has equally suffered from an increasing apathy. Even parks, swimming, athletics, and pigeon racing, traditional foci of local leisure activity, have steadily lost their pull, and are now gradually become no more influential than the much newer institutions speaking a newer language and with a contemporary symbolism, or the use of contemporary method in exploiting an ancient symbolism. The pub, the church, the political party, are answers to questions of living that were vital long before Worktown became a town. The questions—why are we here, where are we going, what is it all for, is life worth living, what else can I do? —are still here. But the actual factual answers are not necessarily the same. There are now a number of alternative answers. The football pools, the cinema, the radio and the *Daily Mirror* give alternative answers to the question, Is life worth living? A hundred years ago the main answers were in a man's own heart, his wife's body, the parish church or the local pub.

There are numerous reasons, the subjects of our later volumes, why these older institutions are up against difficulties inherent in their own structure, organisation and custom, which make rapid adjustment to changing needs or competition difficult. Of the older institutions the pub is in the strongest position in this respect. All the major older institutions have a definitely expressed or felt social function. They have a place in society which is freely discussed, attacked or supported. A long series of customs, traditions and feelings centre around them and are clearly defined—this book in itself demonstrates that. The older institutions, by a long process of adjustment and attrition, have developed defined functions, which include always co-operation for common ends, social groups within the main group (clubs and mutual aid societies, sports groups, outings, and secret societies within church, politics, pub, etc.). Each in a sense aims to provide a cross-section of life's pleasures and hopes. Each has to support itself by selling its attractions sufficiently to make people attend and pay in money. Each devotes the main part of that money to furthering the same sort of activity. If we compare the total takings (mainly from manual workers) of the Church of England and Messrs. Guinness we find somewhat similar proportions are spent on the private pleasures or needs of persons of the upper middle or upper classes, persons earning more than £5 a week.

In the newer institutions there is an important difference. They are willing, and often able, to put out any social doctrine, have any sort of social effect, irrespective of obligation to society and often unaware that they are having any such effect. Their first concern is sales-success. This is also true of the brewers, but it is not true of many landlords, who think of the pub as a place of friends as much as a place of profits. This sort of landlord is gradually being pushed out as the competition becomes fiercer among brewers and of brewers against the alternatives of pools, cinemas, dance halls, television, small cars, and so on. The brewer is being forced along with the whole trend of economics in this society, to eradicate the small and perhaps inefficient old-style unit and develop a massive efficiency which may even involve deliberately upsetting the existing social pattern in the same way as the new cotton combines shut down mill after mill "in the interests of the industry", and so smashed what remained of the mill-home-district relationship, a fundamental one in the whole structure and growth of Worktown. For the competition from the newer groups is tough. Outstanding of these is the football pools, which in the last five years have grown strong enough to start upsetting the cinema interests, their pioneer predecessor (along with the press) in exploiting the social feelings, leisure and wishes of a literate mass. Pools, astrology, press and tuppenny "bloods" have to answer to no one for what they say, as compared with the vast array of law that hedges pub, factory, church and politics—provided what they say it lies within the comparatively few laws that control their new activities. There is no sort of effective or organized, or even informed opposition to the social effect of any of these things

at present, in this country; nothing comparable to the temperance movement or the Labour Party versus *status quo*, or
the Trades Union pressure upward. The newer institutions
are simply out for profits, and they have a pretty well free
hand. They are slowly changing the whole aspect of England,
and no one seems to be noticing it. The brewer cannot make
one move without raising a squawk. If he wants a late licence
on Coronation evening, a rigmarole has to be gone through.
But a newspaper can print a falsified press story front page
and get into the minds of a million Englishmen, and very
few will know. These new groups are currently engaged in exploiting, by methods of science, ideas of pre-science for their
personal profit, and irrespective of the consequences. In this
they are behaving in the opposite way to the scientists themselves, whose equal irresponsibility and ignorance of after-
effects makes for a queer collaboration. The crucial thing is
that these newer drives are *not concerned* with *making a social
group*, except in so far as it is essential to make all those
doing the thing feel that it is a done thing—e.g., by the
sanction of numbers or the participation of important people,
like parsons, or peers, or very rich people. Whereas the pub,
church, politics, sports clubs, depend on the participation of
people in groups which are in active physical and verbal
proximity to one another, and who get to know one another
in the course of sharing the same experiences or interests.
This is not the case in the newer groups.

Pools, radio, press, motor-culture, dance halls too (to a surprising extent), cinema, do not create a social group of people
sharing consciously the same experience. Though all share the
same experience, the emphasis is on each individual experiencing
it, not on any common feeling or interest or talk. Indeed the
promoters for profit of these things find it is best for them if
they can centre the whole socio-human interest of people on
a few central figures which provide the only human contacts in
the affair—Bing Crosby, Joan Crawford or Beaverbrook, "the
Chief" (Cecil Moores, probably one of the most influential men
in peacetime England), Deanna Durbin, Nuffield, Petulengro
and B.B.C. None of these things have permanent local groups
who meet each other and discuss the issues in which they have a
common interest. They emphasize the individual reader or listener
or looker. They thus tend to depart from the older groupings and

to weaken the older groupings, with their definite social interests and controls; this is part of the tremendous shift away from the last centuries' conception of human effort and right, away from fundamentals in Christianity, democracy and scientific research. As part of it, the pub is losing much of its influence in the face of institutions which are providing, comparatively unrestrictedly, to individuals whatever the individuals are supposed to want, or will pay for readily. The *effect* of such activities is not considered. For example, no attempt has been made by anyone in Worktown (or Britain) to find out the exact effect of the films on the life, ideals and actions of the people, and whether the films are "good" or "bad" in the same way as the pub is dubbed "good" and "bad". Rapidly films and pools have become major mental influences in town life, along with its essential subsidiary Blackpool, major holiday resort, run on the same lines as the other newer groupings, with the same objects and effects. The change in Worktown life over the past hundred years has been largely towards an increase in leisure. A hundred years ago all the daylight hours were work hours for Worktown folk. Now this is only true in winter. The pub has not been as fast as some others in exploiting the new leisure opportunities. And its hours have been the principal subject of legal restriction. Originally pubs were open all the day long, drinking was not a matter of hours. But, from the survival point of view the pub has an advantage over its ancient contemporaries, in having direct financially interested persons who demand returns, and thus a quick response to new conditions or a rapid disruption of the financial backing. We may expect the pub to lose a good deal more of its grip on the bladders and pockets of the Worktowner, but not by any means most of its grip.

SORTS OF PUB

Today the difference between the beerhouse and the fully licensed pub is more quantitative than qualitative. It is bigger, and sells more kinds of drinks. A few local licences are also listed as hotels, and in towns of a different character a higher proportion of hotels exists. But with a few exceptions the fully licensed house in Worktown is a drinking place, and not a hotel or inn. A more realistic form of pub classification is one based on the large town centre type of pub, the ordinary beerhouse, and an intermediate type, which may either be a large beerhouse

on a main road, or a small full licence. And also there are a
number of small full licences, not on main roads, which really
belong, from the point of view of size and accommodation, to
the beerhouse category. The form of classification outlined later
is based on this. In order to trace the development of these forms
we must understand that the first inns were lodgings for the night,
the eastern caravanserais. Amongst the Greeks similar institutions
existed, but they had a bad reputation and were not used by
respectable people, excepting those lodgings at pilgrim centres
like Delphos. The use of the inn as a drinking place really began
amongst the Romans. Horace (Sat. 1.5) refers to the inns on the
roads leading out of Rome. There were two types—the diversoria,
which were drinking places, but were not really differentiated
from wine shops and eating houses; and tabernae, at which
travellers put up. Presumably these were introduced into England
during the Roman occupation. The Roman sign for a drinking
place was a bush set up outside, and this custom was also found
in England for many centuries, and still persists in present pub
names; the Chequers also is a commonly used pub name, and this
sign was often found outside Roman pubs.

The Anglo-Saxons had three types of pub—the alehouse,
the wine-house, and the "cumen-hus" or house for accommodation. In the eighth century Ina, king of Wessex, made laws
for the regulation of alehouses. These were used for drinking only,
though sometimes they would provide food for the drinkers.

The connection between the Church and festival drinking
occasions was very close. But also the Church had its own inns.
The famous Tabard at Southwark is an example of this; it was
built by the Bishop of Winchester in 1307, partly as a guest-
house for clerics who came to visit him and partly as a semi-
commercial, semi-holy hotel for the accommodation of the
Canterbury pilgrims.

Noble houses were sometimes used as inns when their owners
were away, and then their arms were hung out. Both the words
inn and *hotel* once meant the town residence of a noble. Also
many large houses established inns in the villages to take the
overflow of their own guests.

In the fourteenth century professional inn the guests slept in
dormitories, brought most of their own food with them, but
could get bread, beer and meat from the innkeeper.

There is little known about the ordinary alehouse of the time.

From current literary references (cf. Skelton's *The Tunnynge of Elenour Runnynge*)[1] it appears they were ordinary cottages whose owners brewed ale and sold it on the premises. But there was no sharp differentiation between a drinking-place and a place for the accommodation of travellers, until the sixteenth century, when a law was made forbidding *innkeepers* to have local people drinking in their houses, and *alehouses* were not licensed to have guests sleeping on the premises. Edicts to prevent local "tippling" at the inns were sufficiently common to show that this regulation must have been frequently disregarded.

The legislation suppressing monastery activity in 1539 upset the widespread system of monks keeping "open house", often a separated "guest house". The independent inn was thus encouraged.

As transport facilities developed, so did the number and quality of inns. The alehouse continued to be regarded as a place of drunkenness, disorder, and squalor. Between the two extremes was the tavern, which had no separate legal status. An early eighteenth century writer[2] observes:

A tavern is a degree or (if you will) a pair of stairs above an alehouse, where men are drunk with more credit than apology.

Contemporary prints show that both the insides and outsides of eighteenth century pubs did not differ in essentials from those of today. The introduction of gin drinking, on a vast scale, at this period increased the number of pubs enormously, and brought into being the large street corner "gin palace". G.Wilson, a grocer, giving evidence before a Select Committee in the House of Commons, 1834, said:

A public house nearly opposite my residence . . . was taken for a gin palace, it was converted into the very opposite of what it had been, a low, dirty, public house with only one doorway, into a splendid edifice, the front ornamented with pilasters, supporting a handsome cornice and entablature, and balustrades, and the whole elevation remarkably striking and handsome.

[1] Skelton was tutor to Prince Henry, afterwards Henry VIII, who permitted the introduction of hops into Kent, and thus, four centuries ago, firmly founded a national habit.

[2] *Microcosmography*, John Earle.

However, the first gin palaces were erected long before this. The eighteenth century brought in a veritable renaissance of drunkenness; in 1722 the consumption of beer per head of population was 36 gallons, the highest recorded figure.[1] In London thousands of gin shops were set up, and gin was sold by barbers and tobacconists, hawked in the streets in barrows. The first attempts by Parliament to decrease its sale led only to universal evasion, as well as riots. In 1743 revenue duties on distilling were introduced, along with a system of licences for spirit selling, and this was successful. Now, apart from the inn and the beer-house, the pub licensed to sell spirits came into existence, a third drinking estate. This tended to alter the character of the beerhouse, making it less of a place for getting drunk in and more the scene of quieter social drinking, since the drunks could go and get so very much *more drunk for less money* at the gin palace.

The beerhouse, always the subject of abuse by the better classes, who drank at home, or stayed at inns, now began to get a different sort of bad name. A brisk bit of reflection, *Reflections on the Moral and Political State of Society at the Close of the Eighteenth Century*, by a Mr. Bowles, published in 1800, says:

> The public houses resorted to by the lower classes . . . almost invariably take in newspapers of a pernicious tendency.

By now, it appears, the name "public house" was in use. This quotation, incidentally, shows that the eighteenth century custom of coffee-house newspaper reading was also found in the working class pubs. At that time there was a tax on newspapers, deliberately introduced to prevent working people from reading them. Hence the pub "News Room", a name that still is found in some local pubs; but there are seldom any newspapers to be found in them now.

Says Postgate:

> There are only a certain number of names recorded of the trade clubs of the eighteenth century, but they almost universally show one peculiarity. Specimen names are: The Marquis of Granby Carpenters, the Friendly Society of Carpenters at

[1] This figure is given in Sidney Webb's *History of the English Licensing Laws*, generally considered the best work on the subject. However, Professor Catlin, on the basis of Lecky's figures, states that the annual consumption was as much as 90 gallons.

the Running Horse, the St. Martin's Painters, the Crown
Society of Coachmakers. . . . Inversely, we find that many
old-established English public houses bear such names as:
The Bricklayers' Arms, the Jolly Painters, the Blacksmiths'
Arms, the Colliers' Rest. They took their names from the
union, as the union took its name from the pub. There is no
reasonable doubt that trade unions originated in the public
house.

Fourteen Worktown pubs have trade names, including two
Weavers' Arms and two Spinners' Arms. The first municipal
elections at incorporation as a borough (1838) were held at five
polling stations—Higher Nag's Head, Red Cross, Church Tavern,
Britannia Inn, Union Arms, Falcon Inn. All pubs. Tories refused
to contest this election, which was therefore a walk-over for the
Liberals; the first mayor was a Unitarian radical.

The first working men ever to get on to the council, called Labour,
but sitting both on Tory and Liberal benches, were elected in
1887, largely as a result of the great engineering strike; several
of the successful candidates had been victimized for their labour
activities. *Three* of these eight were publicans and each was
closely associated with early union efforts. In the words of the
local press:

(1.11.1887)
    . . . The new Labour representative for Exchange ward is
"mine host" *Josiah Finlay*, of the Rope and Anchor Inn,
headquarters of the Engineers' Strike Committee. He is no
orator but a conscientious worker in the cause he has espoused
and possesses considerable business aptitude. He pardonably
boasts he is a self-made man. He is R.C. and a Radical.
    Mr. J. Parkins of Cotton Tree Tavern . . . He was formerly
a cotton spinning operative but his active participation in
the formation of the Cotton Spinners' Provincial Association
necessitated the severance from Park Mill Spinning Co.
    Counc. Hough . . . Landlord of the Falcon Inn, an ancient
hostelry that has seen many bitter political fights. Formerly
employed in the engineering trade at Dobson's and Barlow's
. . . he is an indefatigable worker, a fair speaker and has
considerable critical acumen.

On the other hand, early brewer candidates came in for heavy
political warfare, witness the *Worktown Evening News*, which
published on polling eve, 1892, a letter from "Back o' th' Bank".

Sir,

Mr. Sharman said something about teetotallers pushing their "impudent faces" everywhere. Sometimes he is reviling the Methodists, at others the teetotallers, and really after the election can hardly represent anyone but Bergers Lambs and Dobsons grammarians. But I am astonished to find that he is pushing "his impudent face" tonight on the premises of the Methodist teetotallers! What next? However, when they let him reply to Dr. Thornley's challenge about going to the party at the "Black Lad" in a cab . . . it appears to me that if North Ward men and women are wise they will not have a brassy brewer in the Council but one whose stake in the borough is of a more congenial character if not so great in bulk.

> If you want to have a tip
> Vote for Sharman,
> And when you have a trip
> Vote for Sharman;
> But if sick of Tory rule
> And your not a brewer's tool
> Boycott Sharman.

The result of this particular election was:

| Sharman (Conservative) | 557 |
| Harwood (Liberal) | 537 |

Today the landlords (one an R.C.: none Radical) are still the nearest to working-class people on the council, while a brewer leads the Conservative Party.

MIGHT INCREASE SEDITION?

Politics in the last century centred on pubs. The Beer Act of 1830 made it possible for any one to open a beerhouse. Plenty did. Said Sidney Smith in a contemporary letter:

> The new Beer Act has begun its operations. Everyone is drunk. Those who are not singing are sprawling. The sovereign people is in a beastly state.

Catlin quotes "certain statesmen" as saying that the restriction of liquor might increase sedition. Certainly sedition was brewing strongly around then. But whatever the real reasons, the Act was explained as being to counteract the sale of spirits by that of beer. More beer was sold.

There was no control whatever over the beerhouse; its social status was very low. There were so many of them in comparison to the numbers of the population that their owners can seldom have made a good living out of them. Consequently they were generally of the crudest description, since the landlords could not have been able to afford to lay out money on improvements. Those that did well sought to get full licence. The following ingenious argument made to the Worktown Licensing Magistrates (Licensing Sessions, 1848) is illuminating:

> Mr. Richardson appeared on his behalf, and having stated that the house for which a licence was sought, was that known as the British Queen, near Trinity Church, he observed that in addition to the arguments made use of by Mr. Gaskell, there was one point well worthy of consideration . . . whether the rules of morality and good government were not more likely to be observed in these houses as regular public houses than as beerhouses; the magistrates, under the circumstances, having jurisdiction.

None the less, he didn't get his licence, and the British Queen today is still a beerhouse. At the same sessions a reference was made to the landlord of the Red Lion, who was fined 20 shillings for permitting persons of a notoriously bad character to assemble in the taproom behind the house, which "was conducted by a separate party, and was a notorious receptacle for thieves and prostitutes of the lowest description." We have not been able to find any other references to the custom of having a separate taproom let off to someone else, but since no comment was made about this example, it could not have been an isolated case. This is important in view of the class differentiation (below) between the different types of room in modern pubs.

The licensing laws of 1869, already referred to, besides restricting the number of pubs, presumably resulted in their gradual improvement, since the consumption of drink went on increasing, which meant that a smaller number of landlords were doing better business.

From this date onwards all types of pubs were "institutionalized". Our knowledge of what the inside of pubs were like at this time must be gathered from contemporary fiction. Dickens' descriptions in *Barnaby Rudge* and other works give us a picture that is not very different in essentials from most present-day pubs. The greatest change must have been brought about by the introduction of the beer engine (on which historical data is obscure), which, besides tending to lower the quality of the beer, made it possible for the landlord to keep his barrels all in the cellar, away from the bar, and so serve a larger number of drinkers from a smaller space and with a smaller staff.

The purpose of these very brief historical references is to show that the three types into which we classify contemporary pubs are not simply based on size and layout, but on differences in their character which can be traced back over a considerable period, and which to some extent correspond to the no longer "official" or definite forms—inn, tavern, beerhouse.

THE PUB TODAY: OUTSIDE

The world affords not such inns as England hath.
                    (Fynes Morrison. Itinerary. 1617.)

The height of his ambition . . . is to show some kind of command to the inferior vassals of a Tap-House; where he is only in his kingdome. . . .
                    (Braithwaite. Law of Drinking. 1620.)

A pub is a house. Certain exterior characteristics differentiate it from other houses. All pubs have displayed outside, painted on the wall or on a wooden sign, the name of the brewers to whom they belong. Most, but not all, also have the name of the pub itself similarly displayed. Many have on the windows either painted or engraved the name of the room within or the brewer's name. And many have fixed on either side of the main entrance rectangular tablets with the brewer's name on them. There is no specific pub architectural style. Though false pilasters, porticoes and other stucco neo-classical trimmings are common, many pubs do not have these, and are simply ordinary houses.

The following table is the result of an analysis of the frontages of 12 pubs, 6 of them beerhouses (A) and 3 each of large (B) and small (C) full licences:

Characteristic	A	B	C	Total
Sign with pub name	5	3	3	11
d. brewer's name	6	3	3	12
d. both	5	3	3	11
Tablets on door	2	1	2	5
Name of room on windows	6	1	1	8
Name of brewer on windows	—	—	1	1

Pub signs have never been universal in Worktown; tendency to general decline was recently counteracted by a special exhibition in London, signs by R.A.'s and speech by the Chairman of Whitbread's Ltd., who said:

> "Expression in art must be within reach of the ordinary fellow. If this is so it will meet with an enthusiastic and ready response. Art for art's sake is a noble ideal but it must not be allowed to develop into a selfish thing which does not touch the hearts and emotions of the ordinary fellow"—(*News Chronicle* 7.4.38).

In Worktown the pub façade offers no art-appeal. The only feature common to all is the *brewer's name*. Tablets on the door generally denote a higher class of pub, and name of rooms on windows a beerhouse. More than half the Worktown pubs are beerhouses; there are 19 beerhouses licensed to sell wines; and the rest are fully licensed. This may seem to correspond to the Inn-Tavern-Beerhouse trinity. In fact it does not. Though 35 of the pubs are called Inns, and 63 hotels, only 6 are listed in the directory as providing accommodation. A tour of 19 pubs, of all kinds, asking for accommodation, proved fruitless. The ancient function of the Inn as a place for people to stay at has died away. The ordinary Worktown pub, whatever its title, is not an Inn or Hotel.

All large pubs (i.e. with 5 or more rooms and/or seating accommodation of 150 or more) are full licences; but all full licences are not large pubs, and as far as size, architecture, and general appearance, some small full licences are indistinguishable from beerhouses. The beerhouse licensed to sell wines has a separate legal status, but this status is not reflected in any differentiation in the pub itself (beyond, of course, the fact that you can buy a glass of wine in it).

The majority of pub names have a suffix, such as the —— Arms, Hotel, Tavern. The following, compiled from a list of pub names, shows the relative frequency of these suffixes.

	Inns	Hotels	Arms	Taverns	No suffix
Beerhouses	32	16	50	11	60
Full licences	3	47	19	0	33
Total	35	63	69	11	93

Although the function of the full licence as a hotel has practically ceased, yet traces of it can be found in their names—over a third of full licences are called Hotels, and only 10 per cent of them Beerhouses. Similarly, the suffix "Inn" is almost restricted to beerhouses, only three full licences being so entitled. And eleven beerhouses, but no full licences, are called Taverns.

An article on "Inn Signs" in the *Worktown Evening News*, March 5th, 1937, says:

> In every town or village one expects to find the names of old families perpetuated, and thus inn signs are a valuable adjunct to local history. Worktown's inns do not disappoint us. . . .

And the writer goes on to quote a number of Worktown pubs called after important families, such as the Earl of Bradford, Lord Derby, the Duke of Bridgwater, and so on. In fact, the majority of pub names are connected with dead Lords, Dukes, Kings, and members of the artistocracy. As well as the 69 pubs named the so-and-so Arms, there are 37 aristocratic names or names of kings. Queen Victoria is reflected in two pubs called The British Queen, one called the Victoria British Queen, and another The Old Original British Queen, as well as two Victoria Hotels and one Victoria Inn. Three pubs are called after Nelson, and there are others, such as The Gladstone and The Napier, named after historical national figures.

The next largest category of pub names, is that of animals, the names of which appear in 49 pub titles. Some of these, such as the Ox Noble and the Blue Boar, are connected with the crests of noble families; and indeed, the connection between the hundreds of Red Lions and Black Bulls found on pub signs all over the country, and the families whose totems these were, has long been severed.

We have seen, earlier, the reasons for this connection between the arms of the nobility and the arms of the pub; the later historical connection of the trade union movement with the pub has not, in Worktown, shown itself in the form of many trade names for pubs—there are only 14 of these, and it is interesting to note that 13 of them are beerhouses. Of Worktown's 75 Trade Union branches today, the 40 still meeting in pubs do so without exception in pubs without trade names.

Another type of name, of which there are only a few in Worktown, is the pub called after some place in the neighbourhood. Examples of this are: The Gas Works Tavern, Forge Tavern,

Tramways Hotel, Cattle Market Hotel, The Four Factories (this one is now closed down), Recreation Tavern (opposite the Recreation Ground). Besides the official names, many pubs have nicknames. These are of several sorts. Here are some:

The Greyhound—Clem Dug. (Hungry Dog)
The Great Eastern—The Ship
The Grey Mare—Kicking Donkey (ref. to sign on window)
The Golden Lion—Brass Cat.

Others are based on physical characteristics of the pub:

Wheatsheaf—Roundhouse.
Junction Inn—Smoother (i.e. smoothing iron, because of the shape of the pub).
School Hill Hotel—Skennin Door (squint door, two doors set on angle).
Stanley Arms—Sally up Steps (five steps up to the pub door, and landlady Sally).

Names of landlords and landladies are used also, and often remain after they have died or gone somewhere else:

The King's Arms—Balsher's or Balshaw's.
Nelson Hotel—Owd Flickie's.
Stanley Arms—Pat's Hotel (after ex-landlord Patterson).
British Queen—Owd Pomp's (landlord called Pomfret).
The Old Oak—Owd Kit's.

Other nick-names are connected with the type of customer:

Spakeaisy (this is where Irish labourers go).
Little Lad's pub (this was a place where little piecers drank).
Swine Lodge (people who don't drink there don't like those who do).
Pap Show (reputed to be on account of its being a midday drinking place for miners' wives who came into town with their babies in the afternoon, and would sit there suckling them. Observers have seen this done in local mining village pub).

Then there is the Dog and Kennel, a literary reference, the name by which everyone knows the Park View Inn, some people indeed thinking that that is its only name. Its origin is to be found in the local dialect writings of Allen Clarke, a Worktowner, who wrote, among other things, a number of funny dialogues based on the regulars of this pub, which he re-christened the Dog and Kennel.

Other names, such as the Romping Kicker, for the Nelson's Monument, the Red Rag for the Ninehouse Tavern, the Mop for the Weavers' Arms, Pig and Whistle for the Blue Boar, Sparrow's Tooth or the Boatrace for the Duke of Cambridge, and, most obscure, the War Office for the Recreation Tavern (centre of local pigeon racing, see Sport chapter), are the result of local jokes and allusions, mostly obscure now.

NOMENCLATURE

The only nickname or slang term for the pub itself that we have heard used is "the boozer", though a local drinker tells us that the expression "jerry shop" is used for beerhouses, and according to the *English Temperance Movement*, by H. Carter, the term was in common use in this part of Lancashire at the beginning of the nineteenth century.

Nomenclature of pub rooms varies. Colloquially the lounge or parlour is often spoken of as "the best room", and sometimes "the music room". A slang term for vault, occasionally used, is the "sawdust parlour", a reference that is more comprehensible when it is remembered that at one time the whole vault floor was strewn with sawdust or sand, a custom that no longer prevails here, but has been observed in some small country pubs in the south.

When we come to the "official" names written up on the doors or windows of the room we find the taproom sometimes called the News Room (cf. eighteenth century use of pubs for newspaper reading), and the best room called the commercial room. In other pubs it is named the Bar Parlour. A wide variation from normal nomenclature is shown in the following report:

> . . . the landlord took me round to see the lounge proudly and said "This is what they call the Concert Room". . . . The vault is labelled Saloon and another room Smoke Room. I ask if there is no vault here? The landlord, age 40, well built, pale but healthy looking, in a good suit and gold watch chain, says "This is a real new style pub. Well, this is the vault. It's called the Saloon. That's the thing in the newest. You don't properly have a vault in the town. Vault's outside

the centre. That's the way things are, more highclass." He
does not seem snobbish about this, in fact rather deprecating.
He adds it is also a saloon because it has seats and tables
round it.

The class hierarchy of the various rooms—which we must
now examine—is well illustrated by this, the landlord thinking
that the name belonging to a higher class of room can make the
vault "more highclass". Also the town centre pubs are more
respectable. "You don't properly have a vault in the town"
(this is in fact untrue).

In three or four of the big central pubs that have been rebuilt
or redecorated the south of England nomenclature of Public
and Saloon bars has been adopted. (In one of them castor oil
plants are found in the saloon, as a distinct mark of "class").
Some other town centre vaults are called Saloon Bar. But
normally, throughout all classes of pub the vault remains the
vault. The use of the name Commercial and News Room is mostly
confined to the middling-sized pubs, and in large ones the best
rooms are invariably Lounges.

The sort of confusion that can arise with pub names is well
exemplified in the following report, made by a Southerner, a
non-pub-goer, an experienced observer who had done a year's
work on our politics study, without studying pubs:

> The pub which observer visited was a small but clean one,
> in the heart of the West Ward working-class district. Observer
> intended going into the Vault or Public-Bar, but was confused
> by this name not being posted up. There was only Saloon
> (which in this case, as was later discovered, was another name
> for Vault) and the Lounge part of the inn, comprising three
> rooms. Observer went into one of these rooms, where five
> boys about eighteen years old were playing dominoes for
> money. In the room were also a dart board, a notice saying

ALL OUR BEERS ARE DRAWN THROUGH
GLASS TUBES

and two advertisements stating respectively

"B.B."		EMBEE
Brilliant	and	Amber Ale
Bitter		In bottle
5*d*.		4*d*.

The domino players were seated at a table, and all had half-pint glasses of beer in front of them. The whole conversation that went on, during the half-hour that observer stayed in the room, was on dominoes. About every five minutes one of the players took a short drink, but always alone, and most of the time the liquor seemed forgotten. At one point, however, three of the boys ordered more beer, which was brought by the barmaid, and not even poured out for several minutes. This is how the beer was ordered:

1st boy: (to barmaid) Will you get me one bitter?
2nd boy: And me, one.
3rd boy: Three.
Barmaid: Three bitters?

The same phenomenon was observed later on in the saloon. A man ordered beer for himself and a friend, and the full glasses remained on the counter for five minutes before one of the men took a short drink.

One man did come in, drink half a pint, and go out again, but the other three in the bar were more interested in the game of darts they were playing. The landlady of the pub came into the saloon to take part in the game: she remarked on the poor attendance, and said everyone must be saving up for Easter.

No one consumed a whole pint of beer in one glass, and only the landlady took anything other than beer: she had a small port.

No one mentioned the beer; no one said it was good or bad —it was just beer, and the fact that one paid a halfpenny less for half a pint of it in the Saloon compared with the Lounge did not lower its quality.

The thing that observer noticed first of all and right through the evening was the relative unimportance of drinking. When people drank, in nearly every case they did so without prompting from anyone else present, and were not by any means the centre of attention while they drank. It was more in the nature of an aside, a necessary automatic action which the particular situation demanded, just as the lighting of a cigarette is automatic and habitual.

The following is a complete list of all the written usages for pub rooms that we have observed:

Vault—Vault, Public Bar, Saloon Bar.
Tap Room—News Room, Commercial Room.
Best Room—Music Room, Concert Room, Lounge, Parlour, Saloon, Commercial Room, Snug.

The original of the term "vault" is obscure. The *New English Dictionary* which gives considerable space to unusual and archaic usages of the word, such as an obscure seventeenth century writer who puts it in a context where it means an outside lavatory, simply *fails to mention its current pub usage*; considering it is a term in the daily vocabulary of millions in the North it is an indication of the ignorance of the pub in non-pub-going circles. Certainly the term must have originally been connected with its usage for the cellar. Wine bars in the south, where the term vault is not in use for the public bar, are often called wine vaults. But we have not been able to find any direct evidence of how its present pub usage came about. In this connection there is an interesting Worktown story that under the vault of the Man and Scythe, oldest pub, is a secret passage running to the Parish Church (200 yards). Now bricked up, it serves as a myth-umbilical between church and pub. That the church was once Publican Number One is beyond question. It is certain, therefore, that the pub has directly acquired religious associations. The whole set-up of the vault, the bar severing the landlord from the ordinary folk, the arrangements of bottles on the shelves, the often ornate windows, the beer-engine handles (generally three or four) sticking up like tapered candles, the shortly-to-be-described rituals of toasting, rounds, glass-swiggling—have much in common with forms of religious rite and invocation. The intricate build-up of pub rooms around the exclusive landlord sections is faintly reminiscent of the Catholic Church. And in each you come to the dividing-line between minister and ministered-to for alcoholic liquor.

The function of these different types of rooms cannot be understood until we have considered the types and habits of the drinkers that frequent them. Bearing this in mind we will make the following summing up:

VAULT and TAPROOM, tabu to women, patronized only by working class drinkers, form one group of rooms, in contra-distinction to the

BEST ROOMS (lounge, parlour, etc.) where beer costs a penny a pint more, women are permitted.

THE VAULT is distinguished by the presence of THE BAR COUNTER.

THE TAPROOM, which has the same class of custom, is more of a club and games room.

Amongst best rooms the term LOUNGE is usually applied to the best rooms of the bigger pubs, PARLOUR to those of smaller ones. From now on, the former term will be used to cover all best rooms.

The legal categories of pub cannot be used as a method of functional classification. Age and topographical factors overshadow law or nomenclature.

We will take as typical a beerhouse as possible, of the sort briefly described at the beginning of the book, and examine its features in some detail; then we must do the same with a big town centre pub, and a "middling sized" one. From this we shall be able to see what features are common to all three, what are specific to one or the other type, and what, if any, is the basis of comparison between them.

A. THE BEERHOUSE

For our type of beerhouse we will take the W. It stands at a street corner in a second-class road; there are 6 mills within 500 yards radius; it belongs to one of the chief breweries. In layout, situation, and clientèle, it is about as typical a pub as could be named in Worktown.

There is no sign, and the whole place is no larger than a Worktown under-manager's home; the landlord and family live upstairs. There are three rooms—vault, parlour, and taproom. Under the vault is the cellar, where the beer barrels rest on low trestles, called stillage; from them pipes run up to the beer pumps, whose four brass and white china handles stand up on the bar counter, being, as it were, the levers that control the whole machinery of the pub.

VAULT ("PUBLIC BAR")

The vault is best described from the viewpoint of the barman. At his back are shelves for the glasses (115 half-pints,[1] 25 pints) and bottled beers, and a serving hatch that communicates through the wall into the taproom. His access to the parlour is through the doorway that leads into the passage. In front of him, besides the pumps, is a lead sink and draining board, a brass water tap, and a drawer for money.

From here, behind the counter, the pub is controlled, as a ship

[1] The half pint glasses cost 3¾d.—more than the value of the beer they hold. Pint mugs cost "about a shilling", says the barman.

is from its bridge. (With the barrels, like the engines, out of sight down below.) But from the drinkers' point of view this is the smallest, most inconvenient, and uncomfortable room, little more than an L shaped passage, to whose walls bare wooden benches are fixed, seating eight people. The floor is of bare stone, a continuation of the pavement outside. Walls are panelled with dark brown painted wood half way up, the rest covered with dingy dull red wallpaper. Decoration is confined to an advertisement that reminds the drinkers BEER IS BEST. Along the base of the bar counter, whose top is of well worn, well wiped mahogany, runs a line of scattered sawdust, about six inches wide, on to which people spit, throw fag ends, matches, and empty cigarette packets.

The counter and beer pumps are the main features that sharply distinguish the vault from other rooms in other kinds of not-public houses. In both taproom and parlour, the only articles of furniture there that would not be found in non-pub rooms are the spittoons, round green china bowls, about six inches across, filled with sawdust. These, we shall see, assume a far more important role than simply that of being spit receptacles.

TAPROOM

The taproom floor is covered with dark red lino, and there is the same reddish wallpaper that is found in the vault. Built-in leather covered benches (seating 16) run round the sides, and in front of them are tables, one round and two oblong; under each table is a spittoon. More seating accommodation is provided by two heavy wooden three-legged stools, and three four-legged ones. Another BEER IS BEST reminder hangs on the walls, and a framed and glazed notice saying NO GAMBLING ALLOWED. This is above the table where the card players sit. There is a clock. Also a fireplace, described by the barman as "old-fashioned". Above it is a gilt-framed mirror that runs to the ceiling. (Size of room is approximately 20 feet by 12.)

PARLOUR (LOUNGE)

Now for the "best room". This is bigger—27 feet by 15—and contains new features, a piano (which is sixty years old), wood blocks on the floor, and generally more ambitious attempts at decoration. The fireplace is tiled, red, surmounted by a dark oak mantelpiece, and, as the barman writes in his description, "on shelf of overmantel two figures, bronze, of ladies carrying on shoulders grapes and water respectively".

Advertizing here is also more ambitious—Smith's Crisps, Grapefruit Crush, Craven A, Woodbines, appeal to the non-alcoholic tastes of parlour drinkers.

Benches, upholstered in shiny brown imitation leather, and seating 36, are fixed to the wall, and the 17 stools are light, or varnished bentwood.

There are four round tables, of the type shown in the photograph, whose heavy ornamental bases depict in cast iron figures of Britannia with her arms folded over the Union Jack. And the table tops are not plain bare wood, like those in the taproom, but are covered with a green linoleum-like material, a shade lighter than the green china of the spittoons on the floor underneath.

Some hypothetical observer, who had never seen or heard of a pub before, would be struck by this division into three architectural realms, of different sizes, and of different types. Is, he may wonder, its significance religious, trinitarian perhaps, can

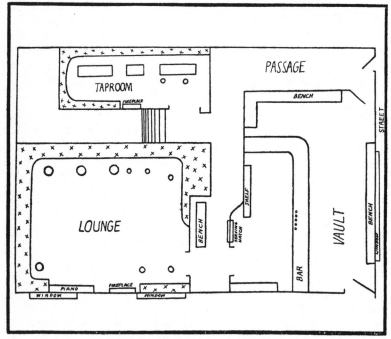

TYPICAL MEDIUM SIZED PUB
(as described in text)

it correspond with different needs of the pub-goer, or does it signify three lines of social cleavage? . . . And he might proceed to make an analysis of the difference between the various rooms.

In the first place vault, tap and parlour are progressively larger, as is their seating accommodation, number of tables, number of advertisements displayed. Conversely, the relation of spitting accommodation to seating accommodation gets smaller. In the vault a sawdust surface of at least three square feet is provided for the spittle from 8 seats: in the tap there are two spittoons for 21 seats, 10·5 seats per spittoon, while the ratio in the parlour is 6·52, or 8·6.[1] But, besides these quantitative differences there are others. What does the parlour possess that the tap has not? The piano, the non-alcoholic advertisements, the lino on the table tops, the wooden blocks on the floor, the bronze ladies on the mantelpiece.

But both parlour and tap have fireplaces, stools, tables, non-stone floors, upholstered benches, and mirrors—all features not to be found in the vault. There is only one thing possessed by the vault which no other room can claim—that is the machinery of beer distribution, which, our hypothetical observer would imagine, was the most important of the lot.

Two points relevant must be remembered here—vault and taproom are for men only, tabu to women, who drink in the parlour. And beer is a penny a pint more in the parlour.

B. THE MEDIUM-SIZED PUB

The next type is the small full licence (or large beerhouse). The differences between this and the ordinary beerhouse are mainly quantitative; the example which we have chosen is bigger, has more seating capacity, and more tables than the previous one. Also there are fewer seats per table and fewer spittoons per seat. All these differences are summed up in the accompanying diagrammatic representation. The vault-tap-parlour division is the same, though the vault is relatively larger in comparison with the other rooms than was the one previously described. Its floor is covered with worn brown lino; the beer pumps, of which there are five,[2] have a blue willow pattern on the china grips. And, since this is a full licence, on the shelves behind the bar are bottles of spirits—whiskey, rum, advocaat,

---

[1] This is unusual. Normally there is relatively more spitting accommodation in the tap. However, there are no "typical" pubs. This is this one's deviation from the ideal norm.

[2] Number of beer pumps depends mainly on the age of the pub.

Geneva, Benedictine, wormwood bitters, peppermint—and wines—
sherry, port, "wine cordial". From the appearance of the labels many
of these bottles have stood there for a long time. And on the top
rows of the shelves stand some ornamental coloured wineglasses and
cut glass decanters. These shelves are further decorated with round
paper d'oyleys that hang down over the edges, forming half circles.

Next to the street door is a small gasfire. On the wall is a
framed notice that says:

GOOD ADVICE

CALL FREQUENTLY
DRINK MODERATELY
PAY IMMEDIATELY
BE GOOD COMPANY
PART FRIENDLY
GO HOME QUIETLY

Let these lines be no man's sorrow,
Pay today and trust tomorrow.

However, despite these added refinements, this vault is very
little different from the other one except in size and seating
capacity, though the presence of spittoons instead of a sawdust
"ditch" has important social connotations.

There are four aspidistras in the parlour—three in the corners,
and a large one on the piano; and there are pictures, one called
"Scotland for Ever!" and representing a "Charge by the Greys";
the other two being coloured Cecil Aldin prints called "The
Connoisseurs" (late eighteenth century costume, folk eating and
drinking with jollity). On the marble mantelpiece are two iron
statuettes of men restraining prancing horses. There is a mirror
here, and another, gilt-framed, at the end of the room.

The music scattered on the piano, the aspidistras, the hearthrug, the pictures on the walls, help to create the impression of a
rather dingy but luxuriant atmosphere of late Victorian "respectability" typical of this sort of pub. In some there are
bronze horses on the mantelpiece, flanking a marble clock that
ticks out seconds below an overmantel craggy with mirrors;
sometimes a plaster trout in a glass case, a large coloured photo-

graph of the Victoria Falls, or three fat, empty Chinese vases, are dominant decorative features. There is always symmetry; and these objects, varying in quantity and quality, in parlours of varying sizes, with shiny, worn leatherette-covered benches built into the walls, round tables on contorted cast-iron frames, flanked with bentwood stools, are typical of the middling-sized pub.

As in the other pub, between the lounge and vault there is a passage. But drinks for the parlour are served to the waiter through a hatch; the passage is wide, and there is a leather-covered bench opposite the hatch; here some drinkers can and do sit. This is a rudimentary passage or "lobby" bar. Here it is unimportant, only used by a few drinkers. But in other sorts of pub and in large ones it can be and is important.

C. LARGE PUBS

The large, fully licensed pub has very variable forms. Our example has more than twice the amount of rooms and twice the seating of the beerhouse, and three times as many tables. Decoration is of more expensive materials than in the other examples; and it is "modern"—plain surfaces, bright colours, and light woodwork. There is no taproom. Its place is taken by a large lobby bar.

The lack of physical separation here between the vault and lobby bar is made up by other factors that clearly demarcate these two areas. The drinker has but to walk round the corner of the vault bar, lean up against the lobby bar, and his next order of beer will cost him a penny a pint more. And, while at the vault side of this region, in a kind of no man's land, there is a space of floor neither specifically vault nor lobby, in one corner of it is a spittoon, and in the opposite corner, well into the more expensive territory, no spittoon is found.

A sharp example of this differentiation can be seen in one of the smaller town centre pubs, which is unique for the fact that there is a vault and a better class bar between which there is *no* physical separation. Half way down the bar counter, there is a gap, and then another bar begins and runs on further. Above the gap is a notice PARLOUR PRICES BEYOND HERE. The vault bar is wooden, the other zinc covered, and in this section the stone flagged floor is covered with mats.

The first time an observer visited it there were eleven men in each of the bars; all the men in the vault part wore caps, and with one exception all those in the other part had bowlers or trilbies. The exception was a small fattish man of about 45, who stood at the end of the parlour bar, wearing a cap; he faced towards the vault bar, and there was a gap between him and the other drinkers in his bar. When this pub was revisited three weeks later the same situation prevailed, the same number of drinkers, the same hat differentiation, and the same little man with the cap standing isolated and gazing at the vault.

The landlord said that he had introduced the division "to make it more select". But since the introduction of the extra penny on beer he had stopped charging parlour prices beyond the division. The notice had been retained "to keep out undesirables". The segregation continues; the higher parlour prices were as much a symptom as a cause of it.

The accompanying diagram, compiled from complete and detailed inventories of these three type pubs, shows the varying quantitative factors, and also those others that are specific to each type.

What emerges from this?

The three pubs are graded in an ascending order of size—number of rooms, amount of seating accommodation, number of tables, and ration of tables to seating. Other differences are found in an increasing expensiveness of flooring material, in a decreasing amount of spitting accommodation. Also, which cannot be shown graphically, there is an increasing elaborateness of decoration, both in the quality of materials used, and such things as the presence of aspidistras in types B and C, plus in C, the castor oil plants in the biggest room.

The main factor that can be deduced from this, is that the qualities that serve to differentiate the three types of pub from one another, are also those qualities that *differentiate the three types of pub room from each other*. The substitution of the lobby in place of the taproom in type C tends to obscure this. Further, just as, on the whole, there is less difference between the vault and the taproom than between those two rooms and the parlour or lounge so the difference between types A and B is less than between them and type C. Examination of the diagrammatic representation of our table will show this.[1]

___

[1] There is an error on the diagram overleaf. "Spittoons per seat" *should* read "Seats per spittoon", and the first figure after this is 9, *not* 8·5. The figure 4·7 should read 5. Decimal points are misleading here.

	a	B	C
number of rooms			
class of rooms	(plant, dominoes, skittles)	(plant, lobby, dominoes, skittles)	(tables, tables, table, lobby, skittles)
seating in rooms	skittles 8 / dominoes 21 / plant 52	skittles 20 / dominoes 24 / plant 52 / lobby 3	skittles 34 / table 87 / table 26 / table 25
total seats	81	99	172
total number of tables in rooms	9	12	36
— in biggest room	6	9	20
flooring / vault / parlour	stone flags / wood blocks	old lino / lino	rubberoid / rubberoid

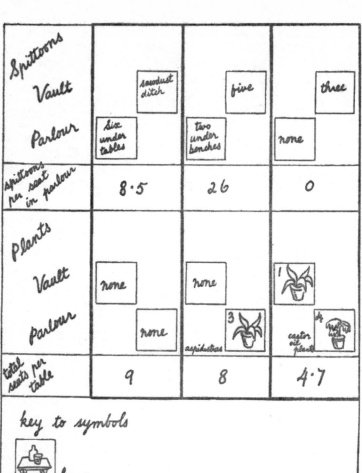

Spittoons Vault	sawdust ditch	five	three
Parlour	six under tables	two under benches	none
spittoons per seat in parlour	8·5	26	0
Plants Vault	none	none	1
parlour	none	3 aspidistra	4 castor oil plant
total seats per table	9	8	4·7

key to symbols

lounge
parlour
tap
vault

DIAGRAM SHOWING
THE MAIN POINTS
OF DIFFERENCES
BETWEEN THREE
TYPES OF PUB

VARIATIONS

Although it is perfectly correct to say that the different types
of rooms in pubs represent a graded hierarchy of class, or rather,
social status, as do the three types of pub; yet a consistent standard of "better" or "lower" class environment is not always
found throughout the same pub—for instance, small beerhouses
exist whose best rooms have that characteristic of size and or
decoration that belong to the equivalent rooms of larger and
better class pubs. The following landlord's remark, quoted in
an observer's report, helps to explain this:

> . . . he (the landlord) got to talking about how pubs here
> were different from those in the south. He said that if they
> were built nowadays they would be made a lot different, they
> wouldn't have so many different rooms, you never got both
> rooms filled—*you either got a vault crowd or a parlour crowd.* . . .

Again, the N——, a small beerhouse, has no parlour, as such.
The taproom, which is barer than the average, having some vault
characteristics, such as a stone floor, possesses a piano, a parlour
piece of furniture. (The parlour or best room of the pub is sometimes called "the music room".)

The presence of potted plants in a room is normally an indication
of its status; but, for instance, the —— Arms, a small beerhouse,
with a stoneflagged vault, where there is on the bar counter an
array of potted plants, and in the summer, vases of flowers, as
well as an aspidistra. In the vault of another, larger pub, we have
observed five aspidistras on the window sills, and two pots (2 feet
6 inches diameter) of them on the counter. The aspidistra is the
front-window, best-room symbol of the private house.

Amongst the town centre pubs the variation in design is too
wide for precise classification. This is partially due to the fact
that when pubs are rebuilt or redecorated their interiors are
"modernized". Variation from our type pub of this class tends,
on one hand, towards an increasing centralization with few and
larger rooms and less physical divisions between them, cul-
minating in the wine bar, which is simply an enormous room,
with bar counters ranged along the sides. The opposite tendency
is towards a greater complexity and decentralization—as an
example of which the X—— can be quoted. This pub has a very
large modern vault, that has no direct customer connection with
other parts of the house; to get from it to the lounges you have

to walk out into the street, and in through another door, that opens to a wide, long passage, in the middle of which is a commodious lobby bar; at each side of the lobby are doors leading to lounges, one of which has a small and separate bar counter of its own on one side. A third, and entirely separate section is downstairs, where there is another very big lounge, accommodating up to 150; at one end of it is a large bar which has its own staff of barmen and its own clientèle of drinkers. This place is really three pubs under one roof. Compare the case quoted earlier of the pub that was fined for general misconduct in the taproom which "was conducted by a separate party".

Now is it possible, on the basis of these facts, to construct a formal scheme of classification?

The three class system of pub and of room are basic; but there are many other factors which tend to obscure this, and which can be best regarded as variations from it.

As when we examined the data of pub distribution, we must take into account the age-factor. For instance, the uniformity of decoration in the parlours of medium-sized pubs reflects the taste and decor of a particular period. The most profitable pubs (which usually means the biggest ones) will tend to be the most often redecorated and rebuilt. Therefore their scheme of decoration will reflect not something that is inherent in the type of pub itself, but a contemporary level of ideas of what looks smart, plus idiosyncrasies and tendencies peculiar to the brewing firm. This is borne out by going along by-pass roads on the outskirts of London and taking a look at the timbered new pubs turned out to a pattern by the architectural department of the biggest brewing firms.

The three class system of pub and rooms is not only a matter of building. It is primarily a matter of the people in the pub. The habits of drinkers, drunkards, anti-drinkites, are keypoint, as we shall soon see.

The pub rooms form a labyrinth. The passage or lobby bar forms the channel between a number of rooms, each with their regulars and casuals, who may never see each other except by chance at the urinals in the back yard.

At a further glance they represent lines of clothes cleavage. The class factor is as confused as are the forms of the class structure all over Worktown, where it is distinct only in death, when you finally come to rest in a grave, if possible better class than your life, class 1a, 1b, 2, 3 or 4, according to the distance away from the path and the number of people who pass by your tombstone and thus how much you pay for your 6x2 feet bit of land (shared with five others).

The real difference between these rooms is in the relationship between the people in them, and the relationship of all the people to the permanent personnel of the pub. Broadly, this is the subject of most of the rest of this book, but it will be useful here to specify some points in the general pattern. The fact that the vault is the place where you often *stand* is first important. *You do not come to the vault to relax physically*. And many of the people in any vault are working nine hours a day on their feet. (The great majority of workers, both sexes, in Worktown have jobs which involve standing or walking about, mainly in artificially hot or damp atmospheres, tropical all the year round, so noisy that a lip-reading system has developed as language.)

Only men are allowed in the vault. There is a sawdust strip along the bottom of the bar, or the derived spittoons with sawdust or (further derivation) without. The seventeenth century usage of vault-lavatory has already been mentioned. There is something of the gent's lavatory and structure in a vault, which is almost always long and thin, and stone floored (in the older pubs). The vault is nothing like home. It is an exclusively male gathering. And the males who come to it come singly. They know that they will meet company there. To the vault you go singly, to the lounge in groups.

There are seldom pictures or decorations of any sort in the vault. There are very seldom aspidistras. There is generally some sort of game, often several. There is usually a bookmaker's runner who comes in at certain times. And the landlord spends most of his time there. There is of course constant contact between the people in the vault and the person or persons behind the bar, who may be a woman, and may then become focus of a whole pattern of banter and flirt. You may spit on the floor or burn the bar with a cigarette, and the barmaid won't reprove you. Indeed, as one pub-goer remarked, "You can do almost anything you bloody well like in the vault, short of shitting on the place."

The vault is thus the place where the male comes to relax mentally, though not so much physically. To meet other men, many of whom he only knows here, who may never have seen each other's wives except on the last half hour on Saturday when the man may accompany his wife in the lounge.

The taproom is the same price as the vault. The same simplicity—it is often like the kitchen of any small farmhouse in the villages outside Worktown. But unlike the vault it is entirely a sitting-room, wooden benches round the wall and wooden stools; unpolished wood tables, spittoons, dominoes. This is more of a club room than the vault. The same people, same clothes, same percentage caps and scarves, but few casuals dropping in. Casuals are somewhat resented if they do drop into the taproom. It would be bad form for a stranger to go in there for a drink. And he would probably notice that the regulars in there were not very pleased to see him.

In the lounge there are padded seats and chairs; a piano with a stool for the pianist; no standing. Aspidistras or other plants in 75 per cent; pictures on the wall, or modern wall decor; never stone floored, but lino, rubbercloth, etc. Generally a hearthrug. No games. Seldom a bookmaker's runner. Often adverts for non-alcoholic drinks. And always someone to bring you your drinks on a tray. You cannot see the bar from the lounge. In brief, the lounge is a large comfortable room with decorations such as may be found in any Worktown home, but on a large scale, on a middle-class level of comfort, with servant and service, every-one in smart clothes. You do not come to the lounge alone. If you do you are conspicuous. You come to the lounge with your social group, ready made, and sit at a table, having no especial intercourse with people at other tables. There is no sex division within the lounge. Each table tends to be a hetero-sexual group—though often these groups are exclusively of men or of women. Sixteen per cent of all pub-goers are women. About a third of all pub clients are in the lounges in pubs outside the town centre. The rest in the tap and vault. Average close on 45 per cent of the people in the *lounge* are women ; in pubs where there are several lounges one will have 90 or more per cent women, it will have become a snug or bar parlour type, reserved for regular women in the same implicit way as the taproom is reserved for certain male regulars.

The saying "A woman's place is in the home" is still current in Worktown where 44 per cent of the adult women earn their own or their families' livings directly (over half these work in cotton mills). And the woman's place in the pub is that part of it which is a home from home, a better home from ordinary worker's home, where —the only time in worker life in Worktown—you don't have to do any more than order someone else to serve your physiological need or wish. And, as usual, the woman's part is the one of cleanness, ashtrays, no random saliva, few or no spittoons. The vault is the place where men are men. In the lounge they are women's men, with collar studs. For that, as usual, they must pay another penny.

Thus it is evident that the pub is not simply an escape from home life into better surroundings. For the men's section is no better, often more dim and crowded than home (but cf. p. 133). And when they come with their women they are only escaping from the home itself, not its associated life. It is also evident that the structure of the pub is not a class-structure, in the ordinary sense of the phrase. Any man can go into the vault. But if he is with his wife or mother or girl and wishes to sit with them, he can't go into the vault. He has to take a step up, a sit down, and pay more for the same stuff. He is not a different class for doing that. And many workers make this vault-lounge (cf. p. 144) move every week-end. The same thing exactly happens on Sunday, and centres around the church-going habit. On Sunday the visible weekday criteria of class-distinctions break down and disappear. On Sunday anyone looks like an Alderman.

THE END OF A PUB

Auctioneer: "It's brick built and it's been very well cared for. It's a good square property . . . a rear room which was probably a snug or something like that in the olden days. There is also a small cellar, formerly a beer cellar, which isn't of much importance and isn't used. But of course it could be an excellent storage cellar. There's a good yard—a large shed —probably in the days when this was used as a licensed house it was used as a cart shed.

"This property was formerly, I believe, a licensed house, but it was delicensed—for what reason I don't know, and of course it doesn't matter. . . .

"Will you give £400 for it. If it had the licence we should be talking about four thousand, shouldn't we? A house like that couldn't be built today for under £600. Of course, you wouldn't build it like that, I know."

And the Merseyside Survey (I, p. 256) expressed the different, more moralist, "social survey" attitude:

Another great obstacle to slum clearance and reconstruction was the enormous cost of acquiring licensed premises in a clearance area. For example, three public-houses included in one Presentment cost as much in compensation as the whole of the rest of the area (534 houses), while in another area it was stated, in the course of the assessments for compensation, that the annual aggregate receipts of three public houses came to about £5,000.

WHAT IS A PUB?

We have seen that no "typical" pub exists. While there are certain features common to the majority of pubs, yet it is possible to find pubs lacking in some or all of these features. The three class system of room, for instance, is not found in the wine bar. The bar counter itself, and the beer pumps, which of all the characteristics that we have examined seem the most fundamental, do not exist in the Park View Inn, which has only a taproom and parlour, and the beer (good beer too) is drawn straight from the barrel in the cellar and brought out and served from jugs. Such a pub is a rarity in Worktown, but there are plenty of them in other places. So, then, a pub is first of all a building, a house. From the outside it is invariably distinguished from other houses, either private or public, by some kind of sign. Inside, the one basic feature is that anyone between certain hours established by law (and often outside them) is free to pay for a glass of mild beer. But even this can be qualified, as this report shows:

> Police station. Man with terrible face (syphilis?) comes in and asks if he can get a card to say face is result of burn. He has been refused admission to a pub on account of it. Cop says "He can refuse who he likes without giving any reason, whether drunk or sober or what. It's his house, it's a private residence. . . . If a licensee wants to refuse you admittance to 'is place 'e's a right". Afterwards cop says to observer that he quite agrees with the landlord turning the man out. "You 'ave to be a bit careful."

Note: The following table is appended giving details of the irregularity of pub distribution, referred to on page 67. The circular areas are divided into four quadrants:

Quadrants	Areas					
	Number of pubs			% of total pubs in area		
	A	B	C	A	B	C
1. North to East	19	52	33	34·6	38·8	41·8
2. East to South	18	35	17	32·7	26·1	21·5
3. South to West	8	24	16	14·5	17·9	20·3
4. West to North	10	23	13	18·2	17·2	16·4
Totals	55	134	79	100	100	100

All these areas are completely built-up, except for some of C that is included in No. 4 quadrant—the corner of a park and the Infirmary grounds.

V

DRINKERS

H OW MANY?

We have already seen in estimating the amount of beer sold in Worktown that there are about 60,000 potential pub-goers; and the evidence showed that, in fact, the whole of this section of the population did not drink (cf. p. 40).

Selley, whose book is one of the few that attempts to deal with the pub as a social institution, says that a census of the public house population "with anything like accuracy is practically an impossibility".

The London Survey and the Merseyside Survey do not suggest the possibility or desirability of finding out what are the proportions of pub-goers in the vast populations whose other activities they have so carefully gone into.

In Worktown neither local temperance bigshots nor the secretary of the Licensed Victuallers' Association would give an estimate.

But it is important to find out. The figure at which we want to arrive is that of the average number of pub-goers throughout the week. A census of all the people in all the pubs at a certain day and time would not have been very useful, because of the large weekly and hourly fluctuation in this number.

The following methods were used:

Sample counts were made in some typical beerhouses on the peak nights at the peak hours—Friday and Saturday between 9 and 10 p.m. From these an average figure of around 60 was arrived at. This number would, of course, be higher in the large town centre pubs, in some of which up to 300 people have been counted. But taking 60 as a basic low figure, with 304 pubs, it means that there are approximately 18,000 people in them at their peak days and hours. This of course does *not* represent the total number of people who came in and out during the whole of the evening.

Then a random count, in 129 pubs, of all types and in different rooms was made. The average figure arrived at from this was 64.8 people per pub—19,699 pub-goers.

Thirdly, the barman in a beerhouse supplied us with a list of all the people who drank regularly at his pub (all rooms) throughout the week. This list contains 62 names. Here again we find the same average figure occurring. Another list, made by a regular of a different pub, gave the names of all the people who came into the vault only on a week night and on a Saturday. Between opening and closing time on the week night 28 came in; and from 7 p.m. to closing time on the Saturday 29 came in; 18 of this 29 went on to other pubs in the centre of the town—a common Saturday night practice, and one that is important in this connection, because it shows that the large numbers on that night in the town centre pubs can represent extra *visits* to pubs rather than extra pub-goers.

If then, we assume a basic low figure of about 20,000 pub-goers, how does it check up with the figures of drink consumption?

Before answering this, we may mention one of the only other *area* counts so far undertaken. This was done by a number of mass-observers while making a study of the social factors in politics in the borough of Fulham, South West London. On a typical Saturday evening in September, 8.30 to 10 p.m., the average persons per pub was 104·3, of whom 36 per cent were women. Unlike Worktown, women were found in every bar, the lowest proportion in the Public Bar and the highest in the Private Bar. Approximately 7,000 drinkers were found, representing 7 per cent of the electorate, and one in every ten adult males. As in Worktown, this is much higher than the maximum numbers in church. But as an actual proportion of population, it is considerably less than Worktown's pub-going community, which is over 15 per cent. For whereas Worktown, with a population of 175,000, has 304 pubs, and averages 62 drinkers a pub, Fulham, population 125,000, has 71 pubs, cramfull at peak times. Fulham pubs average larger, but (see below) distance from home is a factor cutting across size and seating capacity. It would therefore seem as if compulsory inhibiting of drink-opportunity does keep down the *number* who drink in pubs, though many people who live in Fulham drink in adjacent boroughs. With one pub to 1,770 people Fulham (against one pub to 559 people in Worktown) is second least pubbed area in London and one of the lowest in the country. But, as we shall see, this type of teetotalitarian licensing is not correlated with the low drunkenness rate at which it is aimed—largely because crowd social drinking has other major consequences. And the price paid in other, less social or more "anti-social" ways will emerge when we consider the housing estate, as well as in future reports of our London housing researches. While in the next chapter the topographical and historical factors in pub numbers will be considered.

To check against the Worktown figure of some 15 per cent of electorate as pretty regular (at least one night a week) pub-goers, and Fulham's 7 per cent of the electorate, we made counts in certain other areas which have been the subject of special Mass-Observational studies. Counts were made on successive week-ends. Saturday nights, in autumn.

Place	No. of pubs where counts made	No. of persons counted	No. of pubs in town	Therefore est. total of pubgoers
Brighton	39	1,516	380	14,771
Canterbury	26	711	108	2,943
Aldershot	28	1,010	—	—
			(not a licensing area)	

As percentages of total population, these give 9–10 per cent pub-goers. The Fulham data as percentage of total population (not electorate only) is 6 per cent. These figures confirm that on Saturday evenings somewhere around a twelfth or more of the total population of England is consuming alcohol in pubs— a good many more will be doing so at home. These snap counts in selected towns are correlated with a whole lot of other studies, and are still in progress.

To return, then, to the Worktown position.

3,000,000 gallons a year shared out amongst 20,000 Worktown pub-goers works out at a consumption of over 3 pints per head per day. This agrees fairly well with the various averages of drink consumption worked out earlier (p. 40). The figure of 20,000 is, however, not homogeneous—is not always composed of the same people. It can be best expressed by saying that there is a basic low average of 140,000 pub visits per week. There is no reason to suppose that this is an overestimate. And since a great many pub-goers drink less than three pints on the nights that they visit pubs the real figure will be higher than this.

WHEN

It was pointed out that there is a variation in the pub population from night to night. Counts through the week show that this
variation is wide, and is remarkably constant even where small
numbers are concerned. The following table is the result of five
counts, taken during the week beginning May 26th.

	Mon.	Tues.	Wed.	Thurs.	Fri.	Sat.	Sun.
A.	15	25	14	20	50	67	41
B.	28	31	30	28	52	54	38
C.	28	20	23	19	47	61	40
D.	17	18	15	19	39	46	38
E.	45	46	36	52	84	100	87

A, B and C were taken in big central pubs, at 8.30, 9 and 10 p.m. respectively.
A was taken in the lounge, B and C in the vault, D and E were made in an
average corner pub, D represents the total in the whole of the pub at 9.30,
and E is the result of a count made right through the day.

The diagram opposite is based on percentages of the respective
Saturday night figures. The important, and representative count,
is E. The relative abnormalcy of A, B and C in relation to the
ordinary pub is important, because despite this, and despite
the small figures concerned, the correspondence of the curves is
close. And these figures do not vary very much from one week
to another. For instance, C's Saturday night figure is 61. On
a Saturday during the previous month 61 also were counted, at
the same time, and in the following month 60. Bearing this in
mind these curves can be considered as generally applicable. The
Saturday night pub population will be about twice that of Monday,
though this will not necessarily apply to very small numbers, or
to single counts made before the peak hours, the widest variation
from the norm, for instance, being found in A, which was made
at 8.30 p.m. Compare Rowntree's early pub counts at York, 1899,
for six pubs on a Monday and a Saturday, 233 and 342 drinkers
respectively. Then pubs were open all day.

As distinct a variation in the number of drinkers from day
to day, is that from hour to hour. And, just as the week-end
peak is the dominating feature of the weekly cycle, so is the
last hour peak that of the daily cycle. Landlords, when questioned
by observers, have used identical words for describing this.
They all said their best custom was "in the last hour". The table
below and the diagram show this quite clearly. The counts were

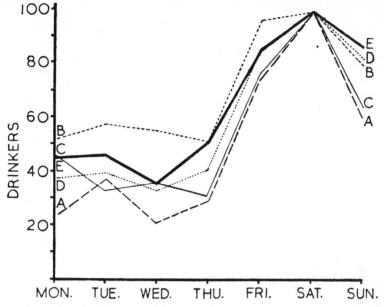

VARIATION IN THE NUMBERS OF DRINKERS THROUGH THE WEEK

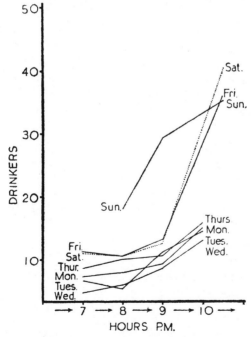

HOURLY VARIATION IN THE NUMBER OF DRINKERS IN ONE PUB

made at the same beerhouses and during the same week as before.

	1 p.m. to 3	5.30 to 7	7 to 8	8 to 9	9 to 10
Monday	8	5	3	12	17
Tuesday	6	6	7	9	18
Wednesday	7	2	4	8	15
Thursday	4	8	10	11	19
Friday	8	12	11	15	29
Saturday	18	12	11	14	46
Sunday	34	—	17	29	38

Note: Sunday hours are 12 noon to 2 and 7 to 10 p.m. The large number that morning was unusual. The barman said: "It's exceptional, it happened to be warm, it makes a difference."

The Friday and Saturday last hour rise is nearly three times as great as that of week nights, while the Sunday rise, though high, is spread out over a longer period.

The analogy between the last hour and the week-end is striking, as is the particularly marked week-end last hour increase, and suggests a possible explanation that will be common to both phenomena. In 1899 York, Rowntree (p. 375) found that with pubs open from 6 a.m. to 11 p.m. "while there is a considerable rush of customers during the hours 12.30 to 2.30 p.m., the attendance during the evening is considerably smaller than on Saturday night", and on every occasion peak time was 9–10, *not* 10–11.

A landlord writes "the most customers only come in on the last hour, unless they are carrying extra cash".

Other comments are:

Landlord says to observer "the drinking is all week-end now". He "thinks" that if the pubs were shut at the beginning of the week everyone would be satisfied; doesn't think lunch-time opening is worth the trouble.

Barmaid: "They just wait for the last hour; never mind what time you open or what time you close. It's all they've got the money for."

The following write up of a local pub-goer (unemployed male) who made a trip down one of the main streets in the centre of the town visiting every pub, contains a number of remarks of this kind, and is worth quoting in full:

I commenced at 7.45 at the C. Hotel. There were seven in Vault, four of whom were Corporation Tram-men playing dominoes and all smoking cigarettes, two were drinking pints, one aged man was well oiled and kept muttering about nobody would take a rise out of him.

I then proceeded to the Q., 7.50, nobody in the house except myself in the vault. Landlord said that the boys would be in shortly, tne dart board was in readiness for them. I then went to the B.C., 7.55, only three in vault, one smoking pipe, and cigarette both were spitting on the floor nothing was said I noticed the landlady's daughter wearing cross round neck, denoting Catholic Faith. There is also a tap room at the rear where dominoes were in progress. I then proceded to the A. Inn, 8 p.m. Only me in the house. I questioned landlady about trade, she said we can't grumble our regulars will be in shortly, could see dominoes were played here. I then went round the corner to the A. Inn, 8.5 p.m. Only me in. I received the reply that it was rather early for much custom to be expected before 8.30 noticed Dart Board in the vault. I then proceed to the B. Hotel, 8.15. there were 6 in vault smoking seemed to be carried on in spasms a few draws and then dock their cigarettes and they light up again a few minutes afterwards dominoes were in progress in smoking room. I proceeded opposite to the O. Arms, 8.20, only me in vault landlord said they would soon have callers the Lido next door would be loosing in about ten minutes. No games noticeable. I then went to the R.C., 8.25. seven in vault one man was chaffing young lady behind the bar but stopped when I ordered my drink he said he thought I was her young man and me being a big-un he better shut up I replied well it wouldn't be a bad idea, the girl said yes I think you would get a black eye off him I could hear dominoes in progress in a side room. I then had a wash and brush up on Nelson Square for which I paid 2d. I then proceded to the P. Hotel, 8.35, five in vault, appeared to be very quiet in here considering the size of the place, particular thing I noticed was the prestige the head barman holds here those under him seem to think he's a God.

I then went to the S. Hotel, 8.45, 45 in vault. There has been an alternation in the vault to make room for a new dartboard which I understand is made out of Fibre an old hand showing me how the dart left no impression on the board after it had been pierced he also said that the darts were heavier than usual. I proceeded to the W.H. 8.55, 120 in the Place. I had a word with the landlord about trade I said I believe this place used to be packed when H.Z.[1] was here, he said "Yes she ruined this bloody town".

[1] He is referring to a celebrated ex-local pub-singer, who is regarded now as a kind of legendary Worktown Mae West figure. More about her later.

I then called at the P.W. 9.10 p.m. (no vault) 6 around bar.
M.A.[1] came in while I was there I saw a young man who stood
near me send in a Pale Ale for her, piano playing in the room,
this is also hang-out for Newspaper Sam. I then proceeded
to another Vault, 9.20, 33 in vault, I must have been getting
a little intoxicated I forgot to look for games the place was
rather full. So I proceeded to the M & L. where I arranged to
meet Tom Harrisson at 9.30. I discovered that it had taken
me an hour and three quarters to walk along the street and I
had consumed

2 half pints of	Mild Beer
1	Hamers
1	Cornbrook
5	Magees
2	Walkers
2	Draught Bass
1	Swales

Total 14 half pints.

I then had two in the M & S and a bottle of Brown Peter in
the G. Total Beer Drank 8½ pints.

WEEK-ENDS

An immediate explanation of the week-end and last hour
increase can be made in economic terms: "The last hour is all
they've got the money for." And when landlords say "the drinking
is all week-end now", the implication of the "now" is that at
one time the town was more prosperous, and many more people
could afford to, and did, drink more and longer during the week.

For most Worktowners paynight is Friday, and that is the
night of the greatest increase in the number of drinkers (and
later we will see that the actual speed of drinking increases
sharply). And the smallest number of drinkers is found from
Monday to Thursday, the hard-up days.

But to explain this in purely economic terms is not enough.
Certainly the greatest number of drinkers are found at week-ends,
when there is most money in circulation. Also, for the majority
of workers the week-end is a period of relaxation and escape from
routine. The fact that they are paid before the week-end instead
of after it can be advanced to prove that such activities as
drinking, dancing, cinema going, are made possible for, and are

[1] M.A. is one of the town's best known women. More about her later also.

indulged in by, the greatest number of people because it is only at this time that they can afford these entertainments. But it can also just as logically be said that the economic factor (paynight) is dependent upon more complex and less easily formulated factors, upon which social habit patterns and choice of activities are dependent. Because why not paynight on Monday?

This sort of thing is a major issue of sociology, and it is particularly relevant to our subject because it keeps on cropping up in relation to drinkers, drinking, and drunkenness, all of which centre round the week-end.

For instance, the actual peak number of drinkers is found on Saturday, not Friday. But Friday is the day on which they have most money. And Saturday is a holiday, Friday isn't. On the other hand, Sunday is a whole holiday, Saturday only a half. But less people drink on Sunday than Saturday. The money factor is not enough to explain this.

Similarly with the last hour—drinkers may only be able to afford to spend an hour in the pub, but *which* hour is not dependent on how much they've got. The fact that the majority choose the last hour means that it must have some special non-economic significance.

It then becomes important to know how much of this Saturday, not Friday, emphasis is especial to the pub, and how much of it is linked to the whole trajectory, or at least the whole drink trajectory, of the week. In this connection a series of figures from a political club, one of sixty-three registered licensed clubs in the town, will show how far the Saturday night climax is peculiar to the pub, and in what ratio it stands to Friday night drinking. These are the figures of total money taken in sales for two typical weeks in February–March:

Day	Week in February			Week in March			Increase or Decrease of second week (shillings)
	£	s.	d.	£	s.	d.	
Thursday	4	19	9	5	10	0	+ 20
Friday	8	6	10	7	15	0	— 12
Saturday	18	6	0	22	0	10	+ 75
Sunday	3	2	0	2	1	0	— 11
Monday	9	3	6	6	4	6	— 59
Tuesday	3	3	6	2	12	6	— 11
Wednesday	4	0	0	3	1	6	— 19

Saturday has well over a third of the total week's custom in each case. The Saturday percentage increase is much higher than that of the pub. A typical Saturday afternoon report shows why:

> Observers who had previously joined the club make a visit at 2.30. On the doorstep they were accosted by a woman, about 25, who asked them if they could sign her in. As the club was not yet open for drinking—Saturday drinking hours begin when the pubs shut, 3 p.m.—she said she'd wait, went off and entered the Wine Lodge. When observers returned later she was already in the club.
>
> At five past three there is a queue of 20 people waiting at the bottom of the staircase, where a table (not usually there) has been set up, and a worried-looking old man sitting at it, signing the people in.
>
> Upstairs, in the room by the bar, are 20 men, and 10 women —none of the club regulars, but observers recognize many town centre pub regulars. The chess room is full, about 60 men and women, in equal proportions . . .
>
> A man is playing the piano briskly; on music stand is a newspaper, open at the sports page, which he is reading. A hunchback, brown suit, bow tie, sings songs about love. People are coming in all the time. When observers leave, at 3.30, there is still a queue waiting to get signed in, and arguments about admission are raging.

Thus the non-club members develop their Saturday drink-up— (it has to be seen to be appreciated)—in this political club. The Sunday drinking is minimum—the club is then open from 1 to 5, and 7 to 10, during the same hours as the pub.

These figures would seem to show that the Saturday and Friday peak phenomenon is common to club and pub. Indeed, it is "well-known" (though that is bad evidence in sociology, as we have often found to our cost) that Saturday night is a big pleasure-night in Worktown. The graph on page 113 shows, however, that the earlier evening hours have more drinking on Sunday than on Saturday.

There is a kids' rhyme (dying-out) in Worktown which runs thus:

> Monday's washing,
> Tuesday's baking,
> Wednesday's cleaning,
> And Thursday's making.

Friday's shopping
And Saturday's playing,
And Sunday's praying.

Like most children's rhymes, it is years out of date—few people
do their own baking now, and Thursday's making is wiped away
by football-pooling for some 60,000 Worktowners. We can get an
angle on the effect of Friday pay-night on another non-essential
pleasure which is in many ways comparable, socially, with beer
and the pub . . . but more directly also a need-food . . . i.e.
fish and chips from the corner chip-shop. The chip-shop is closely
linked to the pub, from which comes much of its custom. Inside
its bar, potato-slicer handle, stone-tiled floors with a single
bench, closely parallel the pub's vault. So does the distribution of clientèle, relations with the landlord, and certain of
the rituals associated with fish and chipping. We may expect
then that the fish sales and those of steak puddings (commonly
sold in chip-shops) should reach a maximum on Saturday, when
also people are out more, and so less likely to cook at home.
To illuminate this point we may use here a fragment from our
work on chip-shops.

Here are the number of clients at a typical chip-shop next
door to a typical pub in a working class district.

	Morning		Evening		
	Steak buyers	Fish buyers	Steak buyers	Fish buyers	Total
Monday	—	—	10	41	51
Tuesday	7	15	5	33	60
Wednesday	9	24	6	19	58
Thursday	7	20	7	31	65
Friday	21,	71	11	70	173
Saturday	12	40	8	61	121
Total	56	170	47	255	528

It thus appears (though these figures are very inadequate) that
more is sold on Friday than on any other day (chip-shops have
recently been closed by law on Sunday, with considerable repercussions). The general tendency, and Wednesday minimum
clientèle, is otherwise almost identical with that in the pubs,
already tabulated, and graphed. A point is that Friday is
traditionally fish day for Catholics, who are fairly numerous in

Worktown. But it will be seen that though fish sales jump on Friday, steak sales do so too. In mid-March there were two consecutive fast-days, Friday and Saturday, as the shop owner, a Catholic, noted on his report (this table is of orders, not clients).

	Number of Fish Sales	Number of Steak Sales
Fast Friday	127	109
Fast Saturday	111	97

(One client often orders for a family. The number of fish orders per client are always higher than steak orders per client.)

The Friday higher sales and clientèle *appear* to be a constant in the chip-shop. The main point here is the general week-end increase. Further study in progress may well lead to revision of these remarks, however. They are only included here for comparison. The average expenditure per client varies similarly through the week; $3\frac{1}{4}d.$ on Monday, $2\frac{1}{2}d.$ on Wednesday, $6\frac{3}{4}d.$ on Friday. The position seems to indicate a closer economic tie-up between chip-shop and pay-night than between pub and pay-night. The chip-shop is more tied to economic and less to psychological factors?

The beer cycle is typical of the purely recreational cycle in the Worktown week. Fish is half-way to the *need* cycle, more closely geared to cash in hand.

Thus the Saturday evening pub-peak can be provisionally placed as part of the week-end complex of leisure rather than the mere direct economic complex which dominates food and credit habits. One of a series of week's statistics from grocery shops all over the town may further clarify—this is a Co-op. grocery branch, May:

Day	No. of customers	Average purchase per customer
Monday	40	2s.
Tuesday	55	1s. 6d.
Wednesday	43	1s. 6d.
Thursday	66	4s. 8d.
Friday	60	6s.
Saturday	78	3s. 9d.

The amount spent on Friday was thus maximum though smaller quantity customers were plentiful on Saturday.

Probably the total amount drunk on Sunday approaches Saturday, because there is then more midday and early evening drinking than on any other day. But Saturday night is "drink night", and also drunk night. Of 1936 drunk arrests, 37 per cent were on Saturday, 11 per cent on Sunday; in 1937, 26 per cent Saturday, 8 per cent Sunday (Wednesdays 11 per cent and 8 per cent respectively). That is to say, more people are run in for being tight on Saturday night than any other, and generally least on Sunday. The influence of Sunday and its special habits is in itself enough to keep down over-drinking among people who are non-church or anti-church. And this is the result of the long church versus pub friction, already and elsewhere discussed. It is far from being a "natural" respect for the Lord's Day. This is very nicely shown when we examine the drunkenness data (in the files of the old *Worktown Free Press*, etc.) for 1837. In that year there were 183 charges relative to drink offences (cf. 184 for 1937). Of these, 36 were for offences committed on Sundays —16 per cent. But the striking difference is that a third were for licensee's offences in having the pub open during improper hours. The rest were for being drunk. These 12 Sunday *licensing* offences compare with the 1937 total of 3 for the whole year and every day of the week. And while there were 12 such Sunday offences in 1837, the total weekday ones amounted only to 15.

Thus, in 1837, Catherine Morris was fined 40s. and 11s. costs for being open from 2 to 5 on Sunday, in January; in February Sam Haslam £5 for being open at 11.15, and the constable said: "It will not do for you to have company at service time, and you know it." In March a publican on a similar charge provoked a dispute on the Bench by pleading that his clients were travellers requiring refreshment—charge dismissed. On Sunday June 5 churchwarden Tom Horrocks—40s. for selling beer after 8. But the churchwardenly repute was retrieved soon afterwards, when one of them found, and arrested, a drunk (Richard Ansby, 5s. and 11s. costs). And just before Christmas the Catholic Abstinence Society (no sign of it now) ran in an Irishman (Mr. Murphy)— another 5s. and costs. The other big drink offence time was Saturday. In April of that year three different landlords were run in and fined 40s. each for selling beer after hours (10.30,

10.35 and 10.40—at all of which times today many local pubs are still illegally open), as well as three others for illicit spirits (big fines for this, £25, £50 and £50). Many of the convictions were actually brought by parsons at those times. They were fighting a direct warfare with the pub for Sunday dominance. The pub's counter gesture was the custom of the landlord to stand a free round at 1 o'clock on Sunday.

TRAJECTORY OF THE WEEK

The trajectory of the Worktown week is one of the dominant factors in every aspect in the life of the town. It affects the numbers who vote at an election, the attendance at meetings, the topics of conversation in the streets, the behaviour of children and the temper of octogenarians. The seven day cycle has got into the whole Worktown mentality, and associated with it the idea of a seven year body cycle, which facilitates the acceptance of those cyclic theories (astrology, theosophy, yogi) so closely correlated with any upsurge of superstition and growth in a power system based on glorification of what has been and denial of the possibility of things that have not been yet, except as rissoles of history. Man as a fly on an ever-rotating band of time is an idea that Worktowners are conditioned to respect by the endless cycle of the seven day week, cut across each seventh day by a slice of leisure (but with few ordinary leisure places open to be enjoyed, except the pub). Saturday is the highspot in the week's trajectory because then things *are* open, people not tired (as on Friday pay-night), and there's no need to get up early next morning. Saturday night is the traditional time for sexual intercourse (often associated with alcoholic stimulation, cf. drinkers' remarks in Drink chapter) and indeed many Worktowners confine it to this night. Others also go to bed Sunday afternoon, 2 to 5, pubs shut, and kids are sent off to Sunday School.

Saturday night is what is left in our culture of the old orgy, the recurring unrepression. It is a small weekly edition of the major Easter, Christmas, New Year and Whitsun orgies, the great religious festivals, pre-Christian and taken over by Christianity, key points in the cycle of the Industrial Year today, days that to the majority of Worktowners no longer have any more conscious religious significance than does Sunday, but days of release from the factory routine (cf. p. 245).

The pub, perhaps more than anything else in Worktown, shows in itself this cyclic tendency. On every day of the week it is open from noon till 2, and from 7 to 10. Only, on other days than Sunday the pub is also open from 11.30 till noon, 2 till 3, and 5.30 till 7. That is, the pub is open for three hours less on Sundays than the 8 hours of other days—but within the same times. And our figures have already shown that the amount of evening drinking before 7 on any day is very small, and only on Sunday is it at all considerable before 8. In the main, then, the cyclic trajectory of pub life, which makes it nearly empty on Wednesday night, packed on Saturday, is not peculiar to the pub, but to the whole lives of the people. And, as already discussed, it is not only economic. The satisfaction of basic human needs has a direct correlation with the amount of money that people have in their pockets. Traditional and mental factors are important (often chief) direct factors in determining which available pleasures they indulge in. The time factor, the way in which, for example, hardly anyone drinks during the times when on a Sunday the pubs would not be open, we will discuss later, when the relevant material has been brought forward. The scarcity of weekday daytime drinking, which we have not yet considered, can now be examined.

MIDDAY DRINKING

On week days the pubs are open from 11.30 a.m. till 3.0 p.m., on Sundays from 12.0 p.m. till 2.0 p.m.

Here is a typical "midday drinking" scene, in the popular S. and G., on a Friday in May:

2.30: No one in the lounge. No one in the passage bar. 2 men in vault. Chaps in vault order pints, drink them in 4 mins. Observers are having shandy. Chaps express contempt. One says "Beer's the stuff". The other "Six pints a day do a man good". They go, drive off in municipal dust-cart number x.

This is an average of the activity in any Worktown pub during its midday opening hours. There were generally so few people in the pubs during this period that observers found it unprofitable to work the pubs except in the evenings, firstly because there was no chance to observe without being oneself observed, secondly because (being so few people about) every visit meant having a drink, and that never helped the afternoon's work. Random visits to different pubs during April–June, from noon to 2 p.m., produced a total average on all occasions of two drinkers per pub per visit. With two exceptions, all were in the vault. Roughly comparable figures for Saturdays gave an average of 9 per pub per visit. Without exception the persons were males on all these occasions.

Figures kept for us at a beerhouse showed a week's total of 75 drinkers during the midday opening period, as compared with 398 for the evening period. (This does not give a precise basis of comparison, since the midday drinkers drink little and don't stay long.) Sunday had the highest midday total, as well as the highest figure for early evening drinking. At the same pub the barman kept figures for each different room on 3 days (a difficult thing for a barman to do). The variation on the previous week's totals is useful data:

	Taproom			Vault			Best room (Lounge)		
	Tues.	Sat.	Sun.	Tues.	Sat.	Sun.	Tues.	Sat.	Sun.
Midday period	6	?	14	4	?	6	0	?	7
5.30–8	4	13	6	6	0	7	0	7	2
8–9	5	16	8	1	3	9	1	9	4
9–10	9	16	12	3	4	9	S	11	7
Total	24	(45)	40	14	(7)	31	9	27	20
		109			52			56	

(Note: This pub has a very small vault, exceptionally large taproom. This explains the unusually high figures for the tap in relation to the vault.)

Thirty per cent of the total Sunday attendance was midday, as compared with 29 per cent the previous week, 21 per cent of the Tuesday attendance was midday, as compared with 18 per cent the previous week.

This table confirms extensive general observations that Sunday night shows a high percentage of best room (lounge) drinking, which of course fits in with increase of female drinkers at the week-end (cf. p. 95).

Finally, to confirm our rather scattered observations, and see if the midday emptiness of pubs, especially their best rooms, was consistent, we took counts every hour for a week in April in four big pubs with large evening attendances—at least a hundred each:

Two Vaults	Time	Sun.	Mon.	Tues.	Wed.	Thurs.	Total (Mon.–Thurs.)
A	12		9	6	8	7	30
	1	21	9	5	6	9	29
	2		3	2	7	7	19
	3		4	2	9	–	
	Total		25	15	30	–	
B	12		5	2	2	4	13
	1	25	2	4	1	4	11
	2		2	3	1	4	10
	3		1	0	3	–	
	Total		10	9	7	–	
Two Lounges C	12		0	0	0	0	0
	1	0	0	0	0	0	0
	2		0	0	0	0	0
	3		1	0	0	0	1
	Total		1	0	0	0	1
D	12		0	0	0	0	0
	1		0	0	0	0	0
	2		0	0	0	0	0
	3		0	0	0	0	0
	Total		0	0	0	0	0

The figures show 12 to 1 as midday peak, Sunday maximum (no Saturday figures obtained). And they show the lounge position adequately—32 visits on week days scored only one drinker—a woman, against the 147 men counted.

Control counts at 9.45 in the same rooms enabled us to compare the number of drinkers at that peak period with the above figures for 1 p.m., lunch hour:

	% increase of 9.45 on 1.0 figures	
	Sunday	Tuesday
Two (large) vaults A	281	820
B	212	500
Two (large) lounges C & D	237	—
Small beerhouse: all rooms	292	300

The factor of drinking most in short periods, of ignoring the long hours available and packing the drinking into the last hour, is thus represented by the increased drinking on Sunday at hours when on other days, including the parallel leisure hours on Saturday, there would be less people. So much to drink and so little time to drink it in!

Most publicans would be glad if midday drinking did not exist at all. It is hardly an economic proposition for those with large lounges and elaborate bars. But, by law, open they must —a time-law whose only parallel is that which says the churches of the Established (Anglican) Church shall be open during day-light hours. The church frequently (in several Worktown churches perpetually) breaks this law. The pub never.

We should note Worktown meal-times, relevant to all these data. The midday meal, always called dinner (except by a few hundred rich people who have "lunch") is between noon and 2, with peak time 12.15 to 1.15, when all factory workers are eating. Office and shop staffs have noon-1, and 2–3 relays. Chip-shops seldom cook after 1, proprietors say there is no trade later than that. Tea, the large evening meal, is mainly between 5.45 and 6.30; supper, a light snack, 9 onwards. On Sundays dinner is generally around 12, and very seldom starts later than 12.30. Tea at 4.30 or 5. This means people are ready to go out earlier than on week days, especially at midday. The mass of Worktown drinking is done on a full stomach and on-the-way-to-digested stomachful.

As this type of research develops it will be important to see how far the different meal habits of the south influence drink habits. At present there is no data available for comparison.

WEATHER PERMITS

In examining our data we have implied the day and time are the only major factors influencing members. Weather and seasons have been ignored.

The main seasonal difference is, according to nearly every landlord in every sort of pub, that more draught beer is drunk in the summer, and less bottled. (Examples of this will be given in a later section.) Weather we have so far ignored because our observational evidence indicates that its importance is slight in either promoting or limiting the Worktowner's use of regular and traditional leisure interests. Whatever the weather he has to go to and fro from work, and this is a training which stands him in good stead on pub nights or polling days. The back of our research headquarters was in a narrow cobbled side street for two years; leaning against it at all times of night and all times of year, hot, rain or snow, one was generally sure to find at least one couple locked in horizontal bliss. Undoubtedly weather is a factor, but Worktown weather is rather unusually equable (thus the Cotton industry), and for practical purposes of a pub study on the present scale the evidence justifies its relegation to a minor place.

Four observers spent some time asking landlords in all types of pub what their own views on the weather factor were. One, a large pub on a main road near the town centre, gave an answer which differed from the rest:

> Landlord said good weather sent people on their motor-bikes to pubs further out. In rainy weather they didn't do so bad, but there was a dance hall on both sides of them, the big Palais took a lot of his trade.

Actually this pub is failing for other reasons, and the answer is a common type of landlord-rationalization. There are four pubs nearer the Palais than his, all flourishing. The number of motor bikes can never be an appreciable factor. A series of other answers gives a good cross section of the ordinary landlord's opinion. The question, introduced during conversation, and not asked directly, or so that anyone could realize that they were being questioned on this point, was "Does the state of the weather affect your trade?":

A. "Oh no, it's about the same, steady you know."

B. Landlord said weather made practically no difference. There was a good steady trade all the year round. Observer asked about rainy weather. He said rather less came then, "When people were not knocking about so much". Observer then said he was surprised, he thought people might have been driven into the pub by the rain. Landlord replied, "Well, it's a funny population, Worktown is. The more it rains the more they seem to come out. I sometimes say to the women that come in 'ere on wet days: 'You must have webbed feet, like ducks, to be out in this weather'". He repeated: "It's a good steady trade all the year round."

C. "Warm weather makes a difference. When it's raining there's not much difference really . . . when the sun shines is the best time." He went on to say that when it was hot a man might have an extra pint before going to work. He talked about a collier who had 10 pints before his tea—but that was before the war. "It's not so now."

D. Landlord very talkative. A colliery engineer, been

in pub 5 years. When he first came in the rates were £27, now £32. "In fact it takes a hundred pound that is everything, before we make a penny for ourselves." Said that weather didn't make any difference to him, "It's all regulars 'ere". Average 4 to 5 pints. "I have one man comes in 'ere, 'e'll be in tonight and he'll drink 8 or 9 pints—he does that every night mind. He'll sit and play fives and threes (i.e. 'all fours'). Even then he hasn't got his talkin'-irons on." Again stressed that only regulars come. "Winter or summer it's all the same."

E. "No, there's not much in it at all" (i.e. weather effect). Shuts up, apparently in a filthy temper.

F. "Well, it does really, especially in the week-time. But at week-ends it doesn't really matter, although I gets a few less in if it's a wet Saturday. You get the regulars so what the weather's like."

G. "It (bad weather) spoils me day trade. But at night it's not effective much, as most of our customers don't live far away. In fact, a wet week-end, especially Saturday, is O.K. for us. People won't go drinking in town."

There are the usual contradictions in these remarks, but they are sufficient to show that the landlord does not feel that his trade is closely dependent upon the weather. While it may influence a certain hour, over the cycle of the week and the rhythm of the regulars, inches of rain have no correlation with gills of beer. The main point is that all pubs outside the town centre rely for the great majority of their trade upon people living in the immediate vicinity.

THE IMMEDIATE VICINITY

We have pointed out that on Saturday nights many drinkers go into the centre of the town to the pubs there. This may mean that they have to take a long walk or a tram ride to do so. The pub from which our example was taken is about a mile from the central area. Is this something specific to Saturday drinking, or is it the habit of drinkers to traverse comparable distances for their ordinary pub-going?

A map of the neighbourhood of the V. Hotel was made.[1] Of 47 regulars whose names and addresses we have, 40 live within a few hundred yards of the V.

First let us find out about these 7 men who live outside this

[1] This, and other maps, cannot be reproduced, owing to the fact that the pub itself and the regulars concerned could be identified from it.

area: 3 of them come from suburbs more than a mile away. But their work is in the immediate neighbourhood of the pub, and they come straight off their jobs to drink. The other 4 live between a mile and three-quarters of a mile away. One works nearby as a corporation night watchman. The other 3 have all lived in the immediate neighbourhood of the pub and have subsequently moved farther away.

Of the 40 who are mapped, all but 2 live within a 220 yards radius from the pub. The V. Hotel and the pub next to it are simply the nearest pubs to where they live. Of the two chaps who live outside this radius, one has to come for nearly half a mile, but he has only the choice of one other pub that is almost as far; he became a regular here at a time when he lived nearer. The other man is about a quarter of a mile away, and there are 7 pubs nearer to him—2 of which he has to pass on his route to the V.

We see, then, that the majority of these drinkers live within a few minutes' stroll from their regular pub; and those that don't either work nearby or have formed the habit of visiting it at a period when they did live close to it, a habit that has persisted, despite the move. This is a fact of significance when it comes to evaluating the relative importance of the alcoholic and social motives for pub-going.

Little can be deduced from the distribution pattern of these drinkers' homes in relation to the position of the pub. The V. Hotel and the pub next to it are in a block between two large factory buildings. The V. (and the other pub) "draw off" the pub-goers from the streets on either side of the block. The main road does not act as a complete barrier here, 12 of the regulars living on the side of it that is opposite to that on which the pub is situated. But the nearest pub on that side of the road is more than a third of a mile away.

A similar map was made, showing the distribution of the regulars of another pub, the C——Hotel, in an area that contains a larger and more evenly distributed number of pubs. The street in which this pub is situated is not a wide main thoroughfare, but it contains a bus route (which superseded tram lines) and has small shops; 48 people live on the pub side of the road and 14 on the other. Here there is no question of a limited choice of pubs. We can suppose that locally there is a natural tendency for regulars to regard a main road as a barrier, and to prefer to go to a pub on the same side of the road as are their homes.

Our map was based on a list of addresses of all the pub's regular customers, 58 of which live within a few hundred yards of the pub. The 4 who live outside this area are connected with the pub for the following reasons—one works in the mill opposite, two have moved out of the district, and one comes from the other side of the town to meet his girl, who lives nearby.

But the distribution is not so simple as that of the previous example. There is a small group of 4 customers who live about three-quarters of a mile away, and who have a choice of 6 pubs within 220 yards of their homes; also, in order to get to this pub they have to pass others; 2 of them work at mills nearby the pub, and 1 comes there to drink with a relative who lives nearby. We have no information about the other 1.

All the others are found within 300 yards of the pub, the majority, as already stated, on the pub side of the main road.

CHOICE

The important point that can be observed in the distribution of these regulars' homes relative to their pubs, is that within the 300 yards radius where the great majority of them live there are plenty of other pubs, many of which are nearer than the one which they go to—which in itself is in no way remarkable either for its beer, landlord, or other amenities. That is, a distance exists (of 300 yards in one case, and 220 in the other—two to three minutes' walk) beyond which the normal pub-goer in normal circumstances will not go to his pub; yet within that distance he does not necessarily choose the nearest pub. The limiting distance will, of course, be greater in districts where fewer pubs per square mile are found. But within the limiting distance nearness to the pub is not the main factor that dictates the drinker's choice; outside the distance it is. The exceptions to the latter rule we have already dealt with, and shown them to be due partly to other factors.

Factors regulating the choice of one pub rather than another within the limiting distance are complex. For instance, one of the regulars at the above pub said he had come there originally because he liked the pianist that used to be there. That was years ago, the pianist died, but the chap still comes. Another said he went there because he used to know the landlord's family when they were children.

In other pubs reasons such as the following were given:

1. An old man, in a pub with an unusually large vault—
"I come in 'ere because there's plenty of room, tha knows. . . ."

2. "I wouldn't go anywhere else all the time they sell
Walkers' beer, and this inoffensive old lady's here." (This was
a reference to the landlady.) Another man, replying to him,
said "It's good beer Walkers', makes you go to sleep, but if
you want to go to sleep for good you'd better try ——'s."

3. "Because Hamer's sell a good glass of beer and he
(the landlord) gives us a good winner now and then."

4. "I only live across the road and I pass a couple of
hours in 'ere ow't' road o't' wife." To which his friend replied "I
come down 'ere to 'ave a drink and a game at dominoes or darts
or owt as is going on. I'm not like some buggers, henpecked."

5. "What the bloody hell's it got to do with you?"

We cannot assume that the normal drinker chooses his pub
deliberately for the quality of beer, type of landlord, etc. We
have gone into the question of the "drawing power" of a good
landlord. These, and other factors, such as credit and games,
are much more likely to be important in *retaining* the drinker's
custom rather than getting it to start with. Assuming that the
drinker's choice of pub lies within a limited geographical area,
the one that he will choose within that area must largely be the
result of his previous relationship with existing regular customers.
This will equally apply to drinkers who frequent pubs in the neighbourhood of their work instead of their homes. They will tend to go
to where the other people from the job go. And if there is a choice
between two or more pubs, the one chosen will be the one where
their friends or the workers in their particular department go.

And once the habit is formed it is hard to break. Many drinkers
rely on credit from the landlord; this, for the hardup, the im-
provident, or the casual worker, can also be both an important
factor in his choice of pub and his leaving it for another one.
The drinker becomes a regular partner in a nightly game of cards
or dominoes, and gets to rely on meeting the same group with
whom he can enjoy discussions on subjects of mutual interest.

THE MEN ARE NOW DRINKING ELSEWHERE

Reference was made to credit as a factor in making drinkers
leave pubs; sometimes they never return, but more usually they
do. A barman writes the following:

The return of a customer who had left in a huff six months

previously because the landlord wouldn't let him have credit again not having paid the previous weeks:

Customer: "Hello, Tom, eh't gooin on. Ah'm faint' see thee, tha see I've cum back, cum 'ere and gi' us thy paw." (Then he kisses Tom and beams with obvious delight.)

Tom: "Well lad, I'm glad to see you. I knew you'd gone off in a huff, but he did you a good turn, and you won't have to pay anything back."

(Tom is the barman: the "he" referred to is the landlord.)

There are other ways in which the connection can be broken. This story, written by a local drinker, shows how a pub lost a whole group of its regulars at one swoop:

Above the door of the "pub" is a notice that reads: X.Y. Bowling Club, Headquarters. Some little time ago there was discord brought about owing to a few of the younger players forming themselves into a group and calling themselves the Z. Arms Bowling Club. Some of their number selected a team, and posted up the notice describing same on the notice board. . . . The X.Y. Veterans, a group of retired men, objected seriously to this kind of conduct. Opinions were expressed on all sides by various individuals, from retired mill cashiers and ex-police sergeants, to the humble (pensioned) bleachworks' labourer, that the "greens" were open to the public, and that although you could have teams representing the park in Inter-parks competition, you could not have one representing the pub there.

The green keeper tore down the notice, and this ultimately led to the group changing its name, and the licensee of the Z. Arms exhibiting the notice aforementioned at the "pub". On a Saturday the group went to a "Saturday Afternoon" bowling excursion and picnic to Southport. When the motor coach is ready to leave for home, Ronny S., a pensioned war-disabled man of about 40 years old, who acts as secretary for the Z. Arms group, stood up in the coach and said "Well, lads, have you enjoyed yourselves?" The group in chorus: "Aye." One of their number, who had a concertina, played "For he's a jolly good fellow." Ronny S. intervened by raising his right arm as a signal that he had more to say: the music and voices stopped. Ronny then asks "Has any on you had owt out o' that two quid as Bob R. geet from t' Brewer?" The lads in chorus: "No-oh!" The concertina then struck up with the tune "In and out the window". But the lads parodied it with: "Slat 'im through the window, Wang 'im through the window." R., the licensee, is a man of a very hasty temper. He

is also a very tall man, as also is Ronny S.—R. made a dive for
Ronny S., but Ronny is no weakling. He made prompt use of his
fist, socked R. good and hard on the jaw and mouth ; laid him out
at the bottom of the coach. He was solemnly counted "out".
The ultimate result has been that the majority of the men have
ceased to patronise the pub and are now drinking elsewhere.

Four months later the writer of this told us that the chaps
were beginning to come back again.

The barman who wrote about the customer's return, told us
that regulars would sometimes drop away on account of personal
dislikes and differences, but they nearly always came back again.
At the same time he said that some people were regulars in two
or three pubs, sometimes going from one to another on the same
evenings, and sometimes visiting different ones on different
evenings. Actual observed examples of the two-pub regulars are
hard to get. Observers have noted regulars whom they have known
by sight, in other pubs, but these have all been at week-ends,
and were far more likely cases of week-end "shiftovers", which
are not invariably to the big pubs. Again, we know that the man
mentioned in the list of the C. Hotel regulars, who comes there to
drink with his relative, also frequents his own local pub (p. 129).

THE PUB AS A HOME FROM HOME

In the taproom of the W. Arms there is a handpainted Roll of
Honour of customers who died in the war of 1914–18, the list
of names surmounted by water-coloured representations of the
allied flags. A regular of this pub won a prize in a local competition ; when someone came in and mentioned it—he had not
yet come in himself—the comment was that they were glad that
one of "our chaps" had won it.

This represents a close relationship between the pub and the
drinker—a state of affairs in which they are part of an institution
to which they *belong*, like the members of a political organization
to their party, or a congregation to its church, in contrast to the
relationship of say, a football fan to his team, ground, and
fellow fans. This last relationship can be compared to the one
that exists between the week-end drinking group to the landlord,
pub, and other groups in the town centre pubs. They and the
other groups are to a great extent strangers to each other, but
participating in the same pleasures at the same time and place.

One of the most reliable ways of telling a regular in a pub is by the degree of familiarity between himself and the staff. The regular commonly gets his drink without having to ask for it, the landlord, barmaid, or whoever it is, knowing what he drinks and drawing it off as soon as he comes to the bar counter. (This will not apply, of course, when he is drinking with a group and ordering for them.) The following excerpt from an observer's report shows the barmaid's astonishment when a man who usually drinks gills orders a pint:

> . . . two old men in the corner at their usual seats, drinking pints of mild. Two young chaps, both missing front teeth, lean against the bar, very drunk indeed, but quietly so. One beckons the barmaid to him—he calls her Madge—and whispers, and later the other does the same, both trying to get her to serve them with another drink, but she will not do so . . . regulars keep arriving. They all call the barmaid by her Christian name and she knows what they drink, serving them without having to be told. They are nearly all old men, pint drinkers. But one man comes in and *orders* a pint, and she, the barmaid, says in a very surprised voice "So it's pints tonight, is it?"

Most regulars are known to the staff by their Christian names, and mostly they address each other in this way. They tend to sit or stand in the same places every night; and this is particularly noticeable with regular groups who stand at the bar; they always retain the same relative positions to one another, and if the room is crowded or they find their usual space in front of the bar partly occupied, though the shape of the group will have to change, their positions relative to one another tend to remain the same.

The degree to which the regular pub-goer can come to look upon his pub as a kind of second or alternative home is shown by a friend of ours, a spinner, who spends almost every evening in a small beerhouse. He goes home after work, has his tea, then comes down to the pub (about 7. 30 as a rule). When he comes into the taproom he goes to a cupboard in the wall, opens it, and takes out his spectacles. Then he puts them on, spreads the evening paper out on the table, and reads it. He always stays until closing time.

SEXES

We have already mentioned that 16 per cent of a large count over a long period in all types of pub were females. But the actual proportion of women that can be observed in different pubs at different times of the week varies considerably from this figure.

In the counts made during the estimation of age groups (January) out of 4,382 people, 19·5 per cent were women. The town centre pubs account for the majority of this figure. The sample counts of 2,790 taken during May–July, for the purpose of estimating the average number of pub-goers, showed 15 per cent women. This count was mainly made in small pubs. Again, there is a greater proportion of female drinking at week-ends than during the week.

The following figures illustrate these points:

(January)	Town centre pubs		Main road pubs outside town centre	
	Weekdays	Weekends	Weekdays	Weekends
Males	667	532	418	513
Females	140	184	39	94
% females	17·4	25·7	8·5	15·5

Percentage weekend increase

Town centre pubs	8·3
Non town centre pubs	7·0

That is, we find nearly ten per cent more women in town centre pubs than in others, and in both classes of pubs there is an eight per cent increase in the number of women at week-ends. The maximum difference between week night figures for ordinary pubs (less than 1 in 10) and week-ends in the town centre pubs (over 1 in 4) is striking.

In connection with these figures it must be remembered that in Worktown vault and taproom are tabu to women; they are only to be seen in the parlours and lounges. So that it is often possible to find rooms in which quite half the drinkers are women.

We can conclude, then, that although at certain times and in certain pubs, a fairly high proportion of drinkers are women, yet regular Worktown week-night drinkers are mostly male.

Incidentally, out of the town's (1936) 143 drunks (arrested) 20 were women—14 per cent, that is less, but not much less, than the average percentage of female pub-goers. In 1937 it was 11 per cent.

AGE GROUPS

Children do not go to pubs. Selling drinks to persons under 18 is an offence, and so is permitting children within the pub. In 1936, out of a total of 994 convictions against publicans in

England and Wales, only 14 were for the first of these offences, and 3 for the second—none of either were from Worktown. Of course, the use of legal statistics is not sufficient to prove anything about pub-goers, unless they are supported by other data. In 4 cases we have seen small children playing about in the vault, but they didn't know that they constituted a legal offence, and they could not very well be considered as pub-goers, for they were the landlord's children. Again, we have observed isolated instances of young people who were probably only 16 or 17 in pubs, but as all the other many thousands of pub-goers whom we have observed and counted have been above 18, we are justified in saying that pub-goers are over 18.

In order to get a representative set of figures for the age groups of drinkers a series of counts were made, in which 4,137 people were classified into 4 age groups. The following groups were used:

> Group 1, under 25.
> Group 2, 25–40.
> Group 3, 41–55.
> Group 4, above 55.

Of course, these ages are only apparent: therefore it was necessary that all the work should be done by one observer, so that a reasonably consistent standard of judgement and error should operate. Checks from other angles of our work indicate a 5 per cent margin of error.

Such methods are necessarily inefficient, but no other is practicable in these particular circumstances. It does clearly emerge, however, in a long and careful series of such counts, taken at many pubs during several months, that the big body of regular drinkers in Worktown pubs are in the 30–50 generation. On the whole, the pub is frequented largely by working men well established in earning industrial jobs, men past the first leisure interests of adolescence and youth, but not yet old, retired from industry or pensioned off. There is a tendency, as usual, for the emphasis in age grouping to shift at the week-end, when the ages of drinkers become very scattered, more representative of the Worktown population as a whole. This is especially the case at holiday times, notably Christmas, when the proportion of young people in pubs tends to go up sharply; this tendency again is in line with the general week-end and holiday trajectory, which is fully discussed in this and other chapters of the present study.

In all cases Groups 2 and 3 are between 85 per cent and 95 per cent of the totals counted. But the percentage of Group varies between 38·5 and 56·1, and that of Group 3 between 37·4 and 54·2. The valid conclusions from this are that about nine tenths of all pub-goers are between 25 and 55, and on an average this figure is composed of proportions of about 4 to 5 between Groups 2 and 3. There do not appear to be any specific differences between town centre and other pubs in this case.

The following is a summary of all age counts:

| | Age-Groups | | | | Total |
	1	2	3	4	
Total number counted	295	1,673	2,070	97	4,137
Per cent of total	7·1	40·4	50·1	2·4	
Total males	259	1,381	1,565	88	3,293
Per cent of males	7·8	41·9	47·8	2·5	
Total females	36	292	507	9	844
Per cent of females	4·2	34·6	60·1	1·1	

This shows a greater preponderance of Group 3 among females than males, and a smaller female percentage in the other groups. Detailed analysis of the sex groups based on the separate figures of the different counts show the same results.

The average age of first marriages (Registrar General's Statistical Review, 1930) is 27·5 for males, 25·5 for females. People below that age are not common in pubs. They are common in dance halls, walking about the streets, going to the pictures with each other. The leisure of the young is largely concerned with courtship—and dance halls provide no alcohol. Once mated, the leisure of a considerable section of the male population (the pub-goers) is concerned with "I pass a couple of hours in 'ere ow't' road o't' wife."

Cost has something to do with it too. The regular who drinks 15 pints a week (which is about the average) spends 6s. 3d. You can take a girl to the pictures or the Palais on Saturday night and go for walks with her on other nights of the week; this costs rather less than being a regular.

There are a few pubs, a couple of town centre ones in particular, which are the hang-outs of the young. For instance, in one of them, 28 females and 28 males were counted, of whom only 3 males and no females were above 25.[1] In the other, on the same evening, out of 97 males and females, only 9 were above 25. Both these pubs have a big custom from adjacent dance halls—which have special drink-intervals—and there is plenty of picking up going on there. (See later for more about this.) The pub motive here is as much sexual as anywhere else in Worktown.

The only data on drinkers' age groups to which we can compare our results are those given by Nicholson in the London Survey. Only 180 people were counted, and they were:

Under 25	8 per cent
Between 25 and 35	18 per cent
Between 35 and 50	40 per cent
Over 50	34 per cent

This agrees with our under 25 figures for Worktown. The different age groups used make other parallels impossible. The 1931 Census gave 33·1 per cent males aged 20–39, 35·2 per cent aged 40 upwards.[2]

SOCIAL STATUS OF DRINKERS

Statistics of the occupations of large numbers of drinkers cannot be obtained on the basis of direct counts or observation. The minimum number of pub-goers is more than a third of all males over 25. The largest single occupational group in Worktown is that of workers in the cotton trades. The following list of the occupations of the regulars of one pub shows the preponderance of this group:

[1] This was in the large parlour, where there is singing. A small taproom at the side is frequented by older people.

[2] To get a parallel on our system the same observers who did Worktown ages did a small sample, 180 people, in north-west London pubs (Dec. 28, 29, 1938). Result:

Pubgoers under 25	1%
,, 26–35	15%
,, 36–50	40%
,, over 50	44%

This approximates fairly to the London Survey count, which failed to specify relevant factors of day, time, bar, season.

Re-analysed into our own age groupings, this London sample gave:

Age group 1	3%
group 2	22%
group 3	39%
group 4	36%
group 5	0%

This implies even less youth drinking at this time and place than in the Worktown averages.

Millworkers	10—6 spinners, 2 fitters, 1 mechanic, 1 carder.
Other factory workers	4.
Corporation workers	6.
Labourers (not included above)	1.
Motor drivers	4—2 commercial, 1 taxi, 1 chauffeur.
Carters	2.
Railway workers	2—1 porter, 1 platelayer.
Tramwaymen	2.
Unemployed	5.
Old age pensioners	4.

And one each of the following—Carpenter, Steeplejack, Gardener, Butcher, Newspaper Canvasser, Window Cleaner, Tailor.

Of these 47, 41 are married, 2 widowers, and 4 single.

This list was compiled from material supplied to us by a regular of the pub. (Incidentally the fact that he was able to tell us the streets in which they lived, their marital states, and in many cases their actual place of work and the number of children they had, is a good example of the highly developed "community" among regulars.)

Except that the proportion of transport workers is high, this is a fairly typical cross section of the town's occupations. Of the 10 millworkers 6 are spinners, who are actually in a minority in the mills, they rarely get jobs before 30, and their wages average around £3 a week. Piecers, of whom there are more in the mills, get between 18 and 30 shillings a week. There are none on this list. Many of them, as well as other workers with very low rates of pay, are not in a position to afford to drink much or regularly. Certainly this is a factor that must be taken into account— but even if it was a fundamental consideration for pub-goers, it could not be assessed on the basis of occupation, since family circumstances and other responsibilities can make a man earning £3 a week have less to spend on drink than another who earns half that sum. And, in fact, it is often the poorest section of the population who spend most, both relatively and absolutely, on drink. The question of status and class is of importance in assessing the pub-goer; and it is unfortunate that this question, which is one of the fundamentals of sociology, has been the subject of so much controversy and so little, so very little, scientifically established fact of the sort that could provide us with social co-ordinates to which we could relate observations. How, for instance, can we tell a labourer from a skilled worker? Are there class behaviour patterns? Extensive work on this in Worktown has not so far given us any very satisfactory answers. Until later volumes in this series we will therefore take simple crude criteria.

The simplest indications of class and status that can be observed in the pub are those of clothes.

CLOTHES

In most vaults and taprooms, on week nights men wear caps, scarves knotted round the neck, and coat, trousers, and waist-coats, of dark materials, that often belong to different suits. Caps are a working class badge; scarves round the neck instead of collar and tie usually indicate middle and lower (unskilled and semi-skilled) working class—but these are not necessarily invariable indications. And a section of pub-goers drink in their working clothes—dungarees of various kinds and bib-and-brace overalls can be seen, as well as corduroys and/or clogs, and old trousers and coats that are stained with earth, plaster, etc., according to the wearer's occupation.

The following are the results of counts made in 9 vaults and 1 taproom, on week nights (January). Group A (2 vaults and 1 taproom) and Group B (4 vaults) were small beerhouses not on main roads, Group C (3 vaults) were larger main road beerhouses.

	A	B	C
No. counted	14	19	26
Caps	14	17	24
Bowlers	—	1	—
Trilbies	—	1	2
Scarves	14	16	21
Ties	—	3	5
Good suit	—	2	—
Old suit	7	12	21
Working clothes	7	5	5

Note: Overalls and clothes obviously stained with earth, plaster, etc., were counted as working clothes. Suits that were clean and without signs of wear were counted as "good", and "old suits" were between these two categories. All these counts were made by the same observer, so that these definitions, though not "objective" in the strict sense, are consistently relative to each other.

The high proportion of caps and scarves plus the majority of old suits, show that these drinkers are working-class. Though these samples are small—it is difficult to count large clothes samples in pubs—they are representative.

There is considerable difference between the above and the clothes worn by drinkers in the best rooms. Comparing the totals of the figures quoted above with a larger count (taken on the following week) in the lounges of 5 similar pubs, we get the following:

Total counted	Per cent of total thus clothed in Lounges	Per cent difference from vault Figures
Caps	45	— 48
Bowlers	13	+ 12
Trilbies	33	+ 28
No hats	9	—
Scarves	14	— 72
Ties	86	+ 72
Good suit	73	+ 70
Old suit	20	— 48
Working clothes	7	— 22

The figures we have quoted were counted on a week night. Results of comparative week night and week-end counts taken in the same pubs on small samples, show that, in addition to the physical week-end shiftover, there is a change in dress. The following figures show this, even allowing for the small number counted:

Two town centre vaults			
	Week-night	Saturday	Per cent change
No. counted	55	88	
Caps	33	30	— 26
Bowlers	3	20	+ 17
Trilbies	12	20	+ 2
No hats	7	18	+ 7
Scarves	19	12	— 22
Ties	36	76	+ 22
Good suit	13	73	+ 59
Old suit	40	14	— 57
Working clothes	2	1	— 2

Though not so marked, and not statistically accurate, all these changes are paralleled in the ordinary beerhouse vault.

Beerhouse vaults			
	Per cent Week-night	Per cent Saturday	Per cent change
Caps	92	80	— 12
Bowlers	—	6	+ 6
Trilbies	8	6	— 2
No hats	—	8	+ 8
Scarves	81	43	— 38
Ties	19	57	+ 38
Good suit	—	34	+ 34
Old suit	81	61	— 20
Working clothes	19	5	— 14

Note how the week-day beerhouse vault figures in this table compare with those of the previous one. Despite the smallness of the samples, and the different districts in which the counts were taken, in one case the percentage of caps is 93, and in the other 92: while the proportion of scarves in one is 86 per cent and the other 81 per cent.

The best room week-end change over is not so strongly marked. Here are the figures already quoted, compared with a Saturday count in the same pubs.

5 pubs Jan. 24–30	Lounges (best rooms)		
	Per cent Week-night	Per cent Saturday	Per cent changes
Caps	45	49	+ 4
Bowlers	13	25	+ 12
Trilbies	33	23	— 10
No hats	9	3	— 6
Scarves	14	3	— 11
Ties	86	97	+ 11
Old suit	20	3	— 17
Good suit	73	97	+ 24
Working clothes	7	0	— 7

The only really significant change is the increase of "good" suits over old ones. The count showed far less uniformity between the clothes of one pub lounge and another than was found in vaults.

It is evident that on Saturday night the general style of dress goes "up" in the pub. There is also a numerical increase of drinkers, notably in the best room. Is this "up" due to an influx of new and smarter week-end drinkers? The answer is clearly in the negative, for the clothes improvement is strongest in those rooms dominated by the regulars. The best rooms have a comparatively high proportion of bowlers and trilbies on ordinary week days, reflecting their better "class", or less obvious workerness. The increase of "respectable" headgear on Saturday night vault men, not in the presence of women, frequently not associating with them all the evening, shows how strong is the ritual of the week and the emphasis on the week-end. The ordinary Worktowner has three sets of clothes—his week-end suit, his week-day suit, and his working clothes (though the last two can be and sometimes are the same). Each year he gets a new suit in the spring, through a tremendous complex of Club or Co-op "cheques", associated with the religious seasonality of the "Sermons" held by every church, elaborate processions, relic of beating of the bounds. This custom is now practically ignored by many who still unconsciously are influenced by it, subscribing to the custom as customers—of clothing clubs and of florists for ancestral graves. Every spring each suit is moved back; one, the third, going off the list.

The "bowler hat index", if we may call it that, goes down again in the pubs on Sunday. Saturday night is, for many pubgoers, their Sunday. We will return to this.

Writes a landlord:

"You will find in pubs that the heavy drinkers has the same clothes on at week-ends as week-nights—not working clothes of course." He also says "the best room people are generally week-end customers."

Summing up, the social composition of pub-goers reflects that of the whole town, though possibly "weighted" in the direction of the medium paid and housed sections.

"DAMES"

We have already dealt with the statistical side of female drinking in this section. But what are the other characteristics of female pub-goers?

To begin with, there are a number of tabus about women in

pubs. Vault and taproom are closed to them. In one small beer-house we have observed a handwritten notice over the taproom door "Gentlemen only". Only once have we observed women in a vault; this was in a large town centre pub, which has a "very good class" vault, with chairs and tables; two women were sitting drinking mild. They were not local, but women from the market, gipsy types, with gold earrings and wearing leather coats.

Also, women don't stand at the bar. Again, we have observed one case of this custom being violated. It was in the lobby bar of a medium-sized main road pub. Sommerfield was drinking with Harrisson, and had just been telling him about this tabu, so when it was broken under their noses there was a certain amount of scorn. But knowing that members of local touring companies put up here sometimes, we went up to her and her boy friend. They were discussing their act. They were Londoners, and middle class ones.

Both these tabus are unbroken by ordinary local working-class women. But they can be seen drinking in vaults, and standing at the bar—in Blackpool, where on holiday week practically every pub custom is broken. (This is important and will be referred to again later, p. 249.)

We have already referred to the form of sexual segregation called the "nuggy hole" (origin of word locally unknown). This, however, is rare in Worktown, though it is found more commonly in the mining villages outside.

On the whole Worktown women patronize the best room. Where there are two of these, one sometimes becomes a sort of women's room, into which men will only enter in company with their wives.

About this, a barman writes:

> A number of men come in the pub with their wives, but separate inside, the wife goes off into the best room while the husband goes into the taproom, either to participate in games or indulge in conversation. Maybe the sexes separate as on tramcars, anyway when the lady has got what she has ordered she will say: "Go to Sam" or Joe or whatever his name is, "for the money". Again, a couple will both go to the parlour, and on discovering that he is the only man present among a number of ladies will leave the wife and go into the taproom, which is men only. And he will say to the waiter now and then "See what the wife's having".

Often the men and women separate like this at the beginning of the evening and then rejoin later on. The reasons for this sort of segregation are not altogether straightforward. On one hand they are connected with the tabu on the pub itself, the idea that it is not "respectable", and that women are more susceptible than men to the operation of this kind of tabu. (The middle-class man who is not a regular pub-goer, but will occasionally drop into a pub and drink with a friend, will not take his wife with him.[1]) But also there is another and much more direct factor to be taken into consideration—the economic one. A report written by a local pub-goer shows this:

> Vault—with a friend and wife. Friend sends wife into the parlour. He remains with me in the vault. Asked him why he didn't go with her—he answered that he would do about 9.30 so as to have "last hour" in her company.
> . . . friend has been approached by the waiter for 8d. for drink in the other room (his wife's). We have had three pints each from 8.45 to 9.20, so asked him if stopping in the vault whilst his wife was in the parlour was so as to enable him to drink more beer than he would do in the other room. Answer was: "There's something in that, but if I was in the other room, the missus would want a Guinness every time I had a pint."

It is generally true that the women accept the position of drinking less in the pub, but that they drink more expensive drinks—not only because they must drink in rooms where everything costs more, but also because they drink bottled beers. The average cost of a woman's drink is 5d. to 6d.: of a man's 2½d. to 3d. The traditions of Worktown tend to lead women to drink at twice the price—and the majority follow the tradition. Many women have never tasted draught beer. Asked why they do not drink it their reactions are generally negative. Lower waged men can hardly afford to accompany their wives and drink as convention demands if they get into company, round for

---

[1] Cf. American middle-class view point. Elliott Merrit, *Social Disorganisation :* "The sight of a 'lady' leaning against the bar of an old time saloon would have brought a thrill of horror even to the most hardened habitué of the pre-war grog shop. Only women of dubious morals were seen in saloons although now and then a daring and unconventional matron risked her reputation by slipping in 'the family' entrance for a glass of beer." Note the use of 'slipping' presupposing that there is something shady about the pub. We suppose the origin of the 'nuggy hole' is something to do with this. It has its own entrance, and if you do 'slip' in and out you needn't be seen drinking in the pub.

round, on this scale. When women are present the round ritual works just as strictly as ever—but the men pay. So the pub regular, living at normal work level, cannot be a regular with a dame; Saturday night and maybe Sunday is all he can manage if he is to have his own beer on week-nights.

A corroboration of the friend's remark that his wife would have a Guinness whenever he ordered a pint is furnished by a story told to us by a barman; its hero is a local policeman who drinks at this pub, and is known as Thirsty. He is famous for cadging drinks and general mean behaviour. He goes in the tap-room, and sends his wife in the parlour, paying the waiter-on for her drinks. (This, the general custom, sometimes results in the husband finding that he has to pay for a big round for his wife's friends, which causes trouble.) Thirsty, although far better off than most of the pub-goers, only pays for mild for his wife, and the cheapest mild at that. She, however, has an arrangement with the waiter-on, so that when her husband orders and pays for her gill, she has a Guinness fetched for her and pays the extra from her housekeeping money. This habit is widespread.

The following extract from an observer's report gives an idea of women in the pub. The parlour that they are in is virtually a woman's room on week-nights. Only on week-ends is it invaded by men.

> Best room, 7.45 p.m. Landlady and four other middle-aged women. Two of them have small Guinnesses, and the other two are splitting a pint bottle of stout. (This isn't allowed.) They are talking about husbands and men. One repeats several times: "I wouldn't give tuppence for a dozen of them." Then they talk children. One complains how hers follow her about, even to the lavatory. Then the landlady tells a story about a man she knew who used to pull a roll of banknotes out of his pocket and say that he had them because he had no kids. Everyone said that this was wrong; it was all right having kids really, and it was miserable for you when you got old if you didn't have any.
>
> Two of the women go, saying "Good night". One says she has to finish her shopping and go to the butcher's.
>
> Two more middle-aged women come in, and then an old one, leaning on a stick. They sit together at a table. Two have Guinness. The older one orders a Falstaff, and when it comes one of the other two insists on paying for it. The old woman holds her glass up towards her and says "Good health".

There is a leather-covered stool in the room which is being raffled by the landlady. Someone remarks that it's useful for sitting on when you wash the kids, She looks well beyond the age of doing this herself.

Another woman hands round a saucer, into which the others put pennies for the raffle, some twice. This woman sits at the table with a notebook and pencil, while the others give her shillings and sixpences, which she puts down in the book. This is in connection with a club.

The old woman tells a long story about how she lost her lodger, who has played a dirty trick on her. The others are sympathetic. One says: "When they think you've got nobody at back of you they shit on you." Another, very respectable looking, hard-faced, adds "They rub it in, too".

More women come in, one about 30, is asked why they haven't seen her lately, and she says she's been hard up. The hatchet-faced one buys her friends another round, and the landlady comes in and joins them, bringing a bottle of Worthington with her.

The talk is now general, loud, with plenty of laughter. It refers back to lodgers, then someone says something about a splendid cheese dish that belongs to her, and how she knocked the handle off the other day. Whereupon the old woman gets up, goes behind the bar and comes out with an *enormous* cheese dish. There is discussion about raffling it; one woman, to whom it is offered for sale, refuses it because it is too big, "and there are only two of us". This leads to talk on the qualities of cheese and its cost, and then generally to the high price of food these days, particularly eggs. A fat woman says "I like duck eggs with a chop, a blue one, not a green one. I fancy green as a rule, but I like them blue. . . ."

Here is a less free and easy gathering in a small best room, which has three racing pictures, a coloured photograph of the Victoria Falls, and a photograph of a football team, and red, white and blue carnations in a vase.

Three women, two have bottled ale, one Guinness. They talk about a film to which one has been. Conversation is desultory, with plenty of silences. Then it cheers up and they whisper to each other, and occasionally laugh loudly. Observer overhears: "She wet me through one night, she cocked her leg over me one night and did it, she wet me through. . . . If she doesn't go to the lavatory before she goes to bed she always does."

After this there is more silence. Then "When did you 'ave your 'air done?"

"Yesterday."

Third woman, apparently referring back to an earlier phase of the conversation, says "They'll be in London now".

"Seven o'clock this morning they left."

"Is their father and mother going?"

"Yes, after they've been to the races they're stopping at the daughter's. . . ." Silence, then she goes on: "I'd like to have a dam good burst at the Isle of Man."

Another bout of whispering begins, about one Daisy, who is always making cups of tea when she should be working. This was still going on when the observer left.

While, in the local pubs, the tendency is for women to get together on their own and gossip, the majority of women in the town centres are accompanied by their husbands or boy friends. Groups of unattached women can also be seen; these often have shopping baskets, and are having a few drinks after their week-end shopping excursion. Others are young or youngish, smartly dressed; their role as pub-goers is discussed later, in the section on sex, where other aspects of female drinking are reviewed.

For some women there is a faint sense of guilt in visiting the town centre pubs (which means drinking amongst strangers) without their menfolk. A remark overheard by an observer one night is relevant to this. A group of three women were talking about going into pubs; one of them, a blonde of about 35, who was not a native, but who visited the town regularly in the course of her work (which was selling electric washing machines), said "You do things when you're away from home that you don't do when you're there." She seemed to know her way about the pub pretty well.

In many London pubs a small section of the public or private bar is partitioned off and has a street entrance of its own, serving as a special tiny woman's bar. We have already referred to the "nuggy hole", of which we have observed three examples in Worktown so small that four old women drinking there give a densely crowded appearance.

LOBBY DRINKERS

Another type of special bar, with its own clientele, is the lobby, referred to earlier. While vault, lounge, and taproom are well defined entities, the lobby bar is not. In its most primitive form it is little more than a place in a passage where chaps can lean and drink; in its more developed forms it has seats, spittoons, and tables of its own.

Assuming that the pub rooms are graded in the order of respectability, the room that has the lowest social standing—the vault—is the one with the bar counter. So that the man who likes to drink standing, and who has social pretensions or aspirations must, in the absence of any other bar counter, either be "de-classed", or give up the method of drinking that he prefers. The lobby bar resolves these contradictions for him.

When we look outside the pubs of this town we can understand more of the function and significance of the lobby bar. In London, for instance, one does not find the actual bar counter confined to one room; it is often the centre of the whole pub, upon which Public Bar, Saloon Bar, Private Bar, etc., abut. But the more "respectable" sort of saloon is not just a "bar" —it is a room with a bar at one side; this bar very often has a superstructure of framed-in frosted glass built upon it, leaving only a comparatively narrow opening through which drinks are served; the opening is below eye level, so that the customer has to bend to see behind the bar. In effect he is cut off from the regions of lower class drinking. The saloon drinker is of course able to sit down at a table and have his beer as if he were in an ordinary lounge. However, if he is a perpendicular drinker, he can lean up against the bar, and yet, invisible to the drinkers at the other side and unseeing of them, he retains his saloon bar status.

The basis of this lies in the method of pub construction—one that is not found in ordinary Worktown pubs but is observable in some of the larger and/or newer houses—the method by which the bar, which can be circular, horseshoe shaped, oval, or rectangular, is the real centre of the pub.

SOME SPECIAL TYPES OF DRINKER

A special type of pub-goer, who doesn't seem to *belong* in any active sense, is the man whom we call the "silent regular".

> . . . 4 men sit on bench opposite bar, talking very quietly to each other . . . 1 other man stands at far end of bar. . . . An old man in corduroys comes in very slowly, does not greet the others, advances to bar and fumbles in

pocket for money. Barmaid comes in and draws off a pint and he hands her money. Not a word has passed between them. He picks up pint, takes a swig, and totters across to the bench where the others are sitting, sits down, drinks his pint in three minutes, and walks out again very slowly, not having spoken a word to anyone the whole time.

This is a large pub, at street corner on main road. No games:

2 men with pints, talking together in undertones. Man in cap, scarf, shiny baggy blue suit, comes in, says nothing to the others, and orders "Pint o' mild" (a stranger). . . .

. . . An old man, wearing clean corduroy trousers, blue jacket, cap and scarf, comes in. He does not say anything but is a regular, and has a pint drawn for him right away; he stays at the bar. The stranger takes a last swig and goes, no one having spoken to him; he does not say good-night.

Another man, wearing a blue suit, cap, and scarf, comes in, goes to the bar, and has a pint drawn without anything having been said. . . .

Both these pubs are on main roads; and we have not observed any silent regulars at small backstreet pubs. They may be simply chaps who drop in for a drink on their way from somewhere, and who have no interest in getting into contact with other drinkers in the pub.

For the last century "the club bore" has been a subject for middle-class humour. The pub bore also exists. Of these a barman writes "Pub bore who always has some relative in a high position, and who knows more about a subject under discussion and won't be crushed. Fellows coming in will always go to the other side of the room when he is present." Related to this type is the man called "the pint 'ole oracle." (Pint hole being a term for a vault.) The following is an account of our first encounter with one of these:

Vault, 7 p.m. 7 men. A group of 4, who had won a lot of money on a horse, were drinking heavily. The drunkest was a Napoleonic little man wearing a bowler hat, who sat at the table and held forth in a loud voice, with wide gestures, often using long words, carefully enunciating them, in the manner of a stage drunk. The others were having a discussion about the central heating that had been installed in the pub opposite. The bowler hat knew all about it . . . there was a lot of scandal about a local plumber who had worked on the job and made a mess of it. The drunk said aggressively "I like to meet these clever people— people who *think* themselves clever". He said this a lot of times. Another man said they had Italians to lay the cellar floor. For some reason the bowler hat man flared up at this, and began to crack up the Italians no end, as if someone had been running them down. "A man only counts from the chin up," he said, and pushed his bowler hat right to the back of his head. "Never mind how big he is, a man only counts from the chin up." The other laughed, and seemed to think he was being funny. The philosophical tone was restored to the conversation by the landlord, who told them what the midwife had said to his grandmother— "man starts to die the moment he is born". No one took any notice of this, and he said "They haven't got onto it yet", and told them the story again.

But bowler hat started to get indignant, waving his arms about and banging the table, endangering the observer's beer "I like to meet clever chaps," he shouted, "barristers and solicitors and suchlike." (Suddenly he changes his tone.) "A man comes to me and shakes hands. He's got galluses (callouses) all over them. I says—I wouldn't shake hands with a chap like you. . . . Ah, I like to meet these *clever* fellows—fellows who *think* themselves clever . . ." And he goes on, philosophically again, about "a man who loses the simplicities, the simple things, loses life". At which the landlord takes the opportunity of telling them about his grandma and the midwife again. . . .

Someone tells the observer that bowler hat is what is known as "the pint 'ole oracle".

LET THE BARKS SPIT ON HIM

In Worktown there are a number of Irish labourers, many of whom live in cheap lodging houses; they, in company with the lowest paid casual labourers and the rest of the doss-house population, form a variety of pub-goer distinguished in a number of ways from the ordinary drinker; and they have their own round of pubs. The following account, written by a local unemployed man, makes clear the characteristics of this type of drinker:

This is definitely a poor working class type of pub, on entering there were nine Irishmen all in working dress, clay on their boots and observer was the only person with collar and tie on. The bar is of the straight type going at right angles near the door is kept in shabby condition of the time that I stayed there I never saw the barmaid wipe the counter with a cloth personally I think its only wiped once a week. There were five spittoons on a composition floor, but these "barks"[1] have no regard to spittoons I saw one spit on the counter. One thing that is different from pubs in other districts is that they have a method of walking about with loaves of bread under their arms. Two men came in while I was there and one had flour cakes in a bag and he had the bag the wrong way up and his cakes were falling in the spit but he just picked them up and put them in the bag. One Irishman said "Be Jasus paddy and youre losin' youre breakfast".

Irishman 2, "Ou sure am, Michael". The difficult part about getting conversation with these fellows is that they appear to get in two's and lean forward and speak in a low tone and it's only when a question is asked in a lively fashion that they reply the same way. I overheard a deputy from one of the spikes[2] telling an Irishman about Mick coming well oiled and to keep him quiet he said, "I sure had to get the frying pan to him". This chap had a mongrel with him and he put the dog on the counter for Alice, the barmaid, to make it beg for lump sugar. Nearly all the speech was inaudible, just slight references made about quarries or navvying but they appear to be a very sullen type of people. There was a lively crowd in the side room singing Irish songs "Mother Macree", "The Dear Little Shamrock", "Does your Mother come from Ireland?" If McCormick could have heard them he would have said he was a Welshman. The waitress waiting on these side rooms was a plump piece well painted and dressed in a flowered cotton frock, she smoked cigarettes while waiting on and had a guinness every other time she had a order also gave observer a smile at the same time. They were still spitting all over the floor when observer left at 8.35 p.m.

P.S. All drinks served in the vault were pints.

(Another such pub, five minutes later):

There were ten men in vault which included three shamrocks. 4 men playing all fours for gills. The three shamrocks were very quiet and kept well away from the other men they were drinking pints and speech was very low and inaudible and after having two pints they went out and made towards Manor st. The only excitement in the vault was with the

---

[1] Bark = Irishman.   [2] Workhouse.

cardplayers who appeared to be regulars. The landlord said that two of them were the best twisters in Worktown. One man replied "We can't twist thee out of so bloody much". First man: "It's a bloody sight better living here than in London, why it were costing me 14s. a week for digs and it only left me a bob to spend out of my 15 bob."

Second man: "I suppose tha lives in't bloody shilling here and spends owt 14 bob?"

First man: "Naw, but I con manage a lot better living in kip houses." Third man: "Go on put thy bloody jack on that makes us two apiece."

Two shamrocks came in with loaves of bread under their arm had a pint each and walked out. A man came in with a accordion and went in back room, the company got lively and struck up with "Does your Mother come from Ireland" but the joke is that the shamrocks don't sing they leave it to the others. Then a man sang "Vanity Fair". The price of these kip houses averages about 8d. a night. There was very little to report about this place tonight and I think that the best place to observe the shamrocks is in the R., and sincerely suggest that John Sommerfield spends a night there from 5.30 to 10 p.m. letting the barks spit on him.

A sub-variety of regular is the wife or daughter who comes round to the side of the bar (the serving hatch) with a bottle or jug to be filled for home consumption. (In a typical corner beer-house in one evening (a Tuesday) to 53 drinkers who came in to drink, 7 came with jugs to take beer home.)

Girl slips in at side bar, holds out empty rum bottle to barmaid, who fills it with mild, without anything having been said. Girl, to tough looking chap who is drinking a pint in the vault:

"What, you still 'ere?"

Tough: "Looks like it."

Girl: "Don't you ever go home?"

Tough: "Aye, for a bit o' food and a bit o' something else."

Girl goes out.

Barmaid, to tough: "Next time she asks you that you should tell 'er it's the same for 'er—say 'why do you keep following me around?'"

We have also observed *men* fetching a jug of beer home like this, but it is uncommon. In numerous visits to local working class homes we have only seen draught beer on the table at Sunday dinner time.

There are types of regulars, such as bookies, prostitutes, hawkers, who use the pub for moneymaking purposes. These will be discussed later.

WHO, THEN, ARE THE PUB-GOERS?

Who are the people who go to pubs? The feature common to every pub is the glass of beer available to all between the legal hours. Similarly, its consumption, or the consumption of some liquid stocked by pubs, is the factor common to all pub-goers. But are there any other factors common to all drinkers that are also specific to them? At the beginning of the fieldwork there was a tendency to assume that such factors must exist. Now, reviewing our data on the pub-goer, we find the external evidence for such factors small.

There are pub-goers amongst both sexes, amongst all adult age groups. Though we have moderate evidence of their occupations, we do not find them to be restricted to any special type of occupation. Nor, on the evidence of clothes, are they restricted to any one social class; though, just as the greater number of pub-goers are restricted to certain age-groups, so are the majority to certain classes—the middle-class pub-goer is in the minority.

Maybe the middle-classer makes up for it by drinking at home. Other slight evidence suggests it, but even so the per head consumption of manual workers is considerably greater than that of the higher social strata. Of the poorer worker it can be truly said that his sixth of a grave is what he fights for when he fights for the second half of "King and Country". For the middle-classes and better-off workers, whose homes are their own, regardless of rent de-restriction, the Englishman's home is indeed his castle. It is rather difficult to get the drawbridge let down. That is why we have only been into twenty odd upper middle-class homes. (As we have said, they are very much in the local minority, and our job has been to survey a cross section of industrialism.) In four homes we have been offered beer, in two of these four wine and whiskey as well. That may be a fair sample. As breweries now have plain wagons for home delivery (which they advertise especially in the local paper) it is hard to say more of the drinking habits of the above-pub people, without carrying out a special investigation into a field that has so far not been our principal concern. But we can say the "best class" people in Worktown do not go into its pubs—this is true of 16 members of leading families known to us. Golf and other *clubs* are their outside drinking places.

SOME WHO DON'T

There are certain local groups who definitely do NOT drink. Such are the church members of the Holiness Tabernacle, the Bethel Evangelical Church, Hebron, Beulah, the Mazdaznan and Truth Centre groups, and certain fundamentalist Churches which are theoretically Anglican. Methodists and Baptists are not supposed to drink, but we have had beer with important lay leaders in each. No minister has ever been seen in a pub by any of our 60 odd observers, nor have any been reported even by rumour. In a nearby town a leading minister drinks and has several times been notoriously drunk. Our evidence suggests that he is the second most popular parson in the area, but his church is seldom more than a tenth filled.

This doesn't necessarily imply that the man who goes to pubs is not the sort who gets to the top. Of the town's Council of 92 we know 10 who are pub regulars (8 of them are Labour). That the man at the top doesn't usually go to pubs is the better way of putting it. Fundamentally the pub is the vault (and taproom), the regulars' room, the place where there is almost always someone during drinking hours. The vault is working class, masculine, with the emphasis on the working rather than the class. Without committees or leaders that community of mild-drinkers runs itself year in and year out, on a common factor of beer.

The churchgoer—or rather, the strict churchgoer—and the political idealist put another continuum of life and hope and understanding first. One of our later books, *How Religion Works and Doesn't*, will deal with that. For the present it will do to suggest, on the basis of our general observations and experience, that for the most part the pub "regular" is not the same chap as the church regular. On the fringe of pub casuals and week-enders there is much overlap, especially among the Anglicans, plenty of whom are regulars. The Church of England's attitude is fairly put by Keast, in *The Church and the Public House* (a small production of the Church Literature Association)— "The Church has always condemned intemperance, but has never

found any wrong in the temperate use of alcoholic liquors."
Roman Catholics, provided they fulfil their normal Mass obliga-
tions, are at liberty to go into any pub they like, and they do so.
The Worktown Catholic Churches are even more dominantly
working class than the pub, and mainly right-wing Labour in
politics.

As control on their drink behaviour the Catholics have optional
restrictions, best shown by quoting a typical local observer's
report on part of a Catholic service:

> Priest then throws his right hand across again, 3 times
> takes the 2 inch circle wafer and holds it with finger and thumb
> of both hands, holds it over the chalice, near the back side of
> it. He then speaks, and the Altar Boy answers. He breaks the
> wafer into parts into the Cup, then puts cover onto it. He
> reads from the board at the back. Choir sing "Miserere".
> Bells ring 3 times. Priest brushes crumbs off the Altar top into
> small silver-looking plate. He empties the crumbs into the cup.
> He then hands the Chalice to the Boy. Pours something into
> it. Then drinks. Then holds it out again. Water is poured into
> it. He drinks it all. He puts the white cloth on top of the cup
> and the purple one on top of that. He stands to the right and
> reads from the board. Faces congregation. Says "Dominus
> vobiscum". Holds his hands up to shoulder height, then turns
> back to altar. He mutters. A child also mutters, has been
> muttering all service; mother tries to keep it quiet, no one else
> bothers except to smile. Priest now closes book. Congregation
> make sign of cross. Priest faces congregation. All standing.
> He waves cong. down again with gestures downwards of both
> hands. He says:
> "Make up your minds what you are going to do in Lent. I
> recommend you to keep the pledge. You may never fear that
> drink will get a hold over you if you can do without it for the
> period of Lent. It is for seven weeks. Don't say it after me,
> but say it in your soul:
>> 'In honour of the Sacred Thirst and in the Atonement of
>> the intemperance of men I solemnly promise Almighty God
>> and the Blessed Virgin Mary that I will abstain from all
>> intoxicating drinks, and may Jesus Christ protect you.'"
> He is solemn, and adds, "I give those who have taken it a
> Benedictus." All heads are bent low. He speaks in Latin and
> makes the sign of the Cross. . . .

MORE ABOUT SUNDAY

We have already pointed out some special Sunday characteristics of the pub. And it is to be noted that the average rate
of drinking on Sunday is 9·7 minutes per gill, compared with
Saturday, 7·9. The clothes data previously given indicated a
considerable "improvement" in clothes on Saturday evenings, a
general step up in the social scale. Similar figures were collected
for Sunday pub hats. They are:

SUNDAY CLOTHES CHANGEOVER
(partly based on figures for beerhouse vaults given earlier)

Men's Hats	Per cent Sunday	Per cent change from	
		Saturday	Weekday
Caps	69·4	— 10·6	— 22·9
Trilbies	4·5	— 1·3	— 3·3
Bowlers	4·4	— 1·3	+ 4·4
No hats	21·7	+ 13·2	+ 21·7
Ties	34·9	— 22·2	+ 15·6
No ties	65·1	+ 22·2	— 15·6
Good suit	26	— 8·2	+ 26
Old suit	74	+ 10·2	— 26

At first the Sunday figures seemed to be contradictory. They
did contradict our idea that Sunday was the "classy" clothes
day, the climax of respectability, setting the tone for its Saturday
eve, and imposing a general pattern on long leisure periods.
(This idea arises from much other data, not relevant to this book.)
Yet on Sunday the percentage of bareheaded drinkers went up,
good suits and tie wearers decreased, though bowlers (hall mark
of respectability) went up a trifle. Because it didn't fit we doubted
our figures. We repeated the survey. The results were confirmed.
It then occurred to us to make our comparisons with week-days
instead of Saturday. An all round "improvement" in clothing
was the result. A comparison of the Sunday pub figures with
part of the very extensive material that we have collected on
Sunday in Worktown from the church point of view illuminated
the whole difficulty, as shown by the following crude preliminary
analysis of some nine thousand people in Sunday streets and
churches, during Spring.

Men's Hats	Sunday Percentages			
	In church	In streets just before or after church	In streets during church	In pub vaults
Caps only	0	12	31	69
Bowlers and trilbies	85	63	26	9
Caps and barehead	15	37	74	91

The church sample is of five churches, of five main sects, in one street, plus the Worktown Parish Church, during two months.

No Catholic church is included. People do go to Catholic churches in caps, but to no other large sects. The large series of street counts show a fall in absolute numbers in streets during services, and a great relative decrease in numbers wearing trilbies and bowlers. The maximum concentration of caps, the non-church unit of headwear, on Sunday is in the pub vault. The less good suits and less ties of Sunday as compared with Saturday, in association with the above facts, suggest an explanation for the data that seemed, at first, to contradict our ideas— i.e. the pub-goer, or rather, the vault-goer, has Saturday night as his "Sunday".

Easter Sunday raises a point here, for it is sandwiched between three other holidays (though most mills work on Easter Monday, and most shops on Saturday). 849 people clothes-counted (Easter) showed the usual ¦cap dominance in the vault, but more variation in other sorts of hat, and a higher all-round cap percentage in other spheres, including churches (the same five samples):

Men's Hats	Easter Percentages			
	In church (evening)	In streets just before church	In streets 9–10 p.m.	In pub vaults (evening)
Caps only	3	17	8	63
Bowlers and trilbies	80	57	43	23
Caps and barehead	20	43	57	77

Easter Monday pub-vault figures compared with parallel street count 9–10, shows a week-day hat-pattern. Drunkenness goes high at Worktown on Easter Monday, though one must go to Blackpool to see a sight such as that recalled by gossipist William Hickey in *Daily Express*, described by his eighteenth century eponym observer William Hickey at Greenwich, "about 200,000 persons present, of whom towards evening 50,000 were sober, 90,000 in high glee, 30,000 drunkish, 10,000 staggering, 15,000 muzzy, 5,000 dead drunk".

Easter Monday figures for 11 Worktown pub vaults were:

	Percentages
Caps only	76·9
Bowlers and trilbies	15·3
Caps and barehead	84·7

The principal pub observer summarized Easter Monday drinking as "like a Friday". After a holiday week-end it is significant that so many are drinking, about 1½ times as many as usual. The clothes pattern in the weekly cycle, class distinction, and behaviour, is vital, providing as it does an immediate tag or identity to each person according to their costume. Further work on this will be necessary.

PUB-GOERS' SABBATH

The evidence strongly suggests the point already suggested by other data—that for many Worktowners Saturday night has gained Sunday attributes. It is as if the pub-goer preferred to keep the pre-Christian Sabbath in a pre-Christian way.

If this is so (and we suggest it as no more than a hypothesis without prejudicing the later sections of the book)—then the opposition between Church and pub has taken a curious twist. Driven by the Nonconformist movement from the free pleasures of Sunday, in a rapidly increasing population where towns were becoming increasingly less easy to get out of, or relax in, some such complex result might well have been expected. For the Church has done little to provide alternatives on Sunday. Only religious activity during limited hours (especially limited among the Nonconformists) is offered. The considerable social life of the Churches is reserved for the week nights. There is, however, sign that the Anglicans and Catholics are further organizing their Sundays to cover social activities, such as films and dances. The most popular single Sunday activity is the social hour, concert-cum-service, held at 8 p.m. in the Y.M.C.A.

PUB AND CHURCH JOKES

Several music hall shows in Worktown have depicted red nosed parsons. It is of course well known that the music hall originated in the public house. It is only in this century that they have become completely separated. The bars in the Work-town music hall are a very important part of it. And the touring company is still on the side of the publican, constantly boosting beer, and often being sarcastic about teetotallers, temperance and parsons. Thus on June 3rd the week's comedian gets big applause for his skit on the Salvation Army, singing "Pennies from Heaven". Observer's report reads:

> With hat and cymbals and sudden, exaggerated gestures, he says "I heard it sung Sunday by the Salvation Army. There was Beastly Bertie, the converted convict, two reformed sailors, two commercial travellers, me, and a man from Darcy Lever—so you can see what sort of people there were. There were 24 in the band—4 playing and 20 going round with the hat."

Darcy Lever is a Lancashire village, and a sort of stock joke, for no known reason (compare Wigan). Thus on August 19, we get another road show, with the comedian gagging:

> "The garden of Eden was where Darcy Lever is now . . . is epistle sister of apostle? The bishop's going on a holiday, so send in your missionary boxes quick." (At the mention of the word bishop he makes with his hands what observer calls "pansy movements"). . . . "There are blank pages in your prayer books for racing tips . . . our new hymn: 'Pennies from Heaven'."

On August 28th at the same place:

> Part of a short sketch is taken up by the vicar visiting a man and his wife while they are having a quarrel. His appearance causes prolonged laughter. His behaviour is stylised in a few movements—perpetual grin, a wagging of the finger. He holds his hands in front of him, the fingers splayed, and incessantly brings in and out of contact the corresponding extremities of either hand.

The Church is not anti-music hall, in Worktown anyway. But the music hall is definitely and frequently more or less anti-Church, definitely pro-pub. Famous brewery firms pay music hall comedians to include the names of their brands in their gags. The pub, on the other hand, is not specifically anti-Church. It never propagandas against the Church. The Church makes all the running in anti-. Individually, however, pub-goers, landlords and a boss of the big local brewery, have expressed distinctly aggressive anti-Church views to observers. A landlord at Christmas-tide told one of us the following story of propagandist sort:

> "A friend of mine went to tea with some others at Christmas time this year with a prominent Methodist chap. This chap told his son to go out to the coalhouse and get some more coal for the fire. The lad took the shovel. He came back with a bit of coal on the shovel, and two bottles of beer in with the coal."

An extensive hospital carnival in a nearby hamlet, organized largely by the Church, last year had as a leading character a collier with dogcollar, parsonic clothes, and a mask that made him appear as big a boozer as any Blackpool postcard figure (see page 221).

Another angle is provided by an observer's Good Friday report—not written down on the spot, but immediately afterwards:

> Peter began to argue that it was peculiar that women should always drink bottled beer. The landlady, aged 72, was emphatic that Guinness was good for women, and was supported by two other women. . . . Three women had been to a cinema matinée. Observer said that he thought pictures would be closed on Good Friday.
> "Oh no. The matinées have been going on for years on Good Friday."
> "It's a very good picture, this *Laughing Irish Eyes.*"
> "A good story."
> A young chap of about 25 was introduced to observer in these terms "He's a fine lad—Good hearted. If it is his last 5*d.* he'd say 'What are you havin'?'" This fellow said "It's funny . . . my sister who is 17 asked me this morning what Good Friday was for—so I had to tell her it was to do with religion and Jesus being crucified." He took a swig at his pint. His brother joined in. "Good Friday is worse than a Sunday owing to the restrictions on refreshments. Pubs close

at 2. The lads (Worktown football team) kick off at 3—so anyone drunk are prowling about the streets. If the hours were extended we should drink a bit more." Says the other. "No one really upholds it. They think nowt of it." Says the first chap "This is the funny thing—He (Christ) didn't die a fortnight before his time. But it's still celebrated. You know how it changes from time to time."

In the following year better prospects for drinkers were revealed in the *Worktown Evening News*, where an advertisement in its 9s. an inch Special Announcements column on Thursday proclaimed:

GOOD FRIDAY

THE ROYAL OAK HOTEL

Will be open for the sale of

BEER, WINES, and SPIRITS

From 12 noon to 10 p.m.

LIGHT REFRESHMENTS, TEAS, ETC.

Provided in Dining-Room

OPPOSITION TO DRINKERS

But from the Churches now the only real and outspoken opposition comes from a number of new sects. These sects, like the pub, permit their members to participate closely, to intervene, cry out, suddenly pray, become inspired by spirit. They have not formalized the service in an exactly defined rota of minister—spectator—chorus—minister, a formality that has now reached its maximum in Methodism and Christian Science. These sects, Hebron, Beulah, Mazdaznan, Advent, Bethel, Evangelical, Holiness, Out and Out, are all comparatively new, small but moderately successful, tremendously intense, utterly anti-pub, anti-alcohol. They generally provide an every evening alternative of organized religio-social activity. They directly compete with the pub, often explicitly.

Holiness Tabernacle, for example, won't allow anyone to join who smokes, drinks, or goes to a cinema: for Communion wine it uses raspberry juice. It is necessary to understand the tremendous power of "Nonconformity" in Worktown, for it influences the

social life and success of the pub. This influence is not at all
"obvious". It would be easy to spend a year in Worktown and,
if you didn't go to church, think the Church was less important
than the tram or the political party. But its leaders are also
leaders of politics, police, magistrates' bench, local press, and
business. And the strong Nonconformist tradition of a town once
known as the Geneva of the North, whose first two Mayors were
Unitarians (in days when Unitarians were "unbelievers")
divides the place into Church and non-Church people. Where
the anti-pub feeling is not explicit it is implicit in all sects—
excepting the Roman Catholics, whose attitudes to drink are
perfectly well defined and necessitate no mental friction or
repression.

This repression constantly bobs up on both sides, a precisely
similar but equally overt attitude exists between churchgoer
and pubgoer over gambling and betting, subjects bound up
with pub life (see later section). And in each case we have a
transitional "sin" crossing the boundary between bar and
pulpit. Smoking, for instance. It is not accidental that a common
symbol of tobacco advertising is the priest, parson, or nun—
for this provides the social sanction that the transitional church-
pub person needs—"The vicar does it".

The other case, in the sphere of gambling (gambling and drink
are the two commonest "social evils" attacked in Worktown
sermons, or at least in the 500 that we have so far studied),
is the football pools. Poolites, too, cut across all social groups,
as do smokers, and also form a special sub-group of their own,
with certain particular feelings, actions, magical interventions,
and jargon, especial to poolites (smokers have similar rites and
magics, such as cigarette tapping, lights, not three to a match,
conventions of offering). Smokers and non-smokers, poolites
and non-poolites, have definite overt oppositions to each other.
(See *First Year's Work*, Mass Observation, 1938.) But none
have any special places to assemble—except smoking and non-
smoking compartments in railway carriages. Representatives of
each attitude occur both in church and pub. The difference is
that in the pub they can smoke or not, pool or not. In church
they can only not.

Both worship and drinking are confined to special buildings,
or (rarely) to homes and certain open air occasions. The Church
adopts a negative attitude to smoking now; and on the whole

an increasingly negative attitude to drink. It is only the new sects that are militantly anti-drink—the sects that have gone back to the word of the gospels and Genesis, emphasizing the second coming's potential immediacy, and the absolute badness of most men and women.

The situation is confused then. And it is symptomatic of the confusion throughout the contemporary doctrine and activity of the older Churches. Those with 100 per cent clear cut and consistent drink attitudes are those that are full in Worktown . . . R.C., Holiness, Bethel, and the vigorous Methodist Mission Hall.

Writing pre-war in an essay competition a leading local Quaker, then a boy, observed: "Perhaps the most effective counter-attractions to public houses on Saturday nights are the 2d. concerts given at the two Methodist mission halls. These are arranged principally by Wesleyans but the concerts are of an unsectarian character. Every Saturday evening 4,500 people fill these halls and enjoy an excellent programme for one and a half hours. . . . Since King's Hall was opened in 1906 over 80,000 people have attended the concerts held there." But the King's Hall concerts have ended; the other hall has its Saturday concert, secular, attended on an average by 1,000. This hall, acting as a church on Sunday, still has the largest congregation (services and Sunday school) of any place in Worktown. Its notice board often displays typical temperance graphs, making up in colour and quality of print what they may lack in objective treatment of fact.

These churches, still with the tough missionary-to-the-worker attitude, are not of course full just because of their attitude to drink. But their attitude to drink is clear cut, because all their attitudes are clear cut, and that apparently is what many people want from a Church. The other Churches are those involved in the complex compromise guilt-feeling elements in pub-going. Many pub-goers do not like it to be known that they are pub-goers—even though they are not church-goers. And most landlords believe that their customers have some secrecies to be preserved—the "better class" the client the more secrecies. Thus when Humphrey Spender was, for the one and only time in taking hundreds of such photographs, caught snapping a scene in a crowded pub, the landlord completely lost control of himself, called in the police, etcetera, etcetera. Spender was within his legal rights, of course, but the landlord was within his moral rights.

Undoubtedly the principal factors of pub-going are social and alcoholic. (How these two factors are completely inter-related we will discuss later.) The pub is the only free, non-esoteric, non-exclusive, weatherproof meeting place for the ordinary worker. Yet very few will say of their own accord that they go to the pub for social reasons—it only comes up in round-about ways. And people will make the most elaborate statements as to why they drink beer—statements that are surely rationalizations and wish-fulfilments. Strong in nearly every Worktowner is the idea that he should-be-good, that he should work on week-days and go to church on Sundays, visit his grandmother's grave at spring "sermons", etc., a code of behaviour that he may not actively subscribe to, but that conditions his attitudes.

And only the Church publicly proclaims against alternative social customs, has organized channels through which it can express its feelings.

It is this position that largely explains the sense of unconscious guilt associated in the minds of many pub-goers with going to a pub. This finds a clear expression in the general attitude of ordinary pub-goers to the only place in the town that specializes in wines. People who don't drink there express contempt for those who do. All sorts of imputations are made about the place's methods, morals, and clients. To outside observers the only special features about it are the wine, the huge square room and the packed mass of people who commonly fill it. But it caters to wine drinkers. An unconscious connection between wine drinking and Holy Communion may be at the base of the strong and frequently expressed aversion to this place. The pub-goer who doesn't go there may be transferring his unconscious guilt feeling about his beer drinking to the wine drinkers?

Worktown has a tremendous Sunday school tradition. Few are the inhabitants who have not been confirmed or initiated into some one of its 27 sects. They have taken Communion and been informed of its mystic importance. It is after the experience of this that so many begin to drop away from the churches as they become "adult" and the more "modern" outlets become practicable. (They are able to keep more or all of their earnings for themselves.) But their first alcohol has been consecrated; "the wine of life" in the sort of doctrine that gets through to the ordinary Worktown Christian's understanding.

It is here, in the sacred quality of drink in the Church, that we can find one reason, largely covert, for opposition to public secular drinking, which becomes more marked when the Churches attempt, as did the Wesleyan movement, to form something of the same simple relationship and week-day evening community in the chapel as exists in the pub. In certain respects the teetotal Wesleyan minister does not play a role so very different from the corner-pub landlord. The symmetrical backset to the bar is as constant in the chapel. In both, the ordinary folk would never dream of going to sit or stand with minister or landlord while officiating; in both there is only one normal occasion for the ordinary person himself to approach this boss, minister or landlord within the building—that is, when he is serving drink.

In most Nonconformist sects, as in the pub lounge, the drink is brought round on a tray (with small wine glasses in the chapel) and you keep your seat. Roman Catholicism, in that it freely permits and never opposes the pub, is also unique in that it does not permit the congregation to partake of the wine. Only the priest does that. The Catholic congregation partakes only of the *body* of Christ. It was against this situation, as much as any other, that the Reformation (formally speaking only, of course) struck. The right of each full member of the congregation to partake of both body and blood, wine and wafer, was proclaimed and preserved in the 39 Articles—Article XXV (the second longest) saying:

> Sacraments ordained of Christ be not only badges or tokens of Christian men's professions, but rather they be certain sure witnesses, and effectual signs of grace. . . . The Sacraments were not ordained of Christ to be gazed upon, or to be carried about, but that we should duly use them. . . .

Since 1562 the majority of English church-goers have taken wine in church at least twice a year, in accordance with the words:

> Drink ye all of this; for this is my blood of the New Testament, which is shed for you and for many for the remission

of sins: Do this, as oft as ye shall drink of it, in remembrance of me.

When reading the sections that follow, on toasting, standing rounds, swiggling, drink speeds, remember that the pub and Church grew up together and as friends. The Reformation shook the alliance. Nonconformity finally smashed it, bringing a discipline of temperance, as well as a good deal of the Labour movement—yet the unions centred largely on the pub, at first not only geographically, but as a real part of the pub social group. There is today in Worktown a definite and evident conflict within the Labour party between Methodist teetotallers and plain, drinking labourites, a disagreement that on the surface is concerned with the value of licensed Labour Clubs to the movement, but that has subsurface implications of importance, not at all helpful to the movement as a whole.

These facts, then, can roughly be expressed thus: The pub with its essential factor alcohol provides for many Worktowners an alternative to the social groups and corporate beliefs of religion or politics, though not necessarily one exclusive to either interest. Religion and politics depend on some desire, however small, to shape, or maintain the shape, of present and future, and the continuum is "idealism"; the release, the immediate satisfaction, is "the feeling of goodness", feeling good, personally and socially. The pub provides a lot of this. Through its liquors it shapes the future in one's mind, does so more personally by obliterating it and emphasizing goodness only of and in the present, with hope and thought stretching out no further than the edges of "last hour" or "closing time". Drink, like its mythology of Lethe and Bacchus, is in this subtle sense a philosophy and ideology almost on its own account, and its feelings are not far from some of those in religion—particularly in religious conversion and absolutism. There is a lot more than drinking involved in drinking.

And the question: Who are the pub-goers? is answered in ways of living, smells of breath, sexual virility, food in the home, language, laughter and sorts of hope.

VI

DRINKING

WRITES A WORKTOWN elementary schoolboy, aged 12:

"Half drunk glasses scattered all o'er.
Spitting buckets scattered all over the floor.
The darts are twanging,
And the old piano planging;
The door keeps swinging,
And barmaid is singing.
Altogether they're shouting for a lot of fresh beer,
And some women are giving a good hearty cheer."

HOW

"The Act it selfe of drinking is varied divers manners of wayes. I will allege some few circumstances. As for example, it pleaseth some to life the glass unto their mouth. Others hang down their lippe, that they might drink with their heads inclining downward. Some joyne two cups one upon another and drink them together. Others take not up the Cup in their hand, but enwreathe it in the crooke of their arme. There are, who set glasses to their browe, that little and little it might descend down by their nose, as by a conduit to their mouth; where in such men have a singular faculty above others, who are well nosed, as having their noses bending down with a beake after the manner of a Parrots bill."

(Braithwaite. *The Law of Drinking*. 1620).

Worktown observer's report:

Drinks slowly and deliberately about half a glass, puts glass down and slides it along table; puts hand round glass, leaves it there a little, then drinks quickly, puts down glass and sucks lips. Two new Guinnesses, both drink together, level, about a quarter of a glass, put glasses down firmly. Both hold glasses off table, talk, swig, talk again, then swill drink round at bottom of the glasses and drink up quickly.

A solitary drinker. Sits with pint mug on table, at his elbow, and reads newspaper. Puts it down, yawns, lights fag, sips half an inch of beer, rests left elbow on table, picks nose and examines result on forefinger and thumb, suddenly seizes beer in left hand, drains mug, gets up and goes without saying anything.

Physiologically, the act of drinking is a complicated combination of both voluntary and reflex movements. The same can be said of it when regarded as a social phenomenon; it is accompanied by a number of conventions and habits which are both voluntary (consciously willed) and reflex (unconsciously reacting from stimuli).

A local drinker who was asked to spend an evening in his usual pubs and write down what he saw, notes in the first report that he wrote for us:

Beers are being consumed steadily at the rate of 15 minutes per gill; at each fresh order an interval of five minutes invariably elapses before it is drunk, and then only a small sip. The three men all follow suit as any *one* reaches for his glass and show wonderful anticipation in drinking equal amounts, so that all three glasses register the same level after each drink.

He uses the word "anticipation", taking for granted that it is a wholly conscious process. This, we shall see, is doubtful. But all our observations show that the majority of pub-goers tend, when drinking in a group, to drink level; and very often there is not a quarter of an inch difference between the depth of beer in the glasses of a group of drinkers. (Gill glasses are about 2½ inches wide.) The greatest lack of uniformity in the rate of drinking in a group is when they are halfway through their glasses; they will, as the report says, start all together, and there is a very strong tendency for them to finish at once, or nearly simultaneously at any rate. The simultaneous emptying of glasses is the most frequent form of level drinking. And it is (for reasons connected with the ritual of standing rounds) the most likely form of level drinking that is due to "anticipation". But glasses in twos and threes, each group with almost identical amounts of beer in them, is not necessarily the result of a conscious desire to drink level. The following incident is difficult to account for on that basis:

Regulars drink quietly. Two ancient women sitting on opposite sides of the room haven't got much face left. (One is syphilitic, previously observed here.) They are joined by an oldish man with similar facial decomposition; he is accompanied by an old woman with a shawl over her head; she supports on her arm a blind man. The three sit together *and drink level.*

After this a sharp lookout was kept for more blind men. Another was sighted two days later; the observer followed him into the pub.

. . . the blind man and three others sit round a table and order pints. As soon as the mugs are brought they lift them to their mouths with a slow "follow through" motion, and keep them there for about four seconds, then put them down simultaneously. All, including the blind man, have drunk about a quarter of the mug, almost dead level. After this they take smaller gulps, sometimes the blind man starting, sometimes the others, in no special order of beginning or finishing; but gulp for gulp they drink level to within a quarter of an inch throughout.

Another observation of a blind man drinking in a pub also showed that he drank level with the others in his group.

Now, if it is assumed that level drinking was a conscious and deliberate process, how do these men, who cannot see the depth of beer in their companions' glasses, manage to keep pace with them? The sound of the glass being lifted and put down, would, of course, give them a clue to the speed of the others drinking; but, in the last case quoted, the blind man sometimes was the first to start drinking. Certainly drinkers themselves do not realize they do this drinking level. Many expressed surprise when told about it, then observed themselves and (usually agreed.)

But level drinking is not an isolated phenomenon. It is connected with other drinking habits, that throw more light upon it.

We have timed about a thousand drinkers. It is very difficult laborious work. And results probably vary by season, class and temperature, factors we have not yet been able to study. There is not an average time per gill. The time varies from night to night. The following table shows the average times throughout the week. The times shown in the second column are based on a smaller number (443), taken at the same times in four pubs, as control, throughout the last week of May.[1] The other times were taken at a wide range of pubs all through the month, and all were between 8.30 and 10; figures are minutes.

Day	Average time	Control average
Friday	7·5	8·2
Saturday	7·9	8·8
Sunday	9·7	9·7
Monday	10·7	12·8
Tuesday	13·5	11·3
Wednesday	12·1	11·1
Thursday	10·7	10·6

The graphical representation of the above shows substantially the same curve as that on page 113, representing the variation in the number of drinkers throughout the week.

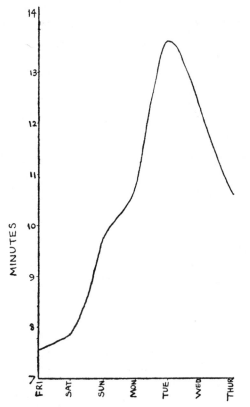

[1] On a November Saturday in Brighton pubs, average time for half-pints was 7·3 minutes.

How "real" are these averages? On all days there are variations from the normal of more than 50 per cent. But there are not many of them. The days that show the most variation are Monday, Tuesday, and Wednesday. The variation around the average at week-ends is comparatively much smaller. This compares with the curves of the weekly counts of the drinkers, the greatest lack of uniformity between them also being on those days.

The variation between week-day and week-end is not so sharp in the case of the speed of drinking, as that of the number of drinkers. None the less, a corresponding week-end peak does exist, if not so strongly marked; and indicates that an explanation common to both phenomena should be sought.

Let us examine in more detail the times for one day. We will choose Sunday, since we have a comparatively large number of times for that day, and also because it is the most "average" of the days of the week.

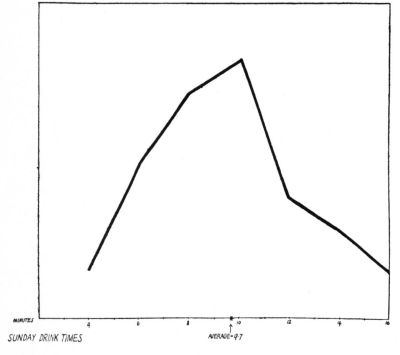

SUNDAY DRINK TIMES   AVERAGE-9.7

The diagram above shows a curve of the frequencies of all the timings between 4 and 16 minutes, for 2 minute intervals—

i.e., all the times between 4 and 6 minutes are added to make the first point of the curve, all those between 6 and 8 minutes the second point, and so on.

63·8 per cent of all times were between 6 and 10 minutes, the day's average being 9·7 minutes. Only 9·6 per cent of the times were under 6 minutes, and 26·6 per cent were above 10 minutes. Also there were 8 timings, not included in the above figures, that were 17 minutes or more, including a group of 2 people who both took 36 minutes over a pint. (Isolated cases of this kind, both unusually fast and unusually slow, are recorded for every day. The fast ones are usually due to people coming in and swigging down a gill and going out again right away; the slow ones are often accompanied by deep conversation—though there are more slowing down factors than there are factors speeding people up.)

Out of the 173 timings for this day, 98 were times for groups of two or more, and 75 were of single drinkers. Tabulating this difference in the speed of single and group drinking for the other days of the week for which we have enough single figures for a basis of comparison, we find that there is a definite tendency for group drinking to be faster than solitary drinking.

AVERAGE DRINK SPEED (minutes)

Day	Groups	Individuals
Tuesday	13·1	15·1
Wednesday	11·0	13·6
Thursday	10·7	10·7
Friday	6·7	9·5
Sunday	9·2	10·4

What are the implications of this? That the social and the alcoholic motives of pub going, instead of being mutually exclusive, actually reinforce one another? The man who goes to the pub by himself and drinks alone would seem to be actuated by alcoholic motives entirely, and the man who drinks with others must to some extent be participating in a social environment. Yet the solitary drinkers drink more slowly. We shall see again and again that these two motives for pub-going cannot be isolated, and are mutually dependent. People don't go to pubs to drink, or for company—they go for both of these reasons.

Other tendencies are shown by the analysis of the 443 control times. The deviations from the day's average shown by the figures for each separate pub are interesting.

	Lounges		Vaults	
	8.30	9.30	9	10
Monday	nil	+ 2·3	— 1·1	— 3·1
Tuesday	+ 2·9	+ 2·7	— 1·8	— ·9
Wednesday	— 1·5	+ 1·9	+ ·2	— 1·7
Thursday	+ 2·3	+ 1·0	— 1·0	— 3·4
Friday	— 1·5	— ·2	+ 2·3	— ·1
Saturday	— ·2	+ 1·4	— 2·9	— 2·7
Sunday	— ·3	— ·6	+ ·7	+ 1·5
Average deviation	+ 0·24	+ 1·21	— 0·51	— 1·49

There is a general tendency for the times in lounges to be slower than those in vaults, and for this difference to be more strongly marked in the last hour.

The comparatively small number of daily timings upon which we have based these analyses do not warrant major conclusions being drawn from them; though the day-to-day variations of

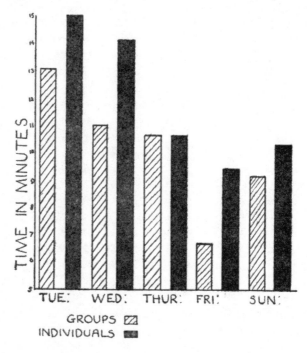

COMPARISON OF DRINK TIMES: PEOPLE DRINKING BY THEM-
SELVES AND WITH GROUPS

the general averages accord so well with all our other data of the pub weekly cycle, that of the validity of the *trend* of their curve there can be no doubt. Criticism of the figures can be made on the grounds that the majority of them refer to town centre pubs. It must be remembered, in reviewing these results, that, in the most favourable circumstances, it takes two or preferably three trained observers, one watching, one timing, and one writing down and checking, to secure 40 or 50 timings a night. It is, of course, essential that no one in the room notices or suspects these activities.

SPEED AND PRESSURE

We have already referred to the immediate economic factors that are reflected in the day to day variation in the number of drinkers. Similar factors can apply to the time variation. The greatest difference between the two variations is found on Thursday. The number of drinkers on that day is low. While the times, both on the general figure and on the small control average, are appreciably faster than those of the previous days, the Friday increase not so sharp. If both the number of drinkers and their rate of drinking are dependent on spending power this discrepancy is easily explicable. Some of those drinking on that day will have got credit and can therefore afford to drink quickly, while others will be eking out their last pence before pay-night, and therefore drinking slowly. Analysis of the average figure of 10·7 minutes shows nearly 50 per cent of the figures are under 8 minutes (week-end time) and nearly 25 per cent of them are between 13 and 21 minutes.

The drinker is hardly likely to order his gill, look at the clock, remember it is Monday, and so decide to drink his beer in 13 minutes instead of the 10 minutes he had taken the night before. But if we assume that the rate of drinking, as well as the habit of level drinking, are not dependent upon *directly* conscious factors, and are inter-related, then the dependency of the rate upon spending power and upon the correlated number of persons present is a satisfactory explanation.

We have already pointed out that we are not at all suggesting that economics are the sole or even major efficient cause for *any* drinking behaviour, but that in many instances they are a direct cause or influence. If you don't get paid on Friday night you may not be able to have a Saturday night drink, but it won't prevent you wanting one. And, as we have pointed out, though week-end drinking is economically dependent upon Friday pay-night, it is also an essential part of the whole rhythm of the working life of this culture, taking the place of the socially sanctioned "breakdowns" of tabus and restrictions that are a part of the life of communities whose work-life rhythms are based on seasons instead of machines.

The increased drink-speed is connected directly with the number of persons in the pub. In general, the more people, the faster the gill is drunk. There is a constantly heightened atmosphere as the numbers increase according to the night of the week. Carbon dioxide, beer smell, speed of service, number of words and faces, music, all climax at the week-end, and influence every one person. In the smaller vault drinking is faster than in the lounge where people cannot crowd so much because seated; the group drinks faster than the single individual. With more money to spend, too, people drink faster in the last hour rather than come earlier and drink like Tuesday. So that not only is more drunk at week-end, but it is also drunk faster, and thus with more "effect". The effect is on sobriety, and we shall see the same sort of social pressure on speed and reaction when, in the next chapter, we get sozzled.

To return to drink times. A local drinker's remark is important and usual. He said: "I can't make a gill last for more than a quarter of an hour. If I've only got enough money for four gills I spend an hour and then go away." This applies to when he is drinking by himself. No one ever sits without a drink. When he is with a group he will have to adapt his pace to theirs. If they come in the pub an hour before closing time with enough money for eight gills, then he will be spent up in half the time. Because the ritual of group drinking means in effect that the man whose turn it is to pay is setting the pace for the group.

DRINKING RITUAL

In a drinking group each man in turn buys a round of drinks for the whole group. So as not to create the situation in which the others are waiting for him to finish before he buys them their drinks, he tends to set the pace for the drinking, in order to drain his glass a little ahead of anyone else. The others, at the same time, are tending to drink level with him. Therefore the speed as well as the amount drunk in the group is influenced by its financial situation. A constant mental inhibition of curious sort is involved.

We must now examine the ritual of group drinking in detail. We call it a ritual rather than a habit because of the strong social compulsion for its observance, the stigma attached to those who do not carry it out, and the resentment expressed by anyone accused of doing so. It is the one invariable pattern of drinking behaviour, and one whose non-observance is never condoned.

A barman writes this of it:

> Treating. Firmly established custom. Sign of friendship. Give a drink but refuse food to an unfortunate friend. Convenience to waiters, and turns to pay are carefully watched. Missing your turn would cause social stigma, anyone so behaving would be called mean, a sponger, etc. People remember who pay, and expect to pay next even if weeks elapse before their next meeting.

Here is the reaction of a man accused of not standing his round:

> Best room. Crowded. Two Irish labourers, one tells the other it's time he stood him some beer, then goes out to urinal. The other sits muttering. "I never passed up on standing my beer yet. . . . Money—suffering Christ—I've handled more of it than any of you. . . . Money—don't talk to me about money. . . ."

Sometimes the rule is relaxed, like this:

> One man in the vault, aged about 42 appeared well under the influence of beer and had about ¾ of a pint in front of him. A friend of his entered and bought a pint of Crown for himself and a pint of best for the drunk. The drunk says "Tha shouldn't 'a done that, mon. I've only just gotten a bloody pint". Friend says "Well, I'll get it made into two gills", and does so. . . . I had the drunk under observation all the time until 7.30 p.m. but he did not pay for friend.

This can hardly be called a breach of the ritual. He was drunk anyway, and didn't want the drink, and his friend was in-the-money (the pint of Crown Ale shows that). Here is an example of it actually being broken, (continuation of same report):

> . . . group of three men drinking pale ale, had three rounds in the hour, one paid only once, and there was a tightening up of the other two towards him.

This is uncommon, but it does happen now and then. The interesting thing is that nothing is *said* about it. In gossip or anger one man may accuse another of not paying his turn, but it is an accusation that is seldom substantiated. The consequences of proving such a thing are too drastic, and would bring about an intolerable situation:

A drunk, labourer, in working clothes, whispers to another labourer, keeps getting up, going to the door, and coming back. Eventually he goes. A discussion on him develops. Chap to whom he has been whispering says "He's no bloody good", but another man defends him. They argue about whether he pays his shot when drinking, but make no definite accusations. One man says to observer, after telling him how he didn't like to go into pubs when he was hard up or out of work, "You can't get drunk when a chap's paying for you, no matter how much you drink."

This is ascribing magical power to the ritual observance.

Indeed, this ritual is of fundamental importance in the life of a pub. A barman, who has supplied us with a lot of information, was asked to write what he knew about people who did not stand their rounds. He wrote:

A group will come in each look at the other for a second or so. The most tender skinned will then say "What are you having?" If they honour the custom one of the others will finish his beer before the others, carefully watching each stage towards the emptiness of the glasses. Says "Are you having another?" then he calls the waiter, and this process goes on until the round has been completed. The type of person who tries to dodge is referred to as the one who gets his hand fast. He will dive into his pocket just as someone else is paying, and says "I'll pay this time!" The hand stays there a bit for all to see, and then is withdrawn. He is generally the one who pays last in the hope that one and all will say: "No, I've had enough." Drink makes some men free with their money, asking all to have a drink irrespective of turns. This type is very popular with the slow motion people, who will stick to the man who is free with his money and flatter him (he likes it) until his money is done. Then they fade away. Then there is the man who hates treating, but accepts a treat without protest. His actions are, he will drink up quickly and pretend he is in a hurry, or hardly touch his drink until the other has grown tired of waiting and ordered another himself. P.C. Thirsty will pay for his own only, but accept it from others.

The gambler will treat round when he has won on a horse, especially if he is usually one who has least to spend, and he is expected to do this by his associates.

Men who have won on a horse, or "come up" on Football Pools, treating all round, account for a number of free drinks that have been stood to observers who are complete strangers in the pubs. The first time it happened an observer was handed a glass of mild by a man who had bought them for everyone in the vault, and who then went out. The observer asked who he was, and was simply told "It's Jimmy, 'e's a good chap".[1]

Standing rounds is a form of social compulsion of great advantage to the brewers. It makes people drink more, and even spend what they can't afford. The following example, which was also written by a barman, shows this:

> Three men drinking in vault, Sunday noon. Each paying for their own. Time, soon after opening. A fourth man enters, orders a pint, which he drinks down to halfway, then says to barman—"Fill us four gills." Talk is then resumed, then, after an interval another man of the group orders four gills. There are two left now who have not paid round, and of these one is unemployed, and the other has been off work sometime. The unemployed man orders round number three. These having been served the man who has been off work rushes off home, leaving half his drink as a sign that he is coming back. He is gone about five minutes, then *comes* back, drinks up, and orders four gills. This completes the round. He told me afterwards that he didn't want to join in treating, as he hadn't enough money, so he had to go home for money. He couldn't get out of it, he said.

The effect of making people drink more than they mean or want is particularly noticeable among large groups of youthful drinkers on Saturday nights. When a group of say, seven, has assembled, it means that each must buy and receive at least seven drinks. It is young men like these who are most self-conscious about pub etiquette. This has two kinds of result.

---

[1] It must also be pointed out that chaps who have won a lot have been seen drinking and not standing anyone anything. Cf. the "pint 'ole oracle" on p. 150. He didn't stand anyone a drink.

We have observed, as time goes on, youths ordering or receiving another round before their glass was emptied, and then ignoring the old glass (as if it belonged to someone else) and starting on the new. And, as we have shown, the one whose turn it is to pay may drink up ahead of the others. So a young and inexperienced drinker who is anxious to seem a regular pub-goer, will try to finish his glass well ahead of the others, who immediately drink up to try and keep pace with him. And the landlord gets a new watch-chain!

Examples of this are shown in excerpts from a report of an evening in a pub where young people drink:

> . . . Five young men come in together at 9.42, and drink with abandon, ordering ahead of their requirements. . . . First round first man finishes in 2 minutes, the next round he takes 5 minutes and another man finishes in 4½ minutes (later) . . . the ringleader of the group shouts out "You bet I can sup that bugger!" and goes out leaving his glass a quarter full. When the group finally go, there are one and a quarter gills left on the table.

Knocking a man's drink over puts you in the position of owing him a drink, even if his glass was nearly empty. An observer once saw this happen to a hawker who goes round the pubs with a basket of hot pies; he knocked some chap's almost empty glass off the table while he was handing him a pie. He took the money for the pie (2d.) and immediately went and bought another drink without anything having been said about it by either of them.

Games are played for rounds of drinks, and in this case the rule of paying in turn does not apply. But complicated situations can arise. A man can come in with a group of friends, drink with them awhile, then leave them to join a four of dominoes. But he is still "in" the round of his original group. If he has paid his turn already and he wins the game as well, then he's lucky, and he drinks twice as much as anyone else without paying for it. On the other hand he may lose his game and find himself having to buy a round for his original group as well.

ORIGIN OF ROUND STANDING

An anonymous pamphlet, published in 1617, called *Young England's Bane*, contains a remark that applies to this:

Truly I think hereupon comes the name of *good* fellow, quasi *goad* fellow, because he forces and goads his fellows foward to be drunke with his persuasive terms, as I dranke to you, pry pledge me, you dishonour me, you disgrace me and with such like words, doth urge his consorts foward to be drunke. . . .

Today's *good fellow* is the man who drinks up quickly and pays for a fresh round, urging his consorts to be gay this way. In Worktown now the toast, the pledge, and the health, are customs not often adhered to. But at one time drinkers always pledged or toasted somebody, and everyone had to drink round then; if you pledged one of your drinking group, he had to pledge you back. It is very probable that the present ritual of standing rounds arose from this; and in any case, it worked out in exactly the same way. The Puritans tried to put it down. One William Prynne, who wrote a pamphlet against it in 1628, called *Healthes Sicknesses*, quoted Alexander ab Alexandro, Polydore Virgil, St. Basil, Atheneaus, Amphyction, Philo Judaeus, and a number of early Fathers of the Church, such as an Augustine, Jerome, Basil, Ambrose, etc., to show this drinking of Healthes one to another in a certain method, order, course, measure, and number, was a common practise, custome, and ceremonie of Gentiles and Paganes who knew not God . . . and he proves to his satisfaction that the custom came from Pagan rites. The custom has indeed an ancient and complicated history, and it almost certainly originated from religious and magical practice, pouring libations to the gods. The Iliad records "but noble Odysseus . . . filled a cup with wine and pledged Achilles; Hail O Achilles". Besides Prynne other contemporary pamphleteers (see bibliography) wrote against the custom, all using as their main argument, not that it made people drink too much, but that it was a sacrilegious and pagan custom.

Besides pledging each other and their mistresses, seventeenth century drinkers pledged public figures and the King. Charles II went so far as to issue a royal proclamation in which he remarked:

There are likewise another sort of man of whom we have heard much, and are sufficiently ashamed, who spend their time in Taverns, Tippling-houses, and Debauches, giving no other evidence of their affection for us, but in drinking our Health.

And considerably earlier, Pope Innocent III in a decree against the drunkenness of the clergy, says:

> For which purpose we decree that that abuse shall be utterly abolished, whereby in divers quarters drinkers do use after their manner to bind one another to drink equally, and he is most applauded who makes most people drunk and quaffs most carouses.

And the Council of Cologne in 1536 made another decree, specifically against the drinking of Healths.

Today in Worktown toasting and pledging is not what it was. Toasts are still given on banquets and ceremonial occasions, but —on for instance the Burns' night dinner (January 25th) 75 people were asked to toast one thing and another, and between them in the course of the evening they drank—8 bottles of lemonade, 6½ bottles of white wine, 4½ pints of beer, 3 small whiskies, 2 sherries, 2 ports, and a bottle of ginger ale. R. Burns might turn in his grave, but the Council of Cologne has been vindicated.

In the Buff's lodge evenings (p. 275) toasts are also used. The first drink has to be accompanied by the remark "The King, The Order, and this Lodge in particular". Also it is a rule that a toast to "absent friends" accompanied by a dreary hymn song, as in many Church services, should always be drunk during the evening.

HEALTH

We have said that the present custom of standing rounds very probably arose from drinking healths; and it appears to serve the same function in contemporary drinking society as did pledging and toasting. None the less, the drinking of healths is not altogether dead yet, although it is not enforced by the strong social sanctions that make the non-observance of standing rounds a serious matter.

The usual formula is for the drinker to raise his glass towards the man who has bought the round, and say "Good Health". Sometimes this becomes a perfunctory gesture of lifting the glass in front of the mouth a moment before the first sip; and sometimes the gesture is omitted, and the words alone used. Among younger people and a number of women the expressions "cheero" and "cheerio" are often used. Facetious healths are given too, such as stereotyped jokes like "down with the drink" —(A landlord's toast overheard (January) was "Beer is best and bugger the Band of Hope")—and the pub wit may evolve his own versions, like this:

. . . Small man with corduroy trousers, faded old dungaree jacket, old gym shoes, pops in, ducks down behind the bar, and suddenly sticks his head up and pretends to the landlord that he has been there for a long time. He is a regular, working on night shift at the factory opposite. He has a gill quickly and says he must be getting back. Before his first sip he holds up the glass and says "Good Health—hope t'queen never gets t'measles."

A fine point of etiquette in regard to drinking healths is shown by the following:

Stranger comes in. Pays for gills round (5). Man who is drinking pints drinks stranger's health from the gill glass and pours remainder into pint mug.

It is a common practice for men to start off by drinking a pint, and then for the rest of the evening getting gills which they pour into the pint mug, usually before it is emptied. But, in this case, if the man who had been treated had drunk the treater's health from his own mug, he would have been doing it with a mixture of his own beer and the stranger's; the gesture was made with a gill glass *before* he had emptied it into his mug.

"PINTERS"

This brings us to the question of "pinters"—men who drink pints instead of gills. According to Nicholson (London Survey) men drink pints because it is something to grip on to. He quotes these words being used to him by drinkers. Also he says, it makes the beer last longer. This again, he bases on what pub-goers have told him.

Our Worktown timings show conclusively that the time taken, per pint, is practically the same whether it is drunk in pints or gills. Observers have reported men drinking pints with a group of gill drinkers, and finishing off their mugs the same moment that the others are draining their second gills. To confirm this, the same observers timed 48 beer-drinkers in London pubs (December); result:

Pints 17·5 minutes average speed.
Halfs 8·6 minutes average speed.

In this small series, pints actually averaged more than twice as long as half-pints.

The fact that the mug "is something to grip on to" has to do with pint drinking. The landlord of a beerhouse who has recently installed gill *mugs* tells us that they are very popular. On the other hand, many pubs do not provide mugs with handles, and serve pints in large plain glasses. The actual size of the glass must also be taken into account in this respect. The habit of drinking gills from pint glasses may be due to this.

Nicholson also says that the majority of London pinters are old men. Our observations bear this out for Worktown too. One of the reasons for this may be purely historical. Before the war, when beer cost a great deal less than now, most working class drinking was done in pints. A factor for changing this may have been the increased price. (We say "may have been", because, although a reasonable suggestion, we have no proof of it, and other factors are involved.) But men who have been used to drinking pints for years have formed a habit pattern which is hard to break, so whenever possible they continue it. Besides old men, the other common classes of pinters are labourers, and people who do heavy manual work, especially foundry workers. In the forge people bring in bottles and drink them off.

A barman writes:

> Pints—depends on how much one can swallow at a gulp. This is entirely a matter of natural growth, and when one has attained the degree of a pinter, a half pint seems insignificant, and you are well steeped in the drinking habit. Seems a matter of choice and habit and maybe length of thirst and pocket.

He is wrong—as those who best know so often are. We see here that the *size* of the pint glass gives the feeling that the men who drink from them must be drinking faster and more than those who drink gills. Connected with this is the fact that the labourer and the outdoor worker who are usually pinters, do very often drink more than other pub-goers, owing to the nature of their work, which makes them thirsty. Hence the feeling that there is something "manly" about pint drinking, and inversely, that it is "unrefined". The landlords of some pubs refuse to serve pints in the parlour. Women do not drink pints—the story of a woman who used to do so bears out these points: it is a discussion in the parlour of a small beerhouse, among a number of women, some of whom are drunk.

> Discussion about a lesbian woman. They concentrate *like hell* to try and remember her name. After four minutes'

working on it and puzzling, one remembers it, and there is joy all round, and the name is reiterated again and again. The following remarks were made about her:

"She be dead and buried now."
"The worst thing about her is neither woman or man."
"'er and Emily lived together."
"She was rather on the vulgar side."
"She was very dirty spoke though."
"She'd stand up at fire." (This mentioned twice.)
"She'd rather have a pint than a gill."

Undoubtedly, the pint mug is associated with labourers, men drinking in dirty working clothes, and old chaps who spit a lot and smoke cheap twist. The association between pints, spitting and strong tobacco is dealt with below. In the lounge of the town-centre pubs, pints are a rarity; while in most vaults they are normal. In the pubs in the "Irish" district, mentioned earlier, to ask for a gill in the vault is to become conspicuous. The first time an observer ordered one, the barmaid repeated "a pint", and there was some difficulty in getting across the idea that a gill was required. A man with a trilby, standing next to the observer, who didn't seem to belong to the pub (he wasn't talking to any of the other chaps) turned and said to the observer in a low voice—"Most of these navvies they come in 'ere and order a pint, you see. . . ."

SWIGGLING

Several observers have, quite independently, remarked that in pubs people are never really still, they are always fiddling with something, tapping their feet, etc. . . . And detailed observations on what is done with a glass of beer while it is being drunk, show that most drinkers fiddle with it, often in a rhythmical way. Some people have a habit of what may be called "swiggling" their glasses, which consists in moving them round and round in circles, either on the bar counter or table top, or in the air. As far as our observations go, these movements are not made by any special types of pub-goer, nor are any section of drinkers more prone to them than others.

The movement of the glass in the air is usually done when it is nearly empty, so that the beer eddies round and round. The wetness of the bar counter or table top, which makes it easy to slide the glass on it, is a contributory factor. People have been observed to move their glasses over from a dry to a wet place on the counter before they begin swiggling. And it is done more frequently on the bar counter, which is usually wet, or has wet places on it, than on the tables, which do not so often have beer spilt on them. The swiggling varies from a definite circling movement, with a radius up to approximately six inches, (either clockwise or anti-clockwise) to a mere irregular pushing about of the glass.

Some may wish to interpret this on the lines of ritual survival, and connect it up with the clockwise port-passing ritual that survives amongst better-off circles. It is certainly pleasant to imagine that the configurations of the idle movements of a sidepiecer toying with his glass are related to the important magic of his remote ancestors who knew that if they neglected their clockwise rituals the sun would stop going round. But it must be remembered that most of the time a man is in possession of his glass he isn't actually drinking from it, and the movements he makes with it are analagous to the cigarette fiddling and tapping indulged in by smokers.

TALKING

The social activity common to almost all drinkers, while drinking, and when drunk, is talking.

What is pub talk about?

Writes a barman:

> Conversation. Typical—what's in the news, sensational, sport main topic among men. Work and past events, good old days reminiscencing. Among women their troubles, especially Marital, but of course children, mainly pride in their own Kith and Kin, gossip, scandal, in fact nothing dissimilar to what women talk about in any other place where two or three are gathered together.

During the course of our observations in May and June, one observer took ten minute sample counts of the subjects of conversations in all the pubs that he visited. Only definite *conversations* on the subjects were counted, not isolated references; at least three consecutive statements on a subject were necessary before the subject was counted as a "conversation".

Of 157 conversations that were classified under our ten heads the relative proportions were as follows:

Pubs and Drinking	18 per cent	
Betting	16 ,,	,,

Personal-topographical	15	per cent
Sport (not betting)	13	,, ,,
Jobs	12	,, ,,
Money	9	,, ,,
Politics	8	,, ,,
Weather	6	,, ,,
Films	2	,, ,,
War	1	,, ,,

These categories can be simplified or recombined. For instance:

Sport and Betting	29	per cent
Jobs and Money	21	,, ,,

Money might also be included with betting. The personal topo-graphical heading requires some explanation. Under this are included all kinds of personal gossip and reminiscencing—discussions that often develop from or into topographical arguments and discussion.

A similar count made by B. D. Nicholson, and quoted in the London Survey, shows the following results:

Sport	37	per cent
Personal gossip	18	,, ,,
Money	13	,, ,,
Hobbies	12	,, ,,
"Shop"	11	,, ,,

The remaining 9 per cent on Politics, Topography, or Religion. The absence of pubs and drinking as one of his categories is curious, in view of our results—indeed his categories are arbitrary, middle-class. However, the important thing that emerges from our figures, is that over 40 per cent of the conversations were about sport or money (including jobs and betting under those heads).

Here is a more detailed account, written by the barmen, of the topics of conversation in a vault one evening (July 6):

Power of earth as source of life—Indestructability of matter—Transfer of a player from the Town team—Food and its adulteration as a cause of national decadence—Power of Dictators, comparisons with Britain—England as a self-sufficing nation—Privileges of the land-owning classes—Allotments, and regulations concerning same—economics of market gardening—Neither pub or pawnshop in Bradford's

part of Great Lever, ground landlords objection, or not?—
Model pub now in Green Lane.

A verbatim record of the conversational "flow" in the same
vault, made by an observer, shows this shift of subject:

> Eh lad, tha gets bonnier every time I look on thee
> through that window—shut t'door now we're all in—wor'st
> reckon off that boxer, didn't see it in this morning's paper, he's
> boun to marry a heiress as soon as they'n gettten' a divorce—
> he'll not be able to box when he's getten her—Schmelling 'as
> to box Louis now—doesn't it show what they're after. We're
> bloody fools for bothering about um—t'Arsenal are a good team
> —Aye they get beaten when they play bad—Bassets bin wi'
> um a long time though—Look 'ere, they got 'im at t'same
> time as t'Wanderers got Taylor, because he should 'a come
> 'ere, Basset, but Worktown thowt he were too little, so they
> let him go, Dick Lyn sent him here—Aye, that's awreet,
> but Taylor's bin wi' Worktown a good while, 'e's 'ad a benefit.
> Arty going to Blackpool on Monday? Aye Ah'm taking t'chilt
> and mother, well, there's a few on us—Oh aye—I might see
> thee there then—Keep away from t'women—Aye, ah will that,
> Ah've getten to that age when Ah can turn me back on um.

Typical small pub parlour talk is different. Out of 13 conversations recorded one night, six were about business (these
were the longest), two about people, including their ages, one
about a bitch who had lost three pups, one about a bus route,
one about bowls and a pub, and one about marriage.

One group (two bowlers and a trilby) in a lobby bar, overheard
from 9.30 to closing time, talked about—horses,—football,—
a booze up last night,—five quid,—a telephone appointment
for tomorrow.

Taproom conversation tends to be more consistent and stick
to the same subject for long periods. Everyone in the taproom
sits, and there are seldom strangers (except interloping observers):

> 9.15, Seven men have ten minutes free-for-all conver-
> sation on the nobility of dogs; then they start to discuss
> all-in wrestling, and the conversation continues steadily, both
> generalizations and personalities, and was still going on when
> the observer left at 9.45, a tough bulldog faced chap repeating
> for at least the tenth time: "It's awreet for them as likes it,
> but I wouldn't let any lad of mine go," as observer walked out.

Talk about animals is common. But we have only once heard tortoises discussed:

Best room, Three women, Seven men, all regulars. At one table a group of three men and one woman. One of the men is large, tough looking, puts his head between his hands and complains of being tired, talks about trade being bad (he is a salesman at the market) suddenly produces a small live tortoise from his overcoat pocket and threatens the woman with it. She screams a little.

"What do you feed it on?" someone asks.

"Milk."

"How much?"

A thin man in a bowler, who is at another table, leans forward and says quickly "A quart and a half."

The owner says "I give it a saucer full on Sunday."

The woman asks how old it is. "Only thirty-six," he replies.

They have long conversation about how you can't drown tortoises, or suffocate them; the only way to kill them is to cut off their heads. "But you can't get at their heads."

Throughout this book samples of most kinds of pub talk are quoted. Political conversations are, as the figures of our sample show, comparatively rare. Political and philosophical arguments that take place are highly personal; as described by a regular:

I first entered the V. Hotel at 7 p.m. Four men were in the vault, F., R., Frank, and S. S. who was in an intoxicated state was talking about R. Owen's Ragged Philanthropist, and was trying to give us the impression that he was a follower of R. Owen. I soon drew a different conclusion about him because he got 6d. out of me for a drink, and his car fare home, and even then he wanted me to carry on as paymaster. He said "I'm a working lad and I could do with more food and clothes". When I asked him how much he spent on drink, he replied, "about 15s. a week" he also said, "I reckon to be skint on Monday". The conversation went on about Darwin's origin of species, and F. said to S. "tha doesn't favour a monkey, but tha acts like one." R. said "I think he's bloody crackers". S. went on to say their house was full of books, so F. said "Don't you think it's about time you started reading them". Eventually between them they got S. that tied up in argument he had to retire, and shook hands with us all and went home. R. went home for tea at 9.15 p.m. he had steak and onions and returned at 9.35 p.m.

Since we are not trying to make a survey of the whole field of what people talk about, but are only concerned with pub conversation, talk is mainly significant if there are any specific differences between pub talk and talk in other public places.

We have a basis for this comparison in a survey of conversational topics made during a year, in Streets, Tramcars, Dance Halls, the Labour Exchange, All-in-Wrestling Stadium, Public Urinals, and Pubs. The method of this survey was not the same as that of our sample count, as it was based on a count of conversational references instead of whole conversations. A detailed analysis of these results, the many variables involved, of the method used, and of the types of category, will be found in a later book of this series, which will also show variations due to time, place, sex of speaking, day of week, seasons, places (counts for Worktown, Oxford, Blackpool, and London). The following is a table of 28 categories, comparing the percentage of their total frequencies to that of their pub frequencies. The present percentage figures are based on about 4,000 references: Streets 1,607, Pubs 642, Trams 332, Urinals 168, etc.

Category	Per cent of total references	Per cent of pub references
Man friend	9·7	11·2
Whistling	9·0	3·8
Laughter	8·7	13·3
Place	7·5	8·2
Woman friends	7·2	6·6
Greeting	6·3	4·6
Affirmative	5·5	3·4
Enemy	5·4	4·5
Goodbye	4·8	7·0
Question	3·7	3·5
Pleasures	3·5	5·7
Coughing	3·5	2·9
Swearing	3·4	4·0
Time	3·0	4·2
Job	2·5	2·8
Weather	2·5	2·8
Money	2·5	1·4
Clothes	2·1	·6
Sport	1·6	1·7
Negative	1·3	·7
Stranger	1·3	1·0
Food	·9	1·2
Holidays, sun	·9	1·5
Health	·83	·15
Children	·67	·31
Sniffing	·54	1·09
News, politics	·23	·77
Bigshot	·07	nil

The only one of these categories that may require explaining is that of "bigshot" which refers to public figures like Hitler, Farr and the Archbishop of York.

Two most outstanding pub deviations from the general figures are found in whistling, of which there is far less in a pub, and laughter, of which there is a great deal more in a pub. Also there is more swearing in the pub, and more talk of time, jobs, weather, sport, food, holidays, news, and politics, places, and pleasures. People sniff more and cough less.

The general trend of these differences emphasizes the social nature of the pub and its talk, and shows a tendency towards more references to the pleasure of life than do the local figures. But none the less, we can conclude that, within the strict limitations of these categories, there is no very marked difference between the topics of talk in the pub and those in other public places.

WHEN

Let us now analyse one complete drinking evening in the vault of a beerhouse. We have already referred (p. 38) to the amount drunk in the course of an evening in one pub. Using the same evening's records we will examine the lengths of time spent in the pub by the drinkers (departure not exactly recorded in 4 cases):

Time spent (hours)	$0-\frac{1}{4}$	$\frac{1}{4}-\frac{1}{2}$	$\frac{1}{2}-\frac{3}{4}$	$\frac{3}{4}-1$	$1-1\frac{1}{4}$	$1\frac{1}{4}-1\frac{1}{2}$	$1\frac{1}{2}-1\frac{3}{4}$	$1\frac{3}{4}-2$	above 2 hrs.
Number of drinkers	—	5	8	3	2	4	2	0	0

That is, nearly half the drinkers (13 out of 28) spent more than a quarter but less than three-quarters of an hour drinking. Now let's take the times they came into the pub.

Time of arrival	Before 6 p.m.	7.30–8 p.m.	8–8.30	8.30–9	9–9.30	9.30–10
Number	4	3	3	7	9	2

Here we see that the greatest number came in between 8.30 and 9.30. There were never more than 17 men in at once; this took place during the last 15 minutes. The diagram (p. 193) shows the course of the evening more clearly than the figures themselves. The time scale at the bottom represents the times of arrival;

the vertical time scale shows the length of time spent; and each upright line represents one of the drinkers and the number of gills that he consumed. A first small group come straight from work to the pub. Then there is a space of an hour and a half before many new people arrive. And in the last hour and a half the main company of the evening's drinkers arrive. For convenience of representation the arrivals are grouped equi-distantly in periods of 15 minutes—i.e. all fractions of 15 minutes are disregarded. This does not apply to the vertical scale

Now compare with the next diagram (p. 195), which represents the same pub on the following Saturday evening from 7, to closing time. Here we see a very different picture. Out of the 29 people coming in, 15 enter between 7 and 7.30; while during that period on the week night no one came in. Again, in the last hour and a half on the Saturday there were only 4 new arrivals, contrasting with 18 in the week day. Now, 15 of them went on to other pubs. These are the times spent: the second column shows the number of those who stayed in the pub and did not go on to drink anywhere else.

Time	$\frac{1}{4}-\frac{1}{2}$	$\frac{1}{2}-\frac{3}{4}$	$\frac{3}{4}-1$	$1-1\frac{1}{4}$	$1\frac{1}{4}-1\frac{1}{2}$	$1\frac{1}{2}-1\frac{3}{4}$	$1\frac{3}{4}-2$	$2-2\frac{1}{4}$	$2\frac{1}{4}-2\frac{1}{2}$	$2\frac{1}{2}-2\frac{3}{4}$	$2\frac{3}{4}-3$
Number	2	5	5	3	2	4	1	1	1	3	2
No. who stayed	—	—	3	1	—	3	1	1	1	2	2

It is only the 14 who did not go on to other pubs who can be compared with the week night figures; 10 of them spent more than an hour and a half in the pub, while on the week night only 2 out of 28 spent longer than an hour and a half. Similarly, the average amount drunk by the week night men was 3·16 pints. Of the 14 comparable figures for Saturday, the average amounts to 4·57 pints—a 40 per cent increase. Of those who went out 13 out of 15 spent less than 1 to 1½ hours.

Summing this up, people come earlier, spend more time, and drink more on the Saturday than in the week day.

We were able to get this data with the help of a regular of this pub, who knew all the other regulars. It isn't possible to make similar diagrams and tables of the drinking in the Town centre pubs—not only because of the impossibility of simultaneously keeping track of a large number of people drinking, but

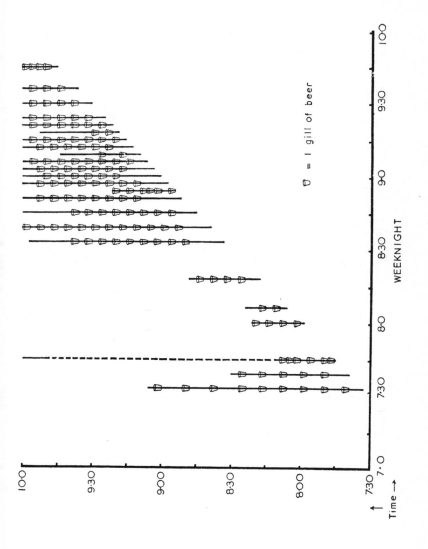

because no one would be in a position to give the same detailed information about the drinkers as can the regular or barman of a small pub.

In the small pub there is a community of drinking. This is shown by the fact that almost invariably the regulars of a small pub arrive singly, while the drinking groups of large town centre pubs tend to arrive together. For instance, out of 64 people counted coming into the lounge of a town centre pub (May) only 3 came out by themselves. There were 15 groups of two, and 6 of 3 or more, including 1 of 9. The regular in his local pub can go there by himself to drink, certain of finding his company there for him; while away from the local, he takes his company along with him to drink.

An evening's observation in a large town centre lounge showed that the majority of people spent less than half an hour there, as the following table shows:

Time	Males	Females	Total
Under $\frac{1}{4}$ hour	14	14	28
,, $\frac{1}{2}$,,	35	16	51
,, $\frac{3}{4}$,,	16	6	22
,, 1 ,,	4	2	6
,, 1$\frac{1}{4}$ hours	2	3	5

No one spent more than an hour and a quarter; 79 people spent less than half an hour, and 33 more than half an hour. This was on a week night. Week-end congestion makes accurate and comparable Saturday night observations really difficult.

The general *opinion* of observers is that week-end drinkers in the town centre pubs also tend to spend more time there than do the week-night drinkers, though this is complicated by the fact that many week-end drinkers visit several town centre pubs during one evening.

TIME

Up to now we have spoken as if the pub shuts up sharp at 10 p.m., the official closing time. This rule is not strictly adhered to. While in London pubs "Time" is often called ten minutes before the closing hour, and the landlord tries to get the pub actually shut at the official closing time, in Worktown the theory is, there should be no more orders taken after 10 p.m. This is demonstrated by the notice in some pubs:

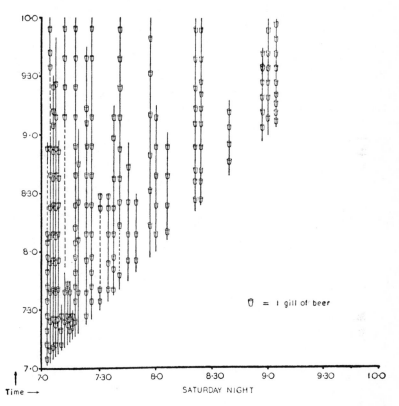

WEEK-END IN BEERHOUSE VAULT, SHOWING TIMES OF ARRIVAL,
DEPARTURE, LENGTH OF STAY, AND AMOUNT DRUNK BY ALL
CUSTOMERS (CF. P. 193)

NOTICE. Will you kindly help us by ordering your BOTTLED BEERS, etc., for taking out before "TIME" is called, as we must refuse all orders after PERMITTED HOURS. THANK YOU!

In the town centre pubs this is kept to usually, but people go on drinking five or ten minutes after the hour. And in Worktown the pub clocks are not put forward ten minutes as they frequently are in other towns. In the smaller local pubs it is normal for drinks to be served up to ten minutes after the hour, time being called then, and people sit about after the glasses have been cleared, sometimes up to half past ten. Drinkers tell us that in many small pubs the regulars are able to knock on the back door and get served as late as eleven. This is not easy to verify; and indeed, the presence of a stranger in the pub at closing time may be a factor in making the landlord brisker than usual about turning people out. Some pubs, however, make a habit of quite openly serving drink until fifteen minutes after the hour.

A report, which shows how it is possible to get drinks served after the pub has shut, if you know how to set about it:

Observer went with Councillor —— and —— an ex-Councillor, to the —— at 10.20 p.m. The ex-Councillor knocked with a key on the glass door—a special knock. We went in and stopped there until 11 p.m.

That this is not necessarily confined to small pubs is shown by the following remark overheard in a big pub:

Time is called at 10.10 p.m. Woman says "It's ridiculous really, Saturday night you can go on until eleven". The waiter agrees.

The biggest and most open infringements of the legal hours that we have observed took place during the Trinity Sunday Roman Catholic processions. Here are excerpts from reports on this:

At 2.45 p.m. we go into pub, ask for drinks. Publican laughs, and says "Do you know what time we close on Sunday?" We say no. He says "2 o'clock," and adds "do we bloody 'ell, I'm going to make sun while the hay shines. And I'll tell you another thing. I'm not closing down for a while yet. It's the first time it's been two o'clock closing and the scholars walking at 2.30. It's a bloody shame!" (Used to be Sunday closing at 2.30. He assumes that everyone should

have plenty to drink before walking in the procession.) A
man comes in and says "I'll be out and have my lunch and
be back again." . . . There are lemonade tables in the less
crowded bye-streets. Ice-cream cars and carts in every side
street. The G. is all shut up, several St. John's Ambulance
men in uniform standing at side door. Nevertheless there's a
steady and noticeable stream towards the pub. Many are going
into or towards men's and women's lavatories, but most are
crushing towards the passage into the pub.

Man 1. "Make way there."

Man 2. "Why?"

Man 1. "It's bloody full up, that's why!"

Man 3. "You can't stir in there!"

Man 4. "It was open to bloody near opening time last
year!" Most of the pushers are R.C.'s from the procession, or
bandsmen. Some miss their places in the procession while
others run after their bands. There are lots of police about.

Large scale open infringement of the law like this must be deliberately ignored by the police.

In the villages outside Worktown late drinking is very common.
An observer reports from a pub in one:

Drink is served until 11 o'clock, people playing dominoes
in front room, with one light on, and constantly going up to the
passage bar for gills. Eight men at once drinking thus at 10.45.
Two are very drunk, and there's lots of noise and good humour.

The actual calling of time is done in a loud voice, and a special
intonation. "Time—Gentlemen—please!" This intonation is
common to almost all bartenders, in other districts as well as
Worktown. The "gentlemen" is sometimes omitted, and sometimes "Time" is simply indicated by "Empty your glasses,
please!" This omission has not been observed in London, where
the closing regulations are most strictly adhered to.

Jokes on postcards sold in Worktown (and in Blackpool) stress
the time element, thus:

Postcard, coloured, showing two rednosed bulbous boozers
leaning against bar-counter, holding up full glasses. Caption:
"What are the vilest words in the dictionary, Bert?" "Dunno!"
"TIME, GENTLEMEN, PLEASE!"

Field research in Worktown and Blackpool have shown us
that vital in human behaviour, story and wish, is the idea of

time. This will be fully dealt with in later volumes, especially that on Blackpool holiday week. Blackpool, whose motto is "Progress", involves many time problems. In the present connection, it is notable that the times of drinking are not based on any logical or mathematical pattern. They centre on short periods, for whose choice there is no direct logical reason, though all kinds of rationalizations are made to explain them.

It is in this field of time that we may expect the earliest "useful" theories of contemporary sociology, predictions comparable to those made in time-physics by Einstein and Planck, who broke up the physical time superstitions which still survive so strongly in sociology and in all inter-human relations. It is in this field of time that we find some of the pub's most interesting phenomena. And generalization, on pub data alone, is tricky. We had for a time a theory that in certain circumstances the closing-time cry was, "Time, Gentlemen, Please" (the only time pub-goers are addressed as Gentlemen); in others "Ten o'clock Gentlemen, please." Until one evening we heard landlord and waiter-on shouting the same side by side in the same pub.

Nevertheless, pub-time is a dominant factor in deciding when people drink, and how much. The *end* of any proscribed period always becomes a complex in Worktown mentality.

Thus two of our full-time observers went to work in local factories to obtain data for our political and industrial studies. Both recorded the same phenomenon, at first very odd to the outsider. Half an hour before the work stops, the workers begin to prepare for its stopping. By 5.10 they have workstuff in locker, outdoor clothes on or ready. By 5.20, everyone is waiting tensed, looking up to one corner of the long workroom, where there is a little electric light bulb. Many look at their watches. Plenty are at the doors. The machines may run (in some rooms, according to nature of the work) but the machinists do not. Then at 5.30 the electric light bulb flashes red, for a second. In that second there is a scamper, a rush, and the whole factory tries to empty itself at one swoop, through inadequate swing doors, down narrow stone stairs, and along slender corridors. (This isn't an "obvious" "wish to be done with work"): nothing like this happens in the morning, when people come in. Then many are early, very early, and the majority are in 10 minutes before work starts. They are almost as much dominated by the idea of being late for coming in, as for getting out.)

Time becomes an obsession with the millworkers; they look ahead to the end of each incident, even in the week's (unpaid) summer holiday. Then they can escape geographically for a little, but not from time. The several painters and poets who have worked with us on angles of Worktown observation find this one especially strange.

The last hour of the night, and the last day of the week, are the drinking peaks. And one aspect of drinking is that it is an attempt to escape from time, to change the rhythm of living, the speed of thinking. Alcohol helps the worker's brain to escape from the speed at which it has to function during worktime. For a short while each week the pubgoer is physically and psychologically emancipated from the restrictions of normal Worktown life.

INDUSTRIAL DRINKING

Writers on drink frequently refer to "industrial drinking". This is defined by Professor Catlin as follows:

> In some cases the worker, either on going to work or at intervals, takes alcohol not only as a drink, but to allay the discomforts of hunger or as a substitute for unappetizing food. . . . Other cases of industrial drinking may depend specifically on the nature of the occupation. In the mechanical work of the hot trades, the need is for large quantities of a palatable and fatigue-dulling liquid. . . .
>
> Again, exceptionally hard or trying work for a man of good physique, or heavy work for a man of poor physique . . . produces a fatigue and depression in which the need for strong liquors is experienced. . . .

We quote from this book because, rather than setting out with the intention of writing an original work Catlin has produced a reference book of Administrative Sociology based on existing authorities, and therefore we can take the above passage as representing a body of opinion amongst writers on this subject. The fact that it makes a number of assumptions as to the cause of this type of drinking, which are largely unsupported by verifiable factual evidence need not be discussed here.

The dominant Worktown feature is cotton mill. In all the older districts there are plenty of pubs in their immediate neighbourhood. In the section on pub names we referred to the pub called The Four Factories, so called because of its situation. This pub is closed now (a Spiritualist Church called the Four

Factories stands nearby) and our evidence shows that many pubs built in the neighbourhood of factories no longer have a special custom from the factory, and are doing very badly. In a small beerhouse beside a mill an observer asked a landlady if she got many customers from it. "Not many," she replied. "A few look in for a drink on the way home."

A report giving a résumé of a long conversation with the landlord of a neighbouring pub quotes him as saying:

> There isn't much in keeping a pub nowadays, you only get good custom at the week-end and in the last hour. The cinemas have taken away a lot of the trade . . . and the men haven't got the money to spend; there aren't any real skilled engineering workers left now, it's all done with apprentices. They don't come in and drink in the dinner hour like they used to! (Not verbatim.)

Another report gives the same picture.

> This is a large pub, it was built to cater for various mills. When they cracked up the pubs custom went; now they have partitioned off half the long vault bar, taken away the bar on the other side, and made a lounge of it, trying to attract a new type of customer. Along with many other of the local pubs this place used to have a great lineup of pints ready drawn when the mill sirens went. The landlord reckoned he used to lose about ten pints in a hundred, the rush was so great. This is all finished now.

Undoubtedly this type of drinking used to exist here; but we have observed few indications of it nowadays. The following report, however, is relevant:

> This pub is in the grounds of a tannery. They own the pub, but Magees run it. There is a back way into the pub from the tannery ground. Plenty of jokes about how a path has been worn across the ground from the works to the pub back entrance. Chaps say people on night work "slip across", also sometimes when on overtime.

This town has passed a peak of engineering prosperity; the population is dwindling. Real wages have fallen, and whereas at one time there were a number of big engineering works, now they are all closed down. Relics of past drinking of this kind linger in nicknames. A pub called the Sunnyside Inn, after the

name of the mills it is next to, is still known locally as the
Klondyke, relic of a boom that our informant, a local inhabitant,
can't remember.

On the other hand, there is industrial drinking resulting from
heavy work. Many midday drinkers are labourers having a pint
with their lunch, and at opening time (5.30) in some pubs
labourers will be found in their working clothes having come
straight off the job.

In *Portrait of a Mining Town*, a kind of journalistic survey
published by an extinct monthly called *Fact*, there is a relevant
reference:

> Steady hard drinking in the public house straight from the
> pit has almost died out—for one thing, very few could afford
> it, and for another there are more civilized amusements these
> days. . . .

The author does not define what he means by "more civilized
amusements" (a phrase which can have little sociological meaning),
but he states that this information was confirmed by visits to
the local pubs. This place is one of those towns very heavily hit
by the various post-war slumps. Industrial drinking of this kind
may be found where there is industrial prosperity. But observation of places where there isn't prosperity shows that it doesn't
exist. Today, heavy drinking is more closely connected with the
speed of race horses than that of industry.

In the *Fact* survey, just quoted, it remarks:

> A considerable number of unemployed people never drink
> at all, and most of the others very occasionally.

Nicholson, in the London Survey says categorically:

> the unemployed regard the public house as closed to them.

Out of the list of 47 *regulars* already given there are 5 unemployed
men; it is a "smart pub" with Neon lights, etc. In this town,
at any rate, the unemployed do not regard the pub as any more
closed to them than anyone else. And to speak of the unemployed
as a separate social group is incorrect. Not only is there a considerable difference between a man "temporarily stopped" and
one whose mill is closed down and has no further prospect of
work for the rest of his life; but a man with a large family who

studies Labour Exchange regulations and rates, may make himself better off out of work than in the mill.

It is an indubitable fact that the more work there is going,
the more people drink, and also that some of the poorest sections
of the population are the heaviest *public house* drinkers. But
explanation of this in terms of industrial drinking is not enough.
The decline of this direct factory-pub relationship may not
necessarily be due to smaller wages. Many authors quote bad
housing conditions as a cause of excessive drinking, and although
today it is possible to find in industrial towns slums that haven't
changed much in the last fifty years, there is no doubt that
housing conditions as a whole have much improved.

The idea that there should be "better housing", closely
associated with Nonconformist, Liberal, and Labour movements,
is the same general idea and trend that has led to less pubs.
The new housing estates in Worktown have ·none at all. On two
there is no pub within a mile. How deeply this affects the social
life of the area will easily be realized, especially when it is added
that there are only two new churches to deal with the new
housing, and no other forms of social centre. It is not our job
in the present volume to describe life on the modern housing
estate. But we may remark that better housing is an idea largely
imposed from above by people who have no direct experience of
working life, and thus little understanding of—though often
much sympathy for—the community values of street, pub and
local feeling. The result of mass transfers of people irrespective of
past habit, ignoring the basic culture units, is at least a two-edged
benefit. It accentuates a potential unsociability and apathy which·is
gradually endangering all our social institutions. The housing estate,
as conceived in Worktown, is another step away from fraternization
and simple democracy. There is no "reason" why it should be—
the conception of the housing estate as such does not demand it.

Another, and a very direct connection between the pub and
industry exists no longer. A hundred years ago it was customary
to pay factory workers *in* pubs on Saturdays, and they would
often be kept hanging around for a couple of hours waiting. In
The English Temperance Movement, by H. Carter, an authoritative and well documented work, reference is made to this
custom specifically as taking place in S.E. Lancs, and the author
suggests that it became quite a racket between the employers
and the landlords—the more the men were kept waiting, the

more they drank. The Rechabites, in 1835, were formed to counteract the habitual meeting of clubs and benefit societies on licensed premises, on the understanding that a sum was spent on drink "for the good of the house".

Incidentally the Centenary History of the Worktown Odd-fellows mentions:

> Action was decided on to prevent the paying of excessive rents by Lodges, this being an attempt to tackle an evil which was at one time rampant in the Friendly Society movement and was known as "wet rent". This custom went back considerably over a century, and originated in the old village benefit clubs whose rules provided that each member should spend a given sum on refreshment "for the good of the house".

THINGS DONE WHILE DRINKING

Accompanying the drinking of beers are many other activities. These can be divided into (a) things done by pub-goers as individuals, such as smoking and spitting while drinking, (b) traditional customs associated with drinking and participated in by the drinkers in a particular pub, and (c) social activities such as talk, music, singing, playing games. This last category, which is very extensive, is discussed in separate chapters. The other two we will go into now.

SMOKING

How many people smoke while drinking? An observer was given the job of counting the number of smokers in all the pubs that he went into during one month, May. As he came into each pub he counted the number of people in the room, and the number with pipe and cigarettes. Out of 590 people:

219 smoked cigarettes	37	per cent
52 smoked pipes	9	,, ,,
319 did not smoke	54	,, ,,

That is, rather more than half the people counted were not smoking. This, of course, does not represent the numbers of all the people counted who are smokers; it shows the proportion who were smoking when the counts were made. Its significance is that it shows that at almost any moment nearly half the people in a pub may be smoking.

The great majority of the smokers had cigarettes. However, this proportion of 4 cigarette smokers to 1 pipe smoker is not constant. Sample counts taken in 3 vaults and 3 best rooms on several days of the first week in June showed:

	Percentage smoking:	
	Pipes	Cigarettes
Vaults	40	60
Best rooms	16	84

We have already noted that there is an association between pints, pipes and spitting. Like pints, pipes are mostly used by older men. And the same classes of drinkers—the older men and labourers—that are pinters also go in for smoking twist tobacco. Local tobacconists said, in reply to observers' questions, that at one time many more people smoked pipes, and that the use of twist was universal. Now it is mostly the older men who buy it. This twist, when smoked, produced plenty of saliva. An observer who began to use it found that it was necessary to spit now and then when smoking, and that the occasional ejaculation into the spittoon was rather pleasurable.

SPITTING

The maximum spitting is found in the pubs in the "Irish" or "Kiphouse" district, and was shown in the report quoted earlier. But while both twist smoking and spitting are mainly restricted to rooms and pubs patronized by a limited section of pub-goers, spittoons are found over a much wider range of rooms and pubs. Writes a barman:

> SPITTOONS. Relic of pipe smoking in pre-cigarette days, for the use of wet smokers, sawdust in them to absorb moisture. Used for waste paper, empty boxes, etc., nowadays.

In fact, today in Worktown the majority of spittoons are not used for spitting into. Their number and usage are indications of the class and status of the drinkers in the pubs. At one end of the social scale we find chaps spitting all over the place, often where there is nothing for them to spit into, while in better class pubs and rooms there are receptacles for spit into which no one does spit. Again in the *best rooms* of the newer "high class" pubs there are no spittoons at all.

In the majority of cases the spittoon functions as a receptacle for ash, fag ends, etc. In our pub-classification we saw how the ratio between seating and spitting capacity varied from room to room in the pub, and also from one class of pub to another. Just as the headgear of drinkers in the best room of the pub gives an indication of the pub's class, so does the spittoon: seating ratio—and in fact they can be correlated. Here is a list, showing the ratio of caps to non-caps and seats to spittoons in the best room of four pubs taken at random (January 24–28):

Pub	Seats per spittoon	Non-cap to Cap	
A	8	1·5	(spittoons dry)
B	5	0·4	(spittoons wet)
C	4	0·6	(spittoons wet)
D	7	1·0	(slightly wet)

Only in A are there more non-caps than caps, and in this case not only is there the smallest number of seats to spittoons but the spittoons themselves showed no signs of having been used. Of course, as the "Drinking Places" chapter showed, there is the widest range of variation in pub-room furniture; with spittoons, the consistent trend is unusually distinct.

In D where the spittoons were only slightly used, there are 7·3 seats to a spittoon and an equal amount of caps and non-caps. In the other two, where caps are in the majority and the spittoons show signs of use, there are comparatively large numbers of them in relation to seating capacity.

Here is a record of one hour's usage in a typical beerhouse vault on a Saturday night (November):

Time	Matches In	Matches Out	Fag ends In	Fag ends Out	Spit In	Spit Out	Number of men present
7.30–45	2	4	—	3	—	3	15
7.45–8	1	6	—	3	1	2	18
8.15–8.30	2	9	1	3	—	4	24
8.30–	1	11	2	6	2	5	32
Totals	6	30	3	15	3	14	
	— 36 —		— 18 —		— 17 —		

18 fag ends to 17 spits is a pretty average Saturday! Observation earlier in the week showed a far lower proportion of salivation than on the Saturday—with 10 men in at the beginning of the

hour and 18 at the end, there was only 1 spit to 4 fag-ends and 9 matches.

The spittoon, which is most commonly of the green china type described earlier, may also be of blue or brown china, cast iron, white enamel (like a dog's dish), and polished copper ones have been observed. The presence of about six of them in a room where they are never used can only be explained on the grounds that they represent the material survivals of a habit that has died out. While the decline of the habits associated with spitting, pipe-smoking, and pint drinking have not left observable material traces, the actual associated objects have persisted, and have partly acquired the symbolic or ritualistic character that, for instance, is inherent in some features of contemporary male clothing, such as the little buttons on the ends of sleeves, which are retained because they have "always been there", and though they serve no direct function yet are "indispensable".

In the zones of maximum salivation—the vaults of beer-houses whose customers are largely labourers and old men—the spittoon itself is not found. Instead there is an area for spitting into. This originally was the whole floor ("the sawdust parlour"). Now in its most primitive form, this area is marked by a line of sawdust, strewn along the base of the bar counter. This area, which we call "the ditch", is often demarcated from the rest of the floor by a strip of lath screwed to the ground. (In vaults that have stone floors this is rare, for reasons of structural difficulty.) We have observed in one pub an interest-ing evolutionary link between the ditch and the spittoon. Here, under the bar, hung on iron brackets and detachable, are two long narrow wooden boxes half full of sawdust, and there is also a smaller one, about two feet long by six inches wide, on the floor near the door. These "spit boxes" present a truly imposing appearance. They are the only ones that we have seen.

Another indication of the transition from the ditch to the spittoon is seen in some vaults where spittoons are present as well as a ditch. This is usually found in vaults with a wide space between the benches and the bar, where it is difficult or in-convenient for sitting drinkers to spit across into the ditch. We can see here, how, with the decline of spitting, the ditch would be the first to go, as it is much more trouble to clean out and refill. Though as a barmaid remarked to a customer one night: "You don't want to come in 'ere when we open, you should come round about six thirty a.m., and clean half a dozen spittoons out."

A few vaults have some kind of tiled or marble flooring, and in these—which are easy to wash down—the ditch is reduced to a minimum, and in some cases done away with altogether:

> There are seven in the vault at 8.45. It is large, with a curved bar. The floor is a sort of dull marble. There are NO SPITTOONS and there is NO sawdust. There are four tables round the walls. Men let saliva drop to the floor directly under their feet.

Spittoons are there to be spat *at*, only incidentally into.

Finally, in connection with spitting, it is very uncommon for *young* people to use spittoons in the best room—i.e., when they are dressed up. The following example is rare. The report describes a group of young men drinking together:

> . . . One, the most drunk, who calls for drink for the others spits nearly into the spittoon under the table, and pleasedly cried "Reet in". Another young man tries, amidst laughter. The first one says "Take it quietly lad, don't rush it". He misses and the first chap does it again, this time hitting the table. He is called a "filthy bugger" and belches in reply. The observer notes: Spitting not previously seen among the young. And adds that when it takes place it is the subject of laughter and notice and backchat.

SNUFF

We have, on several occasions, observed women taking snuff—it is extensively advertised on Worktown hoardings. The first time was in the parlour of a poor type of beerhouse, and both the women wore clogs. The other times it was in a better class of pub. This is what happened:

> Middle-aged woman, dressed in good coat and skirt, fur collar, who is very cheerful and making cracks all the time, produces small tin of snuff and offers it round to four other women in the room. Three, well dressed, refuse it, saying they haven't got handkerchiefs. One, the oldest, who wears clogs and a shawl over her head, takes it. The middle-aged woman says "It stops you having babies" and offers the tin to observer, who accepts a pinch and asks if her remark

applies to him also. She laughs and says "Aye", adding "Eeee, it's lovely, makes your navel perk like a whelk!"

HAWKERS

In many pubs, packets of crisps, nuts and raisins are sold, also pies. But there is not much eating done while drinking; and much of what there is, is supplied by hawkers who go round with hot pies (2*d*.), black puddings, tripe. These hawkers have regular rounds and times of arrival. Usually their relationship with the landlord is friendly:

> . . . the pieman, who does the town centre pubs, comes in. He and the landlord are all pals together, and call each other by their Christian names. A severe thunderstorm now bursts, and several chaps come running into the vault. Landlord offers to lend the pieman an old overcoat. The pieman is very thin, landlord very fat, and there are a lot of jokes about this; the landlord pats his stomach affectionately and says to observer that it has cost him a lot of money.

These piemen don't use salesmanship, they just walk in:

> The local pieman comes in at one door of the vault, walks very slowly through the room, and goes out through the other door, without saying a word. But the barmaid says to a group of regulars "Don't you want a pie?" They don't; anyway the pieman has gone.

However, his life is not always made so easy for him. The one first referred to, who was so friendly with the landlord, used to have a big custom at a pub nearby (the landlord of which, incidentally, is a drinking companion of the other landlord). This pub has recently been redecorated. And now the pieman is no longer allowed in; a great pile of pub pies are displayed on the bar counter, and the waiters walk round with a plate of them now and then during the evening. But the pieman's pies are better quality than the pub ones, and he now stands outside the pub at 9.30, his usual calling time, and sells to the drinkers as they go in.

While on the subject of hawkers, it should be noted that food is not the only article sold by them; one drinker whom we know gets all his contraceptive machinery from a man, who also sells razor blades and "novelties" such as joke cigars, in a few pubs. These cigars are remarkable, brown phallus-like objects, eight inches long, and a little over an inch in diameter, with a glowing tinfoil end; the cigar pulls apart, and inside there is a tube for holding cigarettes. You insert the cigarette, join the cigar up again, and puff at one end. Another novelty is the lavatory in a matchbox ("the smallest receiving set in the world"). We have seen bootlaces being hawked, and once, unsuccessfully, 6*d*. bottles of embrocation. These casual hawkers are sometimes refused admittance:

> An old woman comes in selling shoelaces. Landlady says "Not allowed". Old woman mutters and three times repeats "I'll have to go somewhere else then, where they'll live and let live".

The pie and black-pudding trade flourishes less in the summer months. One pieman whom we know gives up his round then and peddles ice-cream instead—but not in the pubs.

As for getting meals in the pub, this is almost impossible. A few of the town centre pubs that also provide hotel accommodation, serve proper meals in the dining-rooms. And one has a snack bar. An observer who went round several pubs on different days asking for "some lunch" (in contradistinction to "dinner", the main midday meal in Worktown) managed to get in each case after about ten minutes' delay, a couple of sandwiches— and once some pickles with them.

CUSTOMS

At one time there were a number of drinking customs that were trade devices, whereby the landlord provided a free drink on Sunday mornings at one o'clock, free hot-pot or beans and peas, oranges and sweets for the children at Christmas. Of these, which are now prohibited by law, a barman writes:

> These were done through competition rather than desire. If one publican did something fresh, the others followed suit, and I suspect the law restricting their activities was a relief to the publican. . . . He adds: Vault groups of five will ask for "five for a bob" instead of paying 1*s*. 0½*d*. Also landlord expected to "wet a new suit" (treat round).

We have observed one pub where free hot peas are given to regulars on Thursday night (the slackest night of the week) but it is the only case that we have found.

Another custom:

> There was one customer in the pub at this time (out of hours). Being a carter he recalled the good old times when carters were allowed a pint free or half price at all pubs round Worktown, to encourage stabling. And he told of how he himself had often gone out in his working clothes when hard up, and going into a pub would order a pint, and keep rushing to the door and shouting: "Whoa lad," and "Steady lass," etc., though his horse had been at home in the stables for an hour or two, thus letting an imaginary gee get him free drinks.
>
> He also told of a boss who when engaging him told him that he had been very pleased with a carter who had just left, because he was a teetotaller. However, when he took this carter's ex-horse out, it "pulled-in" of its own accord at six different pubs on the way to the next town.

One Worktown pub is famous for its annual celebration of Oak Apple Day (May 29th). This place, referred to earlier on account of its nickname—The Dog and Kennel—is called the Park View Inn. It stands at the edge of a valley, with a fine view of thirty-nine factories.

When the observers arrived they were immediately asked to come and see "Charlie" who was "in the oak". Expecting to see a statue of the late Charles II, they were shown, stuck up on the wall outside the pub and framed with *lime* branches, a possibly Mexican carved wooden painted figure. (Later an expert suggested that it was early Central American Christ.) The figure was sculptured standing in a position that looked exactly as if it was giving the "popular front salute". On its head was a gilt metal crown, evidently a comparatively recent addition. Also added, grafted in, another arm, at right angles —erectly, unmistakably phallic.

Later the figure was put up in the parlour, for the "litany" to be read to it. This had to be done by the oldest inhabitant. He did not turn up. His understudy had left his spectacles at home, so a man nicknamed "the Colonel" had to read it.

When the observers came into the parlour the figure was standing on a round table nearly in the middle of the room, holding in its hand some faded white flowers. Women were sitting all round, drinking and looking. Then one of them got up, stood in front of the figure, raised her arms slowly, and said "God bless you, my brother isn't here to say the litany tonight.

I'll kiss you for him. God bless the king". And she kissed the
figure on its right cheek. (Her brother, who had been the oldest
inhabitant, had recently died.)

It was explained to the observers that you had to be a native
of the place to kiss the figure. In the old times you could become
a native by doing this, but you had to be formally invited,
and then you bought a gallon of beer for the chaps.

The Colonel came in, adjusted his spectacles, and read the
following piece:

Lines written in Commemoration of the Restoration of King
Charles the 2nd on the 29th Day of May, 1660.

O yes, O yes, O yes. It is with pleasure I now behold,
A train of such truehearted Britons bold,
Commemorating in this grand Procession,
King Charles the Second's Happy Restoration.
The lively Genius of Tonge Fold in Trade
Which has for many ages been,
As all the world throughout proclaim,
The first origin of Counterpanes.
It was on this day his birth and restoration,
All was preserved from rumpish Usurpation.
Britannia's Sons let us all due honours pay
In celebrating this auspicious day.
And you young heroes walk in procession grand,
All crowned with oak, each wearing a white wand.
Behave like men and commemorate
The happy restoration of King Charles the Great.
And sing God Save the King.

And he went on, reciting this verbatim off the script, to the
very end:

It was 188 years on the 29th of May last since King Charles
the Second was restored to the Throne of this Realm and
the following lines were written to commemorate the event.

When it was over everyone clapped, stamped on the floor,
and cheered. And a drunk lurched to his feet and began to sing
God Save the King, until told to shut up. As soon as it was
finished everyone sang loudly, a hymn called "All hail to Jesus".
The little room was packed now (18 women and 10 men), and
more people who couldn't get in were standing in the doorway.

When the hymn was over there was a general babble of loud and cheerful talk. The figure was taken into the vault, and put on the table there. People stood round examining it. The landlord said "It 'ud cost above fifty pound for a pup off of 'im". He was going round with a big, white, gallon jug of beer, filling up glasses from it. This was on the house. There was a lot of talk about the figure, and people patted it and called it "Charlie" in an affectionate manner, kissed it, talked of having kids by it.

Then there was a singsong in the parlour, mostly Victorian and sentimental songs; though a different note was struck by a fat, red-faced, cheerful looking middle-aged woman, very respectably dressed, who was asked for a song. She stood up in the middle of the floor and shouted:

> I had a dog called Pompey,
> Pompey he were call,
> And when he went to pee,
> He peed against the Wall.

Red in the face, her hat sliding off, she leaped with extraordinary agility on to a bench, and standing there, sang the song again, even louder, banging time on the floor with a walking stick.

Later, when the observers left, everyone shook hands with them and said it had been "good company". In fact a pleasant time was had by all.

On the following Monday morning the pub was revisited. The figure, minus flowers, was still standing in the vault. The landlord said he would put him away tonight: "After three days, you understand what I mean. He'll have to go away today. He's in our charge. We're responsible for him, see." He told us about the custom in the old days, and how they used to have a procession with hobby horses and everyone was drunk for a week. Discussing the decay in the ritual, he said: "There's nothing that's come for him, not for years, not for forty years . . . it wouldn't get put out only for me. Just hang it out at oak on corner. And there aren't any oaks now, only ash and that . . . it might die out you see, and get pulled down. Many a time they've been short and had one (an oak tree), they've been out and sawed one, you can't do that today, you'd be locked up." He went on to say, of the figure: "I heard one fellow say the originator of that was two hundred years back, and that was thirty years back. He was supposed to be found in a tree one time . . . you'll have a good day's march before you find a statue like 'im, won't you?" In another Worktown pub they used to hang out oak branches on this day, until a few years ago when a new landlord took over, and the custom died out.

These special customs, and especially those associated with the annual booze-ups of New Year's Eve (when you may kiss almost anybody in public), St. Patrick's Eve, Whitsun, Oak Apple Day, Trinity Sunday, June Holiday and Christmas, are a simple part of the pattern of the year, its pre-industrial, pre-christian even, background. A background of sowing and reaping, winter death and spring rebirth, a rhythm that, like the rhythm of the week, determines so much of behaviour (and belongs to a period when Worktown was unthinkable) now dominates Worktowners who never think what it's all about or know the difference between wheat and barley. To put this into proportion consider some comments on the patron saint of Worktowners, and traditional fertilizer, as made by Sir James Frazer in *The Golden Bough*. It reminds of "Charlie" in several ways, and beer:

A LEAF FROM GOLDEN BOUGH

In the East, also, St. George is reputed to be a giver of offspring to barren women and in this character he is revered by Moslems as well as Christians. His shrines may be found in all parts of Syria: more places are associated with him than with any other saint in the calendar. Such beliefs and practices lend some colour to the theory that in the East the saint has taken the place of Tammuz or Adonis.

But we cannot suppose that the worship of Tammuz has been transplanted to Europe and struck its roots deep among the Slavs and other peoples in the eastern part of our continent.

Rather amongst them we must look for a native Aryan deity who now masquerades in the costume of the Cappadocian saint and martyr St. George. Perhaps we may find him in the *Pergrubius* of the Lithuanians, a people who retained their heathen religion later than any other branch of the Aryan stock in Europe. This Pergrubius is described as the "god of the spring", as "he who makes leaves and grass to grow" or more fully as "the god of flowers, plants and all buds." On St. George's Day, the 23rd of April, the heathen Prussians and Lithuanians offered a sacrifice to Pergrubius. A priest who bore the title of Wurschait held in his hand a mug of beer, while he thus addressed the deity:

"Thou drivest away the winter: thou bringest back the pleasant Spring. By thee the fields and gardens are green, by thee the groves and the woods put forth leaves. . . ."

After praying thus, the priest drank the beer, holding the mug with his teeth, but not touching it with his hands. Then without handling it he threw the mug backwards over his head. Afterwards it was picked up and filled again and all present drank out of it. They also sang a hymn in praise of Pergrubius, and then spent the whole day in feasting and dancing

If we knew more about Pergrubius we might find that as a god or personification of Spring he, like St. George, was believed to exert all the quickening powers of that genial season.—Thus Pergrubius may perhaps have been the northern equivalent of the pastoral god *Pales*, who was worshipped by the Romans only 2 days earlier at the Spring festival of the Parilia. It will be rememebered that the Roman shepherd prayed to Pales for grass and leaves, the very things which it was the part of Pergrubius to supply.

These customs of Oak Apple and St. George type are dead or dying. But we came across something as primitive and yet new.

A FOAL CHRISTENED

On Sunday, June 5th, a group of regulars in a small pub in a working-class Worktown area brought a young foal into the tap-room and christened it after the landlady. When asked about it she was rather embarrassed, and said "There was no harm in it, just like a flower show." She explained that the foal had been taken into the kitchen to show to the women, and they had all thought it was pretty. She said that the idea had been started one night as a joke, and she'd been against it. But they brought the foal in on the Sunday morning. She thought that it would have been ugly, "with no hair", but it really was a lovely little thing. They held it by a rope halter, poured a little beer over its fore-head and made the sign of the cross. Nothing was said. After that everyone stayed until closing time, and they enjoyed themselves so much that they said the next time they could get hold of a foal they would have another christening. The land-lady said that it would be fine, and it was "good for trade".

Another custom intimately connected with drink that has been observed is that of telling fortunes with the froth on the side of a glass of Guinness.

A wild looking woman, about 45, white hair, red rash on face, is ragsorter. She tells a Roman Catholic woman's fortune by holding up half empty glass of Guinness, moving it slightly to and fro, and gazing at the froth and the patterns it makes on the side. "It's a dove, and there's a cat. It's an angel too, aye, and different things an all. There's all sorts. I'll not do it for nowt, tha knaws, threepence it is." The R.C. woman doesn't pay. Later another, oldish woman does it similarly and quietly to an adjacent Irish.

VARIATION AND DRINK DECLINE

Between 1871 and 1875 the average quantity of beer consumed annually per head of the population was 32·5 gallons. In 1935 it was 17·58 gallons, a decrease of nearly two-thirds.

Says the Merseyside Survey:

In general Liverpool and the other Merseyside boroughs have shared in the decline of excessive drinking which has characterised the last 30 years.

And the Report of the Royal Commission on licensing (1932) remarked:

By almost universal consent, excessive drinking in this country, has been greatly, even spectacularly, diminished.

We have seen in Worktown the steady fall in the absolute number of pubs in existence during the last 30 years, and a continuous fall in the number of pubs per head of population. The diagram showing the average amounts of beer drunk per head of population per year in Great Britain since 1860, however, does not present the same spectacle of a steady fall up to the year 1905. After that it was steady. The second diagram, correlating amount spent on drink with wage index and drink taxation figures, shows a very different picture. Here we see increased taxation, from 1900, with a sharp rise just after the 1914 war. This rise was accompanied by an equally sharp drop in the amount consumed per head. But actual expenditure on drink is correlated, not with consumption or taxation, but with wages— a correlation that as the diagram shows, is remarkably close.

The conclusions to be drawn from this are, that while the decline from the number of pubs has been the result of legal restrictions, the decline in the amount drunk is correlated with

AVERAGE BEER CONSUMPTION PER HEAD OF POPULATION, 1860–1930.
(The dotted line indicates the years of the last war)

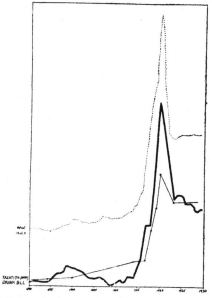

CORRELATION OF NATIONAL DRINK BILL WITH WAGE INDEX AND
BEER TAXATION (BASED ON DIAGRAMS IN "LIQUOR CONTROL"
BY G. E. C. CATLIN), 1890–1930.
The thick line is drink bill, the thin line the beer taxation, and the dotted line
the wage index.

increased *real* price—that is, price in terms of drinker's purchasing power. In *Social Effects of the Business Cycle*, Dorothy Thomas has pointed out that the fluctuations in per capita consumption of beer show a fairly high positive correlation with the business cycle, but the maximum consumption is reached a year or two after the peak of prosperity. The writer has taken a complex set of economic factors for graphing the business cycle, in which wage levels are not the main factors. This lag, we suggest, is due to the lag of wages increase behind the general indices of increased business prosperity. The writer says that the correlation of spirit consumed is much lower than the consumption of beer, an important point (cf. chapter on Drink). Beer is drunk by wage earners, not-beer largely by classes whose incomes are directly dependent upon investments or upon salaries.

Further statistical data relevant to this will be found in the next section.

It should be pointed out that this general decline in drinking cannot solely be put down to economic factors. In the days of big drinking there were no cinemas, radios, no dog races, no big League football, Littlewoods, mass circulation newspapers. The social alternatives to drinking were things like religion, playing games instead of looking at them, the various forms of mutual improvement societies of a cultural, religious, or political nature that were widespread amongst the working class at the time. Shorter working hours to-day may appear, on one hand, to give more time for drinking, and on the other, to produce less inclination to drink as a reaction from fatigue. But while today in Worktown the cotton workers spend less time than ever before in the mills, the actual intensity of the work is very much higher ; and if the assumption is made that people seek drink as a reaction from the strain of hard work, shorter hours and improved working conditions will not necessarily explain why people drink less to-day. In Thomas's book referred to above, it is stated, after pointing out the correlation between drink consumption and wages :

> There are probably psychological factors involved in this increased drinking. The general good feeling and optimism engendered by prosperity lead to an increase in conviviality. Likewise the strain of overtime and general pressure of work requires the relaxation obtainable through alcoholic stimulation.

Which is to say when people have more money to spend, they

spend more money on drink. But the important thing is that they don't spend such a high proportion of the money on drink today as they used to. That Beaverbrook, Metro-Goldwyn-Mayer, Littlewood, the hire purchase firms, and the manufacture of mass-produced radio sets, all flourish indicates this. They are selling a type of culture that is basically different from the culture of the pub which, though economically equal to a picture palace, both places being run as places for the sale of commodities for profit, produces a very different set of responses from its clients.

In the cinema man is individual and passive; in the pub he is part of a group, and active.

In this connection the decay of drinking and of pub customs, such as those described, is significant. In London, where singing and home-made music of all kinds is prohibited in some nine-tenths of the pubs, the radio is common, and so are the various slot machines in which elaborate and mechanical games of chance are played. Some years ago a Worktown brewery tried to stop dominoes being played in all its pubs. In many other towns pub games are either directly prohibited or discouraged. On the other hand, seeing further ahead, Walker and Humphreys, brewers who own many local pubs, stimulate darts and dominoes in their houses.

The pub as a cultural institution is at present declining. And the decline in drinking itself is not only due to its increased price; it is also part of a general trend in the cultural life of industrial England, which is shifting the emphasis of people's leisure from active and communal forms to those that are passive and individual—passive in the sense that the cinema audience can have no influence on the course of the film that it is looking at, and individual in the sense that the members of the audience are brought into no relationship with one another. The most extreme form of this is the radio audience; even the football crowd is in some degree participating in the spectacle and can influence to a certain extent by yells, rattles, and in extreme cases (never recorded in Worktown) the hurling of hard objects. But it is still extremely profitable to provide a man with a glass of beer and a place to drink it in, and leave the rest to him. The pub stresses the fact that you are living among your fellow men, that the issues of life, whether faced or escaped, are not solitary but communal. The Church and the political party say the same thing, in a different way. The films and pools do not.

They say that I am I, and you are you; they emphasize the separateness of the individual, and they do not ask him to know anyone. They do not suggest that he has any duty to help anyone else but himself, and maybe his wife and kids and old sick mother. In this sense these Hollywood and Littlewood philosophies are anti-social. Their enormous influence and success has been made possible by the same processes that have put mass-producing and mass-distributing units in place of craftsman and small trader. The mass production of commodities is paralleled by similar processes that supply mass culture. These economic processes, weakening the numerical and moral power of Church and politics at the same time, have also sapped in advance their resisting power to new manifestations of mass-production culture, such as the Pools, Press astrology, and jazz music.

DRINK IN FILMS, ART, ETC.

It is interesting to note in connection with the cinema audience ''passivity'' that drinking ranks high amongst the activities that are displayed before them in all sorts of films. Dr. Dale, in *Content of the Motion Pictures* (results of a detailed American study), makes an exhaustive analysis of a group of 115 typical films; 78 per cent of these contain what he calls "liquor situations", and in 43 per cent of them intoxication is shown. Similarly frequent references to drink appear on the radio. In a correspondence, started in the B.B.C. weekly paper, *The Listener*, December, 1937, (and going on till September, 1938!) the secretaries of the National Temperance Federation pointed out (29. 12. 37):

A well known firm of distillers boasts in its annual report that by negotiation with concert parties, variety artists, etc., it has been able to get its products mentioned in their programmes. Some of these programmes are relayed by the B.B.C. which (maybe unwittingly) lends itself as an instrument of liquor trade publicity.

And the editor replies:

The B.B.C. does not invite well known propagandists of the liquor trade, as such, any more than it invites well known teetotallers, as such, to the microphone.

Thus we see one form of social and commercial activity which has had an adverse influence on another such form, being used in its turn to propagandize for that which it has to some extent replaced.

Examples of these variety artists' cracks about drinking come pouring in to us in the reports from the Lancashire seaside resorts. Here are some, from pier shows:

Woman. "What would you do if I died?"
Man.   "Drown you."
Woman. "Would you drown yourself?"
Man.   "Yes in Beer."

A song contains:

"We never call for common beer
  Mine's a gin and grape fruit, dear."

Other jokes in same show are:

1. "Very well, Miss Vere, go to the Pier
    and have some beer."
2. "You aren't exactly a bottle of brandy to me."
3. "The inventor of steam was W-A-T-T, and a Scotsman"
   "Watt, T.T. and a Scotsman—he couldn't have been.".
4. "I'll have a glass of water."
   "Water? Oh yes, I have heard of that stuff. No, but you
    can have a glass of beer."
5. "Whiskey please."
   "I've been abroad for ten years and I find people don't drink
    as much as they used to."
   "Perhaps not, but we've not a lot of teetotallers yet" (says
    barmaid). And two reeling drunks come in. One says:
6. "My wife threatens to leave me if I don't stop drinking beer.
    I shall miss her."

And a joke about children being called after their father's trade —Jinnie, for a publican's daughter.

A report of one show, which contains no drink jokes, shows the direct form of brewer propaganda:

Curtain rises to reveal a rustic scene with remote mountain background. In the foreground is a pub, with a big sign— DUTTON'S ARMS. And in the window of the pub is MERCER'S STOUT.

Dutton and Mercer are local brewery concerns.

Blackpool, as well as selling rock made up in the form of property Bass and Guinness bottles, presents a continuous non-stop art gallery in the form of hundreds of joke postcards, stuck up in the windows and on racks outside almost every kind of shop. In a sample collection of 224 of these, the largest number of jokes were about sex—31 per cent. Second most frequent were drink jokes—13 per cent. All illuminating as attitudes to drink; typically:

I. Scene: A cellar. Little man in cellar leans on big barrel marked xxx, holding mug under tap.

Caption : BEER FOR STRENGTH! When I got this a fortnight ago I couldn't shift it—NOW I CAN, EASY!

II. Scene: A drunk climbs on shoulders of another (both identifiable by red noses) and takes down a brimming tankard out of a big poster announcing BEER IS BEST.

Caption : Steady, lad—we don't want ter spill it.

On all postcards a drunk is distinguished by:

(a) Bright red nose, which may be bulbous, or long and pointed.
(b) His collar is always torn away from the stud.
(c) A dilapidated umbrella (this is sometimes missing).
(d) His eyes are closed or bunged up.
(e) Either he is sagging at the knees, or his feet have a pronounced turn inwards or outwards.
(f) He is having fun.

We have referred earlier to drinkers' "Stock responses" about why, what, when, they drink. This is a good example of a stock response to the idea of a drunk—an idea that has no correspondence with reality, but communicates itself perfectly by means of a series of generally understood symbols or hieroglyphs. Similarly, the jokes themselves are stock responses to an "idea" about drunkards. And though these drunks are ridiculous figures, their ridiculousness does not interfere with or invalidate the beer propaganda.

Only the Churches do not seem to have stereotyped the drunkard. They most often speak about drunkenness as a general, and generally deplorable, condition. But sometimes the word is given its wider connotation, as by this Anglo-Catholic preacher at St. Mark's, Worktown (précis of part of sermon, his words):

"To be a shepherd is to be sober. . . . They said of Christ that he was mad. In the East they treat a man who is mad as a person blessed by God. . . . No one could read the Gospels for one minute without realizing that He is more than an ordinary man. The disciples made the people think they were mad. Yes, they were drunk with the love of God."

VII

DRUNK

There is no more striking proof of man's inferiority to animals than alcoholism. . . . It soon overcomes the strongest man and turns him into a raging beast who, with empurpled face and bloodshot eyes, bellows forth oathes and threats.

Richet, *Idiot Man*.

> I want a beer the drunken man said,
> As against the bar he leaned his head;
> The beer came up all frothing and round,
> And he drank it up without a sound.
>
> On the counter he put a shilling,
> I want another glass a filling;
> His wife walks in and bangs the door,
> She seze you've been here since half past four.
>
> Come on home and have your dinner,
> You bad old man, you drunken sinner.
> He walks out with her as quiet as a lamb
> And again we hear the door slam.
>
> Worktown elementary schoolboy, aged 12

DRUNKENNESS IS THE officially recognized aspect of pub life, has plenty written about it, and is recorded statistically by the Government.

In 1936, say the licensing statistics, 7.52 per 10,000 of Worktown's population were convicted of drunkenness: 143 people, 123 men, 20 women, according to the local Chief Constable's Report to the Watch Committee. (This is 2 more than for the same date a hundred years ago, when the town had about a quarter of its present population, and nearly the same number of pubs.)

But these figures by themselves have not much significance. They are dependent upon such things as the geography and chronology of policemen's beats, etc. Also, they are expressed as a ratio of the whole population, and the whole population doesn't drink. The number of drunks expressed in terms of *pub visits* perhaps has more reality. If we take a very low estimate of 150,000 pub visits per week in Worktown—nearly eight million a year—we find that the probability of the ordinary drinker getting "had up" after an evening in the pub is one in 60,000. If he goes to the pub five nights a week it might, at that rate, take him two centuries before he was had up for being drunk. He would have died before then; most pub-goers do die before they get had up for drunkenness.

For every two pubs in Worktown, there is one drunk case a year. For approximately each five thousand hours a pub is open, one of its clients is drunk and disorderly.

However, despite the comparative fortuitousness of arrests, and the variable factors and probabilities concerned, the official figures do have a certain correspondence with the amount of drinking that goes on. For instance, we know that weekends are the times of maximum drinking:

The following are the days of the week, throughout 1936 and 1937, on which drunks were arrested:

Year		Number of drunks						
		Mon.	Tues.	Wed.	Thurs.	Fri.	Sat.	Sun.	Total
1936 Males	9	8	11	16	19	46	14	123
Females	—	1	5	2	4	6	2	20
Total	9	9	16	18	23	52	16	143
1937 Males	23	19	13	16	30	44	14	159
Females	2	2	1	2	5	7	—	19
Total	25	21	14	18	35	51	14	178

That is, during the last two years, over half of all drunks arrested were taken up on Friday or Saturday. This agrees with the other figures for drinking that we have recorded. In the Sheffield Licensing Survey it is pointed out that the majority of arrests for drunkenness were made on Saturdays, though figures for this are not given. And the London Survey says "These convictions refer very largely to drunkenness at week-ends (Friday, Saturday, and Sunday) when the publicans reckon to do about 70 per cent of their business."

Similarly as far as the very limited number of ages—37 Worktown drunks—that we have been able to obtain, we find a certain correspondence between them and our general observations of drinkers' ages (cf. p. 136):

	Groups			
	1	2	3	4
Per cent drunks	10·8	29·7	37·8	21·7
General per cent of drinkers	7·1	40·4	50·1	2·4

The real value of the official drunkenness figures is, however, found in the study of their fluctuations. Taking the local monthly figures, as given in the Chief Constable's report for 1936, we get the following:

	Jan.	Feb.	Mar.	Apr.	May	June	July	Aug.	Sept.	Oct.	Nov.	Dec.
Arrests	11	16	14	4	4	12	11	12	10	10	18	21

The Chief Constable's comment is:

> The . . . monthly tables show that 27 per cent of the persons prosecuted for drunkenness were dealt with in November and December, while April and May accounted for only 5·5 per cent, a remarkable variation which seems totally out of proportion to the reduction one would normally expect to result from the advent of the lighter evenings.

He implies that "lighter evenings" are a factor. It is interesting to compare this with the sales records of the same year in a typical beerhouse (which is shown on page 32). Here we see that with the exception of December (Christmas) it is the time of the year with the lightest evenings upon which they sell most beer. Five per cent of the year's drunks were arrested in April and May. Fifteen per cent of the pub's yearly beer sales were made during those two months. Similarly, during April, May, June, July, August and September, half of the year, only a third of the year's total drunks were recorded. During the same period the pub sold a half of its year's beer—i.e. only a third of the drunks in the summer, with over half of the year's drinking.

The validity of such skimpy statistics is slight. All drink *statistics* ignore behaviour. They are related to a large number of variables, such as the distribution of holidays, weather, police instructions, economics, town centre and outlying pubs, lounge and vault customers, age groups—all lumped together in a crude police figure. Thus the 1937 figures for Worktown drunk convictions needed an entirely new rationalized police explanation, for the two *lowest* months of 1936 drunkenness had second and seventh *largest* totals in 1937. Actually May was a drunk record month for Worktown, because of the Coronation; but at that time drunks were, within reason, left to stagger or sick at will. In 1837 we find April as second highest drunk month, but only 8 per cent in November and December, 1837. And so on. . . .

	Jan.	Feb.	Mar.	Apr.	May	June	July	Aug.	Sept.	Oct.	Nov	Dec.	Total
1937	8	8	13	21	11	17	9	8	14	17	6	32	164
1837	15	13	6	18	9	15	20	9	3	9	7	3	127

Figures are not complete in every month.

FLUCTUATIONS OF DRUNKENNESS

But when we take large figures on a yearly and national scale, the fluctuations have a high degree of correspondence with non-pub factors.

Pub-keepers generally confirm this position, e.g. one landlord and two landladies, April:

1. "If you take bottled stuff in with the draught there's not much difference (between winter and summer). In the summer more draught beer is sold—then people go off the bottled beers. There's one man who drinks Guinness during the winter and then about April starts to drink draught beer. . . . It depends on what kind of man comes into the vault. If you've a good vault, with lots of Irish navvies, they drink more after a day's work in the summer."

2. "Summer's a bit better, but on the whole it's the same all the year round. There's not much difference."

3. "Oh! When the weather's good we do most then—I think men drink spirits when it's very very cold. But more beer in the summer. But there's not much difference."

Dorothy Thomas has pointed out that "Prosecutions for drunkenness show a high positive correlation with the business cycle". The diagram (over) shows very clearly the correlation between the average percentage of unemployment and the figures of drunks per ten thousand of the population of England and Wales. Beveridge has already tabulated and discussed aspects of beer consumption (cf. his book) in relation to bank rate, etc., and observed:

The influences which favour matrimony also favour drinking. The yearly number of prosecutions (for drunkenness) per 100,000 of the population tends to rise and fall in close dependence upon the bank rate, the employed percentage, and all other indications of prosperity.

His figures were to some extent handicapped by lack of adequate unemployment data for those dates (up to 1937).

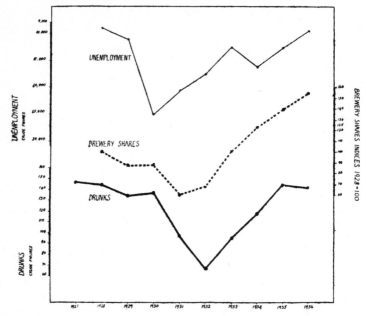

LOCAL FIGURES OF UNEMPLOYMENT, DRUNKS PER 10,000 IN-
HABITANTS, COMPARED WITH VARIATION IN THE PRICE OF
BREWERY SHARES

Taking crude Worktown figures, our diagram shows, of
course, that this correlation is not so close when small figures
are concerned. Also the *trend* of the drunk figures shows a
considerable lag behind those of unemployment.

Actually, the local drunk figures correlate far more closely with
the general business-brewery cycle—for our index of this we have
taken the value of brewery shares, the figures being based on the
Index prepared by the Institute of Actuaries, 1928 equalling 100.

Thomas also notes a cirrhosis correlation:

this close correlation between deaths from alcoholism and
the business cycle is rather surprising and seems to show
that alcoholic excesses take their toll very quickly, for the
lag is about the same as that of the consumption of spirits
and the business cycle.

Worktown figures for this are too small for it to be shown
locally. In 1936 there were 5 deaths due to cirrhosis, only one
of which was classified as alcoholic.

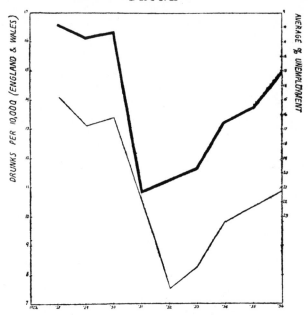

CORRELATION OF DRUNKENNESS WITH UNEMPLOYMENT. FIGURES
FOR ENGLAND AND WALES

Thick line represents per cent unemployment. Thin line drunks per 10,000
inhabitants

Worktown's figure of 7·52 drunks per 10,000 is below that of the
national average, which is 10·9. Similarly the number of pubs per
10,000—17·58—is below the national figure of 18·29. However, the
figures of both vary widely, in each case from under 10 to over 40.

TOWNS WHERE A LOT OF PEOPLE ARE DRUNK

Let us see how Worktown's figures compare with those of
other towns. The following has been compiled from the list of
84 county boroughs given in the Government Licensing Statistics
(re-analysed for present purposes):

	Drunks per ten thousand, county boroughs				
	Under 5	5–10	10–15	15–20	Above 20
Industrial towns	10	19	13	5	8
Non-industrial towns	13	14	1[1]	—	1[1]
	23	33	14	5	9

[1] These two are Blackpool, 14·71, and Brighton, 24·91.

Worktown is in the largest group. Of the non-industrial towns only Blackpool and Brighton, which are industrial holiday places, have rates above 10 per 10,000.

Out of 52 *counties* (whose figures do not include those of the county boroughs) 34 are in the first group of under 5 per 10,000, 14 in the second, 4 in the third, and none at all above 20.

It can be seen quite plainly that a high rate of drunkenness convictions is an industrial phenomenon—and also one of large

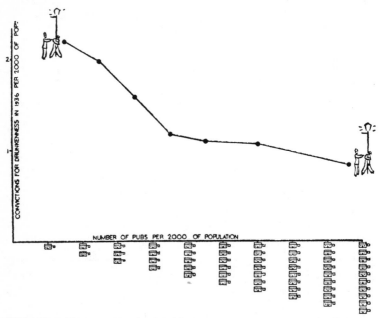

AVERAGE NUMBER OF CONVICTIONS FOR DRUNKENNESS PER YEAR
IN ADMINISTRATIVE AREAS

Areas classified according to number of pubs per unit of population

aggregations of population. The 4 highest figures are those of London, Birmingham, Newcastle and Liverpool (see p. 304).

When we come to examine the correlation between the number of pubs per 10,000 of the population and the number of drunks, the result is rather remarkable.

This diagram is based on the figures of licences and drunks given in the Government Licensing statistics for all the areas —63 Administrative Counties and 84 County Boroughs. It can be seen that there is a consistent negative correlation between these two factors, which can be summarized in the following table:

Pubs per 10,000 pop.	Number of areas	Average number of convictions per 10,000 pop.
0–10	20	11·02
10–	19	9·97
15–	34	8·01
20–	28	5·96
25–	16	5·51
30–	17	5·32
40	13	4·11
	147	

The conclusion that can be deduced from even a casual inspection of the official annual statistics, does not appear to have been taken into account in the controversies that have raged over the restriction of drinking facilities and the "drink problem"—in which there is generally implicit the idea that the more opportunities there are for people to drink, the more drunk they will get. The place in England where there are most pubs to population is Huntingdonshire, which has 55·5 per 10,000. And only 6·53 of those happy 10,000 Huntingdonians got had up for being drunk in 1936. While 7·87 out of 10,000 of the intemperate inhabitants of East Ham, despite their minute allowance of 2·62 pubs, managed to end up drunk and arrested. Of course, the pubs are nearer in East Ham and there are more policemen to have them up than in Huntingdonshire, but there are a lot more people for them to keep an eye on too.

Summing up the figures so far—they show that drunkenness is *not* necessarily dependent upon drinking facilities, *is* considerably connected with industrial concentration of population, and its variation is largely dependent upon how much money there is about. And you are more likely to die of alcoholic diseases when there is a boom on than during a slump.

Further research is needed on the factors influencing drunkenness. The present official statistics are based on a confusion of a word with a state of behaviour. But even these official statistics will not support the argument upon which their use is based. The number of drunk convictions is inadequate indication of the pub's place in local life and vice. The number of pubs is no more significant—pub space, percentage, drinking standing, wage levels in main industries, distribution of pubs in relation to town centre, total beer consumed, are some other factors equally or more important. The basis of sound legislation must surely be the stabilization of what goes on *inside* the pub, not the number of pub exteriors, or the minority that reel out from them blind-to-the-world and disorderly enough to attract a P.C.

Pub control, pub numbers, and a keen leisure-pleasure of about one tenth the adult population, depend very largely on the local licensing authorities. Yet, whereas in Section 40 of the Licensing (Consolidation) Act of 1910, it was determined that "no justice shall act for any purpose under this Act who is, or is in partnership with, or holds any share in any company which is a common brewer, distiller, maker of malt . . . or of any intoxicating liquor", no similar provision excludes those with interests *opposed* to licensing. Moreover, in the words of the Royal Commission on Licensing (1929–31):

> "The sole issue which the licensing justices have to consider in such circumstances (that is, the issue of the licence) is whether, having regard to all the circumstances, it is in the public interest that the licence should be granted."

But the licensing authorities have no way of determining the *public interest*—nor, for that matter, did the Royal Commission attempt to do so; it thought that "authorities", experts, vested interests, were sufficient witnesses. The "public interest" is what the justices make it. It is at present based neither on facts nor the public. The Royal Commission similarly rejected in two sentences, a suggestion, made forcibly by several witnesses, that licensing bodies should have the status of courts of law. The reason they rejected it, in their own words:

> "While we appreciate these arguments, we believe that they are based on a misconception. Such status would, we think, be inconsistent with the free and unfettered exercise of their (the licensing justices') discretion in the public interest."

Whose is the misconception? Unfettered seems to be the operative word. They can, and do, use their discretion from the angle of their own opinions, unfettered by public intervention or appeal. The public of this democracy have no nominee, no representative, no effective voice in this as in so many other matters which concern them. The result is a continual inhibition, a conservatism from necessarily aged persons who are also automatically too high up the social scale to know much, if anything, about ordinary pubs. Not only pubs, but hotels and restaurants all over the country are affected, even to the detriment of tourist traffic. Recently, in a letter to *The Times*, Sir George Reeves-Smith, managing-director of the Savoy Hotel, pointed to a particularly interesting instance of such licensing inhibition. He described how, in three minutes, the London licensing authorities refused confirmation of a licence to the Savoy for a branch of their old English restaurant, Simpson's. The new branch of this world-famous restaurant and tourist centre was to be in the West End, costing more than £65,000 to do up. The Strand justices who heard the first application for a licence, granted it. But Quarter Sessions, the general London body, refused unconditionally. As Sir George Reeves-Smith pointed out, if they won't grant one to Simpson's they won't grant one to anyone else. "This places London as an international centre in the position of not being allowed to have any new restaurant of the first order."

This matter was the subject of comment in the House of Commons, May 17, 1939, when, according to the Official Report, Captain Evans, M.P., after quoting Sir George Reeves-Smith's letter, discussed its implications and went on to say:

> "It appears that since the confirmation of the licence refused by quarter sessions investigations have shown that some of the justices who adjudicated were actually shareholders in companies operating, or financially interested in, restaurants or hotels in the district concerned. It is true that those companies cannot be said to be principally concerned in retailing intoxicating liquor, but the fact does remain that they are connected with restaurants or hotels selling intoxicating liquor in the district concerned."

At this stage in his remarks, other members intervened, thus:

> *Mr. R. Morgan :* Will the hon. and gallant Member state what these companies are?
> *Capt. Evans :* I hope that the hon. Member will not press me on that matter. I am not anxious to give names here, but I can give them privately.
> *Mr. Wedgwood Benn:* Is it not usually held that the conduct of justices should not be impugned except on a substantive Motion?
> *Mr. Speaker :* That is so.

Captain Evans then replied giving the specific information for which Mr. R. Morgan had asked, and went on to say:

"Here is a case, a definite case, a specific case, where justices were
interested, and it does not seem right to me that when justices
come to consider the granting of facilities to a new restaurant they
should be personally concerned in any way financially, either
directly or indirectly, with the profits or losses of other restaurants
in the district. The sole test should be the public interest."

To remedy this, Captain Evans (Conservative M.P. for S.
Cardiff; he lives in Park Lane) obtained leave to introduce a
Bill requiring justices to *declare* that they are not in any way
interested in licensing, for or against (May, 1939).

Captain Evans' Bill deals with an alleged abuse. It still does not
touch on the Nonconformist or teetotaller acting in the licensing
authority, does nothing to gain any representation of public interest
in the form of the public, pub-goer, non, etc. The assumption
that mere NUMBERS, statistics, of the most obvious kind,
are the only relevant pub facts continues. Among these obvious
external factors on which the issue of licences are judged, is the
number of hours for which the doors which open into the pub's
interior are open to the public, pub-goers. The limitation of open
hours has been an inhibition imposed on the masses by the
magistrates as strongly as the gradual inhibition on the actual
number of pubs. It is an absolutely basic assumption in contemporary licensing practice that the length of time a pub is open
directly affects drunkenness. It is no better supported by demonstrable facts than the other assumption (about number of pubs);
the experience of nearly every country on the Continent rather
disproves it. And we have already seen (Chapter V) that when
Rowntree made some counts thirty years ago in York, during the
period when pubs were still open all day, there was no Last Hour
Rush, indeed custom declined in the last hour. We have suggested
that this inhibition on the pubs' times, the rigorous enforcement
of time limits on drinking, has had an effect in making the pub
seem in a special way "immoral", its code constantly fringing the
boundaries of the law and its last permitted minutes a special
period for as-near-as-possible defiance. Without going into the
psychological subtleties of this, particularly among males,
anyone can observe it for themselves, not only in the pub, but
anywhere else where time is arbitrarily limited and the end of a
pleasure (which seems "harmless" to those enjoying it) threatened
by automatic and external forces, which make an extra minute
an "offence against the law".

Writing in the *News Chronicle* (2.6.39), Doris Langley Moore remarked:

> Licensing regulations, like many other old-fashioned methods of dealing with potential evil, were framed under the simple illusion that you can prevent people from doing something they want to do by placing difficulties in their way. The most acute students of human nature have long been aware that, on the contrary, difficulty frequently acts as a first-rate incentive, and forbidden or partly forbidden fruit tastes far sweeter than that which drops into the hand. . . .
> I believe that, if we were given the freedom permitted in this respect to Latins, Hungarians, Rumanians, Yugo-slavians, and almost all the other peoples of Europe, there might be at first some slight excess, but in a very short time we should adjust ourselves to the idea of being treated as rational creatures, and would behave as such.

It is difficult to believe that in limiting the hours during which pubs are open you limit drunkenness, any more than forbidding abortion prevents some 90,000 working-class women aborting per annum. First, people do not go to pubs to get drunk. Second, their drinking is limited by their spending capacity. Thirdly, as our timings all show, they could easily get drunk in the available hours if they wanted to do so, by coming in earlier instead of during the later hours of open time. Fourthly, unlike the last century's drinking, nowadays a primary reason for pub-going is not the desire to escape from appalling home life. There may well be other reasons for limiting hours, e.g. in the interest of the publicans, though it is doubtful whether these interests are best served by the present system, including the fact that pubs are compelled to open all the available hours every day, which effectively prevents small-pub people from holidaying. A recent poll by the British Institute of Public Opinion gave a nearly equal number of people for and against extending licensing hours but more than that in both of these groups put together wanted the hours left the same. Unfortunately the poll failed to differentiate between those who use the pubs and those who don't, and is thereby rendered relatively meaningless in so far as no qualitative weight can properly be attached to such quantities of opinion.

There is in existence a system which seems almost legally to admit the doubtful validity of closing time. Under the Licensing Act, 1921, licensing justices are empowered to vary the provisions as to permitted hours of opening by adding half an hour to them, fixing drinking to end at 10.30 instead of 10.0 p.m.

Of the 990 licensing districts outside London where this can be done, in 1937–8, 99 allowed the half-hour to be added for the whole year, 350 for part of the year. Thus 5 out of 11 varied hours from the "normal". 1938–9 showed a further step in the same direction; 101 districts added the half-hour for the whole year, 358 added it for part of the year, making 46 per cent extension from the "normal". There was NO INCREASE in drunkenness or associated offences in these districts as compared with the others which allowed no extension. The Act defines that the extension may only be allowed if the licensing justices are satisfied that the special requirements of the district render it desirable that it should be made. The position is, therefore, that nearly half the licensing districts in this country have been judged to have "special requirements". The word "special" seems to have a very remote meaning in such circumstances. In fact, the "special requirements", key-phrase of the Act's Section I are, as the trade paper *Morning Advertiser* remarked in a lengthy editorial on the subject (5.6.39), "words about the precise meaning of which nobody is quite sure". In Wisbech and in Bradford litigation has followed licensing decisions on the subject, and the results have not finalized anything. The *Morning Advertiser* makes comment relevant to our own theme:

> It is hardly fair to expect the courts to define phrases which Parliament presumably had found impossible to define; just as, in many cases, it is even less fair to expect the ordinary man-in-the-street to keep within the bounds of a law the meaning of which may be quite clear as to its tendency, while it is completely lacking in clear definition.

And, after discussing the recent case of Blackburn, which, once having granted an extension all the year, unusually rescinded it—on doubtful grounds—the editor ends his column:

> It is a point which perhaps some society such as "Mass Observation" could clear up once and for all.

We are doing our best. And we shall presently give other data relevant to licensing methods, especially in connection with the inhibition on social life in Worktown pubs; also the notorious cases of Liverpool and Glasgow. In the meanwhile. . . .

A DETAIL

So "unexpected" are the previous figures on the lack of correlation between pubs and drunkenness (p. 228), that it will not be out of place to give the following table, showing the scatter:

Pubs per 10,000 of population

	Convictions for drunkenness per 10,000 of population in 1936 (Number of areas)																							Total
	0–	1–	2–	3–	4–	5–	6–	7–	8–	9–	10–	11–	12–	13–	14–	15–	16–	17–	18–	19–	20–	25–	33	
–5		I		I		I																		3
5–			I																					1
6–			I		I			I												I				4
7–	I	I																				I		3
8–						I								I	I									3
9–						I	2											I			I		I	6
10–				I				I		I														3
11–		I																I				I		3
12–			I				I	3				I		I										7
13–								2							I				I					4
14–					I			I																2
15–			I	I	I	I	I	I				I	I	I							I	I		11
16–			I	2								2								I	I			7
17–	3				3		I								I	I								9
18–						I																		1
19–	I	2			2			I																6
20–		I		I	2																			4
21–			I	I	I	I		2			I	I	I											9
22–			2	3	I	I			I			I	I											10
23–				I																				1
24–			I	2				I																4
25–			I	I	I			I																4
26–					I																I			2
27–			I	I	I																			3
28–					I	2			I															4
29–	I	I			I																			3
30–		2	I	I	I		I	I	I				I											9
35–		I	I	3	I		I		I															8
40–			I		2	2	I			I														7
45–	I																							1
50–55	I	I				2	I																	5
Total	2	10	16	20	16	16	8	18	6	4	3	6	4	2	2	1		2	1	2	4	3	1	147

GETTING TIGHT

Says the 20th annual report of the Worktown Temperance Society, 1854:

> That drunkenness is painfully prevalent in the Borough a thousand facts bear most painful testimony. Men and women staggering along the public streets, fights and brawls of the most barbarous character. . . .

In its Jubilee (1936) report it notes:

> Amid conflicting "isms" teetotalism is the only one producing immediate and lasting social effect.

What is drunk?

T. Heywood: *Philocothonista* (1635) speaks of a man being drunk as:

> He is foxt, he is flawed, he is flustered, he is suttle, cupshot, cut in the legge or backe, he hath seene the French King, he hath swallowed a haire or a taverne-token, he hath whipt the cat, he hath been at the scriveners and lerned to make indentures, he hath bit his grannam or is bit by a barne weesell . . .

Worktowners speak of a drunk as being boozed, pissed, kettled, canned.

> "The evils of today," said a local clergyman preaching Sunday, July 18th, "are drunkenness due to the activities of the brewers, gambling, wrecking homes, and pleasure seeking. . . ."

During this, notes the observer, he twisted his mouth in getting his words out. It was 6.59 p.m., one minute before opening time.

But what do they mean when they talk about a man being drunk? Is it how much he has drunk, or how he is behaving? In a pamphlet given away by the Worktown Temperance Union, Sir T. Lander Brunton is quoted as saying "Alcohol produces paralysis of judgment, and this begins with the first glass."

Remarks Professor Catlin:

> The effect of a given quantity of alcohol varies greatly from one human being to another . . . to ascertain the nature of the effects of alcohol upon the human system various

physiological experiments have been carried out by Furth and Schwartz, Dodge and Benedict, Hellsten, Rivers, Vernon, and others. Where these experiments have shown positive results, they have indicated that alcohol tends to impede the strength and speed of muscular activity. . . .

Koren, however, in his authoritative *Alcohol and Society* points out that most of the experiments made to ascertain the effects of alcohol on the system, were conducted upon abstainers with empty stomachs, who were given small doses of raw alcohol; this is certainly not the usual procedure of getting drunk in Worktown.

Even the police and doctors can't agree what is "drunk". In 1938 two Metropolitan magistrates said they preferred police to medical evidence, drawing protest from the Medical Practitioners' Union (*Reynolds*. 2.1.38). Police tests include chalk line, bringing tip of outstretched hand quickly to the point of the nose. But nervous diseases will give similar results, while doctors—stressing pulse rate—do not know the rate of the particular person.

Let us see the effect of 13 pints of mild on one drinker, and a pretty large quantity on a number of others:

As Observer and P.J. enter vault they are greeted by shouts of "don't cross the line" "stay over this side", etc. There is a lot of backchat over this that continues when the observers do cross to the window end of the room. There is no real line, but in fact, it represents, for this evening at any rate, a distinct opposition between the two ends of the room, which is carried on with backchat, until the vault is filled up. One man, with slow gait, fattish red face, gets up to have a pint from the bar and is greeted with cries of unbelief from chaps at the other end of the room, who stare at each other, mute and gasping. It appears that this is Jack S., and it is his thirteenth pint since 5.30. He carries it well, though slowly. But he is always slow, seldom speaks, "it seems to be an effort for him to say anything" says P.J. "He comes in here when he finishes work and God knows when he goes away". He is second engineer in a big mill nearby.

A clerky man comes in at 8.55, and has his pint redrawn. A postman, with Jack S., who is also under the influence of drink, yells at clerky man and barman "That's the same pint as you drawed him first but you drew it twice and he's satisfied. . . . Aye, a fastidious old bugger, that's what you are, a fastidious old bugger." Postman tells this man that he'll get his tap (credit) stopped if he isn't careful. To which he replies "I'll get nobody's tap stopped—I can drink here till 12 o'clock if I like." Postman starts noisily again "I was 59 on the 29th of April last year" and he bets he is older than Jack. There are derisive comments and assertions. Postman talks of his own age and seniority, then switches on to a friend of his. "He reckons he's seen Kruger. But 'es never seen bloody Kruger. Kruger was in America. . . . I seen De Witt. . . . I were in South Africa in 1899". A lot about this, with plenty denials from the others. Clerk steps up to postman's table and shouts "I'll bet you a shilling I'm not older than thee." Postman roars back "I'll not bet you a shilling, I'll bet you a pound". And he comes back to the war, where "The Lancashire Fusileers took Spion Kop. Certainly they did. I was there".

A man from the other end calls out "You bloody liar", and there is general laughter. Postman replies "All you bloody co-op men are the same."

Clerk. "You said that you'd bet me he's older than me."

Postman. "Well, if you lose your bet you'll get bloody divvy off it." And adds "What does your wife say. Are you any good on soft dirt." (Laughter.)

Clerk. "You never seen South Africa."

Postman. "Neither have you . . . medals, more bloody bars on them than they have on step ladders. I'll bet you a pound now that I was in South Africa and I was a bugler."

Clerk. "Well, you must be an old ancient bugger then."

Postman. "I wasn't in the Worktown infantry, you know. I've pinned many a medal on to a strap in Preston."

Clerk. "You never got a single medal in your life."

Postman. "You never saw a South African medal."

Clerk. "I know more about South Africa than what thou does."

Postman. "You know bugger all. . . . You didn't see *me* come back. I was with the lads . . . (pause) King's Bodyguard, that was me. I seen Queen Victoria."

Clerk. "Never in your life."

Postman. "I seen her in reality. I seen King Edward. I went to t' proclaimation of King George. Medals—what are you bloody well talking about. Medals. Medals. . . ."

Says a chap from the other end, raising a great laugh "He sold all his bloody medals to Bessemer's."

This conversation is ended, except that the postman reiterates every minute or less "Medals . . . medals". After which he has an argument with Bill S. about who is the older, ending with the statement "Thou's an old-fashioned bugger", at which Bill grins. He has only drunk an inch off his pint in the last twenty minutes.

These men aren't drunk in any legal sense. But they certainly aren't sober. In order to be able to analyse the behaviour of drunks, we will give excerpts from a few reports that show typical drunk behaviour.

The commonest is the cheerful, argumentative type. Here is 10 minutes verbatim from a group of this kind:

Seven men, three sitting at domino table. A. is young, has a cap and tie, all the others are middle-aged and wear scarves, old clothes. B. is one legged, with a couple of crutches and a red scarf tied round his neck.

A tremendous argument about the Farr-Braddock fight is going on, with all kinds of side issues, one of which develops on to the question of what is a novice and what an amateur. No one is very sober.

A. A amateur is a chap who fights for nothing—for the sport o't'. Now a novice——"

B. Now then, did you know Braddock before 'e fought this man . . . Burr . . . Barr . . . what's it . . .

C. Baer (pronounces it "beer").

B. That's right, Baer.

C. Give 'im 'is due.

A. The point is Primo Carnera was the champion of the world.

C. 'e was knocked out more than any man in the world.

A. They gambled on 'im . . . well, the point is—did you know an old chap that beat the lot of 'em, and 'e was beaten quiet easily——

B. Was 'e ellfire, it was young Siki——

A. 'e can't complain——

D. (sitting down, now joins in) 'e 'ung round what they call the spakeaisys.

A. That's where Siki was stabbed. . . . Carpentier made a fool of 'im.

D. Did you ever read Carpentier's life, I've been reading it in a illustrated paper. 'e thought 'e was on a easy thing 'e never trained. Battling Siki knocked everything out of 'im.

A. 'e only 'it 'im once.

E. (sitting with D) Siki knocked 'im out anyway.

D. (who is drunker than anyone else, and getting more so

all the time—in a suddenly irritated voice) I'm not talking about 'im, I'm talking about Bombardier Wells.

A. Did 'e ever fight again?

E. Yes, 'e did, two or three times.

D. 'ave you ever in 'is life?

A. D'you know Carpentier 'eld at least seven championships, not one—seven——

F. (who hasn't spoken before) Yes, 'e did.

D. (furious) When did 'e ever win the lightweight championship of the world, when did 'e ever win the bantam weight championship of the world, when did 'e ever——

A. (not waiting for him to stop) I didn't say the world.

B. (suddenly) 'oo's the middleweight champion o't' world now?

D. Mickey —— (inaudible).

B. 'oo's the last chap 'e fought 'ere.

D. 'oo did 'e fight for the championship of the world.

B. Did 'e 'ellfire.

C. 'e got beat, what are you both bothering about.

E. 'e fought (inaudible) in France.

A. What's that.

G. (joining in, and for no apparent reason) I know I'm right too, mate.

B and C have been having a side argument. B suddenly says: Sit down there.

C. I'm not going to sit down.

A and E join in, and there is a lot of shouting for a moment and then suddenly everything is quiet.

B. (starting again) Sit down!

C. Will I 'ellfire.

E. (pacifying) Come on, Albert, come and tell us all about it.

B. (moving towards E) 'e fought Kid Lewis, Carpentier.

D. 'oo should of won? (Suddenly he starts singing in a loud flat voice) *It's only a chi . . ild*—(stops) When a man's in the ring 'e's in the ring.

B. 'e knocked out Bombardier Wells twice in July '28.

At this point there enters a middle-aged man in dirty clothes, wearing a new and expensive looking bright green trilby hat, sideways, napoleonic style. He has a scarf knotted round his neck, and another, woollen, cream-coloured, wound round and hanging free at both ends.

All shout "'allo Jimmy."

Jimmy advances to the bar and tries to bargain his white scarf for a drink. He unwinds it and hands it to the barmaid, who won't take it.

Barmaid. No, I don't want it, Jimmy. I don't want it. I won't have it.

A loud singing arises from the parlour. Jimmy says something inaudible to the barmaid, who replies—Now don't start showing your bolshevik blood to me.

D. is singing again—*Do what you can If it's only a smile I'm somebody's chi . . ild . .*

Jimmy, holding out scarf to B. I'll sell this for a tanner now.

B. I couldn't buy a woodbine.

D. Starts another song, very melancholy—*Do you recollect that. my 'appy days. are 'ere again* — — — And he falls backwards off the stool, flat on his back. A and B pick him up, and pat him all over, as if he was a dog, saying "Come on, oldtimer". He starts singing again, waving his pint mug. *You made me cry. . . .* Then points to Jimmy and shouts to the barmaid—Hi, make 'im up a bucket (pint).

Jimmy. I slept out a week tonight.

B. Well, can't you sleep out another week.

Everyone is quiet now. Jimmy gets his pint. Then the Farr-Braddock fight starts again.

This, and the report previously quoted, both show an accentuation of certain characteristics of ordinary pub talk (q.v.)—a great deal of repetition, rhetorical questioning, and apparent irrelevance (free association). In the first one there is a disposition to make "cracks" at each other's expense, accompanied by boasts; in the second the most drunk has a tendency to start singing —now and then—sentimental songs; that is characteristic. Also, the back-patting, soothing remarks of "oldtimer" when he falls over are typical of drunken "good fellowship".

But accompanying these traits, in both the cases, there is an aggressive tendency that comes out into the open occasionally. This commonly manifests itself in the form of apparently gratuitous offensiveness:

Two drunks were very talkative, had been having a good day drinking champagne, whiskey, sherry, and beer. The elder man says "You're not driving that bloody car tonight or you'll get pinched", the other man replied by singing *"When the moon says something to the mountains"* and the first one kept interrupting him about driving the bloody car, and went on to say "I can lend anybody a bloody fiver". One sober man in the vault says "If you can put your bloody hand on fivepence I'll have a pint". The drunk said "You

can have nowt wi' me, Walt". (Later.) One man was handing
him his glass and he said "Stick it up your flaps" . . .

The following personal-political argument is another type of
aggressiveness. (The argument can be about anything, of course):

Two men, about 50, caps and scarves, shiny worn blue
suits, quarrelling about politics. One keeps saying "If tha'
doesn't like t'country why doesn't thee go away. No one stops
me getting a living." Then he suddenly shouts "Why shouldn't
t' king and queen be there. I'm for them. They should be
there". Other replies "Why should they be there?" "I'll not
argue that", says first man aggressively. And they begin to
shout at each other.

The landlady says "Now shut up". The others standing
round laugh, but the landlady comes round into the bar,
looking threatening, and the others stop laughing and also
say "Shut up" but in a helpful way. Landlady collars the
anti-monarchist and says "No politics, now shut up will you".
The other drunk turns away and looks complacently virtuous
(thinks observer) while his mate is being lectured. The anti-
monarchist calms down quickly, but keeps shoving his head
past the landlady's bosom (no mean feat this) and saying to
his mate provocatively that he doesn't mind shutting up
because he won the argument. When landlady turns on to the
other chap and tells him that it's his fault too, he becomes
indignant, protesting that *he* wasn't arguing. Then they both
suddenly shake hands and get friendly, one saying "I like a
chap that speaks out, speaks his mind". But about ten minutes
later, as observer is leaving, they start arguing again, about
Hannen Swaffer, the other chap shouting "but he's an educated
man, speaks six languages".

Sometimes a fight results:

Shouting and screaming outside after the pub had shut,
the bang of a bottle on pavement as prelude to what follows:

Jack—"You're a bonny bugger, you are. You're not fit for
decent company." And he grabs Peter by the tie, shaking
him. Women rush to aid Peter, interrupted by rescue party
Jack breaks loose, takes bottle out of his pocket and hits
Peter with it twice. They are separated again, each trying
to get at the other. Peter's woman attacks the aggressor and
is taken away. Goes to her man and says "Never mind him,
love."

Observer hears that Jack does not like his wife to associate with such "not quite respectable people".

Another row, this time between husband and wife:

Two men in vault, one woman (a hawker) sits between them. Men pay in turn for drinks for all three. One of the men has been sacked and paid up the same morning. They soon get to the stage of telling each other what fine chaps they are and what they did in the past, etc. This reminiscencing is rudely disturbed by the voice of a woman. She opens the door and shouts in "Come out of it, you dirty stop out all night" and bounces out, to patrol the street opposite. She is wife of the man who was sacked. He betrays uneasiness, which he pretends to laugh off. Wife comes back to the attack, and another woman asks her to come and have a drink. She refuses, shouting at her husband. Goes away again to patrol street. The two men peep over the window to see if she has gone —wife sees them—dashes in again, says "What, you'll laugh at me". Kicks him and thumps him, making growling noises while doing so. Says "Go on, hit me—that's what I want you to do, I'll report you to the Chief—go on, hit me, I've been working all morning while you're boozing in here, you dirty stop out all night, why don't you come home." Husband does not retaliate, merely grins. Woman becomes more infuriated, kicks him again, both go out into street. Landlady says "Don't hurt her, she's only doing what's right". Wife takes off a clog and cracks husband on the head with it. Husband finally hits her—she goes away at this. They, the two men and the woman, stay on till pub shuts. The woman attempts to get off with erring husband, but he doesn't.

(A postscript on the report says "Erring husband gone to sea—Oct. 16". That is nine days later.)

Another kind of drunkenness manifests itself in the form of a more or less incoherent "free association" of ideas, often bawdy ones. The following example shows other traits—boasting and complete lack of consistency between different statements of the same speakers:

(This takes place after the fortune-telling episode quoted earlier.) She ends up with humour about the crown on the glass. A younger woman comes in, and another remarks to her "It's time you did something." She replies "I just done something" and there is loud laughter.

"There's nowt in t' Coronation. I can see nowt int'," remarks a woman. The ragsorter says "I've supped ale till I'm sixteen and I'll sup it till I die."

Old woman: "I got throwed out last time I was here. I'll get throwed out this time, out of front and in at back."

The ragsorter starts talking about her separated husband again. He nearly throttled her on Easter Saturday. A small man, but he boasted "as if he were eight foot". . . . "He just wanted to have a look at me. Any man's big enough for that. There's a bit of love, like. I got a letter since. He said dear darling, are you still troubling. I got a bit of beads, and a brooch. I've been father and mother all my life—four of 'em." She describes how she had arranged to meet him and a girl of his. She said "I'll be in here about nine o'clock—and I'm waiting—this is the pantomime, it's time this. In 'e comes with 'er. Orders a Guinness, I blinded 'im with a pint. I plastered—I said I'll give you something. I drowned 'er, and I gave 'im some spit."

Old woman: "Thank God I got one of the best. I 'ad operation six years ago. Doctor towd me to be easy for six months, but that's been for six years. Never 'ad to make no beds, do no polishing, no brewing—brew our own beer—then while t'owd man's doing the work I run out and see me friends." (Loud laughter.) "When you get 71 you done your share," comments one woman.

She goes on—"He were too old to work when he were 62, I worked last year from last week in August till Christmas week —picking up taters—never mind—four and six a day, it was my own money. I could do what I liked with it. I've been a collier all my life." (Loud laughter.) "I worked since I was 19 and when I want halfa pint of beer I shall have it. I never start boozing till half past ten. They open our place half past ten. Then I drink as much as I can till closing. All while the war was on I worked—I worked in my trousers and coat. I had 13 kids, I buried one in t' war. My youngest baby, he were 31. He's a young baby. He was the youngest of 13. And I buried 2 or 3 besides that. I always worked till a fortnight before I 'ad them. And I never was in t' house above a fortnight. I'd take 'em to be christened Sunday morning and be there to work on a Monday morning. And I 'ope as soon as I done working and drinking the beer the Lord'll look upon me. We've a big garden—apples and plums. . . ."

At eleven o'clock everybody goes, the ragsorter winding up last "I'll have to get the Duke of Windsor next."

CHRISTMAS EVE

All these are examples of individual drunk behaviour. There is also something that can be called "social drunkenness"— group intoxication of large numbers of people. One example has already been given earlier, the Trinity Sunday Catholic procession. The following report of Christmas Eve (written by a local observer, religious, non-drinker) shows effects of big scale drinking:

Passing down the street observer saw a man of 30 running across the road, through the entrance of this pub, up the steps and shouting. The next second the sound of breaking glass. The man then comes tumbling down the steps with another man on top of him. They begin to fight in the middle of the street. The man who put his arm through the window of the door is mopping off the blood on his arm.

"I'll show that bastard; I never said nowt to him—Christ I'll show him!" He made a lurch towards the door, but two others from the pub, came out and grabbed the back of his jacket. Then a chap of 22 came out of the pub and nearly fell down the steps.

"Where the bloody hell is he? He wants a fight, does he? Christ!" Other men got hold of him and held him back.

Just then a sergeant with a stick and a P.C. came up: in no hurry they came to the door.

"What's the matter? What's it all about? Now then, come on there, get out of it, *get out of it!*" They pulled two men out of doorway—saw the window:

Sergeant: "Who did that?"

The landlord came out, rushed to the sergeant and shouted: "He did it, that chap there; take his name, will you, officer." The sergeant went up to the man who was standing in the middle of the street, using his handkerchief to get the blood off his hand.

Sergeant: "Did you do this?"

Man: "Aye, but he tried to throw me out."

Sergeant: "Well, go over there a minute."

Man goes over to the other side of the street and leans on a windowsill. Just then the group on the pub side gets noisy; the sergeant says to them: "Come on now, get a move on, get off home will you?"

One of the men, drunk, says: "O.K., sergeant, we'll take him home; come on you silly bugger. Can't you bloody see what'll happen, he'll pinch you." They all hung on to the drunk who got noisier still, but he got sight of the sergeant and said: "It's all right, I'm going." To the men with him: "Come on, what are you waiting for?" They go off up a side street, shouting and singing. One of them is singing: "Daisy, Daisy, give me your quinsey, do". At this they all start laughing, all have arms round each other; they go into an alleyway (courting place, very dark).

Then out of the pub come three girls of 20. One of them shouts: "Eh, wait for us—they're buggering off with the bloody port-wine!"

The two police are standing in front of the pub, talking to three men, two of them young.

Two men of 22 come up the road, they are dead drunk and have difficulty in walking. They get to the corner and begin to cross the road. A car comes up the road at 30 m.p.h. Observer yells "Stop!" as the car was 20 yds. from the men who had fallen in the road. Car pulled up with a screeching of brakes and turned at an angle, having pulled up in 12 or 14 yds. Two girls standing on the corner ran into the roadway, both of them laughing and smoking. They picked the young men up and took them off down the alleyway, came back to the corner 10 minutes later.

The two police now began to try to get into the pub. The lobby inside doorway was full of men of 20 to 25, and women of same age. The door with the broken glass would not open with the crush.

The landlord is trying to pull a young man of 25 out of the bar. "Who you bloody pulling? Leave me alone, I'll break your bloody jaw." At this the sergeant turns to the young P.C. "Get him out of it!" So P.C. grabs him by the arm and shoulder. The young chap starts shouting "Leave me alone, you broke my bloody shoulder last time you got me. I know what you'll do, bloody well baste me when you get me outside, *leave me alone!* He begins to tear backwards to get into the pub. The P.C. pulled at his coat: "Come on, you're coming out!" Man: "Leave me bloody suit alone, will you?" He comes out. But before he can get out he has to pass landlord and a soldier. Landlord: "Haven't I tried to get him out quietly, soldier?" Soldier: "Yes, that's right, you did, anything you say goes, he did, officer."

P.C. jerks the offender from between landlord and soldier, he comes toppling down the steps and goes away shouting.

Observer then goes to the corner further up the street. There things are quieter, but a group of five girls of 18 to 20

are smoking and laughing on the corner. Three young men
of 18 to 20 come out of the pub and talk to the girls; they
begin to kiss them to the screams of the girls—laughing
screams. One of the youths gets hold of the girl and bends
her right back, making him bend over her; all the time kiss-
ing her; when finished he says: "God she's bloody hot."
Girl: "You're not so bloody cold yourself."

The young men go inside and bring out two bottles wrapped
in light brown tissue paper: they give these to the girls. They
bring out two more young men, one of whom says: "Which
is her?" They all ten go off down the alley.

Observer then heard a shout and looked down towards the
other pub. Here a man was running followed by the barman
and the policeman, both running. As he runs another chap
is thrown out of the pub; this one is 25, he has a thick ear and
his mouth is bleeding.

Woman: "He got what he bloody asked for."

Man: "I never saw anybody get it like that."

The sergeant comes back to the front of the pub, takes a
few notes from the chap who has been kept waiting with his
hand bleeding.

Observer talked to sergeant.

"They're not real boozers, they only get a bit and it goes
to their heads. I went in with that chap: I thought it would
all be over, and damn me if as soon as we got to the door one
of the other fellers didn't lash out at him, called him some
bloody thing, and hit him. I made after him, but I had this
coat on: he could run, the barman couldn't catch him. We
went in after one chap and he made off through the house.
He dropped down a twenty foot wall, I thought he would be
killed: anyway he's all right; he said he only wanted to get
away; when he saw us he sobered up."

The crowd of approximately thirty men and women made
off slowly and stood at the end of the street. Here they began
to row again. The two police broke them up: "Move on there,
move on!"

A woman of fifty stood at the corner. "They're only a lot
of silly young buggers, they get a couple of gills and they
think they can best each other. I left my daughter in there.
I've got two bottles in there, but I daren't go for them 'cause
of the cops."

The daughter came up, a girl of 18. "It's all right, silly
devils, I'd show 'em what to do."

As four of them pass her, she calls to one with a grin on
his face: "Eh, go on home, you silly devils!" In reply to

Observer, remarks: "Who, him? He daren't say anything—I've been with him—he's nowt. I'd pull his pan handle." Mother and daughter laugh. Mother grabbed the soldier and shouted to him: "You don't want to be finished in your uniform do you?"

Soldier: "I don't care a fart, I'll bash him."

The third woman began to cry as she held on to one of the men. The daughter grabbed another fighter by the shoulders: "Go on home, don't be a fool; eh, you, is he your chap? Why don't you get him out?"

All three women had hold of three men.

A girl of 20, blonde and who had come out of the pub said to another girl: "He called me a bloody whore he did; if he doesn't bash his face in for that I'll never speak to him again." She went up and put her arm through the soldier's. "Come on away, sod him."

When the soldier got away all quietened down; the police came up walking quietly and said: "Come on now, clear off." All cleared off.

High point of mass drunkenness takes place at Blackpool, during the Worktown holidays, and also at week-ends when thousands of Worktowners come over on excursions. Here is a general impression of the streets at closing time:

At closing time back and front streets crowded, some people dancing, men and women doing foxtrots and a group of women trying to do a fling. Three observers independently estimate that at least 25 per cent of the crowd are drunk. . . . (Later.) Along promenade the air is full of beersmell, that overcomes seasmell. It arises from people breathing. A swirling, moving mass of mostly drunk people, singing, playing mouthorgans, groups dancing about. Chaps fall over and their friends pick them up cheerfully and unconcernedly. At one spot a young man falls flat on his face, his friend picks him up and puts him over his shoulder, and lurches away with him. Immediately a fight starts among four young men: the crowd simply opens up to give them elbow room as it flows by; some stop to look on. One of the fighters is knocked out cold and the others carry him to the back of a stall and dump him there. Back streets are not so densely crowded, but even more drunks. In a litter of broken glass and bottles a woman sits by herself being noisily sick.

Convergence of crowds round Central Station. Most departing males are drunk, have bags of rock and pockets full of beer bottles. Some sleep on steps or seats in the station, nursing bottles.

In the Blackpool pubs peculiar and unusual things happen. The ordinary clothes standards go—sometimes you see plenty good suits, bowlers and trilbies in vaults, and sometimes mostly caps, scarves, in best rooms. Also women are commonly seen in the vaults.

For instance in one vault (Sept. 4; 9 p.m.) there were 29 men, 8 women were drinking, 4 of whom were standing at the bar. In another, earlier the same evening, 52 men were counted and 12 women, 2 of whom were at the bar (cf. p. 144).

We have no age group figures for Blackpool, but all observers are agreed that a very much higher percentage of young people are seen in pubs there.

The following report shows another aspect of Blackpool holiday drunkenness:

> The parlour is crowded. At one side of room 2 girls in black coats and skirts, white blouses, are singing very loudly a very dirty song, using words seldom heard in Worktown pubs, and never from women. It is a parody of Old King Cole and it goes on and on, getting bawdier all the time. Many join in the chorus. However, a rival group at the other side starts bawling "The music goes round and round" and after a period of complete pandemonium, win—*everybody* in the room taking up the chorus.

> A Salvation Army girl comes in selling the *War Cry*, which two men buy, one looks at briefly, and puts down, the other does not look at, and puts in pocket. No one says anything to the girl.

> A man by himself at a table in the middle keeps on shouting, for no apparent reason, "Order, please, order, please". No one takes any notice.

> Now independent singing develops, various groups starting to sing on their own, sometimes one group's song being taken up by others, sometimes several groups going at once with several songs.

> In the middle of this uproar two very old ladies, sitting side by side, next to the dirty-song girls, wearing fur coats and hair-nets, remain impassive, say nothing, do nothing, and, as far as observer can see, have nothing to drink.

> The dirty girls come back again with a spirited rendering of "Oh, oh, Antonio" which everyone takes up. Then one of the girls gets up, and goes over to a group of chaps who have been signalling to her for some time. She sits in the middle

of them and sings "Down at the old Bull and Bush". One of the men implores her for "When your hair is turning grey". By now some of the younger chaps are yawning and lolling drunk. Suddenly the whole crowd is singing "Lily of Laguna". Then a young man sings a "heroic" sort of sad song. He sings this sitting down, while his mate, sitting opposite, holds his (the singer's) face very carefully between his hands, but not interfering with the movements of his jaws.

People are coming in and going out all the time, and there is a constant stream of women to and from the lavatory.

Now the dirty girl comes back to her friend, but sits next to observer. Two men buy the two girls drinks (I.P.A.). These two are, it turns out, an engine driver and his mate. The mate is small, round faced, and the whole time he is trying to sing a sad Irish song in a thin reedy tenor, of which no notice is taken, except by the girl next to him, who turns and laughs at him now and then. Later, Irish songs develop generally.

At 10 the singing dies down a little. A loud remark suddenly emerges from the (comparative) silence. "Mae West is the best football player in England." The girl next to observer is now nuzzling at him with her head and crossing her leg over his thigh, while she talks to him about all-in wrestling. The girl opposite (Alice) produces from handbag a large photograph of *le mannequin pisse*. One of the old ladies leans forward excitedly and says "It's in Brussels, I've been there often." Then subsides. The engine driver counters by producing a homemade pen drawing on a piece of paper. It is pornographic. The girls then tell a number of dirty stories. Observer does not find them very funny or original, but they are some of the dirtiest stories that he has heard. *There are no tabooed words* whatever. The girls, the man, and the old ladies, all freely use the odd half dozen common words that at the moment are never printed in England.

Later the observer and the girls, plus the two other men, went and had fried fish and chips. The rest of the evening passed soberly and chastely. The girls were subsequently contacted in Worktown, in a pub, where they behaved perfectly normally, just like anyone else. It is important to note that all this "breakdown" behaviour does not apply to abnormal people, but exactly the same types of drinker who have been observed behaving quite differently in the Worktown pubs. Another brief example of "breakdown" behaviour in Blackpool pubs is this:

Lounge is densely crowded. From remarks overheard observer judges the people to be Worktowners. At one table are 7 men and 7 girls, all drunk, ordering Crown ales rapidly, and singing Victorian music hall songs. Considerable erotic squeezing. One girl, a blonde, about 17, has long kiss with youth, lasting nearly a minute.

WHY GET DRUNK?

Now is it possible, on the basis of the above examples, to come to any conclusions about the behaviour of drunks?

It must be remembered that the examples chosen have not been included because they are "special", but because of their typicality—each showing characteristics of behaviour that have often been observed. Taken in conjunction with the typical behaviour of ordinary not-drunk drinkers, they show an accentuation of that behaviour. The aggressive man becomes more aggressive, the mild man more mild? People argue more, and at greater length, repeat themselves more. But, on the other hand, there are tendencies to boast, to sing, to say things that are not normally said and behave in ways that are not normally countenanced. Drunkenness manifests itself in the form of either the expression or removal of individual "repressions"—and when this takes place on a large scale, the removal of social repressions—the breakdown of conventions and tabus.

The material that has already been brought forward indicates that the pub is mainly sought as a social rather than an alcoholic environment. But it is a form of social environment that is only possible plus alcohol. And therefore a whole range of the social life of the ordinary pub-goer (who is one of the main sorts of "ordinary man") is bound up with the idea of drink. The social and alcoholic aspects of pub-going cannot really be separated.

The Chief Constable of Brighton, in his report to the General Annual Licensing Meeting (1938) gave the results of an analysis that he had made of the reasons given by over 300 people, arrested for being drunk, as to why they had got drunk. The following are his results:

A. Celebrating with friends	136
B. Habit	89
C. Depressed and worried	52
D. Medical reasons	18

     E. Daily visitors   6
     F. Lack of food   5
     G. Pension day   3
     H. Not used to liquor   2
     I. Mixed drinks   1

The first two categories are "social", and between them they account for 72 per cent. C—depressed and worried—which accounts for 17 per cent—is important. These are people who are getting drunk *because* of something, *in order* to forget they have lost their jobs, are miserable at home, etc. (compare our examples). While the rest are getting drunk socially, because "it's good company", and others are getting drunk too.

We get the apparent contradiction of one set of people becoming drunk because they are miserable, and another because they are happy. But both are getting some sort of "release". This release, the breakdown of personal and/or social barriers, is seldom the result of the purely physical stimulus of alcoholic substances. It takes place in a social environment, that itself is partly promoted by alcoholic stimulation, and the environment itself is a factor in bringing about the "release". Confused is Thomas's data-less deduction to explain socially her valid statistical data:

> Theoretically, the greatest psychological need for drunkenness would seem to arise at the time of greatest misery. But, however sordid the surroundings, and however intense the desire to escape from them, the ability to make such an escape is a function of the ability to purchase.

SOCIAL INTOXICATION

Instead of considering drunkenness primarily as the result of alcohol, we must look upon it as a social phenomenon, as a pretty regular minority social process of self-liberation from the week-routine and time-clock factory-whistle dimension of living, that in this culture is often entirely accomplished by alcoholic stimulation, but in other cultures can be and is equally produced by music, dancing, the social taking of drugs, oratory, or religious ceremonial—indeed the hysterical forms of revivalism and mass enthusiasm produce substantially the same effects as drink in an industrialized culture, and tend to replace altogether the need for alcohol in the individuals concerned. The behaviour of a cup final crowd, as observed by us this year around Wembley, was not very different in kind before opening time and after closing time—and this behaviour, shouting, linking, singing, occasional quarrels and fights, wearing coloured hats, is very similar to the all-summer crowd behaviour at Blackpool.

Looking at it in this way we may say that the behaviour of the ordinary Worktown week-end group of drunks manifests itself in the breaking down of *personal* inhibitions, and therefore automatically social inhibitions, thus influencing other persons, many of whom may be less drunk than the drunks. It isn't just a question of how many people are drunk, of a lot more drunks—a lot more people free from personal inhibitions than on a Wednesday; for by many doing so, a social sanction is obtained on the breach of these inhibitions generally, and the numerous tabus, the attitudes of quietness, shyness, reasoned conversation, respect for the law, from which the drunk is for a time liberated, tend also to disappear for everyone, drunk or sober. Similarly, the prostitute is picked up in a pub or after closing time, not in a milk bar or at tea-time.

This is a matter of general interest, in a culture where no one has yet exploited widespread mass-focus techniques, now so fully used in "undemocratic" states. In our Blackpool book we shall necessarily deal with crowd psychology more adequately and with more evidence, so for the moment need only note the conclusion of an American sociologist, D. Martin, who has made special study of the subject:

> The crowd is always formed for the unconscious purpose of relaxing the social control by mechanisms which mutually justify such antisocial conduct on the part of the members of the crowd.

With this relaxation the police invariably collaborate to a "reasonable extent", and with it alcohol is always linked. The dominant theme in these breakdowns is the negative pleasure goal. There is little destructive interest or hate. Outside pub buildings themselves, we have never—even on evening of May 12, 1937—seen drunks or crowds in Worktown damage anything appreciably. Le Bon, long considered classic crowd-expert (*The Crowd*, 1896), developed his theories in the best European sociological tradition, infusing the crowd with his personal feelings of aristocratic anti-mass. "Crowds are only powerful for destruction," he said (p. xix), and (p. 6) "What really takes place is a combination followed by the creation of new characteristics." Of these the latter statement approximates more nearly to observed fact; but there is no creation of novelty, rather a simple mechanics of numerical effect such as we have seen in the speed of drinking a gill of beer. Pub space: Saturday night: more money: more people: less space: more drinking: faster drinking: more effect: more drunks: more noise: song: maybe brawl: more police cases. The people are people just the same, the drunks drunks, the beer beer. The relative quantities of each alter, but there is no evidence so far for McDougall's mystical obscure "sympathetic induction".

"Primitive" or "savage" society is full of restrictions, conventions, tabus. And its way of life is rigid. There are no alternatives to it. Our society, though increasingly offering alternative ways of living and thinking, is no less full of conventions and restrictions. But they are conventions and restrictions imposed in a different way than those of primitive societies—purchasing power instead of magical power giving one the power to override them or make use of them, convention being enforced more by economic than religious sanctions. And while in primitive societies there are ritual and socially accepted occasions of breakdowns of tabu, our "feasts", holidays, etc., don't work out in quite the same way. Today in England, for instance, there is no occasion when the breakdown of sexual tabus and conventions is "officially" recognized, though Christmas (above), New Year, Easter and Holy Trinity come near it. In the life of the ordinary Worktowner no occasion arises when he is officially sanctioned and encouraged to dance in the streets, unless the Monarchy is involved in some ritual climax. But it is all right for him to do it in Blackpool, and he often does, not necessarily because he has been drinking a lot, but because a lot of people have got drunk and don't care any longer for the social conventions that forbid them to dance in the streets.

The conclusion to which evidence points is, just as there are two aspects of pub-going—social and alcoholic—that cannot really be separated from each other, so there are two aspects of drunkenness—individual and social—that are inseparably connected. And on occasions these two aspects are synthesised in the form of "social intoxication."

VIII

SINGERS AND PIANISTS: BOOKIES
AND PROSTITUTES

THERE ARE PEOPLE who go to pubs to make money.
One type, singers and pianists, are paid or otherwise rewarded
by the landlord; their function is that of attracting other people
to the pub. The other sort, bookies and prostitutes, also act as
attractions to sections of pub-goers; but they make money from
the drinkers and not from the landlords.

MUSIC

Pub music plays, and has played, an important role. Says
the report of the Worktown Temperance Society for 1852, giving
an example "illustrative of the evil effects of singing saloons":

> Two young women . . . visited one of the singing saloons
> for the first time. One of them attracted the attention of a
> young man there, a perfect stranger to her; he artfully per-
> suaded her to leave the room in his company. The sad result
> was, she became a mother.

There do not appear to be any figures, either for that time or
for today, of the effect of pub music and singing on the birth
rate. And it does not appear likely that the present declining
birth rate can be correlated with the decline of pub music! Today
the authorities tend rather to correlate it with drunkenness.
Says the Worktown Chief Constable in his report for 1936:

> I am rather inclined to believe that the increase (of drunks)
> may be to some extent attributed to the attractions—which
> include organized competitions, concerts, and variety enter-
> tainments . . .

He, the Chief Constable, while recognizing that there had been a
general increase in drunkenness throughout the country that year,
pointed out that the local increase was higher than that of the
national one. A glance at the diagrams already given, will show

that his interpretation, though clearly offered in the best of good faith, was a mistaken one, since there was not a straightforward correlation between national prosperity indices and those of Worktown, and the national increase in employment and drunkenness since the lowest period of the slump (1932) had taken place less regularly in Worktown. None the less the Chief Constable circulated a letter to all licensees prohibiting the employment of singers and variety artists in their houses, and he says in his report, since then "the practices have apparently ceased". Apparently is the operative word.

In the parlours of most pubs there is a piano. All customers are welcome to play it, and sing with it, and on week-end nights playing and singing is usually going on. Above many pianos a placard will be found, saying "Voluntary playing only allowed". This is usually a sign that on at least one night a week someone is being paid to play. In the lounge of almost all the really crowded and popular pubs there will be a pianist playing for most of the evening on week-ends. And from week to week it is usually the same pianist. It is not likely that such regularity is un-rewarded. Although it is not necessarily paid. Writes a barman:

> The pianist is the most important person in the pub concert room. He is generally a light that has failed, whose indulgence in pleasures of the immediate surroundings keeps him from seeing further afield. In most pubs in these days business is bad and payment of good players is a matter of difficulty, so people play who are content to sit and tinkle all night for a few drinks providing a sort of wireless background to a buzz of conversation. To stimulate the artist a custom prevails in Lancashire. That the landlord treats one who has sung two songs. He must do or business suffers.

Anything from 7s. 6d. to half a crown a night is the fee for a pub pianist.

> In the F. I got into conversation with the waiter-on who had been there 15 years and was aged 35. A very tough little chap. The new manager had been there only 12 months, and the waiter-on was very angry against him. He told me how this pub's business which was once the first in Worktown with 64 barrels of beer a week has now fallen right away, so he had made the new manager get in a pianist against police regulations —in fact he said to the manager, who is a very timid man "Oh

surely you know how to get a man to play and pay him and tell him to keep his mouth shut about it!" This pianist was an awfully seedy-looking object, but one of the finest that I have heard in Worktown and for an hour and a half he played beautifully, the most sentimental jazz tunes.

Before the official ban on paid entertainers, pubs would hire good variety artists and advertise them. Some are remembered and discussed today, one in particular has become an almost legendary figure.

> Fish and chip shop, man of about 40, proprietor, and observer talk about singing. Man says that it has been stopped in the pubs here. "Done the town a lot of harm." "It's taking the money out of Worktown" says fishman. But they go on to say it got to be a bit of a scandal. They were advertising for auditions in the pubs and girls came along got up as if they were going on the stage. They refer to V.Y. who was famous for a comic number "when they clapped her she used to pull out her tit and clap on it—she 'ad fine big ones too . . ." And he made an indicative sketching gesture with his hands.

This girl used to sing at the pub referred to in the previous report. She emigrated to another town nearby, and for quite a long time many Worktowners used to go over to visit the pub where she operated there.

A landlord who was asked whether he thought music made people drink more said:

> "Where there's entertainment there's more drinking." He also said of the Chief Constable "He used to send his men round in plain clothes to see if they were playing for money." And he told a story about one cop who dressed up as a navvy and went to a pub. "He stayed all day there. He sang for them when he left 'I shall come home when the ebb tide flows', and next day he raided 'em."

More than a year after the prohibition of this paid entertainment, when the 1937 drunk figures were announced (nearly 25 per cent increase) a further statement was made by the Chief Constable, who said (Report to Watch Committee for 1937, published 1938):

> It has now become apparent that certain licensed houses are again catering for this form of entertainment, and various

subterfuges are being adopted to assist the licensees to break the law.

And he adds:

> While no attempt will be made to suppress the occasional use of a piano on week-days in the case where friends meeting in a public house may play and sing for the entertainment of one another, the practice of holding what amounts to weekly concerts must cease.

It was too early to see what the effects of this would be before the war stopped this study. The initial effects of the original edict were more widespread than might be imagined. The pub concerts were a great attraction for people from the suburbs and surrounding villages who came into the town at week-ends on shopping excursions.

Now:

> Pub in X. Singing and music are of course permitted here; one pub has a jazz band. Until Chief Constable stopped singing in Worktown many went there at week-end to drink; the buses were packed. Now this movement has stopped. On the other hand plenty of Worktowners come out to drink in X. The people here are agricultural labourers, and also bleach workers. A man says to observer that Worktown "seems dead-like, no life in it, no music, no singin',—nothin'." He says none of them keep to one pub, but they have a local round and tend to end up here. "There's a good crowd 'ere—not the same as it is in Worktown."

The effects of this are both economic and cultural. The people of these villages are tending no longer to look on Worktown as a centre for enjoying themselves. The whole focal effect of Worktown, whose population of some 170,000 is about a quarter of its generally assumed "shopping area", has been upset, its week-end function of bringing people in to shop, cinema and drink, from the many small hamlets all round. And the effect has actually been reversed even from Worktown centre. Says a publican:

> "It's taking thousands of pounds out to surrounding places and going to the pubs there, where music is permitted, to drink and sing."

A trip round the outskirts on the following Friday confirmed this; landlords of surrounding hamlets said there were Worktown people in, and that many more came over on Saturdays.

In banning organized music the Chief Constable—whose powers in such matters are considerable, though subject to the Watch Committee, the Anglican churchwarden chairman of which goes on his summer holidays with his family along with the C.C. and his family—has hit a vital element in pub culture, one which each evening transformed the individual units of drinkers in all rooms into a harmonizing whole, who send themselves often into a sweat with laughter and melody. Worktown people love music of simple sort. They love singing. There is nowhere else where they may sing the songs of their own choosing. In a town which has practically no native painting or poetry or literature, the curtailing of music is a serious matter intellectually. And the action has evidently done nothing either to stop drinking or drunkenness. It has practially nothing to do with either—far less than darts, dominoes or the Police Sports, which is the biggest local sporting betting-cum-booze-up of the year. But in making such decisions it is doubtful whether those responsible, despite their intelligent and sincere interest, are competent to make judgments based on understanding either of drinking people or drinking fact. The Chief Constable of Worktown is a teetotaller. Neither he nor the Chairman of the Watch Committee, nor the religious leaders who are active in restricting pub activities, ever go into Worktown pubs. Indeed, nine out of ten of all the well-to-do in Worktown never go into pubs.

Those well-offs who drink do so at home or (a large number) in the Golf Clubs, which are open all hours, including Sunday (excepting the Municipal Golf Course, where Sunday golf is prohibited). Such a position is typical of the contemporary English scene, where those who legislate for the poorer sections of the community have little accurate knowledge of what they are doing or where it will lead. Classic example was that of the recent Royal Commission on Gambling, which called nearly a hundred witnesses, representing every sort of interested organization imaginable, but not a single ordinary person, not a punter. In an almost casual sentence it advised that the whole of Football Pool betting be made illegal; it called no witness who had filled in a pool form. It can have had no *social* understanding of what it was doing; its conclusions cannot have been arrived at on the basis of impartial analysis, objective human facts, or social realities. Naturally, the Commission, like so many such Commissions, produced a report which could not and cannot properly be put into practice, at least with useful effect. The local police are in the same boat. On crime they know their stuff well enough. When they start tampering with the normal, inhibiting pleasures generally regarded as "legitimate", complications are bound to ensue. The pub is the one "normal" place which the police can closely control and command. They are unable to tell churches that they must not have Liturgical Services or Sung Eucharists.

So far few Worktown pubs have radios. When they become popular the pub atmosphere will have changed quite a bit. For the radio does not cater especially for large, amorphous groups who come to *participate*. The pub-goer is not just a listener and looker. He is active in drinking and talking about all sorts of subjects and with all sorts of people, many of whom he would never meet in any other way. So he or she needs accompaniment rather than complete entertainment, at least for most of the time. Music in the background, songs which everyone knows, largely sentimental songs.

At present, therefore, the musical side of pub culture is getting involved in a sense of guilt and repression, another one of the several already associated with the pub. Pianists are still being paid, but in secret; two reports on this:

C. Arms. 9 p.m. Approx. 70 in all rooms; 35 in main singing room, where an old man, black suit, bald, pince-nez, plays piano and sings, making cracks in music hall patter style between songs. (Rector of Stiffkey, just deceased, was mentioned.) All join in the singing, very loudly indeed, also those in the next room, who usually finish a whole bar later than in here. The entertainer is an ex-pro. and in observer's opinion is certainly paid by the landlord.

Best room. Piano being played by young woman in brown dress, who has glass of Guinness at her side on the end of the keyboard. Over the piano is the notice "Voluntary playing only". Two young men are fraternizing with the pianist, then exchange jokes with the landlord. The pianist says to him "You look tired" and he says "I am tired, me 'eart's broke". She plays loudly and sings "Somebody stole my heart away". The young men join in loudly, slapping their knees and beating time with their feet. Then she plays another jazz tune, and then some old ones, such as Burlington Bertie, which are very well received.

All observers report that the sentimental and old-fashioned songs go much the best, and also the sad sort of Irish songs are popular. And though mostly jazz songs are played and sung, the evening nearly always finishes with old-fashioned ones.

Sufficient examples of ordinary voluntary pub singing have been given in reports in earlier sections. We are able to give the pub pianist's point of view, written by himself—the account actually is of a Christmas club, and also contains material relevant to our next subject:

About the end of August the ladies frequenting the parlour decided to have a saving up club for Christmas. Some of them wanted to have curios as well. (See later about this.) . . . Anyway, the landlady objected, so this was just a saving club, no limit. Five of them drew out their money before the time. The remainder were paid out last night (Dec. 22). They all turned up for their money and the landlady paid for the contents of a large potato pie, which was made by a customer. She no doubt was actuated by the thought of a presence of so much money, and the hope that some of it might be spent in the house. Ladies drifted in about 8 onwards, until the appropriate moment, everyone being paid out, the pie made its appearance. This was sold at twopence per plate, the money pooled in front of the secretary. This pie was sold in all parts of the house. While this was going on a weary and neglected professor of music was thumping tunes out of a dilapidated piano.[1] The pie finished, it was decided that each contribute to the accumulated heap of pence, then to have Guinness round until it was finished. Tense moments were experienced when the drinks were being paid for. The last round was bought before anything like a convivial atmosphere prevailed. Everyone was satisfied when it was suggested that the three-pence left over should go to buy the pianistic drudge a beer. He responded to the noble gesture by playing Christmas carols, Noel, and Christmas Bells. There was singing of a community type and a little dancing. Time was called, and round empty tables talk centred round the family life and the good old times. They drifted out in ones and twos, the pianist

[1] This piano once had a gallon of beer poured into its works by a drunk. The writer is the only person who can produce anything recognizable as music from it.

gathered up his music, patted the dog, and made his way home full of potato pie and free beer!

BOOKIES

Betting is important in the pub, takes various forms. One form is centred around activities that take place *within* the pub. This is dealt with later. Another form centres round activities that take place *outside* the pub. Betting of this kind involves the largest sums, and is carried on through the medium of the bookmaker and his runner.

Writes a landlord:

Betting is forbidden by most pubs, but the pubs that do the best trade are those that have a means for that entertainment, a good bookie is a great asset to a pub.

This is corroborated by the following, written for us by a local drinker, who was asked to write up what he knew about a leading local pub bookie:

This man, known as Nero, employs about 170 runners in Worktown and district but has no particular pub where he stays for a long time. At one time when singing was allowed to have full swing in Worktown he used to follow a niece of his around wherever she was engaged in that capacity. It is always noticeable when he enters a public house where any of his agents are employed. He is a tall man, thick set, with thick gold chain very prominent, he also has the usual cigar and a very prominent display of gold rings on his fingers I personally have counted as many as six rings on both hands and when he is drinking usually rests one hand on the counter to display the same. He is always welcomed by the landlord owing to the fact that through his business he is responsible for probably half the custom that enters these places. The word goes round the house that Nero has arrived and all the customers in the lobby get as close as possible so that they can be in the first order. The vaults clients usually voice their protest through the agent who very often is permanently placed there and the drinks are on Nero. He usually has a large following of relatives but these are deteriorating at present owing to the fact that they are employed as checkers and trusted servants to get the slips in from agents, consequently one or two of them have been putting slips in after the race has been won, so poor Nero can't even trust himself now. He is expected to contribute to all annual picnics or bowling handicaps the usual contribution being £1 so that his prestige runs very high to the people who buys his cigars and rings. The agent also holds a position of esteem in the pub especially during the dinner hour of a working day the position is that the client wants a bet and the runner being in the pub causes the client to enter to make his bet and this helps the landlord to make a sale. There is also the fact that a client that has a method of selecting winners and enters the pub to receive his winnings very often calls for a drink and the agent receives one also so that one can see how profitable an agent can be to the Licensee. I personally would suggest that instead of a brewery advertising "Guinness is Good" it would be better to say "Nero's agent calls here". The agent also has a great deal to do with arranging domino sweeps, bowling handicaps, picnics, etc.; money lending is also another feature of his business because he works on a weekly basis of payment with the bookmaker all winnings being paid in at week-end so that the agent has always a surplus of money during the week, this enables him to lend money to his clients. So that we can weigh all the facts together and find that the agent is more prominently placed in the pub than the Licensee himself. The Licensee therefore has to give a great deal of Latitude to the agent so that when he puts his betting dice on the table the licensee has to close one eye and be content to have his card posted up "No betting allowed".

This account covers the whole field of bookies' pub activities. As the writer says, betting is usually done in the dinner hour:

Midday, vault. The bookie's runner comes in and has argument with the landlady about her yesterday's doubles. Betting slips and newspapers are produced. She then makes bets on the day's races. The runner has a gill of mild.

Of course, all this is illegal. Transactions usually take place unobtrusively, like this:

Vault, 5 men with caps and scarves, talking about work and wages. Man, blue suit, no hat, comes in, says nothing, gives half a crown to a chap. Blue suit leans against door for a little. Nothing has been said so far. Then the man to whom the half-crown had been given says, husky and questioning, "Pint?" and goes to bar and gets a pint for blue suit.

But the police are aware of it, though perhaps not exactly when, where and who. Our old friend P.C. Thirsty bets heavily in his local pub. At this pub the local bookie sometimes doesn't come round at midday, but sends his wife instead. Barman suggests that he knows the place is being watched on those occasions.

Though almost every pub has regular betting, convictions are rare. It is an accepted breach of the law, and one that the police themselves often commit. In the following case a landlord in a small pub on the edge of Worktown was fined £10 and costs (4s.) "for permitting the use of a betting house"—the bookie was not penalized; ditto the bookie's runner. The press report of the police court case reads:

A man named X—then said in the presence of Y: "I've got a good thing for the 4.30 race at Pontefract. I have a friend who sends me tips." X wrote out a betting slip and showed it to the officers. Y (the landlord) was still in the room, about six feet away.

Z then shouted across the room "Be sharp with that bet. You are going to be too late." Z then went to the table where the officers were seated, produced a betting clock, and taking a betting slip and money, put them into a betting clock bag. Between 2.30 and 3.13 the majority of men present wrote out betting slips. . . On the following Saturday . . . in the room were 15 men and the man Z was sitting at a table about three yards from the licensee. Z was counting about 15 betting slips at the table, and did something with them that the officers could not observe. Sporting papers were also in the room, and the licensee was present at the whole of the time, except when serving drinks.

When Dt. Insp. ——, Sergt. ——, and other officers, executed a search warrant at 2.50 on June 12th Z had in his pocket three betting clocks. He was seen to tear up some betting slips and throw them under the seat. In two of the clocks were 35 betting slips, representing 131 bets ranging from 3d. to 1s. 6d. to a total value of £3.

When charged Y said "They did it all unknown to me. I knew the fellow Z came in, but I never saw a bet passed." Gambling brought no reward to the licensee. There was a notice prohibiting betting. It was detrimental to the licensee, and put him in danger of losing his house and his occupation. He had been a licensee three and a half years, and did not gamble, and had never seen a betting clock. He did not hear the remark about the betting clock. If he had he would have ordered the man out.

Incidentally, in a main street in the centre of Worktown there is a large cigarette shop that doesn't sell any cigarettes; there are dummies in the window, and the counter inside is only used for passing bets over; everybody knows about this, including the police, since anybody can walk in.

It is, amongst pub-goers, a known thing that the bookie's runner acts as moneylender. Verification of this can only be laconic and unexciting, such as the following note given to us by a pub-goer who has helped with this work:

> August 1st. Two instances of the bookmaker's runner lending money occurred at the V. Hotel on the above date about 9 p.m. Two regulars, one borrowing two bob, and the other one shilling.

But the connection between the speed of horses, credit, and the consumption of drink, manifests itself in other ways:

> People drinking at table on one side of the room are very loud and cheerful. Little sharpfaced woman, very old, is rather drunk and talking bawdy about little men and copulation. The old woman says "What about flies, they do it all right" and everyone laughs. She tells a story about her husband (also a little man) urinating out of the bedroom window one night and nearly having a regrettable accident, owing to the window suddenly slamming down. She then says that she is going to G— tomorrow, to the barracks, where she will drink in the canteen with generals.
>
> This group are drinking on credit, the man who orders the rounds writing them down on a piece of paper. He has won on a horse, and collects tomorrow, he says.

The illegality of pub betting, and the consequent surreptitiousness of the transactions, makes it easy for an outsider completely to overlook the place of the bookie and his agents in the pub. On the other hand it is easy, as does the writer of our report on Nero, to exaggerate the importance of the bookie as a pub figure. The real importance of pub betting in the life of the pub is that it makes possible for "week-end drinking" to take place amongst isolated groups on any night of the week, when a member of the group has come up on a long priced winner. The economic importance of the bookie, to the landlord, both as a "draw" to betting customers, and as source of rakeoff in drink profits on the occasions of big winnings, is self-evident.

PROSTITUTION

In Worktown, a town in which strangers are not common, and whose transient population is small, prostitution does not flourish: the full-time prostitute is a rarity. The small band of them that exists are to be found in a few town centre pubs. They circulate within this limited orbit of a few hundred yards. One of these pubs in particular is regarded as their headquarters. A local pub-goer who spent an evening there acquiring what information he could, wrote the following account:

> I received some very interesting conversation during my stay there, I got into touch with a man who spends on an average a pound per week on prostitutes. This man pointed out all the prostitutes as they came in and their methods of operation. In the first place he gave me to understand that a great deal of jealousy attached to this particular pub owing to the fact that where you find a dozen prostitutes in a particular pub at one time they watch one another for stealing their clients. They also observe what clients their rivals pick up. To give an instance of this he tells me a story about himself and two prostitutes that attended there regularly and he says "I always interrupts by saying I can get eight in a night" . . . An elderly prostitute then entered with a client I felt sorry for him because I know she has had about 3 packets.
>
> When I asked him how much they charged he replied there are types that will do it for free drinks, those are the type that are married or receiving some income from elsewhere, then there are those who manage to scrape enough together by backstreet methods, prices varying from 2s. to 5s., but the real professional type that take their clients home charge from 10s. to any price according to what they think a client can pay.

Another local pub-goer gave us the following dossier on some of the pub whores:

> *The Z——.* Well noted for Married Women Type of Importuning.
> *May X.* Resides in the vicinity of ——. Visits the ——. Can be seduced after two bottles of Guinness. Many boys have missed the last car to bed.
> *Fannie Z.* Frequents the —— in preference. Mother tells fortunes. Very low class type.

Miss ——. Frequents (three pubs). Clean professional type. Always requires pay, before Business. Very generous will treat patron to a good drink. These women generally want 10s. and supper, have only one man a night, and let him sleep.

The most common type of pub prostitute is semi-professional, of the sort referred to above, girls who work and who sit about in pubs waiting to be picked up and stood drinks; they will go home with the men who stand them drinks, or rather let the men "see them home"—the town's irregular sex life is consummated in the back streets, which are narrow alleys running behind houses parallel to the road in which the houses stand. The peacetime street lights go out at 11.15 p.m. This makes casual intercourse uncomfortable, but available, and is one of the reasons why so few Worktowners have recourse to professional prostitutes.

This type of amateur prostitute is mostly found in the pubs frequented by young people, referred to earlier. Here is an excerpt from a report from one of these pubs:

Next to observers were two young women wearing green coats, fur collars, thick make-up, veils. Also (a) a respectable looking young millworker, (b) thin, cheeky young man, and (c) man of about 30, pockmarked, with glasses. The girls try to get off with observers (who are both wearing prosperous overcoats) by saying at different times "Are you enjoying yourself?" "Been on whiskey all the evening then?" "Is your name Sattiwell?" and "Been here before?" After ten minutes the young man (b) got into conversation with these girls. (a) took longer. The girls paid for their own drinks; it was about this that (b) got into conversation. He said "You know the bargain, don't you—the price of two Guinnesses and I'll take you home, front door or back". (Both observers felt that had it not been for the hope held out by their prosperous overcoats this offer would have been accepted.) But the girls left, unattended, at 10.5 p.m., having arrived at 8.41 and had only one drink, no cigarettes. They said twice "beggars can't be choosers you know". Just before they left (a) joined in backchatting to them, but they didn't take much notice of him.

Directly they had gone animated conversation developed, (a) saying "I knew you wouldn't get anywhere with 'em", at which (b) said vigorously he never expected to.

(*c*) "The only way you can get anything from them is for money." (Another man, sitting by, solitary, says "I weighed them up in three seconds." And he never spoke again.)

(*a*) declared it was impossible to get anything out of them anyway. (*b*) agreed. (*c*) said "There's about as much chance . . . (thinking hard) . . . as an Eskimo getting sunstroke." He then told a confused and improbable story about how at one time when he had a lot of money and was going on a trip up to London and wanted to take a girl with him, he dated up one of these girls for the week-end. (He got very confused with his dates, speaking of meeting her on various days.) But she said she wouldn't come unless he came across with a Guinness immediately. So, as he said "I took 'er at 'er word and didn't turn up meself on Wednesday."

(*a*) "They're just gold grubbers."

(*b*) (very cheerfully) "All they want is Guinness, 'ere every night for it."

(*c*) in the face of strong opposition, seemed to think that there was a chance of something further, though he admits "You pay for 'em inside the pub, you pay for 'em outside and by that time you're inside out". At the end he summed up, in his peculiarly difficult style "It's like a motorbike—pitting your skill against hers."

The interesting thing about this conversation, notes the observer, is that not one of them considered the possibility of *paying* for the girls; it was something outside the range of their ideas.

The observer's comment at the end of the report above shows the attitude of the ordinary Worktowner who wants a casual girl; and explains the small part played in the life of the pub by prostitution.

HAWKER PUB-GOERS

Hawkers have already been discussed, from a different angle. They form no groups, neither do they act as an attraction to pub-goers. But many in their private life capacity go to pubs. The 1931 census lists over 500 hawkers in Worktown. A pub opposite the open market is a special hangout for many of them.

Certain newspaper sellers, who have a regular pub round, are popular as individuals, and in a very limited sense can be said to be part of the pub social life. Most famous of these is an old, amusing, loud-shouting, back-chatting, paper-seller called "Chronicle Tommy"; his real name is unknown.

Where these hawkers differ from other pub-goers is that they are permitted to come in and go out again without having a drink. So are Salvation Army lassies. They are accepted as part of the Worktown landscape, though not necessarily with good grace. And it is significant that several prostitutes, in one pub particularly, do not drink alcohol unless they are with men. They drink grape-fruit, and it is "done" for them to do so, no one regards it as odd. They thus put themselves somewhat outside the pub life, dissociating themselves (partly for practical and physical reasons) from the basic pub item of alcohol. In the reverse direction, the bookie is generally expected to stand a round when he enters, acknowledging a special pub status. He is the centre of the betting, which comes second to drink as pub interest, first as an all-round working-class leisure interest generally. The methods of betting, raffling, sweeping, gambling, will be shown when, in the chapter after next, we describe the sporting life of the pub. Before that we must briefly examine the sub-groups with no definite money-seeking figure as centre, the secret societies and pub-clubs. The bookie, prostitute, pianist or hawker are persons out not so much to enjoy as to acquire; they come from outside, and focus certain human interests, of food, gamble, rhythm, news, sex, which are not catered for in the structure of the pub itself, or are actually forbidden by law in the pub. The sub-groups in the pub, subject of the next chapter, have similar interests, but run them from within the pub, with the assistance of appointed regulars, and the positive approval of the landlord.

IX

SUB-GROUP PUB GROUPS

In the pub, amongst pub-goers, groups exist whose activities, though they are not directly connected with drinking, play a considerable part in the life of the pubs.

These activities range from the highly organized groups of societies such as the Buffaloes and Oddfellows, to the transitory clubs formed to get up outings or picnics and dissolving once these aims have been carried out.

In the section on music there was a report of a savings club. This is an example of the group of an unofficial kind, got up informally amongst a crowd of regulars, as contrasted to the more highly organized type, which may be held under the auspices of the landlord or of the brewers, or which may be some outside organization that uses the pub as its headquarters.

SAVINGS CLUBS

Of the first type, savings clubs are the most common, often run in connection with picnics, and outings. The formation and history of one of these is described by a barman:

Four years ago the men had a picnic. A notice was posted up in the taproom in order that those wishing to go could write down their names. This work was done by a self-appointed customer with a liking for this kind of work. When enough names were on the list a meeting was called. It was decided that each would pay in each week a fixed sum and that donations would be sought from those traders who supply the pub with goods including the brewer, tobacconist, and of course the landlord. Various means were resorted to in order to swell the funds—surreptitious raffles and curios, until the time came for deciding the place to be visited. Their decision started with Blackpool but this was changed to a spot near by. This was again changed as someone bluntly suggested that as it was going to be a boozing expedition they may as well go to some pub in the neighbourhood of Worktown, then there would be more money for booze. This found general favour.

The weather was glorious, and using the town's transport facilities, they all arrived at a country pub, neatly attired, cigars and buttonholes, for an afternoon at bowls, tea afterwards, and then to settle down to the real business of soaking. This thoroughly accomplished they drifted back in small groups mainly through the help of sympathetic bus and tram conductors, in time for a drink before closing time at the pub.

This picnicking is not done so much now, as charabanc owners have found a wider field. Commission was given to the organizers of these stunts.

Here is an account of a more lively outing, by charabanc this time:

A local pub arranged a picnic to Southport. The members, all who frequented the pub regularly and knew each other well by sight had paid a small sum per week to pay for the drive and tea. My informant went in place of a woman who could not go at the last moment. About 30 people were in the party. The coach was due to start from the pub at 1.30, but the members agreed to arrive at one and have a drink before starting.

This picnic was full of incident, first of all the coach was ready to go at 1.30 but they were waiting for someone, no one seemed clear who it was but it turned out to be somebody's *man*. (My informant said: "Everybody was with somebody else's husband or wife.") At two o'clock the lady finally said she'd bring him in, and did. She marched into the vault (he was playing dominoes) overturned the table, and made a scene. They came out together. She said "I wish I'd come my bloody self". He said "Well, I didn't know you were waiting! You knew where I was". Finally they got in and away they went.

They had a great big meal half way to Southport at a large pub that caters for such parties. They had, of course, stopped at a few pubs on the way. Arriving at Southport, after a great tea, the party broke up into small groups and went in different directions, some to the fair grounds, some to the gardens, some to the prom. and so on, but all met at different pubs during the evening. One woman had won a case of cutlery on the fairground. Much drink was had by most of the people.

On the way back the coach stopped at several pubs, and at one some of the elder women had cups of tea. At this place some male member of the party had a fight with someone. They were away from the coach for a long time and when they came back this man had been fighting and wanted to go back and fight some more. But his elderly mother-in-law quietened him, she gave him a crack with her umbrella, and said be quiet.

The party arrived home about midnight. My informant described them as some very nice people, and some lowlife folk. The very nice people kept together and held aloof from the fights and brawls.

These picnic and savings clubs (some of them called 'diddlum clubs')[1] are got up for a specific object, and apart from that objective do not have any separate existence as a social group in the pub. Another type of club, formed with similar objectives, to run picnics and outings, and to hold raffles, etc., also has regular meetings and rules of procedure, and does not go out of existence (as do the others), as soon as the accumulated money has been spent. Here is a typical meeting:

Sunday, midday. Small stone-flag taproom, with benches and three-legged stools. Large kitchen range at one side. Waiter-on is a monstrously fat man, who wears waistcoat, jacket, and bowler, despite his personal perspiration. He is a spinner and famous for never taking off his bowler, not even in the mill. There are 29 men present and 26 of them have pints. At the centre of the long table, sits the chairman. He calls for "the glasses" and two gill mugs (the only gill mugs in the pub, and not used for drinking purposes) are brought in and put in front of him. People hand up blue cards which have the name of the club printed on them and he takes subscriptions, putting silver in one mug, copper in the other.

A white china gallon jug full of mild is brought in, and everyone's mugs (including that of the observer, who is a stranger here) are filled from it. This is paid for out of money left over from raffles and other activities.

A man pays threepence to the chairman and says he can now swear as much as he likes. And a little later, he gets to his feet, doffs his cap, and accuses various other chaps of having sworn. Each time anyone rises to address the chair they doff their caps. Fines of a penny and two pence are paid for

[1] Reasons given for this name are: (a) that the treasurers often abscond with the funds, and (b) that sometimes large parcels full of nothing are raffled; in both cases the members are diddled. The term also covers savings systems mainly run through mills and churches, where you start with units of a halfpenny in the first week and increase your subscription a halfpenny per unit per week up to one shilling, i.e. 24 weeks, then down a halfpenny a week to a halfpenny again. Then draw out.

swearing. The interesting point about this is that very "bad" swear words that are seldom used in ordinary local pubs (though they are common enough in the south) are used frequently here, the men laughing and paying up immediately.

The chairman discusses next week's outing. A man proposes someone as a member of the club, who wants to come on the outing. Another man objects, on grounds that are obscure to the observer. There is some shouting, and everyone else is against the objector, and they want him to be fined, but this doesn't happen.

Raffle tickets for a budgerigar are circulated. And the chairman announces that next Sunday a buttonhole show and competition will be held. Seven of the men present today have fine carnation or sweet pea buttonholes.

Later, a member of this club wrote up an account of it for us, with some general remarks about similar clubs:

How formed? Some man or licensee suggests it, and the members of the public frequenting that pub acquiesce, because they know they will get more than they pay in if a club is formed. Meetings are held every Sunday at noon drinking hours; other meetings, if any, by a small committee along with the licensee, to arrange for motor coach, teas, dinners, paying out, and what not.

The Rules. These are made usually after a Chairman and Secretary and a small committee of about 4 others have been appointed. They raffle various things from parcels of grocery or "joints" to such things as canaries and cucumbers. They also have flower shows or buttonhole shows. In this case[1] they make a profit of about 7s. 6d. in the space of the 2nd hour, 1—2 p.m. . . . Other members, such as Mr. L. who has a hardware business, will give small articles on occasion as a kind of advertisement for their goods, as well as assisting the club.

The outing: The cost, I don't suppose, will be above 6s. which will include a feed at about 2s. or usually 2s. 6d. per head. The coach ordered will take 32.

There are no specific amounts to be paid, and although payments are optional, the club doesn't usually encourage contributions of less than sixpence. It is certainly optional to a member to save up as much as he likes, because less the cost of the outing, he receives back what he puts in plus his share of the club's profits.

[1] The writer is now referring to his own club, the one described in the previous report.

He describes procedure about paying fines for swearing, already referred to:

> . . . there are also other offences, such as a member addressing the "Chair" with his hat on, for which he is mulcted the usual penny fine. One member was fined for placing his hand on a certain part of his "Anatomy" in order to convey to another member a meaning, which, if the words had been used, would have certainly meant a fine against him. For making use of this subterfuge he was successfully "brought to book". The following is the manner the accusing member used. Taking off his bowler hat and rising to his feet he addressed the Chairman. "Mr. Chairman and fellow members, Ah propose that Brother so-and-so is fined for indecent be'aviour. 'E 'as put 'is 'and on 'is body in a way in order to insult Brother so-and-so. Ah should like a brother to second that."
>
> "Ah'll second Bro. R's proposal, Mr. Chairman." (This member was subsequently fined for addressing the Chair wi' 'is 'at on.) The Chairman rising, addresses the members thus "Fellow members, it 'as bin moved un seconded that Brother so-and-so is fined a penny for indecent behaviour. All in favour please show. Carried. Take 'im the glass."
>
> The fines collected in the glass are counted at the end of the meeting and the amount made known to the members. All moneys received are recorded each Sunday and the takings are generally, in most if not all clubs, handed over to the Licensee for safe custody. The Licensee, as the time of the "outing" approaches, usually apprises the "Brewery Co." people of the event; this is traditional in these parts, and generally receives the "Brewery's" approval along with a nice donation of a couple of quid.

Another sort of selective pub group with rules of order, passwords and taboos, is the Dolly Club. The password is, so to speak, showing your dolly. Every member of the Dolly Club (which has no formal constitution) carries a small cheap doll. When one member meets another, both must produce their dollies. If one hasn't his doll with him, he pays 2*d*. or some other fixed sum into the pool, for drinks. Membership is purely masculine, and it is a little strange, perhaps, to see a miner meeting a navvy in the street, each producing dolly.

There is, as we shall see, a great deal in common between clubs of these types and the more organised semi-masonic gatherings that take place in reserved rooms and in secret, in pubs.

SECRET SOCIETIES

The Ancient Noble Order of United Oddfellows and the Royal and Antediluvian Order of Buffaloes have rooms and hold regular meetings in Worktown pubs. Both these and the trade unions, sprang up in the form of autonomous local benefit and mutual aid societies, centred around the pub in which they met, and often giving their name to the pub. And both passed through a period when they had to function as secret societies, so that the rituals and passwords in which they indulged had or took on a practical import.

As a Worktown drinker put it:

"The Buffs are a kind of Masons, they're a beer crowd and the Masons go on whiskey . . . a chap asked me once to join, I told 'im I can drink my beer all right without having to pay ten bob to join anything—they've smoking concerts you know, I've seen the beer going up, 20 or 25 gills at a time . . . funny, they never seem to drink pints."

An observer who made enquiries about joining the Buffs was told by one of them, "We're good company," and he added, "You get four pound when your wife dies"—an indication of the exclusive masculine attitude of this organisation. It is not difficult to join. You have to be proposed, seconded, not black-balled, pay 10s. 6d. The elaborate initiation rites may be summarized as follows:

1. Initiate is taken upstairs in the Pub.
2. He is blindfolded.
3. His proposer and seconder knock three times on a wicket.
4. Whispered conversation and passwords with doorkeeper.
5. He is supported by elbows and led into large room.
6. A man shakes hands with him, asks if he joins of his own free will and whether he has tried to join any lodge before.
7. He is led to other side of room and all this repeated.
8. Declaration of Buff principles, in 18th century "Rights of Man" style, is read aloud to him.
9. "Litany" chanted by all present; words inaudible.
10. A long churchwarden pipe (clay) is handed to him.
11. His right hand is placed on his heart, and pipe pressed there.
12. Pipe is explained as symbol of purity, friendship, peace.
13. Oath of secrecy, read out to him, he repeating.
14. He snaps pipe with both hands.

15. Bandage taken off his eyes, revealing . . .
16. The Worthy Primo (chairman) in chain and regalia, standing on canopied dais before "altar" with a red and a blue candle (The Royal Lights).
16. All present "Form the Link", dancing round him and singing "Auld Lang Syne," etc.
17. Speech of welcome.
18. Drinks all round.

This sort of ritual is characteristic of the Buffs and other such societies; it is at its simplest at initiation. Ordinary meetings are held once a week or so. When a member enters he must knock three times, give the password, then, when (and only when) the door is closed, come forward and face the Worthy Primo on his throne with his right hand on chest, second finger in waistcoat buttons, and say "Worthy Primo, Officers and Brethren, I bid you good evening". He then signs his name in the book, pays 4d., and orders a drink. Before drinking it he must adopt the above position again ("upstanding") and say "Worthy Primo, have I your permission?" Beer must always be called "gat", tobacco "weed", penny "dee", door "tyle", etc—fines for failing to preserve these usages. No christian names may be used, all officials to be addressed by full titles, no swearing. Fines for infringements. Meetings alternate between periods of Strict Business Order and Liberty Hall. In front of the Worthy Primo and his assistant (the City Marshal) are revolving wooden plaques with one side the letters S B O, on the other L H. When these are turned, both officers knock three times each with a gavel. S B O involves largely the raising of funds by raffles, "curios", subscriptions and fines—members often deliberately infringing rules to be fined. Another official, the City Constable, walks round with a small truncheon and a long collecting box during S B O. The main features of L H periods are drinking, piano playing, telling "stories", singing.

Very important in Buff life is the process of "raising"— that is, of going up one degree on the Buff's ritual ladder, and thus gaining new titles, rank, badges, taboos, secret words. We have fully described the exceedingly elaborate nature of these rites in another book and so need only point out here that in many respects the ritual itself, and much more so the spirit of it, resembles very closely the degree-taking rites and chief-making social ladder of the cannibal tribes in

Malekula, Western Pacific, as described in *Savage Civilisation* (by Tom Harrisson, Gollancz). Swords, aprons embroidered in gold, stiff purple velvet gauntlets, Guards of Honour, numbered stages and steps and ribbons, changed titles and stepping up, are part of these rites, The ceremonies have, of course, much in common also with the rites of Freemasonry. For example, the Buff's raising to "third degree" (Knight of Merit) approximates in many respects to the first degree initiation in Masonry, where, to quote handbook: "The candidate is divested of all money (to symbolise the buildings of Solomon's metalless temple) and metal, his right arm, left breast, and left knee bare, the right heel slipshod, is blindfolded, and has a rope called a cable to put round the neck, with a sword pointed to the breast." He is asked if he can feel the sword ("poignard") and replies, Yes. He is given a 24 inch gauge, a gavel, a chisel, plumb lines, a tracing board— craft implements. A Freemasonry song goes:

> Thus, symbols of our order one,
> The compass, level and the square,
> Which teach us to be just and fair,
> And that's the craft of Masonry.

Thus "on the level", "are you playing square with me?" etc. Second degree masonry is similar to first (but without sword or blindfold), unlike the Buffs, who make second degree much more ceremonious. The Masonic doorkeeper is called Tyler, as with the Buffs, and his function is similar. So is the ritual of opening the lodge for "refreshment" and closing it for business.

Similiar too is the nomenclature for business. The Buffs have a "Governing Authority" which, by their constitution, "shall consist of a CONSTITUTION", which consists of:

Prov. Grand Primo, Immediate Past Prov. Grand Primo, Deputy Prov. Grand Primo, Prov. Grand Secretary, Prov. Grand Treasurer, Prov. G. Chamberlain, Prov. G. Tyler, Prov. G. Constable, Prov. G. Registrar, Prov. G. Ald. Juniper, Prov. G. Ald. Benevolence, Prov. G. Minstrel, Prov. G. Trustees, and Prov. G. Waiter, together with Past Prov. G. P.s, Past Deputy Prov. G.P.s, and Delegates appointed in writing from each minor lodge.

Special rules cover the Jewels, important part of Buff property, provided from a voluntary fund. "R.O.H. jewels must be obtained from G.L. through the G.A.", warns the Buff Code book. And, unusually, a special rule forbids the suspension of standing orders under any circumstances. The Knight's Chapter sees that "cere- monies are carried out in uniformity, according to the Rules of the Order from time to time ordained"; they also look out for cases where members need help of any sort, "cultivate a spirit of brotherly feeling among the members", "promote the welfare and well-being of all enrolled".

The Buffs are a small but vital part of Worktown pub-life, and they are never associated with any building other than a pub. The only outward sign of their existence to the ordinary drinker in any bar is a notice (usually behind the bar) saying that a Lodge of R.A.O.B. is held at this pub. There are thirty lodges in the Worktown "Province". The Observers who collected the above and much other material mixed in with them, personally experienced and recorded the rites. But the Buffs are only one of the secret societies of masonic type among the working classes. Another is the Oddfellows.

ODDFELLOWS

The Oddfellows resemble the Buffs in general principle, and are even more intimately linked with Worktown, where many claim one of the earliest and most important lodges was formed. A Buff indicated the difference in a conversation with an observer; "The Oddfellows are more of a benefit society—we are more like the Freemasons," he said. But the Oddfellows are equally jealous of secret rites, which, like the rest, they trace back to pagan faith. Oddfellows tradition gives descent from the ancient Jews; a Jewish Roman legion introduced the cult to Britain—the Masons have a similar belief and their third-degree rites state "our traditional history, which mentioned the death of our Master Herrim", chief builder of Solomon's Temple, who was murdered; the candidate goes through positions and conditions connected with this murder and parallel in some ways with the Catholic "Stations of the Cross". Whatever the Oddfellow origins, however,—and it is not improbable that secret cults of this sort have survived, more or less unchanged, for centuries— its British form has been largely affected by the period of early working-class and illegal craft-organisation, centred on the pub, and persecuted by the upper classes. As the *Oddfellows Magazine* (1880) says: "Those who have made it their study to dive into the hazy past incline to the belief that the Oddfellows are revivals of the Old Trade Guilds that flourished in the 16th century."

The Industrial Revolution with its urban upheaval of poverty, social chaos and craft, stimulated the growth of secret groups among the poor, stimulated the pub as social centre, as well as Nonconformity, enemy of the pub and of squalor. The Oddfellows' odd name is most plausibly explained by the suggestion that they were people who, unlike masons, carpenters, etc., had no special craft, being "odd" in the old sense of the word, and with a composition rather like that of the Transport and General Workers' Union today. Others say Odd equals God, god's fellows. The idea of ascent towards god is indeed essential in the origins of these degree-taking societies, in Malekula as in Masonry. As a masonic text-book says of "The Climax of Royal Arch Masonry":

> This sublime degree is the Climax of Masonry and is intimately blended with all that is near and dear to us in another state of existence . . . suffice to say this degree is founded on the name of Jehovah.

Undoubtedly Oddfellows, Buffs, Foresters, have also borrowed bits direct from Masonry, the socially senior esoteric society. The present organisation of Oddfellows in Worktown is extremely complex. Owing to disagreements and difficulties, ritual reasons, historic growths, the organisation has broken up into many separate and distinct bodies, including (in this area), the Worktown Prosperity, the Manchester Unity, the Notts Imperial, the Lancashire Imperial, though all are loosely associated with the United Oddfellows, and have degree ritual with elaborate insignia, sword and mask rites, etc. In Worktown today the Oddfellows are less active and concerned with the pub than the Buffs. Many of their meetings are now held in nonconformist chapel rooms, as for example one advertised for 8 p.m. at Clean Road Spiritualist Chapel, which an observer tried to enter, with the result as indicated in his report:

> There were 12 men present. Two at table near door. One was standing book in hand, and immediately asked observer what he wanted, as it was a private meeting and only members were admitted.
> After apologising, observer pointed out that he wanted to join, and seeing the advert in paper, had come along. The

bookholder glared, then said one could not attend this business meeting but could come next Friday at 7.30 and join.

Obs. asked if there wasn't a lodge nearer where he lived.
Glarer: "Why?"
Obs. "It's a long way to walk."
G: "Walkin' is good for the soul, they say."

FORESTERS AND TRADE UNIONS

Third of the working-class secret societies, and furthest from its origins now, most emancipated from the pub too, is the Ancient Order of Foresters, claimed as "founded from time immemorial", thriving in 1790 especially in the Worktown area, where they are first definitely recorded in their present form in 1823, while nearby the initial "Court of Antiquity" (governing body) attempted to dictate to the whole movement, causing a considerable section to break away and form a new authority, with officials titled in the usual esoteric way: High Chief Ranger, High Sub-Chief Ranger, High Court Treasurer, High Court Senior Woodward, High Court Senior Beadle, High Court Junior Woodward, High Court Senior Beadle, High Court Junior Woodward, High Court Junior Beadle, High Court Secretary. By the end of 1835, 342 courts of the original "Royal Order" had joined the new "Ancient Order", which held its first "High Court" 12 miles from Worktown in that year. As the Foresters themselves put it in a handbook of theirs:

The ceremony of initiation adopted contained many elements of religious significance. Candidates for membership were required to undergo tests of courage by defending themselves with swords against any member in the Court Room. Cudgels were substituted for swords at a later date. This ordeal was called the "Combat" and upon the issue of it depended the acceptance or otherwise of the candidate into the ranks of Forestry. When the "Combat" ended, the Chief Ranger enlightened the candidate as to its meaning, stating that it was symbolical of the fight which all good Foresters should wage against the world, the flesh, and the devil.

The early members of the Order commenced all their proceedings with prayer. There were four authorised lectures entitled respectively—the Introduction; the Initiation; the Installation; and the Illustration, all of which contained many biblical references.

There was also a "grip", a "sign", a password. New ceremonies and "lectures" were adopted in 1857, modified in 1879, used still. An extraordinary feature of the organization, persisting 80 years, was that by the constitution the Order's central office *must* be shifted to a new town each and every year. This entailed great inconvenience, which was only increased by the rule that all the executive had to be drawn from the office-area each year. Yet (such is the power of ritual and tradition) only recently, after numerous unsuccessful attempts, the rule was altered.

Like Buffs and Oddfellows, the underground stage ended with the passing of the Friendly Societies Act in 1850, which legalized them. Lloyd George's legislation on working-class insurance brought them, as Approved Societies, prosperity, and changed their aims considerably, made them much nearer ordinary insurance societies. Today some seven hundred thousand adults use the Foresters as their Approved Society. From a beginning of poor men's pennies, like trade unions and the Co-op., this body has grown to have a ratio of solvency of 21s. 4d. per £, assets totalling millions. The youth section, started in 1840, now has 200,000 members, and it thrives in Worktown, where the juvenile secretary is a retired ironmonger. His section carries on the Forester tradition of archery even today, when it is organized by the society's collectors, of whom there are eight. About early June all children are urged to come out and shoot on Saturday afternoons in open places outside town. Slightly more girls than boys respond, and they are better shots at the four foot target, stuffed with straw, the arrows tipped with brass. Worktown Foresters possess 2 bows, 12 arrows.

All through, all these societies sprang from and continue in the working-classes. They seek no eminent patronage and they make no fuss about their functions. What the Foresters say about themselves in one of their booklets applies well enough to all the others:

Foresters' Courts have provided large numbers of members in all parts of the country with their first experience of mutual enterprise and their first insight into the problems of common government. They have instructed them in many branches of work in which they could have no other teacher. They have taught men to control themselves by working with others. They have taught them how the systematic savings of the few resulted in the accumulation of funds which could be directed wisely and well, and how the public services and social developments could be fertilized thereby. Participation in the unobtrusive but intensely valuable and practical work carried out in their Courts has equipped many thousands of members for useful service in other fields. . . .

Of other fields for which they have been equipped, the largest is the Union. The Trade Unions grew from the same roots as Buffs and Oddfellows, started as secret societies of craftsmen meeting in pubs. 40 of Worktown's 75 Trade Union branches still meet in pubs, some weekly, some fortnightly, some monthly. The close association between pub names and unions has already been analysed.

The following from the 1936 report of the Worktown Trades Council (co-ordinating body of unions in town) is illuminating:

> This year we have had correspondence with the Licensed Traders of the town requesting Trade Union Branches to hold their meetings only on premises of landlords who are members of their organisation. This was readily agreed to as a matter of principle, we replied in the affirmative. When, however, we suggested that they should return the compliment by engaging Trade Union labour to assist in their business and deal only with the firms which observed standard conditions and paid the recognised rate of wages, no reply was forthcoming.

A local union leader writes:

> Bleachers' and Dyers' Foremen's Guild meets in R—— Hotel. At branch meetings guest speakers are sometimes invited from Manufacturers' and Trade Organisations who stand Drinks round during the meetings. Drink is not served during Committee Meetings but always at Branch Meetings. Small rent is also paid for the use of room.

The Union meetings are less cut off from the pub than are those of the Buffs, as it is common practice for some of the members to stay in the pub after the meeting is over, or to come down from the room after they have paid their dues and have a drink.

WEDDING PARTY

Finally, in the following story we have an example of a completely transitory pub group, existing for only two evenings, but during its existence held together very strongly by non-pub considerations.

This is an account of a wedding party that finished up in a small beerhouse one evening. It is written by a waiter-on:

"Good evening."

"Aye, they're getten t' job o'ver. This is 'er and this is 'er 'usband. They were married this mornin'."

The party consists of bride and bridegroom, their parents, best man, and friends, and occupy the far corner of the parlour, where they will not be disturbed. After a long wait during which they have a whip round for drinks, each contributing what they can afford, the money piled up in the centre of table. The first round is ordered—2 small Guinness, 1 pint stout, 5 beers, and 2 shandies, these latter for the younger members of the party, not fully qualified drinkers. Quiet for about half an hour, then one of the chaps starts tinkling at the open piano. Ordinary customers file in and conversation starts. People go to the young couple and wish them much happiness, shaking their hands.

Cries of "Here's Tom. Hey, Tom, come an' give us a tune." "Can't just yet, I'm busy." Lady gets up saying "Can Tom come on 'ere and give us a tune, I'll wait on", pushing him to the piano. Tom obliges with an Irish jig and before this has finished the magic of music has worked and chap wants to sing Pennies From Heaven. The place fills rapidly as noises of merriment pervade the street. People come in to see what's up. Singers vie with each other for best applause. Lady brings down the house with imitations of film stars. Another with snappy choruses, such as Goody Goody. Old time songs are sung, such as On your Wedding Day—and Dear Old Mother. Thick sentiment, old girls weep. Army songs such as Are you from Dixie, Pack up your troubles, amid confusion of scuttling waiters, loud laughter, and free conversation. At 10.30 the happy couple depart, and there is a quieter atmosphere. Old people start talking of struggles when they were married and bringing up families, and the party ends here, perhaps to finish up in their own homes.

One week later same members of bridal party come in to drink together sitting in exactly the same places, and behaving the same.

X

SPORTS, GAMES AND GAMBLING

Perhaps the strongest early stimulus to the embryo pub in ancient Greece was the Olympic Games. Today the pub is the stronghold of sport, while tennis, golf and cricket clubs are also pubs for middle-classites.

The pub sports collect groups around them, similar in several respects to those described in the last chapter, and some transitory, spontaneously organized within the pub, some extending over long periods and not necessarily organized amongst a wholly pub group. Examples of the first kind are pub games such as dominoes and darts, of the second, bowls, angling, and pigeon flying clubs—whose meeting places are in the pub, and in the case of bowls the pitch on grounds adjacent to the pub.

PIGEONS

Of the well-organized groups the most elaborate are the pigeon flying clubs. Many of these are called after the pub in which they meet. Pigeon flying itself, a highly-developed form of active and co-operative culture, is on the decline. Reasons for this are indicated in the following material, and it also must be noted that the decline of this sport is symptomatic of the decline in a whole range of communal and non-commercial forms of culture.

Pigeons flutter around the Town Hall, roost in public buildings. Some prefer public houses. A Worktowner's write-up of pigeons who became pub regulars shows this:

PIGEONS: Many migrants are now spending their time on the electricity station in Vale Rd., but of all these migrating pigeons from the Town Hall, St. Patrick's (R.C.) belfy houses most. I watched these birds flying in and out of a Shamrock-shaped hole in the building, and on to the slates of the pub, the New Zealand Chief. But they entirely ignored the offices of the Unemployment Assistance Board which are directly

opposite. I went in to have a chat with the licensee, on Sat.
Oct. 3rd, and he told me that he bought grain and fed the
birds. He liked the birds, he said, and they would fly down
and feed from his hand. "They'll never go back to the Town
Hall whilst I am keeping this pub. Any of them will fly down
on my hand that are up there. . . ."

Pigeon flying clubs meet in the pub. Their notices are posted
up in it. Here is one:

RULES AND CONDITIONS OF THE X ARMS
SILVER CHALLENGE CUP

1. That it must be flown for annually from this club house,
   the X Arms.
   That it shall be a open spin sweep the spin to take place
   at this club house not later than one month before the date
   fixed for the annul sweep.
3. That the date of the said sweep shall be fixed by a general
   club meeting.
4. That the date having been fixed up a general meeting must
   remain as fixed.
5. That the annul date after haveing been fixed and found to
   be unsuitable may then be rearranged by an agreement
   of club members at their general monthly meeting.
6. That the Cup shall be held by the winner of the sweep
   for one year, less one month when it shall be returned to
   the club house.
7. That the commite of the club shall be held responsable
   for the care of the cup.

———

The donner will also present the winner with a miniture
repleca of the original cup.
And any further rules the club may wish to add it is free
to do so.   ———

This document is understood and appreciated by the club
members, who, in carrying out their sport show ability to master
intricacies of topography and organization. And in the course
of training and breeding their birds they show themselves
capable of acquiring an extensive empirical knowledge of genetics,
bird psychology and the conditioning of reflexes.

Every club has to have a mapper. The following is from a
local flyer's written account:

These regular "mappers" of the clubs are regarded as experts at the job; but, of course, if there is any doubt about places and distances the matter is submitted to the council of the district. Other members of the clubs also possess maps, and certainly need them for training purposes. The majority of the clubs have what is called a centre, such as, in the case of the S—— Hotel Club, the Hotel itself: where the licensee, himself a member, has his cote. Other methods—according to what the members decide—are also employed. The map of the district is spread upon the table, and a "spinner" is used. Wherever this brass spinner falls, the pigeons housed nearest to the point of the spinner is mapped from. . . .

My method of training . . . is what is known as "roading" a pigeon. As with a young pigeon, having to fly to his home for the first time (perhaps guided by an old hen), so with all the other birds being trained for a "Sweep". Supposing the mark I am to fly from is one hundred yards up the Lane. I get out the map, take a piece of string, and from the position of the starting point to my cote I get a line. This is then as the pigeon flys. I then make points at stages. These points may be 5, 6, or 7, according to my judgement of the bird and the weather conditions likely to be met with. The first point may be 100 yards from the cote, at the gable end of a shop, or even in a garden. If I cannot get permission to toss in the garden I take the nearest point to it. It is certainly true that pigeon flyers meet up with opposition from other people. Birds of mine have had stones thrown at them by farmers, and others, and on one occasion when I was training a bird for an important match and had a point on a back doorway the owner of the premises threatened to shoot the bird if I came again. But it was imperative that I should toss the bird (the best in my cote) several times from this mark during the month's training. . . . (He goes on to describe how he fetched the local secretary of Short Distance Flyers' Union, who told off the property owner and threatened prosecution if he carried out his threat.)

It is essential to fly to a "set" time during training. The watches must be set accurately (chronographs), a time indicated to the man at the outer end when to toss, and the inner end men know to a couple of seconds when to expect the pigeon. At both the inner and outer ends there should be timers and tappers, as in an actual match. At ten seconds before the time to toss the timer says Get ready! and begins to count, one, two, three, four . . . eight, nine, Up! At this last remark the pigeon is tossed. At the inner end the men are waiting for the pigeon, knowing to seconds when it will arrive, the tapper is looking upwards as soon as the starting time is reached, and immediately the bird comes in sight raises his hand ready to tap the timer's shoulder. If the bird alights within ten yards of the centre of the cote the tapper will tap the timer, crying Let! Usually a trained pigeon makes a bee-line for the cote and enters it nearly as quick as lightening. . . .

It is the policy I have always pursued to have my young birds flying from a mark that some of the old birds are on. It has been found by purely training the birds—giving them two fly's in the space of an hour—that the bird will do the better time on the second outing rather than the first . . . the policy is to fly the bird a trial an hour before the match. Say you have matched a young cock—4 months old, with a 2 years old hen—then you will have the opportunity since he will have become a parent a couple of times before the September young birds "sweep" of finding out whether he flies best sitting, driving his hen, or to the young ones. The hen mate of this age is more of an attraction for him and it is also likely to keep him steady. . . . She will be proud of her cock and ever ready to fly to him, the eggs, or the young, just as the case may be. . . .

He now describes in detail the elaborate methods used during an actual match, the synchronization of timing, and what means are used to ensure that there is no cheating, then:

. . . it is absolutely essential in the case of this place, they are such bloody thieves and rogues. A man who was at one time a member of this club, was found to have altered his mark and was disqualified. The mapper was in a rage at this trick that was alleged against a member of the divisional council and thoroughly investigated the charge and proved it to the satisfaction of the council. Tappers (particularly since severe unemployment in the collier fraternity has come to be known) have been known to accept bribes. A bribe would induce (providing it was large enough) the timer and the tapper at the outer end, to allow the pigeon "up" five or six seconds before its time. This, and other methods, such as men being hired to fire stone from behind a hedge, or to fire airguns in an attempt to injure or drive the pigeon off its course, are not uncommon.

He writes more on training methods:

With a cock bird I have taken his hen away from him a fortnight before the race, boxed him up for a few days in the dark, and then, after feeding his hen well during this time, have put him back to her seven days before the race. There is an immediate reunion with his well fed mate. . . . On the Wednesday night I give the cock two cod liver oil capsules and clear his bowels. From Thursday onwards I prescribe for both birds a mixture, baked into a cake. . . . This consists of Rape, White Millet, Dandelion, Sesame, Lettuce, Hemp, Linseed, Golden Pleasure, Mauve, White Spanish, and Thistle seeds. The latter are very dear, costing 1s. per oz, but the pigeons crave for these after eating them. The seeds are made into a sweet cake by mixing a little Demerara sugar and a gill or more of Sherry. . . . The motions of the birds are carefully watched, and should be jet black with a smear of white on top. On the Saturday morning I give the cock bird a beak full of Parish's food and a wee bit of the cake. Then he is boxed up for an hour or two (because in the dark he will settle down to rest) after which he is put in a trap cage where he can see his hen being fed on the very best food half an hour before the race, whilst he can't get to it. When the time is approaching to take him up to fly, the best tit-bits that a pigeon could desire are placed in front of the cage, and he is released. As soon as he begins to feed . . . he is grabbed, put into the carrying box, and taken to fly for the money. It sometimes happens that he is ready and about to tread his hen on being released. He should be grabbed and put into the box, and off for the money. He will come like hell in either case. Another trick is to put a large mirror in the cote on the Saturday. This is much better than putting in another cock to make him jealous, because the other pigeon may be able to knock the stuffing out of your flying cock, or seriously exhaust his energies. When released from the dark box he spies his opponent in the mirror and pecks at him without being injured in return. Then when the time has arrived to take him up you put down his hen's food and tit-bits and food he should have; let him see them in addition to his imaginary opponent in love, then grab him and take him up to fly for the prize. If he has trained after the method I have described he will take some beating. . . .

About betting on the race:

So confident are they in their pigeon's merit to win the race, I have seen the Landlord of the X Arms have a side bet of a 100 black puddings. This is of course in addition to the money bets that have been wagered over a course of several weeks. After the race, when the men are in the Pub vault, the pudding man would bring his 100 puddings all piping hot, and Jim would say "Get into 'em, lads". An hour after there would be the skins all over the vault floor. I have also seen side bets of sacks of potatoes, a sack of corn, flour, case of oranges, joints of beef, legs of pork, etc. I have betted a fishmonger a box of kippers that my bird would beat his, and won handsomely. My brother has also had such bets on my birds, as of bottles of Whiskey and Rum, and I remember him betting a local tripe dresser a dozen pounds of tripe on my bird. We ate the 12 lbs. in the pub Saturday night, used up a couple of bottles of vinegar on the job as well.

It can be seen that the groups of flyers and the whole social side of their elaborate organization and knowledge, centre around the pub.

Raffles—which play a large part in the life of all pub clubs— are organized by the pigeon clubs, and take place in the pub. One of these is described later in this section.

Writes another local flyer:

Really I'm fascinated with the hobby, and I regard them as such, and I like them for the lovely creatures they are, their beautiful types and characters appeals to me. . . . I think it's folly to enter in this sport with your outlook from a money making proposition, it simply isn't done, I venture to say not one per cent make this hobby pay, never mind showing a profit. . . . A hobby or sport presents you with as much returns as you put into it, not from a Capital standpoint, but from an interesting, social, and perhaps some little rewards for the patience you endow to it. . . . To my mind the racing pigeon is one of the Greatest sports it is possible to imagine.

A man asked in a pub if he found pigeon racing exciting replied:

"Why, how long is it sin' Jim Hardy dropped dead at a pigeon match, Bob?"
"Oh, it's good while sin', Jim."
"Aye, Ah know it is. Weren't 'e buried on the Saturday that (inaudible) won?"
"Aye, 'e were, Jim. 'E were fifty-one year owd. 'E were so excited about 'is pigeon that dropped dead."

Another report, taken from a local man's account of a race, shows the intense feeling that flyers have for their sport:

The spectators were doomed to disappointment, for the pigeon did not come in during the two minutes that the times allow for the distance. In fact it hadn't come in after four minutes, and produced from the throat of its owner the despairing cry "It's bloody well lost". He meant that the pigeon itself was lost, not so much that he had lost his money. It was a study to see the features of this man (who was unemployed). The tenseness on his hollow-cheeked, mal-nourished face was that of a man who was awaiting the verdict of a court. I felt great pity for this man. I had chatted with him going across country, and had found him what I should say is the ordinary working man down on his luck. When he asked the timer "What time has mine done?" his face was eager. But when the reply came—"It's not come" his look altered to one of despair. He said "I've only been roading it a week, because I didn't know whether I could get enough money to enter it. It serves me reet, it's my fault, not the bird's."

But despite organization of the sport, and the enthusiasm of its followers, pigeon flying is on the decline in Worktown. The unemployed man's statement above is one clue to it. Writes the secretary of the local district clubs: "The Short Distance Union is a great organization that caters for the humble working man." He is appealing to us for help "to bring back Short Distance Flying to something like its normal strength, owing to circumstances over which we have no control, namely bad trade and depression, we have dwindled down considerably. . . ."

An observer who asked a collier if a local pigeon club was still going got the following reply:

"Nar, they are broken up, tha knows what wi' one thing and another, un t' pits not doin' so well, thee geet short o' money, un this stated 'em fawing out among theirselves."

Asks the observer "Are many of them unemployed?"

"Aye, ayther that or they're not arnin' bloody salt" (earning their salt). The collier points out a nearby pigeon cote—"'e's 'ad some o' t' best birds in England."

Observer then goes into a pub and talks to chaps about pigeon racing. They say "It's gone bump about a couple o' year or more. The buggers were aw skint wi' bein' out o' wark—bar a few like owd Bill R. an one or two more . . . one or two on 'em are still flying. . . ." "There were sweeps every two-three week, mebbe ten bob a pigeon, un thee carn't do it." Observer asked if there were other factors, such as a few experts winning too many races, that were responsible for the decline. "Aye, I dar say there is sumat o' that in't." One man said "Owd Puffy's won 'is share, but 'e's buggert now, poor bugger carn't walk. . . ."

Pigeon flying is traditionally a sport indulged in by colliers, and they have suffered probably more than other sections of Worktown people from unemployment and short time. Though the decline of the sport can be understood on economic grounds, it is also correlated with the decline of many of the local forms of culture that are skilled, active and communal, in favour of newer and passive forms of leisure activity.

The present situation is that few of the clubs are actually functioning, though many individual ex-members still keep some birds, and sometimes race them. Talk in pubs where pigeon fanciers hang out is of past glories. One tells this story:

"It were nineteen 'undred when Joe Chamberlain won Pitman's Derby (Northumberland Plate). We 'ad a slip made out for every 'orse int' race—nobody about 'ere 'ad a telephone in them days. Well, one o' our men 'ad a fast pigeon as ud come straight un fly o'er cote. 'e took it in a box down ta *Evenin' News* place—gets it out in 'is 'ond und lets it 'ave a look round und puts it back again. Winner o' race is give 'im by a pal in there afore it 'as getten into print. It were number eight. 'e fastens it ont' pigeon's leg un quicksticks 'e tosses it up. In 'arf a minnit it were o'er our 'eads at t' cote. Number eight Bob, go on, gerrit on quick. Well you know, no bookie ever dreamt us would know t' bloody winner. Aye, isn't that reet, Jim? 'e took t' bloody bet as comfortable as you please, but 'e ad to pay out about thirty pound to us t' same neet. Thee carn't do that now, now wi' near everybody 'aving a telephone, tape machines, un aw that sort o' thing."

FISH

Some pubs are the headquarters of fishing clubs. A local brewery organizes a big annual angling competition. This takes place at Salwick, on the Lancaster Canal. Teams are of four. There were 464 individual entries for the competition that year. The teams go there by train, and the match starts at 10.30 on a Sunday morning. It lasts for two hours. Afterwards, some stay and go on fishing, others go to Preston and have pints, and others take bus or motor trips to the coast towns. The whole procedure, except for the two hours' angling, is very like the outings organized by the pub picnic clubs.

At five pubs owned by this brewery only one knew anything about it. On the other hand one pub entered 12 teams. An observer's report of the match:

. . . people fishing all the way at pegs ten yards apart except where the canal is obstructed by weed. Wearing a dark suit, was conspicuous: anglers mostly wore check suits and light tweed caps. While fishing a match there is intense concentration, some having barely the time or the wish to smoke. The fishing equipment of these men must run to thousands of pounds. Rods, lines, reels, keep-nets, bait cans and baskets, top boots, rubber boots, etc. To pass by a line of them a couple of miles long is to get this astonishing impression almost at the beginning.

Secretary gave out rules before the start. Stood on a table he said "There is a printer's error in the tickets, the man who gets B 100 will go that way, but the ticket is marked A 100, through the printer's mistake. Now there is no blood-worm or bloodworm feed to be used. No man must have above two hooks on his line. If any man is found to have broken these rules his team will be disqualified without the option. As soon as you get your team's tickets get to your pegs. Match starts at 10.30 a.m." The committee conducts the draw for numbers. The tickets in each series are mixed up and then one from each placed in a packet (A, B, C, D series), thus team mates cannot fish near each other.

Typical conversation recorded amongst the anglers:

"Who's gerrin ar tickets, Squire?"

"Gi' us a tin."

"Nay, theau's getton three bloody tins awready. Theau come wi' no bait, we've g'en thee three tins o' bloody maggots, un then theau wants more."

"Ah copped a Bream just under 3 poinds weight last wick i' this length."

"This bloody weed's stopping me fra doin' owt."

"There's a barge coming."

"By Christ ah'm bloody glad too, it u'll shift this bloody weed, happen."

"Whor is it, owd lad?"

"Perch—Christ cum eaut. 'e'll atta 'ave 'is jaw cut awf, ah'm not wasting my time maulin abeaut gerrin this 'ook eaut." (Cuts fish's jaws open with scissors.)

"What's good a buggerin' abeaut wi them lickle weights. Get four eaunce purron mon."

"Ah'll bet thee a bloody quid there's four eaunce, nar mind what theau says."

The weighter and checker on C section took such a long time to weigh each man's fish that they came in for a few curses.

"They arr a bloody farting numb lot arr you two, by Christ!"

After the match is over two hundred people go on fishing, most of them in entirely different places from where they fished during the match. Observer enquired the reason for this. Practically every man gave the same answer, either "Ah were on a bad peg", or "Bloody place ah worr at wur full o' weeds, an' ah couldn't get deawn."

Those who went on fishing did not drink during the afternoon, and caught the 7.20. On the station they went to the Gentleman's. Says one "By Christ! ast ever seen a free shit 'eause on a railway station afore? Ah've not. It's too bloody good almost ta be true. Ah ah dree-aming, Joe?"

"Ar'ta bloody 'ell, it's reet enough."

"Then ah'll 'ave a free shite afore t' train comes in."

Coming out this individual got in a carriage with the others and commented further on the "free shit"—"Theau con tell thi pals at wark, Joe, that ah 'ad a free shite at —— station."

The prize giving, which takes place ten days later upstairs in a pub, is a sociable affair. The following is part of a local working man's report on this:

. . . On the large table was a large silver cup in a mahogany case which is presented by the brewers. The landlord of each pub pays 2s. 6d. to entitle his team to enter. The cup is held by the winning pub for a period of 12 months and the concert is also held at the winning pub. They used to present medals also, but now give money prizes. There were 464 entries this year and in addition to the cup £37 10s. plus ten pounds from the brewery was given as prize money.

. . . The Chairman started off by calling upon the pianist to give a piano solo; quite contrary to the *Evening News* advt. the pianist said "I can't play a solo but I'll play 'Old Folk at Home' in different times." This was followed by "Bells of St. Mary", "On the Missisipi", and "Swanee River". There was loud applause and the chairman called on Mr. S. to entertain. S. sang "Because" and received loud applause, a man saying "He's a good singer, yon man, but yon pianist'll knock bottom right owt o' two pianos if 'e plays like that all neet." There was more singing, by a bass who sang about Devon.

Immediately the talk starts about fishing, so asked one man was there so much interest in it. He replied "Aye, once tha taks a mon fishing an' he gets a big un he never forgets it". Then a conversation developed about the journey to Salwick. There is plenty of technical fishing conversation—samples:

"I allus uses maggots on a match."

"Ah could a gotten a bream if ah'd t' right maggot on."

"I were sittin' there three hours under t' bridge and ah did well."

"Last year on biscuit meal I catched 16 roach and not one were under 'alf a pound."

Then there was more singing. The waiter then came in and said "Sup up, we're havin' one on t' firm", and the man next to me ordered ginger beer, and said "I never drink anything else".

The writer goes on to describe the presenting of the cup, which was done informally, the winner replying in a short speech in which he remarked "You know, we don't want record catches, what we want is an average catch for an average angler". A vote of thanks was then given to the landlord and everyone's future patronage was asked for. There was more singing until closing time, some of it voluntary.

DOGS

Important and regular dog shows are held in two big local pubs. They are run by canine societies, which are not sponsored by the pubs, but whose landlords are on the committees. They hire a special room for the evening. Exhibitors come from all over the area, seldom more than twenty from Worktown itself. Terriers are the principal interest. We learned the function of the fox terrier's stiff upright tail when we saw owners lift their dogs into different positions in front of the judges, tails used as handles. Most of the exhibitors drink beer between the classes, but there is no special drinking activity.

Practically every Worktown pub has a sweepstake on the Waterloo Cup, the year's major greyhound race, run near Liverpool. Tickets from 6d. to 2s. 6d. This survives as a tradition, though interest in coursing is now slight. There is also a greyhound stadium in Worktown, with a bar exclusive to club members. Observers have not recorded a conversation about greyhounds in any pub.

Ordinary dogs are talked about. And freely admitted with their owners. In a pub near our headquarters a man regularly sells dogs, brings puppies into the vault. If there are any strangers present, for the price of a round of beer he and his fellow regulars will give a display of tricks of his Alsatian. This dog does all the traditional Rin Tin Tin stuff rather better than Rin Tin Tin, or so it seemed to two (sober) observers present on such an occasion.

Cats are seldom seen in pubs, much less than in London. No cat shows are held in Worktown. Canary and budgerigar shows are held, but not in pubs.

BOWLS

Other groups around the pub are the bowls players. Like pigeon flyers, their activities as a group take place *outside* the pub, and are not directly connected with drinking. But their link with the pub is closer than that of the pigeon fans, since much of the bowls played in Worktown takes place on greens belonging to the pubs.

The game played locally is "crown bowls", which takes place on greens of fine turf that are not quite level, having a "crown", or slight convexity, that raises the centre of the green a few inches higher than the edges. (In the south bowls are almost invariably played on a flat green.) The game is played by teams or individuals bowling round wooden balls (about 8 inches in diameter) at another smaller ball, called the jack. The "woods" have a bias, are flattened so as to be slightly elliptical; considerable skill is required to allow for this bias. Each player bowls two woods at the jack, the nearest wood in each case scoring a point.

There are many bowling clubs, some connected with the pub at which they play, others organized by the workers in various factories, etc. There are inter-club leagues, and handicaps, often organized for charitable purposes, between clubs and individuals. Besides all this, unorganized individual games are played. (There are municipal greens in the parks, as well as those belonging to pubs and clubs.)

The following is part of a description of a typical match between two well-known players, one from another town:

Observer went through the lobby bar, and across the pub backyard on to the green. . . . The two players stood in the middle of the green, with the judge, a middle-aged man

in a brown suit and cap. . . . At the end of each set the judge
calls the score out to the spectators. At first B. runs up after
his wood all the way each time, while M. goes about four
paces after it, then stops, watching its course. He gestures
to it with his arm, calling "Get along". Later, after M. has
bowled and gone up to stand by the jack, he watches B's
wood approach and gestures it away with his hand. At certain
times (which the observer cannot as yet differentiate from
any other occasions) B. runs like blazes after his wood as soon
as it has left his hand, so that he reaches the jack almost as
quickly as does his wood. One time, as he goes by, he is heard
muttering to himself "Should make summat this time,
shouldn't I?"

Chaps are calling out to each other "B. is cracking." "'e's
stalling." "Better take 'is shirt off." "'e carn't stand t' pace."

. . . Observer begins to come to the conclusion that the
running up after the wood and the magic gestures made with
the hands are done increasingly in proportion to the player's
uncertainty as to the course of his wood. This seems to be the
only explanation of their behaviour, since sometimes they
charge up the green the moment the ball has left their hands,
while at other times they do nothing until they have watched
it travel some distance. And sometimes they simply stand
still, with arms folded, and watch it. . . . This also applies
to the amount and intensity of the arm gestures that they make
as they run after the wood. These gestures are always made
inwards, so that they use the right arm in order to encourage
it to go towards the left, and vice versa. However, this does
not apply to another sort of gesture, which is done very
quickly, moving the hand from the wrist, as if beckoning. . . .

By the entrance to the ground is a small bar, with a sort of
serving hatch connection to the ground. Some chaps stand
and drink there, others take glasses and stand with them at the
edge of the green. Throughout the game there was a steady
trickle to and from this bar.

There is plenty of betting going on.

. . . one man calls out "Ah'll tak two dollars" several times.
Man in front of him immediately calls "I'll take 14 bob to 8."

"B. carn't win this game."

"I'll take 5 to 4."

"Ten bob to eight."

A man passing "Ten bob to nowt!"

Two bookies' runners sitting on the bottom step of the stand
suddenly begin a furious argument (incomprehensible to
observer) which one eventually offers to settle by betting a

pound, which he clutches in his hand and shakes under the other's nose. Nothing being done about it, he then walks off, and sits down about ten yards away, threatening to punch the other's nose. Nearby spectators are amused, make remarks about "When bookies fall out . . ." Other bookies and runners are taking bets on slips of paper. . . .

Now there is more intense gesturing going on in the game, as it nears the end. At one point M. runs so fast that he overtakes his wood as it is slowing down; he lies down, one elbow on the ground, bends his head low over it, and whispers. And B. watches M's wood intently all the time, making adverse gestures at it.

B., the local man, wins. The players' gestures and adjurations to their woods, and *against* (when things get tense) those of their opponents, are among the most exciting things one can observe in anthropologically exciting Worktown. They cannot, of course, influence the ball; "obviously" they are expressions of the players' feelings, and serve the purpose of relieving their tensions, but the form that they take is that of sympathetic magic.

Saturday afternoons are the times for important bowling matches. These sometimes end up with a big drunk in the evening.

FLAT GREEN BOWLS

Flat green bowls, though not a local pub game, is played in some of the parks, organized mostly by church groups, who have been discussing the possibility of forming a league.

The jack in this variety of the game is small, about the size of a cricket ball, and white.

CARPET BOWLS

There is an indoor variety of the game, called carpet bowls. This is played on raised carpets, and the woods do not have bias. It is seldom played here, and never in pubs, mainly in connection with church groups.

Bowls is one of the oldest sports practised today. It originated in the 12th century. As far as Worktown is concerned it is the only pub game that is also frequently played elsewhere. Darts and dominoes, for instance, are rarely seen outside the pub. Also, it is through bowls that the pub links up with "official" non-pub life—the Infirmary Handicap, for example, played on pub grounds, organized partly through the pub and partly through non-pub important people, the Mayor as Patron. It is a link between the pub and municipal affairs.

Another point peculiar to bowls is the lack of any class characteristics in the game. In the south it is played mainly by middle-class, and "old gentlemen". Here, all sections of the community, of all ages, join in it. And they play *together*, especially on the municipal greens, numerous players criss-crossing their bowls and jacks on the same green.

Women also play bowls—but not on pub greens. This is important. The games described later in this section—cards, dominoes, darts—are vault and taproom games, and so only played by men—exceptions being landlady and barmaid, to whom vault and taproom are not tabu.

There are certain things common to the above sports. In each case the pub is the social locale of the groups that engage in them, in many cases being the actual meeting place of clubs, which are named after the pub. Then, there are always prizes, cups, certificates of merit—compare the remark on the pigeon flying official diploma "Great achievements merit honour and recognition" with the Buff ritual speech that "It has long been the most ancient custom of mankind to honour its leading figures." These are presented in the pub, on "climax" occasions, usually followed with or accompanied by plenty of drinking and singing.

The pub games played indoors need no such build up. And, connected with all of them, as well as with the games that take place outside the pub, and with pub-clubs, are betting, lotteries and raffles.

GAMES PLAYED INSIDE THE PUB

SMALL GAMES

A barman writes:

Games played are darts, dominos, cards, these are subject to rule that no gambling takes place, the writing of betting slips is prohibited, the licensee being technically responsible for proper supervision. Regulars may play for drinks, and so the consumption of drink is encouraged, and such artifices run through the whole business, for the stimulation of trade.

Card game played is all fours—play partners, 4 players, for who pays for drinks, spectators will have bets in among themselves, but it's done surreptitiously. . . ,

As well as the games mentioned above, quoits are played in a few pubs. There is no shove ha'penny, or skittles, both common in some districts.

Commonest game is cards—all fours—played with a reduced pack, for "tricks" which are marked on small board full of holes, into which are inserted pegs (often matchsticks) that are moved forward as each player scores a trick.

DARTS

Darts, which went out in Worktown before the war, is now coming back again rapidly. The highly organized brewers' darts league and clubs, common in other districts, have not yet made their appearance here. But a few pubs, belonging to a Manchester brewery, have participated in a league. A landlord of a pub who had belonged to it said that they had given it up as "It didn't pay. Someone always got dissatisfied. They have a meeting and propose a resolution and then someone objects and has it altered. It's the same with the dominos league now. They want to be top dog. They're like a lot of kids."

Because of the lack of organization of darts playing, the rules here have a certain fluidity. At one time in the north of England darts were played on a comparatively small board (about 9 inches across—100 years ago on a 6-inch board, the darts blown through an 18-inch blowpipe) divided into quadrants numbering from one to twenty (not consecutively). Around the edge was a double line, about a third of an inch across. This was the "double", and a dart hitting the board between the lines counted twice the score of the respective quadrant at whose edge the line was. Now this board is being replaced by the larger type used originally in the south. The southern board, also, has a "treble" inner ring, as well as a "bull" in the centre, counting 50, and a ring around the bull, counting 25. The method of play used in most parts of the country, is that a double has to be scored by each player before the game can begin, and then the players have to score 301, finishing on the correct double—i.e., a player who wants 19 to reach 301 must score a 1 and a double 9, or a 3 and a double 8, etc.

This method is rarely used here. Instead, most games are "round the board"—the players having to score 1, 2, 3 and so on up to 20, and then finishing on the bull. In most pubs players are allowed to count any double under 9 as the equivalent number from which to follow on—so that a player getting 8, then a double 9, can go straight on to 19. There are also variants about getting both the inner and outer bull, and the double 20 as well as the 20. But there is no standard method of scoring common to all pubs.[1]

Each player has three darts, wooden and/or brass-shafted. Games are played between individuals or pairs, mostly the latter. From the spring of 1937 to that of 1939 the number of pubs at which darts are played in Worktown has more than trebled. And many of the places which originally had the old type of small board have replaced this with the bigger southern board. But as yet few darts clubs have appeared.

This great increase, common to the whole country, is largely due to a little episode at Slough, Bucks, where on December 17th, 1937, the King and Queen, inspecting a Social Centre, casually threw darts at the dartboard there. A press photographer snapped it. Big news! Royalty as worker! Since then, darts—though always popular among pub-goers in parts of London and the south—have boomed everywhere in pubs, clubs, schools, hostels. The *Sunday Chronicle*, nine days after the episode, put it:

WOMEN FLOCK TO FOLLOW THE QUEEN'S LEAD AT DARTS

THE QUEEN HAS MADE THE WOMEN OF BRITAIN DARTS-CONSCIOUS

Since she played her first game of darts at Slough nine days ago thousands of women have asked where they can have tuition in dart-throwing.

Mr. R. B. Tillock, hon. secretary of the British Darts Council, told the *Sunday Chronicle*: "During the last few days the British Darts Council has been snowed under with inquiries from all parts of the country." By the way, there is now a darts room in the servants' quarters at Buckingham Palace.

And next day the *Daily Express* has a special map, and head:

[1] Recently Professor H. Levy has written a book called *A Philosophy for a Modern Man*, which tells people that they must be scientific about themselves, without giving either actual or factual examples of method. Early on this book has a diagram intended to demonstrate "statistical order" in human behaviour; in fact it demonstrates the difference between the theoretical idea of behaviour and what really happens. Diagram shows a normal dartboard, with dart pricks distributed in a concentric pattern, described in the caption: "The perforations due to the darts are most closely packed near the bull's-eye, and fall off according to a definite law as the distance from the bull's-eye increases." This is an example of a typical academic social philosopher, imposing from above a theoretical pattern of behaviour which is *not* found in fact, among ordinary people in every-night life.

IN ONE TOWN IN ENGLAND DARTS IS FORBIDDEN
THE TOWN? HUDDERSFIELD

In the 250 public houses in town are two where the game is known, where darts—of a kind is permitted. But the arrows have rubber suckers. Or they are made of sharpened wood. . . .

No one knows why the ban was put on. But there is a Public Health Act of 1871 which stops the game. Magistrates have power (by the same Act) to allow the ancient game to be played.

Since the King and Queen played applications may soon be made to the courts to let Huddersfield do the same.

While the weekly *Answers* occupied a whole page of the *Daily Express* with a coloured advert. of a dart board, as part of their "50th Birthday Celebrations" . . . "*Every Home should have one of these superb dart boards.*"

In common with all other games darts are not played in the home-from-home part of the pub (i.e. lounge, snug, best room) but in vault or taproom, usually depending on which of these rooms is most patronized by the regulars.

QUOITS

Dying out in Worktown, now seldom seen, is quoits, played with small rubber rings that are thrown against a shield-shaped board with projecting hooks on it. The hooks are numbered from one to twelve, and have to be ringed consecutively. In those pubs where quoit boards are found we have seldom seen them being played. And during the period of our observation, plenty of quoit boards were replaced by darts. There are few quoits fans. Said one "It's a bigger game than darts." And he told us the story of the ace local player who could put five rings into a gill glass, and how he would stand at the end of the bar and ring all the beer pump handles, and finish up with the small tap on the strong ale barrel.

DOMINOES

Despite the increasing popularity of darts, dominoes are still the most popular pub game. Dominoes is played with oblong bone, wooden, or composition pieces, about half an inch across and two inches long. The face of the pieces is divided into half; on each half are a number of dots. In the form played almost everywhere else in the country, the dots number from one to six Worktowners, however play with dominoes whose dots range up to double nine. Players receive nine dominoes, and the game is to construct a chain of them by matching the number on the free ends of the chain—i.e. if the first domino put down has three dots on one side and four on the other, the next player has to put one down with either a three or a four on it, and so on. Until no one is able to match the numbers on the free ends of the chain. When this point is reached the numbers left in each player's hand are added up, the one with lowest number being the winner.

A board, with raised edges to prevent the pieces falling off, is often used to play on: while in some pubs there are special tables for the game.

The pieces which are left over after the players have each taken their nine, remain lying face downwards on the table, and the chain is started by placing the first dominoes on top of them. At the end of the game the used pieces are turned over and mixed with the unused ones; this is done by stirring them all round, usually in a clockwise direction. The dominoes are always held in the players' hands—which means at the start, five in one hand and four in the other, difficult until you are used to it—instead of being stood up on edge.

Dominoes are found in about two-thirds of the local pubs, least of all in the town centre houses. One or two of these, however, have several tables, and are well-known hangouts for domino fans.

The outstanding difference between all these games, which take place *inside* the pub, and the sports connected with the pub that take place outside, is that the outside activities are well organized into clubs, leagues, etc., with a highly competitive background, while the inside activities are for the great part *unorganized*, their competitive elements unstressed, and the players held together as pub groups rather than games groups. Pub games are male and do not involve large or permanent teams. Almost invariably the competing unit is of either one or two persons.

There is no connection between the pub and either football, cricket, tennis, or golf, in Worktown. The two last are mainly "class" games, involving considerable capital and current expenses. Tennis and golf players are seldom pub-goers, generally earn more than three pounds a week, often have their clubhouse as a pub serving drinks at all hours and doing very good business in this respect. Cricket, on the other hand, is played by all sorts of people in Worktown; working-class teams are largely financed by their mills, never by pubs, and the pub link is unusually weak here. All these sports involve special clothing. None of the pub sports demand any change of clothes.

The pub spirit is not the team spirit. It is the freedom of each individual to do as he wants, an unregimented, individual, "democratic" spirit, the right of each person to play and back himself for a small bet, in a game that does not involve any differentiation of function between the players, any authoritative leadership, or, for the games inside the pub, any elaborate preparation, or length of play.

The pub is the only institution which positively encourages this sort of play.[1] In general other institutions tend to stimulate what is often called "the team spirit", which assists them in organization and in linking individuals of different interests into one machine. And often these other institutions, who link all ideas of traditional British sportsmanship to the team spirit (nearly all our team games have comparatively recently become so), express some active resentment against the pub technique of games. Amusing aside on this appeared in *The Times* during April, 1938:

> The Rev. Ralph Allpor, a Weymouth Methodist minister, on Saturday condemned tortoise racing, which is gaining popularity in South Dorset. The contests take place on billiard tables, the tortoises carrying toy jockeys. Mr. Allport said that many public houses in Weymouth were exceeding their legitimate function as places of refreshment. They were being turned into fun fairs, and their proprietors, having exhausted the possibilities of darts and mechanical games as a means of retaining custom, were resorting to silly stunts. Dumb animals which had been bought as children's pets were being dragged out of their natural environment. Mr. Cyril Frampton, who introduced tortoise racing, said, "It is all harmless fun, entirely free from cruelty. We do not allow betting."

[1] Football, like the musichall, is closely associated with drink, though not with the pub. The top of the huge stand at the Worktown football stadium is decorated with enormous letters that spell the name of a local brewery. During the interval the bars are crowded (interval 3.45). Another advertiser here is the Y.M.C.A. The position was well put by a leading Quaker 20 years ago (MSS. given to us): "All the work in connection with the stalls is voluntary, and all sorts of teetotal drinks, mineral waters, and meat pies, are sold in such large quantities that in spite of an increased yearly rental the profits increase from year to year. Many men now find that a 2d. cup of coffee makes them warmer than a glass of beer, and often drunkards from the liquor bar are considerably sobered down after further quenching their thirst at the Y.M.C.A, stalls." This is still true, twenty years later.

Other side of the tortoise picture is Liverpool, where good statistics and some social data are available. As regards its pubs, Liverpool is well below the national average of 18·29 per 10,000 population, for it has only 15·02 per 10,000 (H.O. Licensing Statistics, 1936). As regards drunkenness, Liverpool is well up; against the national average drunkenness convictions per 10,000 of 10.9, Liverpool averages 27.37, a figure only surpassed by London and Birmingham. In view of these facts, and also because of our ideas of the pub as a social unit, we were therefore impressed by a passage from the Merseyside Survey (III, 286):

> Very few public-houses in Merseyside provide facilities for activities other than drinking. A few supply food, but provision for games is rare, and it is understood that the licensing authorities ten to discourage the use of public-houses for playing games. Some public-houses have bowling greens, and others . . . have billiard tables. But games such as darts and shove ha'penny are practically never found.

These two facts—the exceptionally high drunkenness rate and the exceptionally severe ban on pub games—seemed possibly significant in connection with the theme of this chapter, so that we sent over a skilled observer unit without giving any idea of what we were interested in; instructions were to find out, first by observation and then by conversation with landlord and regulars, about pub games.

Result of observation :

      0 per cent had pub games
      6 per cent had slot machines

A typical strip through the town-centre showed:

	Number of pubs	Games	Machines
Main streets	13	0	1
Side streets	17	0	1

Result of conversation :

Here are typical comments selected from a whole series, many of which are almost word for word the same and which reflect a decided local point of view:

1. "No games here."
2. "No. You'll not find any games or that in this town. Yer daren't speak above a whisper—yer not allowed a sing-song even."
3. "Yer daren't change yer mind—niver mind play darts or cards in this town. You have to go to Manchester for games."
4. "This town, it's dead for things like that. They're not allowed." Man of 50 intervenes, "It would cost too much. If they gave a dart board to one, everyone would want one!"
5. White cockatoo kept on saying Hello-Hello! Observer thought he had made a find, seeing a penny-in-slot pin table. Obs. went to play, and asked if there was anything to be won for a good score. Says landlady "Oh no, it's for amusement only." Obs. asks about games. "Oh! no not in 'ere you won't." Man, 60, cap, "No son, they'll not 'ave darts nor dominoes in this town—you would get a sing-song in the suburbs. They're not allowed—but yer can sing in the doorway outside."
6. Man in naval uniform, 50, says "Oh, no—it's the worst town in the country for that kind of thing." Another "I don't see why men shouldn't have a game if they want." Barman "It's the police—yer can't change yer mind unless they're on top of you 'ere."
7. "Ye'll not find a dart board in Liverpool—all they want is for yer to get in an' get out again, that's all." Barman told how a man had been fined for running a raffle in the Vault on the number of a cigarette card, fined £3. "When next 'e comes up for th' license renewal he'll be—phuff" (he makes rude noise).
8. "No, it's the police 'ere—not so long ago you got into trouble if a man was reading a racing paper in the bar 'ere."
9. "This is the worst town in the country. Yer not even allowed to swagger a bit—before yer up."
10. "It's the council in Liverpool—it's like nothing on earth. They don't allow any games at all."
11. "Naw there ain't nowt in this town excep' th' booze."
12. "There's no games in Liverpool. Yer just come in and go out."

DRINKING IN THE RAW

Here, then, we get drinking in the raw. And, say the statistics, drunkenness—though of course on such data there is no suggestion of a positive correlation between less games: more drunkenness.

But it is perhaps worth noting that an observer casually timing men drinking gills of beer standing at the bar in a Liverpool pub on a November Tuesday got an average drink speed of 5 mins. 34 secs., no one taking more than 11 minutes. The Worktown Tuesday *average* speed is over 13 minutes. It is quite possible that people drink faster in the unsocial atmosphere of Liverpool pubs; we have already seen that on the large series of Worktown figures, people drink appreciably slower in company. Faster drinking is an important factor in getting drunk.

But there is another interesting aspect of the Liverpool position. On April 20, 1939, Mr. A. P. Herbert, Independent M.P. and friend to the pub-goer, asked the Home Secretary in the House of Commons:

"What is the statutory authority by which licensing justices are able to veto games on licensed premises; and will the Home Secretary draw the attention of all licensing benches to the Report of the Royal Commission on licensing?"

The part of the Commission's report to which Mr. Herbert refers is contained in paragraph 243:

We have indicated . . . the importance which we attach to any influence which will help to modify the insistent emphasis on the sale of intoxicants. It has been suggested to us that entertainment and the sale of intoxicants should be kept severely apart; but, apart from any question of the reasonableness of suppressing legitimate amusements in places of wide public resort, we believe that games, music and the like, have a definite value as distractions from the mere business of drinking.

Yet most licensing authorities, including (very emphatically) the Worktown ones, tend to inhibit the playing of cards and pianos in pubs. Or rather, it would be more accurate to say that the Chief Constable of many places, including Liverpool and Worktown, do so. For in these matters, the opinion of the Chief Constable is generally the dominant factor. Frequently his opinion runs contrary to demonstrable fact and contrary also to recommendations of the best available experts. The whole position in which the Chief Constable determines the contours of pub leisure is at the same time undemocratic and unconstitutional. Commenting on this, the Royal Commission (which reported eight years ago) paragraph 244:

Complaints were made to us that in some districts the police, presumably with the danger of gaming in view, had purported to forbid the playing of various games on licensed premises. . . .
The police have, of course, no statutory authority to forbid such games, and the licensee is under no obligation to comply. We hope that steps will be taken to secure the discontinuance of any policy of discouragement of lawful games on licensed premises. . . .

This is the curious position that Mr. Herbert recently set out to remedy. Emphasis was given to it by the reply of the Home Secretary to his Parliamentary question:

"The licensing justices have no power to veto any lawful games and I am in general agreement with the views expressed by the Royal Commission as to the desirability of encouraging such games 'as a distraction from the mere business of drinking'."

Encouraged by this answer, A. P. Herbert issued a public challenge to Liverpool. Pointing out that there was no legal validity on the darts veto at all, he urged publicans to play the game. One only, the Royal Yacht Hotel, responded. The reason is simple. The whole autocratic control of licences by the licensing justices working in conjunction with the police, makes it everywhere possible for these authorities to go beyond the law and intimidate publicans into obedience to any regulation. Arbitrarily and without appeal, a pub can have its licence taken away. That is a permanent disaster for the publican and his family. He can't take the risk. The Liverpool authorities are actually cutting down on licences all the time. Although the number of pubs is well below the national average, they have cut the number of Public Houses from 1,217 in 1935 to 1,195 last year; the number of Beerhouses from 70 to 65. On the other hand, and consistent with their idea of what drink is for, they have only reduced the number of Off-licences by 1 over the same period.

In Worktown the attitude of those controlling pub licences seem to be moving in the same direction. And another great city, Glasgow, has apparently adapted the Liverpool method. On April 12, 1939, the licensing bench decided that "dominoes, darts and games of any kind" must no longer be played in the city's 1,100 pubs. The reason given: "games encourage drinking." Although no date was given for the orders coming into force, every pub stopped games immediately; at least 200 Glasgow pubs have darts teams, many of them playing regularly in League matches.

Liverpool certainly proves that people will go to pubs to booze and talk without being able to play any games. If the licensing authorities would prohibit talking, we should have an excellent control on all our pub generalizations about social factors, etc. But the Liverpool pub, like any other, is stronger than the restrictions on it. Its future should be watched with interest by all those concerned in alcohol, for or against. We have strayed from Worktown. Back there. . . .

RAFFLES

Here is a raffle report from a Worktown pub:

> They decided that owing to the blind ex-soldier being present in the pub he would be the person best suited to give the draw an air of respectability, and that they could tell their friends at home that the numbers were drawn by a blind man, which would consequently help to allay their fears, and keep their patronage for other draws to come.
>
> The first remark as the blind man took hold of the bag of tickets was "They're shook up, David." "Never mind that, lad," says David. "I'm going to give them a good shake now, and every time I've drawn a number. Leave it to me."
>
> Voices heard. "D. Warburton, he has aw't' Chorley lot." "Bring a blue un out, David." "What colour's that?" "It's a whiteun." "Five, seven, eight, buff colour."
>
> "Nar, they durn't go back in t' bag."
>
> "We carn't purrum back in t' bag, Johnny."
>
> "Buff colour again, two, ninety-one."
>
> "Go on again, David."
>
> "Where is that dickey bird?"
>
> "It's a white un, two forty-one."
>
> Secretary—"Two forty-one, white, is E. Hart, E. Jones' card."
>
> "Bloody hell fire."
>
> "Bring a blue un out, Daff."
>
> "Who's won that?"
>
> "Peter McEwan. Hey, bloody hell, they're gerrin aw t' lot."
>
> "There's another prize yet, gentlemen."
>
> "Gerra blue one out, David lad."
>
> "Right, I'll do me best for you."
>
> "Wheer's wife to neet Henry. Is 'er up t'Elephant?"

"Nar, 'er's ut Clayton."

"Well, gentlemen, that concludes the draw," says the president. "I propose we give David a pint—all in favour?"

Grunts of approval. Voice at back "Give 'im a shillin'."

"Is it moved that David 'as a shillin'?"

"Aye, und seconded, lad."

"Moved and seconded that we give 'im a bob. All in favour?"

"Aye, gerrit 'im."

"Right."

Secretary—"Gentlemen I should like to tell you that we 'ave sold two thousand four hundred shares in our draw. It is not a bad number, but I think we can do better if we try."

The first prize was 10s., then 7s. 6d., 5s., 2s. 6d. (twice), 1s. 6d. and 1s.

Gambling and raffling, though theoretically prohibited, takes place among drinkers generally, as well as among the more limited groups already described, and in addition to the betting that takes place with bookmakers. For instance, the raffling of a pie is common:

Vault. Barman comes round with a small canvas bag, jingling it. Asks observer if he wants to come in a penny draw for a pie. So observer pays his penny, puts hand into the bag, and draws out a worn brass disc, about the size of a halfpenny, on which is stamped RIGGS' PIES, and a number. The draw for the winning number did not take place in the vault. Number 9 wins; it is one of the men playing dominoes; he gets a small hot pie, the sort that you can buy for fourpence.

The raffling of what are called "curios" is a common local custom. Here is a description of this by a local pubgoer:

Parlour. Conversation lively, especially of two stout women who are talking about why or why not to have children. One young woman (the most attractive in the room) is going round to customers inviting them "to have a penn'orth in our curio". She wheedles one or more pence out of everybody present, and then goes into the vault and taproom. No person appears to have the moral courage to say "no" to her request. The "curio" idea is that each week some member of a prospective picnic party (in this case the women customers of the pub) gives a small object to be raffled off, the proceeds— which are all profit—go to the pool to be shared out at the "dividing" which takes place a day or so before the actual picnic. The "curio" takes many forms, sometimes useful, as a small parcel of grocery, sometimes humourous, and sometimes lewd. Its value ranges from half a crown down to a penny or so. In about 25 per cent of the cases it is given back to the "club" to be raffled again, unless it is grocery, when the winner invariably keeps it. On an average from 4s. to 10s. profit is made on each "curio", and invariably results, over a period of about 3 months, in a "free" picnic for the members of the "club" . . .

In this case we see the raffle being conducted for a picnic club, but amongst all the drinkers in the pub.

Curios are also raffled amongst the Buffs, and at one Lodge a member brings some pies every fortnight and puts them up for raffling. The Lodge has special wooden counters, with numbers on one side and one of the ritual Buffalo words on the other, which are used for raffles.

We have seen a large range of objects raffled and bet, from 100 black puddings to a small pie, a box of kippers to a fireside stool. We have even heard of a game being played for socks:

The landlady told observer that a man who used to sell silk stockings from door to door, came into the pub and played dominoes with her for a sock a game. She won three and a half pair, but "was so greedy" to make up the fourth that she lost them all back to him again.

All pub games are played for some kind of stakes—usually drinks. A landlord said "No one wants to play cards for love". Games are also played for money. To refuse to play for a stake is bad form:

Stranger comes in and pays for gills all round. He suggests a game of all fours (cards). After the first round the game is abandoned, owing to the stranger refusing to pay a small wager on the game. His attitude is resented by all present who say that he is unsporty, though he had paid for treat earlier.

OBJECTIONABLE PRACTICES?

At the Worktown Annual Licensing Meeting, 1852, Mr. Taylor, a temperance man, said:

"The objectionable practices which are now associated with the public house embody raffles, clubs, bowling greens, theatres, music, singing, dancing, and in some cases, brothels, and the police know it".

Most of this still applies. In fact, apart from drinking but bound up with it, the pub has a cultural life, and/or "objection‧able practices" of its own. They comprise all the non-drinking activities that go on inside the pub. Selley sums up the material of his book on pub-theory plus some observation:

> My observations show that in most public houses intoxicants are objectionably prominent. The majority of public houses are "drink shops" pure and simple, and a large proportion of them are not fit for the purpose of social institutions. . . .

The merit of Selley's work is that he, despite strong prejudice, does recognize that the pub *is* a social institution. But the con-clusions that he draws do not agree with those that are suggested by our observations. No pub can simply be regarded as a drinking shop. It may be lacking in facilities for games and music, present no organized forms of social activity, and its actual accommo-dation be of the crudest; but none the less the activities of the drinkers are not confined to drinking. To say that they come there to drink is true, but an incomplete truth; just as it is an incom-plete and misleading truth to say that a cinema is the place where young men go to feel girls' breasts.

The pub is a centre of social activities—for the ordinary pub-goer the main scene of social life. Worktown working people rarely meet in each others' homes for social activities in the way middle classes do. For some there is the social activity of politics, football or cricket clubs. But participators in these activities are a small minority. The place where most Worktowners meet their friends and acquaintances is the pub. Men can meet and talk of the way of their womenfolk.

A drink is the only price of admission into this society. And so, for the pub-goers, drink becomes inseparably connected with social activity, relaxation, and pleasure. And the picnic, the out-ing, the angling competition, the bowls match, the savings club, games of cards and darts, betting—all these forms of non-pub social activity become connected with the pub, and thus are "incomplete" without drink.

The pub-like places in which drink is not sold, such as the milk bar, the fish and chip shop, are not used by their frequenters as centres of social activity; they are—so far—shops in which the goods sold are consumed on the premises. (People don't stand each other rounds of milk shakes, or fish and chips.)

The forms taken by pub social activity bear on the conclusions that we have drawn from the behaviour of drunks. Here, too, the social and the alcoholic motive cannot be disentangled. The alcoholic motive itself is primarily social, if it is given a long term definition; it is a motive that seeks the breaking down of barriers between men, the release from the strain of everyday life in the feeling of identification with a group. And the rituals of the Buffs and the clubs, the merging of groups in singing, all in different ways are part of this process.

But as well as this group-forming process that takes place in pub social life, there is another and apparently contradictory form taken by the pub social and cultural activities, one that is shown most clearly in the hierarchical organisation of the Buffs, and that also appears in the playing of games, pigeon-flying and angling competitions. This is the form of behaviour that is governed by motives of exceeding and beating the other man, of being the best in the group. And it must be recognised in a concrete form, by regalias and medals, by prizes and cups and diplomas. "Nobody wants to play cards for nothing." The winner of the domino game is getting more than prestige, he is getting a free gill.

These two motives, of being the winner, the best in the group, of rising in a social hierarchy: and of getting something for nothing, plus the excitement of the game or of waiting for the result of the race so that even if you lose you still have had something, are characteristic not of pub society, but contemporary industrial society as a whole—indeed of animal life. And they are the opposite of the democracy of drinking, that manifests itself both in the merging of individuals into groups, and also in the basic ritual of drinking, that of standing rounds. This, the most fundamental and regular of all the pub rituals, is based on an assumption that all the members of the drinking group have the same amount of money to spend, a truly "democratic" assumption in a wage-earning personal-advance society.

The competitive side of pigeon-flying, bowls, angling, takes place away from the pubs; but the groups participating in these activities of trying to excel one another, then come into the pub, sit down, and form an essentially communal, equalitarian, leaderless drinking group—they go to the democratic vault or taproom, not the best rooms (lounges), in which the groups are isolated from one another, middle-class either in fact or space or dress.

Whatever forms of pub society that we analyse we find this contradiction manifesting itself in some way or other. It is, in the last analysis, a contradiction found through all forms of human society, the mutual irreconcilable of everyone's desire. Increasingly complex societies impose increasingly more restrictions upon their members, while at the same time freeing them increasingly from the restrictions of their conflict with "natural" (non-social) forces. In the jungle you are free from the factory siren, but you've got to watch out that your neighbours, animal and human, don't kill you. In Worktown you are free from the shadows of sudden violent death and starvation, but a lot of the money you give for your beer goes to pay for unobvious guns. And you never know when your mill is going to shut down.

So you hope for a fortune from Littlewoods, for the Wanderers to be top of the League, to beat the others at darts, to back the winner; you put on a bowler and go into the parlour on Saturday. But you all get a bit drunk together on Saturday night, forget your troubles, be good company. You work co-operatively, create nothing yourself, but as part of a process with thousands of others who between them turn out in a day more than they could make as individuals in a year. Then you go to your own separate house, your own separate family, sit down to your own separate tea.

The Worktowner's culture (between home and work), as much as the time that he spends at home and work, shows these fundamental contradictions of a society whose ways of thinking and whose ways of living reflect two different aspects of social organisation, pulling "human mind" and "animal body" in the dimension of time.

It is fundamental in the pub, inherent in the whole arrangement and feeling of pub social life, centred in beer, that *there are no drinking matches*. Beer is outside of (escape from) the personal advancement ethic. During over two years in Worktown, we have never come across any case of any kind of drinking matches nor have we heard of them anywhere, outside Oxford, and Cambridge and parts of London. There are eating matches though, mainly pies and kippers. They are rare, and we have not observed one. But a friend of ours, who has worms and a pushcart, claims to out-eat all comers, to manage a pushcart of kippers. He attributes his success, which is generally admitted, to the fact he only drinks beer before and after, not during, the match. These matches are always between males and in a pub.

XI

NON-DRINKING

A N ENQUIRY, IN six ordinary working class streets, on who drinks and who doesn't, was carried out in January. The approach used was informal—"I'm sorry to disturb you, but we are making a licensing study of this area . . . we want to know if the drinking facilities are all right." Then they were asked— "Do you use the local pubs . . . clubs . . . off-licences?" If they didn't, "Are you teetotal then?" And so on.

The following are the results of detailed informal interviews:

		Percentages	
		Males	Females
1. DRINKERS			
(a) Pubgoers	Local pubs	47	27
	Town centre	7	4
	Both	5	0
Total Pubgoers		59	31
(b) Non pubgoers			
	Clubs	2	0
	Off-licences	7	4
Total drinkers		68	35
2. NON DRINKERS			
Not "teetotal" but don't go to pubs, hardly ever drink		17	42
Teetotal		15	23
Total non pubgoers		41	69

Assuming, for the moment, that this is a crude sample on this one point (the figures don't conflict with our other statistics and estimates) there is more drinking than non-drinking, and amongst males a little more than one in four are non-drinkers. And one-fifth of all the people in all our Worktown surveys *said* they were complete teetotallers.

EARLY AND ABSOLUTE

Hop, pub, God, parson, have grown hand in fist. Before Henry VIII hops were "wicked weeds", but Henry (whose tutor was the pub-poet Skelton) sanctioned its introduction to Kent, earned the doggerel:

Hops, Reformation, Boys and Beer
Came into England all in one year.

Remarks the *Report of the Bazaar for the Liquidation of the
Debt on the Temperance Hall* (1859), "In few towns has the tem-
perance enterprise been rewarded with more success than in
Worktown." Says the *Worktown Chronicle*, March 29, 1859:

> The bazaar which was opened in the Temperance Hall . . .
> eclipses all other alike in its splendour, in the tasteful decoration
> of its varied contents, and in the manner in which it was con-
> ducted. Early, despite the rain, there was a constant arrival
> of equipages, and by the hour of opening, the hall contained
> a large and fashionable assemblage, presenting, with the
> magnificent decorations around them, and the well-appointed
> stalls under the direction of richly attired ladies, a spectacle
> in this town perhaps unparalleled for beauty.

On the second day things weren't so good "owing to the
unpropitious weather" until the evening "when a considerable
number of the working class availed themselves of the opportunity
afforded by the reduced charge for admission." At the end, the
workhouse children were admitted in a body, shown round, and
each presented with a currant bun. Gross proceeds from sales,
admissions, etc., were nearly £900. Such temperate splendour has
not been seen again in Worktown. The hall is now a cinema, and
as such is as much an enemy of the brewer as ever it was.

The origins of the national Temperance Movement were in
this area. It is often stated that, nearby, 1832, seven Nonconformists got together and signed the following:

> We agree to abstain from all liquors of an intoxicating quality,
> whether ale, porter, wine, or Ardent spirits, except as Medicines.

Short and to the point, this was one beginning of a non-drinking
movement that spread over all the country. The next year missions
were sent out to other towns, including Worktown. But a centenary volume of Worktown's Holy Trinity Church mentions:

> The first Temperance Society was formed on July 20th,
> 1831, at a meeting held in the Parish Church Schools when
> Canon Slade was elected the first president, and Rev. J.
> Jenkins the first secretary.

Jenkins, first incumbent at Holy Trinity, was a friend of
Lord Lonsdale, member of the Pitt Club, and later a J.P. The

church school was later sold and converted into the Lord Clyde beerhouse.

Less coherent efforts had been made earlier than that. One is described in the *Memorials of the Independent Methodist Chapel, Worktown :*

> The very great impression which Mr. Hunt, in 1819, made upon the inhabitants of Worktown, by advising them to abstain from the use of excisable articles, and more particularly from the liquors of the alehouse, is worthy of record, and would have been still more worthy of record had the impression been permanent.

Apparently:

> Mr. Hunt addressed the inhabitants in front of the Swan Inn, and, among other good advice, he desired them to combat their enemies by that abstinence which would benefit themselves. So great was Mr. Hunt's influence, that scarcely a person was seen in the public house for several weeks, and some of the Worktowners have resolutely shunned them to this day . . . the landlord of the —— Inn, told that such was the effect upon his business, that he lost five hundred pounds by it, and, with other difficulties, it led on to a train of disasters that had made him bankrupt.

Worktown was for many years a centre also of temperance literature, which is much more numerous than pub literature. The national organ *British Temperance Advocate* was printed here from 1849 till 1879 when it removed to Sheffield. The quality of this literature is best indicated in Fawcett's *The Temperance Harmonist*, songs with music that summarize the temperance tendencies and simple honesty. For example, *The Temperance Star, a Round for 3 Voices :*

Thou heav'nly boon that forms the spring, Thou priceless gem, of thee I sing:

While man-y drink a health each day, In draughts which take their health away,

In wa-ter pure, this toast be mine, The temp'rance star, long may it shine.

While the stirring *Temperance Tea Table Song* goes:

(1st verse)
> Around the social board we meet,
> With Temp'rance viands richly crown'd;
> To pass an hour in converse sweet,
> Where harmless mirth and love a-bound.
> The feast of reason and the flow
> Of soul, which poor Inebriates boast,
> Is but an empty, noisy show,
> Where reason in the bowl is lost.

(2nd verse)
> The cup which does our spirits cheer,
> Expands and elevates the mind;
> The pleasures we partake of here,
> Will leave no serpent-sting behind.
> Our banquet rang'd in order stands,
> And while the fragrant stream ascends;
> We rise and with extended hands,
> Bid kindly welcome to our friends.

The Worktown Temperance Hall's 20th report (*c.* 1852) shows a record of regular weekly meetings, monthly sales of 150 for the *British Temperance Advocate*, 600 new members for the year.

Carter points out that around the 1850's a conflict arose in the temperance movement between suasionists and suppressionists. The original movement was suasionist, moral instead of legislative. In 1851 the state of Maine, U.S.A., introduced prohibition, and there were wide repercussions from this in Britain. The details of the conflict are tedious, involved, and obscure; the modern results well known. Those interested are referred to Carter's book. He says:

> It is contrary to historical fact to assert "the main objective to which the Temperance Movement has been steadily marching for a century is the Prohibition of the liquor traffic" . . . the conquest of intemperance was the goal of the reformers . . . their original objective was moral, not legislative.

After 1860 there appears steadily less of the crusading and missionary spirit about the temperance movement. It got institutionalized, concerned with legislation, received Archiepiscopal approval. This is strikingly true of the state of the movement in Worktown today. Barely do memories remain of the crowded days of Rechabite Tents, Progression, Blue Ribbons, Good Templars, Gospel Temperance Men. Their alcoholic counterparts—Foresters, Oddfellows, Masons, Buffs—carry on.

TEMPERANCE NOW

Enquiry from the Sons of Temperance (now a benefit society) for local drink statistics, was met with a blank, the observer being recommended to go along and see the Secretary of the local Temperance Union for this. He did, and was given a leaflet, the annual report, a pamphlet entitled *End this Colossal Waste*, by the Rt. Hon. Philip Snowden, foreword by the Rt. Hon. David Lloyd George, O.M., M.P., and a blue-covered booklet published by the Independent Order of Rechabites, and rubber-stamped Worktown Temperance Union.

The 1936 report was Jubilee. It opens "We can look back on a record of 50 years of unbroken public service, personal effort and social achievement." They had 187 indoor meetings, estimated attendance 10,725; 21 meetings were held on the Town Hall steps, estimated attendance 7,143. (We do not know how they reach these figures. See below for reports of the meetings.) They have a Temperance Queen. She and her maids of honour "joined the Infirmary Pageant and excited much interest and appreciation on the route of the procession". The organizing secretary "has had a busy year in connection with lectures, general organization, finance, Licensing Sessions, office work, etc." Re finance, income for the year was £490 8s. 6d., the biggest slice of which—£225—coming from the Temperance Hall Trustees Grant. The main item of expenditure is the organising secretary's salary, £250. Balance carried forward £21 3s. 7d.

The "Points and Paragraphs" is a mine of quotations and figures. Solomon, Chaucer, Thomas Edison, Edgar Wallace, Lindbergh, and Dr. Philalethes Kuhn, are among those quoted.

The secretary holds meetings on the Town Hall steps. An observer's report says:

> Three men come together on the steps of the Town Hall. Speaker is man of 55–60. They gather a group of 8 men, 1 woman. Speaker says, "You hear of men who say they can drink 14 pints. Is there anyone who can say he is capable of knowing what he is doing at all by that stage. . . . Can you deny that it is a waste of money when you have ceased to have any knowledge of the supposed enjoyment. . . . Do

you think that the brewers spend vast sums of money on advertisements with little idea of for what purpose? Anyone knows that if you spend something, no matter how little, on such as drink that you can buy what I call necessities with it if you did not drink it. . . . The brewers use the modern type of advertisement because they know that by employing the best type of artist and slogan they can catch the eyes. And this is what is happening, the young people are being taught that they are not ill-using themselves by a little drinking." He speaks for 20 minutes, little interest in most of the few people who listen. Five are present for the whole 20 minutes.

Another time:

. . . he tells the story of a man who says to a business colleague "Let's have another drink, and then get down to business", and then they have another and another. This chap feels good and comes home saying that he has done a splendid stroke of business. But when he wakes up he is not so sure. . . . Three people listened to this during the early part of the meeting, and two far away, sideways, and a policeman. Later, about 9 p.m., there are 35.

MILKBAR

The great hope of temperance reformers is the Milkbar. But is Milkbar ideology temperance? Nomenclature of a notice:

MILK COCKTAILS served hot or cold at popular prices. CREME KICK. GOLDEN GLEAM. BROWN KNOCK. STRAWBERRY FLAME. PURPLE KICK. ROSY DEW. SEZ-YOU. PINEAPPLE FLIP. LEMON BITE. SUNSET RAY. DAY BREAK. DRY ROT. HORLICKS.

The last is indubitably "soft", but the one before it, Dry Rot, has an alcoholic *sound*!

The single Worktown milkbar was opened in 1937. At first slack, its trade now covers three floors, and is increasing. In several respects the bar resembles that of a pub. But you are not expected to drink milk standing. A high percentage of the clientèle is under 25, the rarest age group in the pub. The total number of milkers, however, is not appreciable in relation to Worktown's 304 pubs. The milkbar, when filled to capacity, won't hold more than a big pub—although its floor space is as large or larger than that of many big pubs. A number of landlords

see the milkbar as a threat to their business. Our figures,
however, show a milkshake, soup, and Horlicks drinking peak
at 10.30—i.e. when people have been turned out of the pubs,
but before the cinemas come out. Women slightly predominate
up to ten o'clock, but not after. We also know a number of pub-
goers who regularly go to the milkbar after closing time.

The milkbar may well be another contribution to the weakening of pub influence, and has already developed some of the
social interests of the pub. On the other hand, the milkbar
forms pub-like social groups who are not themselves pub-goers,
especially among young people. There are, however, difficulties;
you cannot sit and drink milk by the hour. Twenty gills of beer
can be consumed by a practised drinker without him getting sick,
but half that amount of milk in an evening would need a special
stomach to digest it. Milkbar drinks cost more, and show a larger
profit to the landlord, than do those in pubs; but the amount spent
per customer cannot compare with that of the pub. You've got to
keep your customers moving; therefore social difficulties.

The brewers are not happy about milk. They cannot be happy
when the young are being educated along a non-alcoholic channel.
A report in the *Daily Herald*, April 18, 1938:

BREWERS ARE PLANNING BEER AND MILK BARS

Three men go into a public house. One says to the girl
behind the bar, "One bitter and two pineapple milk shakes,
please." And the girl produces the bitter—and the shakes.

Fantastic now, perhaps, but the brewers are planning to
make it possible. Disturbed by the success of milk bars—
there are now some 2,000 of them—they are considering going
into the business themselves.

That the Milk Board has been approached was indicated
by Lieut.-Colonel J. F. Duncan, a member of the Board, in
a speech at Southampton.

Inquiries made by the brewers leave no doubt that many
thousands of milk-bar customers are young men and women
drinking their milk shakes as part of a daily "keep-fit" ritual.

We have seen (p. 136) the scarcity of youths in Worktown's pubs.

MORE TEMPERATE

We have quoted from reports of the Temperance people's
activities at the Licensing Sessions. The Temperance Secretary
told an observer:

They are going to oppose the brewers' attempt to get an extension at the Coronation. He said that before he started working here the brewers never had any difficulty in getting extensions, changes of opening hours, etc., but now they have to brief a barrister to represent their case before the licensing authorities. At the conclusion of the interview he said he was interested "in the scientific side of the drink question".

However, he is not alone in his opposition on these occasions. The *Worktown Evening News* reports:

> Objections have been lodged by the Vicar of Worktown (Mr. D.), the Rev. H., and others; on their behalf Mr. G. submitted that so far as they were concerned there was no lack of patriotism or loyalty to the Crown. . . . Extension would mean 11½ hours' continuous work for public house employees. There was no special occasion—the principal part of the Coronation was taken up by a religious service. . . . Evidence was given by Mr. D. and Mr. H. . . . The former, under cross-examination, submitted that . . the Coronation was a day of such a special nature that it was not an occasion for the extension of drinking hours.
>
> Mr. M.: "Does your objection arise on the grounds that drink is a bad thing in itself, or because you are of the opinion that it is not a special occasion?"
>
> Mr. D.: "From the latter."
>
> "You do not believe that a man has a right to drink if he thinks fit?"
>
> "I do. I am not a teetotaller."

This (Anglican) attitude is a long way away from the declamations of the Rev. Garrett, who in 1867 filled the Worktown Temperance Hall with 2,000 people to hear him declare that the working man "if he will insist on clothing the landlord and landlady in purple and fine linen, must be content to remain in poverty and rags".

CHURCH AND NON-DRINKING

The two clergymen referred to above are the leading Anglican and Nonconformist local figures. The Rev. H. has a Nonconformist hall, a large one, in which temperance meetings take place.

One of these is this year's annual meeting of the Temperance Union:

It takes place in a small room, containing tables, about 40 bentwood chairs, and two harmoniums. There are 13 men and 7 women present. Only two of the women and three of the men are under 45. Two men have beards, most are bald or whiteheaded, and one of the women has a long black moustache. Two of the oldest men doze most of the time.

The year's report was read and adopted, and officers re-elected; everything was run very briskly and unanimously, except for some diversions from an old gentleman of 94 (he stated his age frequently) who made a number of speeches that were incomprehensible to the observer, delivered in a booming and oratorical style. The theme of his remarks appeared to be about the Roman Catholics, whom he disliked, and seemed to have got the idea into his head that they have drinking orgies going on in their churches. While he spoke the chairman and secretary fiddled with papers, yawned, and displayed ostentatious boredom.

After the formal business a discussion developed about young people coming from dance halls and drinking during the intervals. All agreed that this was a bad thing, and there was a lot of it. They would like to prevent dance hall managers issuing pass out checks, but came to the conclusion that it would not be possible. . . .

Then an altercation broke out between the hon. sec. and one of the trustees. It appeared that a letter had been sent to the trustee from some leading Temperance committee asking him to bring something up at the meeting; the hon. sec. said that he wouldn't take any notice of anything unless it was sent to *him*, in a proper manner. There was a lot of personal back and forth of increasing acrimony, enlivened by the very old gentleman's search for his hat which was going on at the same time; everyone was pointing and whispering to him that he was sitting on it, but it took him some time to discover this.

The altercation was terminated, not settled, by the chairman briskly closing the meeting with a short prayer. It had also been opened with one. Neither of these prayers mentioned temperance.

The President of the Union, who is a Baptist clergyman, was not present at this meeting. The following extract from an observer's report perhaps will explain why:

He (the President) says, of the secretary, "He's as keen as mustard". And goes on to tell the observer of the old Temperance Hall, that was sold for six or seven thousand in order to pay for a permanent secretary. He says this man (the secretary) "is very keen on the legal side, but the education side has lapsed. He's a rather older type, and that's not pulling today". The President says that he himself is not really keen on temperance work, except on the educational side: "I've been dragged into it really . . . the temperance people are such fanatics and their committee had got into such a state they couldn't do anything with it and so asked me if I'd go and be chairman and keep order." There is a dominant man who is 94, an extreme fanatic, and "he spoils it". The movement was gaining ground until 1932 when the brewers launched a three million advertising campaign and got it all back. Nothing can be done about temperance as long as the present system of money distribution exists. Since 1932 the amount of drunkenness has increased steadily in the country and in Worktown. He thinks that every child should be taught the hygienic effects of drink and "the habits it engenders".

And the Temperance secretary's attitude to the Church:

In answer to an enquiry if the movement was started by the Church he (the secretary) said "If we had waited for the Church we'd never have got started. We used to have the Temperance Hall—it has served its purpose . . . too big a thing altogether . . . what we're up against now is people saying 'we know all about temperance. . . .' The Sunday schools and Churches are too contented, full of complacency, they say there's no drunkenness—we know that's rubbish. All the Bands of Hope seem to have gone. . . . If the Church is really keen for the kingdom of heaven they ought to be more active. Where any temperance work is being done in the Church it's the work of one devoted man or woman . . . there's no temperance teaching in the Sunday schools. We sent a circular to all the churches asking if we could discuss together the problems of temperance teaching, and we had four replies. Two said they were satisfied and the other two said something and we're still waiting for them to do it."

Some leading local clergymen's views about pubs are relevant here. The Rural Dean of Worktown writes in answer to our questions:

My views are bound to be one-sided, for I know nothing of the inside of them, and what I do see of the influence of them (pubs) is all the bad part—men and women spending too much time and money there, to the spoiling of their lives, and it's at that point generally that I come in, to try and patch up the damage and restore, if possible, the spoiled lives.

My impression, however, is that there is not so much of this sort of thing nowadays as there was when I was a curate in London twenty years ago and more; this may be due in some part to the milder sort of beer which is sold, but I also think it is due to the wider interests of working men, and other attractions, such as sport and the cinema. I am also prepared to believe that there is a real friendliness among the habitués of the public house; though I am convinced that it is a very superficial thing, and not worthy to be called "fellowship". . . .

Such convictions are common among clergymen.

It is perhaps particularly significant that the origin-legend of bottled beer—the thing that has made drinking outside the pub easiest and which has increased in recent years—traces to an Anglican Dean. Alexander Nowell was Dean of St. Paul's in the days of Queen Mary. He was fishing in the Thames with a stone jar of beer beside him, when someone rushed up to tell him he was being sought out as a heretic. He quickly buried the beer, and got into a boat bound for Holland. Some years later he was able to return. He made for his beer. Unearthed, opened, the effect was sensational. "It was no beer bottle but a gun, so great was the sound at the opening thereof." The Dean found the beer much strengthened and "brisker". That, says the story, started deliberate bottling, bottled beer.

A leading Worktown Congregational Minister wrote us:

I am ready to accept the weight of scientific evidence as to whether moderate drinking is harmful and the verdict, as I have understood it, is that even a small dose of alcohol does harm . . . and I am therefore an abstainer.

As alcohol harms the body which is the instrument of personality and the dwelling place of the spirit of God immanent in man, I regard drinking as to that extent an act of irresponsibility unworthy of a man who is seeking the highest moral life.

(He goes on to say that he is actively interested in the temperance movement and thinks that Christians should be total abstainers, though he thinks that temperance legislation will have to come about gradually by "the weight of public opinion". He puts down the recent increase of drinking "to the success of the

brewers' vigorous advertising policy", the more plentiful supply
of money and a general decline in idealism.) As to the number of
churchgoers who are also pub-goers he says:

> I only know Congregational churches well, and my own
> intimately. Not 1 per cent are pub-goers.

Another local clergyman writes:

> I doubt if more than 1 in 25 of the churchgoers at D——
> visit a public house.

As, at a broad estimate, there are about 30,000 pub-goers
and 30,000 churchgoers in Worktown, this figure doesn't seem
probable; but 12,000 odd of the churchgoers are Catholics. He adds:

> I wholeheartedly believe that on moral and physical, to
> say nothing of certain social grounds, abstention is best . . .
> the volume of drinking is slowly declining, and the cause is
> the multiplication of interests, at least in part. Cycling, motor-
> ing, cinemas, wireless, have played their part. Further the
> work of Temperance organizations and scientific medical opinion
> have borne fruit. Again, modern machinery and traffic conditions
> make demands inconsistent with habits of drinking.

"Wayside Pulpits" outside local churches often try to counter
the enormous BEER IS BEST advertisements opposite. Here
are a few samples:

> LORD BADEN POWELL SAYS: "KEEP OFF LIQUOR
> FROM THE VERY FIRST. TOTAL ABSTINENCE IS
> BEST!"
> TOTAL ABSTINENCE IS GOOD FOR POCKET, HOME,
> HEALTH, CHARACTER—TRY IT.
> THE "AUTOCAR" SAYS "NEVER DRINK WHEN
> YOU'RE DRIVING!"

But without use of colour, illustration or market research,
such propaganda has no observable effect and is today really
no more than a protestation of faith. Pitted against Temperance
is the up-to-date and volatile technique of business advertising,
though nothing we have seen in Britain quite equals in subtle
disarmament the widespread American advert. of the United
Brewers' Industrial Foundation (September, 1938):

BEER PROPOSES A PROGRAM . . .
AND INVITES YOUR SUPPORT

There are some people who still believe that the use of beer is sinful or harmful. The scientific evidence is overwhelmingly against them.

The great majority of Americans accept the truth . . . that beer is a mild, wholesome beverage . . . that "There is nothing more promising to combat the evil of too much alcohol than the opportunity of drinking good beer".

And so on. . . .

Their dot-dot-dots.

Besides the connection between the Church and temperance, there are other close pub-church relationships, such as the drinking already described at Catholic processions. On the Protestant side, there is a local custom, already referred to and generally known as "Sermons", where on a certain Sunday of the year, varying in different churches, the congregation has a local march round through the streets, with banners, collecting money. Quite often collectors go into the pubs. During a procession:

> 7 men stand in front of pub watching. Says one "They would have sung for us if we'd asked." Another says "We can do all the bloody singing here." (Laughter.)

And an annual open air service in the churchyard at D—— (the church referred to by parson above):

> Rain comes down heavily, crowd takes shelter around pub opposite church, 2 men in bowler hats cheerfully converse. "If it was something else they'd call it an Act of God."
> "Aye, last year it was a thunderstorm."
> "It'll be passed over soon."
> "Aye, but t' damage is done."
> Male members of the crowd look in through pub window occasionally. Just before opening time there is a movement towards the pub doors. Immediately they are opened a rush takes place. The bowler hat says, still very cheerful, "They ought to get an extension for these Sermons". Everyone comments on rain, and how it always does come down at the Sermons. They appear very cheerful about it. Except one

oldish man, who complains "It's a fortnight since I put on short pants, and I've been bloody nigh froze since". Groups of women greet the barmaid, who says "I was waiting-on upstairs last time". She is referring to the Sermons last year.

A barman writes:

Chap called B. belongs to the Salvation Army. He is a well known toper. Gets up and testifies on Sunday evenings. He got up and said "Before I joined the Army I had nowt, but look at me now, nice suit of clothes and a watch and chain." Cries of Glory to God and Praise the Lord. This was at 8 p.m. At 11 p.m. same man was crawling upstairs at the S.A. hostel on his hands and knees, blind drunk. Two captains pitched him out.

A landlord on non-drinkers:

He said he couldn't understand teetotallers. Some of them were as "narrow as the edge of a cigarette paper". He reckoned that "—— (naming leading local clergyman) could knock back a pint as quick as you or me". And he told the observer how, where he used to live, the clergy drank—he had been on a bus with one of them one hot day, and mentioned how he would like to have a pint. The clergyman said he'd like one too. So he offered him one, and it was accepted for later on "when people weren't looking—now that's what I call broadminded". And he went off at a tangent about narrow-minded people, giving as an example (still on this bus) the sort of people who kicked up a row when you sneezed and said "He's sneezed. We can't see out of the window."

PUB-GOERS ON NON-DRINKERS

Pub-goers do not like temperance people. Some previously quoted remarks show this. Drinkers in a Vault asked outright what they thought of them said:

(a) "There's a kink in their brain, I think" and (said ominously) "They're worth watching." This man added "If you come out of a pub at half past ten and stand on the flags outside a policeman'll come and move you on. You go along where the Victoria Hall comes out of a Sunday afternoon, you have to get off the pavement for 'em. The policeman'll get off and walk round them too. But you're suspect if you've had a pint of beer."
(b) "They're entitled to their own opinion."
(c) "They should be able to please themselves."
(d) "As a general rule they're not to be trusted, and they're

usually disliked by the opposite sex. I'd suspect them of
having worse vices than drinking."

(e) "Don't think much about them, I hate bigots of all kinds."
Conversation went on to say that all knew several really fine
fellows who didn't drink, and gave several instances of chaps
who did not drink but paid for booze with the rest.

ATTITUDES; AND A DIGRESSION . . .

Attitudes such as the above show an unawareness of the
other point of view, which is of course characteristic of pro-
and anti- in spheres of social behaviour. It has become a habit
amongst considerable groups of younger people to use as a term
of insult the epithet neo-Wellsian for anyone who suggests that
a wider understanding of the other point of view is necessary.
Nevertheless such an understanding is, from any point of view,
necessary. But it is inherent in the structure of opposing groups
that they are unable and/or unwilling to appreciate, even
objectively to observe, the motives and methods of their
adversaries. The role of honest reporter is left to the scientist.
So far scientists have not been very scientific about English life.
They have confined science to limited fields of research, and
the same man who is a scientist in his laboratory is generally
noticeably "unscientific" outside it. An objective and reasonably
impartial sociology does not yet exist in Europe, though it did,
for a time, in Austria. The English work, such as the surveys of
certain areas undertaken by University bodies, has been what we
can best describe as "Administrative Sociology"—that is to say,
it has started off by accepting all the usual assumptions as to the
social role of pub or pool or unemployed. It has hardly used the
valuable techniques of anthropology, and has produced few
generalizations in the magnificently rich and easily worked home
field, which can be compared to those of Malinowski, Rivers, Firth,
Layard or Haddon for "primitive" communities. The persons
(such as Ginsberg, Laski, Hobhouse, Tawney) who have made
valuable contributions to social theory in this country have been
economists and others acting intuitively, as social philosophers.

A word of explanation here. We're not trying to make out
any case pro- or anti-academism. We want to avoid being "as
narrow as the edge of a cigarette paper". But it *is* difficult not
to be puzzled by English academic attitudes in a field where
unacademic approach is clearly essential, at least unacademic
approach to the exceedingly unacademic human study material.

Our own attitude and our feeling of amateur enterprise have been summed up by Professor Bronislaw Malinowski, who in our first year's Report (Lindsay Drummond, 1938) describes how he first met one of us reading a paper to the Institute of Sociology:

> He started with the time-honoured abuse of things and men academic. My prejudice did not melt. Then he came to the point. I was puzzled, at times irritated, but realized more and more that I had to become acquainted at first hand with the movement. After a careful perusal of the published results I veered round in my opinion almost completely. I found that the movement was in no way a caucus or cabal, but a scientific undertaking, in the sense that everything was being done above board. An occasional *boutade* or joke apart, the workers were keen to work hand in hand with academic interests and institutions.
>
> Wisely perhaps, they embarked on the large enterprise without too many doubts, self-criticisms and cavilling uncertainties. They had started from the side of rough and perhaps crude empiricism. They also did not encumber themselves with either an heavy initial outfit of methodological scruple, conceptual precision or terminological consistency. On the point of these deficiencies, full reparation will have to be made by the authors.
>
> The leaders of the movement being ready to meet us halfway, we professional students of social science have also to make our move. Personally I am convinced that it is both wiser and more profitable to co-operate rather than to put obstacles in the way; to criticize constructively rather than to ridicule.
>
> My reasons are clear and simple. The basic idea of the movement is 100 per cent. right.
>
> The movement is a natural out-growth of the best tendencies in modern social science. It represents a type of research which has now become inevitable. It would be an unpardonable waste of initiative, enthusiasm, and accomplishment, if, for lack of intellectual support and financial backing, the work were allowed to peter out. For it would have to be restarted, most likely under less favourable conditions, and with a less competent personnel.

There is no question of restarting us, for we're going on. We started with no money, no personnel, and no useful existing technique for making objective study of normal behaviour. Our main asset was that all the people who began this job had direct experience of working-class life and had earned their own livings as unskilled workers. Three of us had been to universities but none had stayed too long. Now we have many skilled investigators, and thousands of part-time observers also, from all walks of life and parts of the country.

In view of all these circumstances, we are fully aware of the numerous limitations from which this work suffers, but we do not apologize for them except in so far as we must apologize for the human sciences in this country. Directly we start from the field of administrative and official statistics with their massive appearance of reliability, we go into fields that have scarcely been charted except in a specialized way by a very few novelists. This book suffers more than its successors from lack of a native sociological tradition, from methodological difficulties because it has been done by a few persons, is thus the most subjective and the least comprehensive; it provides therefore the best introduction to the limitations and scope of such work. This work naturally has as one of its aims the analysis of sympathetic and of conflicting trends within this civilization. "As narrow as the edge of a cigarette paper" is false from an external, objective-angle, but true in terms of the person who thinks that way. Social life consists not of judgements by scientists, but the history of ideas, conscious or unconscious, "true" or "false", in the mind of each and every person involved in the civilization. The social scientist must describe these, for better or for worse, as far as it is possible. And the factor "possible" should be decided simply by the methods that he can devise, for measuring what people do and think. Of course, nearly everyone thinks that they are right. In arguments about alcohol this is especially so. The main argument in favour of alcohol comes down to the right of the individual to enjoy his own leisure within reasonable limits. The main argument against alcohol is generally stated as being based on the best interests of the individuals themselves. But the Churches that advocate abstinence show (in Work-town anyway) no equally explicit attitude about nutrition or dole. Similarly the brewers, when they say "Beer is best". These sorts of "social conscience" seem to suffer from distinct limitations.

TEMPERANCE HOTEL

The town, it should be noted, has a temperance hotel. Observers' first contact with it was when one walked in, thinking it was a pub. Its exterior features form a strong parallel to those of pubs of its size. The name runs across the façade in the same way as does that of the brewing firm on the pub; and on either side of the entrance (which is like an ordinary pub door, ground glass with brass rail across) are oblong tablets of the kind that are seen on many larger pubs, advertising the brewery or a particular type of its beer. In this case they are inscribed with the name of a mineral water.

The porter here used to be a barman; and now he has plenty of his old work to do, going across the way to fetch drinks for the residents, most of whom are commercial travellers. Meals are served here to non-residents. In fact, except for the absence of the direct sale of alcohol on the premises, this place is far more of an "inn" in the strict sense of the word than are the majority of other local pubs.

HOUSING ESTATES

An important aspect of non-drinking is that which takes place in the absence of pubs. In the new housing estates there are no pubs. What happens about drinking?

An ex-landlord, who lives on a housing estate, says that some 50 per cent of the men drink. "They make tracks to their old localities." But he points out that they can only afford to do this at week-ends, "because of the finance". "When they are placed in better surroundings they go in debt for wireless . . . (rent) . . . have less to spend on drink." The following extracts from a write-up on the housing estate by an unemployed man who was moved out there as a consequence of slum clearance, have an important bearing on the whole subject of pub-going:

> Whilst it is fairly common for the street dweller (male) to have a "mate" or "boozing partner" living in or close to his own street, the average estate man who takes a drink, apparently prefers his own company, or relies on meeting friends in his perambulations in the town. The estate man completely changes his social activities on removing from the street to the estate, sometimes breaking down the habits of a lifetime.
>
> To my knowledge a man may have for years frequented a particular pub 5, 6, or 7 nights a week, but living on the estate his jaunts are restricted to week-ends. Possible reasons are
> —Reduced economic circumstances.
> —Restricted facilities (no pubs on the estate, therefore necessitating travelling).

—Prudence dictated by a sneaking regard for the "authorities" who appear to act in a mysterious way as "distant guardians" of the behaviour of their tenants.

The estate seems to develop along the lines of "communal life" . . . for instance, the "village" atmosphere, where "everybody knows everybody else", is very noticeable.

. . . in this respect the transport facilities of the tenants is a good instance of this unusual joviality. The conductors are invariably on intimate terms with most of their fares. . . . He, the conductor, knows a large number of the passengers almost as personal friends, and most journeys to and from the town are enlivened by the wisecracks passed between him and his friends. . . . It is particularly marked on the late Saturday night buses. . . . Several of the passengers have provided themselves with liveners for the morrow, in the shape of pint bottles of beer or stout which advertise themselves by a passenger's difficulty in passing down the gangway owing to numerous mysterious bulges in the pockets of the men.

. . . The jollity, although very noisy, is never wranglesome. Sheer drunkenness is rare. I have seen no instances where people have been more than fuddled. . . . The bus appears to be the connecting link between two worlds as typified by the town and the estate, and is the scene of more exchanged intimacies than any other place. In this respect it particularly takes the place of the absent pub. It is the meeting place of the estate, and the "bus stop" at the shopping centre becomes to a limited degree the centre around which the estate revolves.

Generally speaking, it is as if the sociability of the estate is hurled into the town at week-ends, to drift back into the estate bus load by bus load . . .

The presence of a public house on the estate would I think be welcomed. Its absence is the cause of comment on numerous occasions when people meet. . . .

He goes on to describe, at some length, the important place taken by gardening in the estate, and the development of a community of gardeners. Similar to pubgoers.

Now these points are of the utmost importance in assessing the role of the pub. Firstly, ordinary week-day social drinking becomes impossible. Week-end drinking, which, as we have seen throughout the book, represents a different set of satisfactions, however continues. But the ordinary pub-goer becomes a non-drinker as far as his usual week-night pub habits are concerned.

And, if we are to take the writer's statement as true—much other material confirms it—new forms of social intercourse arise. The bus, gardening, the "village atmosphere". We are not, of course, suggesting that the absence of pubs alone is responsible for this. But if we have been correct in evaluating the social motives of ordinary week-night pub-going, then these are just the sort of compensations that we could expect to arise in its place. Another new and important feature in these housing estates is the rise of Tenants' Associations, which are spreading rapidly in Worktown. These are a new form of working-class organization, growing up on new estates all over the country. But here again the absence of pubs, which means that a large proportion of the adult male population are deprived of their normal social life, must result in some compensatory form of social institution.

The reason why there are no pubs on the estates is best expressed by a report:

Observer talks with —— (Town Planning Committee member) who says his authorities have no objection at all to pubs on housing estates. But licensing authorities are definitely anti-drink. No brewers may be on licensing authorities, though they have representatives on the magistrates' bench, who exercise considerable influence. He thinks it a disgrace that there should only be lay magistrates in a town the size of Worktown, whereas if there was a stipendiary it would remove a lot of graft which he definitely states goes on. However, these conflicting brewers do not want a pub on a housing estate because "they want a monopoly" and cannot agree as to which of them should have the pub there; if one is allowed there's no reason why there shouldn't be others. They think that if they have no pubs there at all and run no risk of outside competition, the people will come and drink at the existing pubs. This man thinks that the result is a good deal of dissatisfaction; and lacking social facilities people tend to discuss "dissatisfaction issues" which would not arise if there was a pub; these ideas can't be anything but against the status quo. That's bad, he says.

At any rate they discuss the status quo of housing estate, not the status quo of traditional Worktown. The municipal authorities thus limit social life on their estates, and induce people to take considerable bus journeys towards the town centre for shopping, cinema, drinking activities. There is a lack of local life or loyalty on the housing estate; at least none is encouraged by the corporation. Recently, however, the estate tenants have formed into the vigorous associations mentioned above, a new and militant departure of local organization. This might well have been anticipated where large numbers of persons, uprooted at random from streets which have all sorts of personal and family values to them, are plonked down in outlying areas where there is no communal meeting place, not more than one church, no pub or club. It takes more than a semi-detached house and a small piece of garden to destroy the Worktown worker's feeling for fraternization. The persons, half a dozen of them, responsible for the replanning and rehousing of the area, are not persons with any direct knowledge or understanding of working-class social life. The two most active have very large houses, incomes, cars. Fired by the best liberal traditions of decent reform they have assumed that it is essentially good in itself to shift a worker from a house in a continuous row without a bathroom to a house in an interrupted row with a bathroom. Nothing else is necessary for the good life? The profits (for the corporation) on the roundabouts mean some losses on the swings (for brewer and boozer). While further and detailed research is necessary, we venture to suggest that in Worktown the consequences of restricting the normal pattern of any local group life are considerable, and tend to lead to attitudes which some people call "anti-social" and "apathetic".

THE REVOLUTION . . . .

Or, as the Worktown temperance report pointed out, Hitler, Mussolini, and the Mikado are teetotallers. Baldwin, Marx, Engels and the Duke of Windsor are not.

The story of Marx, who for a bet succeeded in having a drink in every pub along a densely pubbed two-mile stretch from Tottenham Court Road to Hampstead, does not find parallels in the lives of 1939's dictators. Summing this up neatly, Minister of Pensions Major Herwald Ramsbottom, said:

> Beer is a peaceful drink. Beer is the drink for the ordinary, kindly, simple workingman in the street—the man who can be found in millions all over the world. If he could get together with his fellows in other countries over a pint of beer, we would hear much less of dictators and all the other high and mighty political personages that at present bully and bewilder the ordinary man. In these unstable, quarrelsome days I think

I can give you a slogan for all peaceful, genial, companionable
folks of all countries:
"Beer Drinkers of the World Unite!"

In thus revising the traditional slogan rally-call of working-
class militants, Conservative Ramsbottom states the case for a
big slab of English civilization to whom the pub—whatever its local
varieties, basically the Worktown pub described in this book—
is the most important centre of leisure and pleasure and peace.

A theme well-developed by wide-awake brewers; in a recent
Sunday Times advert (their italics):

> To drink beer is for your country's good as well as for
> your own. Every time you raise a glass of beer to your lips
> —you do *double* good. You not only benefit *yourself*—you
> help to keep the country's flag flying. Think of this wherever
> you go—into a little country inn or a bar of a town hotel.
> Say to yourself "for the country's well-being as much as for
> my own—beer is best!"

For the usual opposition, equally sentimental, ideal, a typical
advert (*Strand Magazine*, April, 1938):

> The drink question today is very different from what it
> was fifty or even twenty-five years ago. Values have changed.
> There was greater prosperity and less competition, less "struggle
> for life" and more equable atmosphere. In those days, if a
> man over-indulged in alcohol, provided he did not do it in a
> socially reprehensible extent (and society was distinctly toler-
> ant), it mattered comparatively little. We will not go as far
> as to say that over-indulgence in alcohol was the rule rather
> than the exception, but the thriving times lent themselves
> to an expansiveness which we cannot afford today. Today
> professional men, business men, writers, artists, brain-workers
> of all sorts, dare not make a habit of festivity, or live too richly.
> There is too much competition. It is, for better or for worse,
> the day of the very abstemious if not the ascetic. Unfortunately,
> habits are tenacious things and not easily discarded; and the
> most tenacious of all is the drink habit. We are not here referring,
> of course, to the hopeless drunkard, but to the respectable
> man who, through never letting a day go by without consuming
> a certain quantity of alcohol, has become to rely on it. Once
> alcohol ceases to be a slave and becomes a master, he (if we
> may think of alcohol anthropomorphically) develops into the
> worst form of tyrant, whom only a revolution can displace. It is
> the function of the Turvey Treatment *to make the revolution.*

XII

THE LAST HOUR!

Beer drinking is one answer to the solution of the personal problem of existence, the personal revolution. It provides a mechanism for dealing with situations which appear to be recurrent and almost universal. There are few races in the world who do not have some similar method of physiological change as well as a "spiritual" one—religion, an intellectual one—a magic or science, and a physical one—sport, dance, etc.

The work-life rhythms of pre-industrial civilizations were bound up with those of their cultural life; they both arose from the same sources—the seasons. In the mill, where it is perpetually sub-tropical summer, what you do, how and when you do it, is independent of time and weather, which are the governing factors of men's work in agricultural societies. The sowing-reaping cycle, not only governed men's working lives, but set the rhythm for their religious and cultural activities. In an industrial society, whose religion is still based on the seasonal cycles of primitive communities, as are many of its cultural traits—spring cleaning, for instance, children's games, adult sport (the football fan's life in the summer is not the same as in the winter). The ordinary daily activities by which people get their living are conditioned by dynamo and steam engine instead of sun and moon.

The pub is still essentially very much a pre-industrial institution. Format, ritual, traditions, nomenclature, games, have not changed very much in the past hundred years. It still caters in the simplest way for leisure hours of working people living in the immediate vicinity, but with one portion for better off folk (and irregulars and travellers). Today the pub is a sort of bridge between the older institutions and those new ones catering for people strictly as individuals, but on a mass basis. The recent experiences and contemporary difficulties of the pub are closely similar to those of its opposite number, the Church. Their Cain and Abel history has already been discussed. But the Church, and the pre-Christian trajectory of year, still decides the dis-

tribution of and emphasizes social activity throughout the year
and the week. The pub is ruled by that rhythm too, but is more
directly subservient to industrial variations.

The cycle of working life determines, if not directly *how* leisure
should be spent, *when* it should take place. Evenings, week-ends,
Blackpool holiday week represent, to a different degree, periods
of freedom from certain constraints. At work a man's actions
are being imposed upon him directly by material circumstances
over which he has little or no control.

We have already suggested that both holidays and drunkenness
represent breakdowns, the lifting of restrictions and tabus.
Human societies have only been maintained by limitations of
their members' freedom, by restrictions, tabus, laws, barriers
between man and man. The internal stability of a society is
dependent upon the general observance of these things. They
have to become "natural", so that the ordinary individual in
the society considers his way of living to be the normal, sensible
one, and other ways stupid, crazy or immoral.

But they are also "unnatural" inasmuch as they tend to
repress, constrain, and modify powerful instinctive urges in
connection with sex, eating, aggression, etc. Therefore the
machinery to preserve the stability of the society must include
safety valves, that allow a partial release of accumulating
tensions.

The most stable societies tend to be the more primitive ones,
which have the most definite and organized ritual breakdowns
of tabu, unrepression and "intoxications". It is in these societies
that magic, ritual, and convention are most highly developed.
One of the features that differentiates our "civilized" society
most clearly from other and more primitive forms is the weakening
of these forms of restriction, so that it is possible for many
people not to accept the idea that the way they live is "natural".

But while these restrictions have weakened another type
has become very strong—those imposed by the actual economic
structure of the society. The economic restrictions, not imposed
by religion, magic or convention, are none the less "unnatural",
and the need for their breakdown is just as strong, (possibly
stronger) as it is in other forms of society. But there are only
few and feeble sanctioned breakdowns of contemporary restrictions. The Christmas feast, the Cup Tie, the wedding party,
the week-end drunk—these are our forms of release. But they

are feeble—there are, for instance, no real and sanctioned occasions of sexual freedom—and though the economic restrictions can be temporarily forgotten, yet they are actually present because so often the whole thing is dependent upon how much money people have got in their pockets while they are celebrating. No breakdown provides free beer for all. It is in this respect that we see the importance of the pub democracy, exemplified in the ritual of standing rounds.

The decay of the organized occasions of breakdown of social restrictions has not been accompanied by any real relaxation of those restrictions, or of the need for their breakdown. The yearly holiday and the week-end intermission from work have taken their place. And, no money—no holiday.

While the ordinary, week night, quiet evening at the local pub represents social relaxation, "week-end drinking" (in its extended sense) is playing the same sort of social role as the Cup Tie, the Coronation, religious and political revivalism. As contemporary industrial society becomes more and more un-stable, manifesting this in fears of wars, unemployment, revolu-tions, lack of confidence in the future and of certainty that we live in the best of all possible worlds, the need for breakdowns becomes greater amongst those who have no adequate set of values to deal with the situation. But drunkenness is not on the increase. There is, however, as will be shown in other books of this series, an increased belief in magic, luck, craving for "mystery", gambling, a whole series of alternative values, passive, personal and non-participative, though of course with the necessary social sanction that large numbers of other individuals —some of them famous or royal—do the same thing.

One big function of the pub is thus being undermined, from other angles, by other groups whose principal motive must be the making of profits. But there is still no other group interested in providing a place to which ordinary people with ordinary incomes can come without formality, swear with impunity, meet strangers and talk about anything, and maybe spit on the floor.

OTHER INTERPRETATIONS

Finally, we should look at some other points of view on the pub. The list of books at the end of this section is not intended to be a full bibliography. It is only of those books actually referred to during the writing of this one. Most of them are of little use to anyone who wants to get to know anything about the pub as a living social organism.

They can be divided as follows:

1. (a) Historical. The majority of these are sources of quotation. No kind of comprehensive history of the pub as a social institution exists. In order to find anything about it, it is necessary to consult broadsides, pamphlets, plays, poems, in which chance remarks can be found that throw a light on how the people of the period regarded the pub, and what they did in it. Our selection of sources is naturally limited; we have not attempted to write a history of the pub.

1. (b) Contemporary works which are specifically about the history of the pub or which include passages relevant to it. Of these, antiquarian, like R. V. French's *Nineteen Centuries of Drink*, or the useful work of Firebaugh, Marshall and Gregory; and sociological, like Sidney Webb's work on the Licensing Laws; a few others have been relevant to this study.

2. Scientific works. (a) Physiological. Of these there are plenty. And as far as they go they are adequate. But, cf. Koren's remarks on how experiments on the effects of alcohol are carried out. There is nothing in any of these books to show, for instance, what the effect of drinking beer *in a pub is*. They contain material about "subjects", not pub-goers.

2. (b) Sociological. There are plenty of these too, some specifically about drink, and others which treat of drink. While most of them contain a lot of statistics, they are concerned with the "drink problem", not the pub. The titles of those we have listed show this quite clearly. The sociologists and the sociologically minded temperance writers have not considered the pub as a social institution. To them it comes under "Crime and Delinquency" (cf. *The London Survey*).

That the physical, moral, and statistical results of excessive drinking are interesting and important is not to be denied. But they are the results of an *abuse* of the special functioning of a social institution. And writers have studied these results as a "problem" divorced from its real background. It is just as if the problem of unemployment was to be studied without any reference to, knowledge, or understanding of the social and economic system in which it took place.

The trouble is that sociologists and temperance men are seldom pub-goers. To them, as to Worktown's Rural Dean, the pub door opens on to mystery. Who goes in and what happens there they don't know. But from this doorway there reels a succession of figures that can be recorded under the headings of drunks per ten thousand of the population, and later as victims of cirrhosis. We have seen how few of the people who come out of these doors actually are had up for being drunk or do die of cirrhosis.

The ordinary pub-goer has no official existence. It is typical that the *New English Dictionary* gives no pub use of the word "vault" and that for the *Encyclopædia Britannica* the pub only exists in relation to the liquor laws (to which one-eighth of a paragraph is devoted) and the legal aspect of public house Trusts.

The *Fact* survey quoted earlier speaks of people seeking "more civilized" amusements than pub-going. The idea implicit in this is that it is more civilized to go to the pictures than get drunk. Well, most pub-goers don't get drunk anyway, but is it more civilized to go to the pictures than get drunk? It just depends upon what your ideas of civilization are. The film is nearly 100 per cent celluloid, beer 3½ per cent alcoholic. In terms of stupefaction content the film wins every time. Yearning after Garbo instead of flirting with the barmaid is a lot less trouble. This is an idea of civilization that is based on self-culture.

3. Books that contain accurate descriptive material about pubs. There are very few of these. *The London Survey* (drink section by B. D. Nicholson) and Selley's *English Public House as it is* we have frequently quoted. Also Rowntree's pioneer study. The first, though limited in its scope, contains more fact about pubs in its few pages than can be found in all the other books listed here. Selley's book is written from a temperance point of view, assuming that the pub must be bad. And Rowntree shows a good deal of prejudice at times. These writers have *observed* pubs, and their conclusions are based on something else than the study of official statistics and the bumps on dead men's livers.

There is also a whole pile of "Ye Olde Inne" books, of which a few are listed here. (p. 345). These are of little use for the understanding of the pub today or at any other time.

Thomas Burke's *Book of the Inn* is a good anthology of passages from various writers about inns, and contains a lot of material about the use of the inn as a place of accommodation and eating. It is a pity that he gives no details of the works—beyond the writer's name—from which these references have been taken.

Most of English literature contains descriptions of inns and inn scenes—Chaucer, Skelton, Dekker, Shakespeare, Fielding, Smollett, Dickens, are examples. But they contain little that is enlightening on the function of the inn as a normal place, or a social hangout for the locals. The descriptions are of people eating or sleeping there, and of adventure and encounters for which the inn is simply a background.

Amongst contemporary novels there are plenty of pub scenes also, the most outstanding being Joyce's pub stuff in *Ulysses*, and a short story in *New Writing* (1938) by H. T. Hopkinson. But no one—say an educated Indian—ignorant of the pub, reading modern novels would be able to get from them any understanding of what the pub really is and who uses it. We have thus had to leave out most literary sources and we have learned, above all, to distrust (i) data from "official" sources, from interviews with leaders and persons who have vested interests (psychological or economic) in the subjects involved, (ii) from written sources of all sorts, whether historic, contemporary, or questionnaire—wherever and whenever these sources claimed to speak for anyone other than the person speaking. The difference, for example, between what an Anglican clergyman says happens in his church, and what he knows happens, between what he knows happens and what the verger knows, and what the choirboy does, is often sensational, and in each case differs in external circumstances from what *happened*. . . . For any incident consists as much of invisible as visible components, is as much an expression of opinion as of fact. Each interpretation can also be called a misinterpretation, each and all must be included in a sociological decision of "truth". The difference between what is supposed to happen and what does happen, between the written law and the law as enforced, between the press report and the observer's report, is a constantly recurring, and at first bewildering factor in the study of this civilization. Indeed it appears to be a diagnostic character of the key institutions in our civilization, and one which is constantly raising grave and (on present methods) insurmountable problems. This type of discrepancy between fact, fancy, fallacy, decides many of our judgements and personal attitudes—including, no doubt, those of all mass-observers. And the channels that claim to represent public opinion or accurate fact are silted up solid. Clearly we get involved in the same position in Worktown. But we try not to forget that every expression of opinion, act or word, is valid and potentially significant as part of field-work material.

A typical case of such expression (and relevant at this point) is provided by two articles in Worktown's weekly *Journal and Guardian* in early 1938, showing the process of reportage and remoulding, which makes the externals of English culture at first a fog and a wilderness to the groping researcher.

(*a*) The *Journal and Guardian* carried a four-column centre page item called "Weighing-up Your Neighbours", with a heavy caps para to start off:

> Most of us like to speculate upon our neighbour's habits. As a rule, it is an idle form of harmless curiosity but recently, it has been elevated into a pseudo-science "Mass Observation". Worktown has been one of the experimental stations of the mass-observation movement and some months ago its citizens were assailed with the question "Why do you drink beer?"

The journalist goes on to say how silly this pub-research is, and to analyse the Chief Constable's annual report to the Licensing Justices for 1937:

> The most curious information is that Monday and Tuesday, along with Friday, are the days when Worktown goes on the "binge". I wonder if the mass observation people can tell us why? In the meantime whilst waiting for their reply I myself . . .

And he proceeds to explain everything, using neither data nor humour. We must suspect his line of approach from the start, because the word "binge" is not a Worktown pub-goer's word; "on the piss" would have been right, or if his paper can't face that fact, getting kettled, canned, or boozed up. His first explanation covers Monday as binge night. "That shilling left over from Saturday and Sunday nights determines where he shall go." It is not clear why a shilling should determine the place, for beer prices are uniform.

The writer implies that a Worktowner gets arrestably drunk on one shilling (the price of two pints). He then steps on to safer ground of Monday Bank Holidays, etc., before going on to ask, with a usual vagueness:

> But what of Tuesday? Baking as a rule, does not usually drive the man of the house from his home. So the solution

must be found elsewhere. I have an idea that market day on Tuesday provides the answer. It provides the one necessary excuse I can think of for coming to town. Carrying a shopping bag has led many a man to the altar. What better reason then, than going to town to give the missus a lift with the marketing does a man need for meeting his cronies of the pub? And this, my mass-observation friends, is, I think, as near a solution as any you will arrive at.

The above statements contain the following erroneous conclusions:

1. That people need an excuse to go to a pub.
2. That they actively help their wives with marketing.
3. That to drink on Tuesdays they come into the centre of the town.
4. That being "driven from his home" is the most probable impulse to pub-going.
5. That most Worktowners still bake their own bread.
6. That people go to the town centre pubs to meet friends; just the reverse, the local pub is for that.
7. That men carry their wives' shopping bags.[1]
8. That carrying a shopping bag has led many a man to the altar.
9. That his mass observation friends can't arrive at something nearer to what he calls "a solution".

The writer carries on his laborious pilgrimage of rationalization throughout every day of the week, and ends up with considerable éclat, "Any sharp rise in the returns of drunkenness should be strictly investigated, especially in view of the tendency over post-war and pre-war years to a decrease".

The futility—from an administrative point of view—of such generalizations is immediately demonstrated by a glance at the drunkenness figures for the previous year, 1936, when there were less people drunk on Monday and Tuesday than on any other night. While Thursday, of which this journalist says an "empty purse automatically rules out having a binge" (he doesn't know about the pub credit system) has only three less drunks than Tuesday in 1937, twice as many as Tuesday in 1936.

(b) On another page of the same issue of the same paper a special article by a staff reporter describes a series of University

---

[1] A Tuesday night's observation at the market showed only one in one thousand men carrying his wife's shopping basket; the majority of women were not accompanied by men.

Extension lectures being given in Worktown. It mainly deals with a series of questions set as a sort of examination after the latest lecture. It says:

> They were interesting questions too. The first one was "What is democracy?" That's a stiff question. Even when one is attending three lectures on "The Theory and Practice of British Democracy". But when the lecturer goes on to say that he wants the answer in the fewest possible words, and allows about three minutes for the answer to be written then it becomes a really tall order. Did it worry members of the audience? Not a bit. They wrote swiftly and silently— some kneeling on the floor while using the form as a desk— and then waited calmly for the next. And although I have no idea what sort of answers were written I am quite sure no one wrote anything like "Government of the people, for the people, by the people."

The writer of this is an expert on local opinion, contributing extensively to both the leading Worktown papers, which enter 96 per cent of its homes.

Actually these questions were designed and set by us in connection with our political research, and in collaboration with the lecturer. Of the 52 Worktowners who were at this lecture 13 *actually and exactly used the cliché* whose non-use the reporter was sure of. Thirty-eight (73 per cent) used forms of it which included the phrases "by the people" and "of the people".

The article ends by quoting with approval a statement, which is clearly correct, from the lecture syllabus:

> Over and above this, it has become especially evident in recent years that no democracy can hope to survive unless, in regard to subjects with a close bearing on public affairs, its people are given full opportunity, with fair guidance, under conditions of free inquiry, to learn and to think for themselves.

Quite so.

But along such routes of purely pious and decent *hope* there seems no likely lasting achievement. It is imperative to face the *facts* of contemporary culture. Until we do that our good intentions are mostly futile. The correlation of fact-finding sociologist with act-making humanist, reformer, reporter, reactionary or revolutionary, is essential?

LIST OF RELEVANT REFERENCES

IN THIS BOOK we have had to make the best use possible of the scanty material about the pub itself. America, richest sociological source, has no pubs in our sense, unfortunately for this bibliography. In this list of publications (excluding fiction) which we have referred to, those marked X have been most useful, and those followed by H have provided significant historical material.

BOOKS

Anon. *A Peep into the Holy Land, or the Sinks of London Laid Open.* 1835.
Atkin, Frederick. *Philosophy of the Temperance Reformation.* c. 1875.
Aubrey. *A Description of Wiltshire.* 1630.

Baker, J. L. *The Brewery Industry.* 1905.
Barley, R. *The Brewer's Analyst.* 1907.
Besant, Walter. *East London.* 1901.
Beveridge, William H. *Unemployment: A Problem of Industry.* 1912. X.
Boomer, Lucius. *Hotel Management: Principles and Practice.* (New York.) 1931.
Bowles. *Reflections on the Moral and Political State of Society.* 1800. X H
Bowley, A. L., and M. H. Hogg. *Has Poverty Diminished?* 1925. X.
Boyd. (*See* Evans.)
Braithwaite. *Law of Drinking.* 1620. H.
Brougham, B. (*See* I. Fisher.)
Browne, P. *Discourse of Drinking Healths.* 1716. H.
Bruce, R. *Lancashire Regional Planning Report.* 1926.
Bruere, M. *Does Prohibition Work?* 1927.
Burke, T. *The Book of the Inn.* 1927. X H.
Burke, T. *The English Inn.* 1931. H.

Carew. *Survey of Cornwall.* 17th Cent. H.
Carter, H. *Control of the Drink Trade in Britain.* 1919.
Carter, H. *The English Temperance Movement.* 1933. X.
Catlin, G. E. C. *Liquor Control.* 1931. X.
Chettle, H. *King Hart's Dream.* 1592. H.
Chisholm, C. *Market Survey of United Kingdom, 1937.* 1937.
Clegg, J. C. *History of Worktown.* 1892. X H.

Dale. *Content of Motion Pictures.* 1921. X.
Davkin, Charles Gilbart. *A Poem on the Evils of Intemperance.* 1838.
Deacon, A. B. *Malekula.* 1934.
Dekker. *Gull's Hornbook.* H.
Dorr, R. C. *Coercion or Control.* 1929.
Dowell, S. *History of Taxation and Taxes.* 1888. H.

346 BIBLIOGRAPHY

B.E. *A Dictionary of the Canting Crew.* 1700. H.
Earle. *Microcosmography.* 17th Cent. H.
Eaton and Harrison. *Bibliography of Social Surveys.* 1930.
Eberlein. (*See* A. E. Richardson.)
Elliott and Merrill. *Social Disorganization.* 1934. X.
Evans and Boyd. *The Use of Leisure in Hull.* 1933.
Evans, R. *Training for Citizenship.* 1935.

Fawcett, John. *The Temperance Harmonist.* (Glasgow.) No date.
Feldman, H. *Prohibition, Its Industrial and Economic Aspects.* 1927.
Firebaugh, W. C. *The Inns of Greece and Rome.* (Chicago.) 1923. X H.
Fisher, I. *Prohibition at its Worst.* 1926.
Fisher, I., and B. Brougham. *The Noble Experiment.* 1930.
French, R. V. *History of Toasting.* 1882. H.
French, R. V. *Nineteen Centuries of Drink in England.* 1884. X H.

Glücksmann, Robert. *Das Gaststättenswesen.* (Stuttgart.) 1927. H.
Gregory, E. W. (*See* H. Marshall.)

Hackwood, F. W. *Inns, Ales and Drinking Customs of Old England.*
    1910. H.
Hampson, F. S. *An Interesting History of the Execution of the Seventh
    Earl of Derby, at Ye Olde Man and Scythe Inn.* 1914. H.
Hannah, Mary. *Brookdale Hall : A Temperance Story.* (Worktown.) No
    date.
Harper, C. G. *The Old Inns of Old England.* 1906.
Harrison. (*See* Eaton.)
Harrisson, Tom. *Savage Civilization.* 1937.
Harrisson, Tom. (*See* C. Madge.)
Harrison, G., and F. C. Mitchell. "*The Home Market.* 1939.
Hayner, Norman S. *Hotel Life.* (North Carolina.) 1936. X.
Highet, R. *Points and Paragraphs.* 1935.
Hogg, M. H. (*See* A. L. Bowley.)
Homer's Iliad.
Horace. Lib. 3, Carm. ix.
Horsley, V. and M. D. Sturge. *Alcohol and the Human Body.* 1907.
Hose, R. E. *Prohibition or Control.*

Keast, H. *The Church and the Public House.* Undated. X.
Kelynack, T. N. (ed.) *Drink Problem of Today.* 1918.
King. *Art of Cookery.* 1776. H.
Kirby, J. (*See* G. C. M'Gonigle.)
Koren, J. *Alcohol and Society.* 1916.

Layard, J. W. *Journ. Roy. Anthrop. Institute,* LVIII, 1928, p. 139.
Le Bon, Gustave. *The Crowd.* 1896.
Lewis, Sinclair. *Work of Art.* (New York.) 1934.
Lyell, A. *It Isn't Done.* (Kegan Paul's Today and Tomorrow pamphlets.)

McBain, H. *Prohibition, Legal or Illegal.* 1928.

McBride, C. A. *The Modern Treatment of Alcoholism and Drug Narcotism*. 1910.

M'Gonigle, G. C., and J. Kirby. *Poverty and Public Health*. 1925.

Maceroni, F. *Defensive Instructions for the People*. (How to defend a pub.) 1832. H.

Mackies, *Worktown Directory and Almanack*. 1849. H.

Madge, C., and T. Harrisson. *Mass-Observation, First Year's Work*. 1938.

Madge, C., and T. Harrisson. *Britain, by Mass-Observation*. (Penguin Special.) 1938.

Marshall, H., and E. W. Gregory. *Old Country Inns of England*. 1912. H.

Marshall, H. *The Taverns of Old England*. 1927.

Mayhew. *London Labour and the London Poor*. H.

Maynard, D. C. *The Old Inns of Kent*. 1925.

Merrill. (*See* Elliott.)

Merseyside Survey. (Liverpool,) 1934.

Miles, W. R. *Alcohol and Human Efficiency*. 1924.

Morrison, Fynes. *Itinerary*. 1617. H.

Moffey, R. W. *A Century of Oddfellowship*. 1910.

Nicholson, D. B. *London Life and Labour*. Vol. ix. (Section on Drink.) X.

Ogburn, W. F., and Dorothy S. Thomas. *Journ. of Am. Statistical Ass.*, 1922, p. 324. (*See also* Thomas.)

Overbury. *Characters*. 17th Cent. H.

Plato. *Symposium*, IV. X H.

Prynne, W. *Healthes Sicknesse*. 1628. X H.

Reedman, J. N. *Report on a Survey of Licensing in Sheffield*. 1931. X.

Reeves and Turner. *The Text Book of Freemasonry*. 1874.

Rich, Barnaby. *Irish Hubbub*. 1617. H.

Richardson, A. E., and Eberlein. *The English Inn, Past and Present*. 1925.

Richardson, A. E. *The Old Inns of England*. 1934.

Richet. *Idiot Man*. 1925.

Rideal, S. *The Carbohydrates and Alcohol*. 1920.

Rigby, Joseph. *An Ingenious Poem, called the Drunkard's Prospective, or the Burning Glasse*. 1656.

Rivers, W. H. R. *The Influence of Alcoholic and Other Drugs on Fatigue*. 1906.

Robinson, W. *Reminiscences of the Temperance Movement and The Temperance Hall, Worktown*. 1890. H.

Rothwell, Charles. *Some of the Obstacles to the Temperance Cause*. 1880. H.

Rothwell, Samuel. *Memorials of the Independent Methodist Chapel, Folds Road*. 1897. H.

Rowntree, B. S. *Poverty*. 1922. X.

Rowntree, J., and A. Sherwell. *Temperance Problem and Social Reform*. 1901.

Rowntree, J., and A. Sherwell. *Public Control of the Liquor Traffic*. 1903.

Scarisbrook, J. *Spirit Manual.* 1891.
Scarisbrook, J. *Beer Manual.* 1892.
Scholes, J. C. *History of Worktown.* 1892. X H.
Selley. *The English Public House as it is.* 1927. X.
Shadwell, A. *Drink, Temperance, and Legislation.* 1902.
Shadwell, A. *Drink in 1914–22.* 1923.
Shawcross, W. *Misuse and Abuse of Alcohol.* (Section in *Manual of Hygiene for Teachers*, ed. Shawcross.) 1927.
Sherwell, A. (*See* J. Rowntree.)
Skelton. *Tunning of Elenor Rumming.* 16th Cent. poem. H.
Smith, C. *Centenary History of the Ancient and Noble Order of United Oddfellows, Worktown Unity.* 1932. X.
Snowdon, Viscount. *End This Colossal Waste.* 1936. X.
Starling, E. H. *The Action of Alcohol on Man.* 1923.
Sturge, M. D. (*See* V. Horsley.)
Sullivan, W. C. *Alcoholism.* 1906.

Thomas. *Philoconothista.* 1635. X H.
Thomas, Dorothy. (*See* W. F. Ogburn.)
Thomas, Dorothy. *Social Aspects of the Business Cycle.* 1925. X.
Thomas, W. I. *Source Book for Social Origins.* (Chicago.) 1909. H.
Tillotson's Directory of Worktown. 1932.
Trusler. *Modern Times.* 1785. H.

Vernon, H. M. *The Alcohol Problem.* 1928.

Ward, S. *Woe to Drunkards.* 1627. H.
Webb, S. *History of the Liquor Licensing Laws in England.* 1903. X H.
Wise. *Further Observations on the White Horse.* 1742. H.
Wright, H. E. *A Handy Book for Brewers.* 1907.

Young. *England's Bane.* 1617. H.
Young, R. *Charge against Drunkenness.* 1655. H.

REPORTS AND PERIODICALS

Amulree Commission on Licensing. 1930.

Band of Hope Messenger. (Worktown.) 1848–1880.
British Medical Research Council. Alcohol: its action on the Human Organism. 1924.
British Temperance Advocate 1849–1879. (This national organ was published from Worktown.)

Chief Constable's Reports to the Worktown Watch Committee., X

Fact. No. 5. A Pocket History of the British Workers. 1937. X H.
Fact. No. 8. Portrait of a Mining Town. 1937.

Gentleman's Magazine. October, 1768. H.
Good of the Order The. (i.e., Worktown Order of Good Templars.) 1873–1874.

Holy Trinity Church Centenary, 1826–1926. (Worktown.) 1926. X H.
Home Office. Licensing Statistics. 1936.
House of Commons Committee on Drunkenness, Report of the. 1834. X. H.

Liquor Problem The. Committee of 50. 1905.

Manchester and District Joint Town Planning Advisory Committee
    Report upon the Regional Scheme.

Peel Commission on the Licensing Laws. 1896.
Public House in the New Housing Areas, The Problem of the. (London
    III Committee on Disinterested Management.) 1934.

Royal Commission on Licensing, Report of the. 1932. X.

South-west Lancashire Joint Town Planning Advisory Committee. The
    Future Development of S. W. Lancs. 1930.

Worktown, Reports of the Annual Licensing Day for the Borough of.
    1848. 1852. H.
Worktown Temperance Union, Reports of the.
Worktown Trades Council Report. 1936.

Owing to wartime library conditions, it has proved impossible adequately
to check the above references. In addition, the following studies in other
fields of sociology have proved particularly helpful:

Allport, Floyd H. *Social Psychology*. Boston (Loughton Mifflin), 1924.
Brunhes, Jean. *Human Geography*. London (Harrap), 1920.
Burgess, E. W. *The Urban Community*. Chicago (Univ. Press), 1926.
Cooley, C. H. *Social Organization*. New York (Scribner), 1909.
Cooley, C. H., R. C. Angell and L. J. Carr. *Introductory Sociology*. London
    (Scribner), 1933. (Popular re-write of Cooley's Works.)
Dollard, F. H. *Criteria for the Life History*. Yale (Inst. of Human Relations),
    1936.
Florence, P. Sargant. *Economics of Industrial Fatigue and Unrest*. London
    (Unwin), 1924.
Galpin, C. J. *Rural Life*. New York (Century), 1918.
Gist, Noel P. and L. A. Halbert. *Urban Society*. New York (Cromwell's
    Social Sci. Series), 1933.
Ogburn, W. F. *Social Change*. New York (Viking), 1922.
Park, R. E., E. W. Burgess and R. D. McKenzie. *The City*. Chicago (Univ.),
    1925.
Rice, Stuart A. *Quantitative Method in Politics*. New York (Knopf), 1928.
Sombart, Werner (trans. M. Epstein). *The Jews and Modern Capitalism*.
    London (Unwin), 1910.
Sorokin, P. A. and C. C. Zimmerman. *Principles of Rural-Urban Sociology*.
    New York (Holt), 1929.
Sumner, William G. *The Folkways*. New York, 1907.
Veblen, Thorstein. *The Theory of the Leisured Class*. London (Unwin),
    1924.

Young, Kimball (editor). *Social Attitudes.* New York (Holt), 1931. This volume, from many contributors, gives an excellent picture of the scope and vitality of Sociology in U.S.A.

Actually responsible for the greatest section of field work to date are Chicago's Park and Burgess, whose University series of sociology books includes the following of special interest:

Anderson, *The Hobo* (1923); Cressey, *The Taxi-Dance Hall,* (32); McKenzie, *The Neighbourhood* (29); Mowrer, *Family Disorganization* (29); Shaw, *The Jack Roller* (23); Thrasher, *The Gang* (27); Wirth, *The Ghetto* (28); Zorbaugh, *The Gold Coast and the Slum* (29).

Perhaps the most penetrating work on method is that of Thomas, Loomis and Arrington (Yale, 1933). Dollard's *Class and Caste in a Southern Town,* Thomas and Znaniecki's volumes on the Polish peasant, the Lynds' *Middletown* and *Middletown Revisited,* Gosnell and Merriam on the non-voter in American politics, the University of North Carolina's Society Study Series, and the volumes of the Payne Fund's Cinema Research are significant also.

In conclusion it must be emphasized that this volume is isolated from its context as the first and most limited in a series on Worktown life and culture, which will have to await Victory, and after that Peace, for completion. Meanwhile, " The Pub and the People " is by way of work in progress, while those responsible for it are scattered, each trying to help win this war, and presently this Peace, when Worktown pubs may be their confused, contented selves again.